BUILDING BRIDGES BETWEEN CHAN BUDDHISM AND CONFUCIANISM

WORLD PHILOSOPHIES

Bret W. Davis, D. A. Masolo, and Alejandro Vallega, *editors*

BUILDING BRIDGES BETWEEN CHAN BUDDHISM AND CONFUCIANISM

A Comparative Hermeneutics of Qisong's *Essays on Assisting the Teaching*

DIANA ARGHIRESCU

INDIANA UNIVERSITY PRESS

This book is a publication of

Indiana University Press
Office of Scholarly Publishing
Herman B Wells Library 350
1320 East 10th Street
Bloomington, Indiana 47405 USA

iupress.org

© 2022 by Indiana University Press

All rights reserved
No part of this book may be reproduced or utilized in any form or by any means, electronic or mechanical, including photocopying and recording, or by any information storage and retrieval system, without permission in writing from the publisher. The paper used in this publication meets the minimum requirements of the American National Standard for Information Sciences—Permanence of Paper for Printed Library Materials, ANSI Z39.48–1992.

Manufactured in the United States of America

First printing 2022

Library of Congress Cataloging-in-Publication Data

Names: Arghirescu, Diana, author.
Title: Building bridges between Chan Buddhism and Confucianism : a comparative hermeneutics of Qisong's "Essays on assisting the teaching" / Diana Arghirescu.
Description: Bloomington : Indiana University Press, 2022. | Series: World philosophies | Includes bibliographical references and index.
Identifiers: LCCN 2022015381 (print) | LCCN 2022015 (ebook) | ISBN 9780253063670 (hardback) | ISBN 9780253063687 (paperback) | ISBN 9780253063694 (ebook)
Classification: LCC BQ9269.4.C65 A74 2022 (print) | LCC BQ9269.4.C65 (ebook) | DDC 294.3/927--dc23/eng/20220404
LC record available at https://lccn.loc.gov/2022015381
LC ebook record available at https://lccn.loc.gov/2022015382

CONTENTS

Acknowledgments   vii

Abbreviations and Conventions   ix

Introduction   *1*

1. Chan Scholar-Monk Qisong on the Affinities and Differences between Chan Buddhism and Confucianism in "Inquiry into the Teachings" ("Yuanjiao" 原教)   *33*

2. An Eleventh-Century Confucianized and Cohesive Form of Chan: Qisong's Interpretation of "Teaching" (*Jiao* 教) in the "Extensive Inquiry into the Teachings" ("Guang yuanjiao" 廣原教)   *59*

3. Qisong's "Letter of Advice" ("Quanshu" 勸書): An Examination and Correction of the Deficiencies of Confucianism   *93*

4. Qisong on Buddhist Filial Devotion (*Xiao* 孝): A Buddhist-Confucian Comparative Perspective   *125*

5. Heart-Mind (*Xin* 心), Emotions (*Qing* 情), and Nature-Emptiness (*Xing* 性) in Qisong's Thought: A Song-Dynasty Interpretation of Cohesive Chan Practice Intended for Confucian Scholars   *167*

6. Qisong on Universal Principle (*Li* 理), Nothingness (*Wu* 無), and the "Encomium of the Platform Sutra" ("Tanjing zan" 壇經贊): Answers avant la Lettre to Zhu Xi's Twelfth-Century Criticism   *209*

7. Ethico-Spiritual Discipline, Emotions, and Behavior during the Song Dynasty: Zhu Xi's and Qisong's Commentaries on the *Zhongyong* in Comparative Perspective   237

Conclusion   259

Notes   263

Bibliography   279

Index   289

ACKNOWLEDGMENTS

I DEVELOPED A SIGNIFICANT PART of my interpretive study and hermeneutical translation of Qisong's *Essays on Assisting the Teaching* (*Fujiao bian* 輔教編) during an extended period of research in 2017 and 2018. I am most grateful to the Université du Québec à Montréal for support during this period. The research grants permitted me time free of teaching and administration.

First, I would like to thank my family for their unwavering support throughout the project. My appreciation goes to my longtime friend Professor Kirill Ole Thompson from National Taiwan University, whose observations have been invaluable. He attentively read and commented on the entire manuscript and raised important issues that enabled me to improve the quality of this volume. I would like to acknowledge the anonymous reviewers for their detailed, valuable feedback and constructive critique, which helped me revise and enhance my research. I thank them for a fruitful review process and for making this book's publication possible. Obviously, any remaining faults of this work are entirely mine.

My thanks go to Indiana University Press and, in particular, Bret W. Davis, coeditor of the World Philosophies Series, for welcoming my manuscript and recommending it to the other editors.

Chapter 7 is a revised version of an article originally published in *Philosophy East and West* 70, no. 1 (2020): 1–26, "Spiritual Discipline, Emotions, and Behavior during the Song Dynasty: Zhu Xi's and Qisong's Commentaries on the *Zhongyong* in Comparative Perspective." I wish to thank the journal *Philosophy East and West* for permission to include this article in the book.

Diana Arghirescu
Montréal, Université du Québec à Montréal
October 2021

ABBREVIATIONS AND CONVENTIONS

CITATIONS FROM QISONG IN THE CHINESE ELECTRONIC TRIPITAKA COLLECTION, RELEASED BY THE CHINESE BUDDHIST ELECTRONIC TEXT ASSOCIATION (CBETA)

Zhonghua dianzi fodian xiehui 中華電子佛典協會. 2016. CBETA 電子佛典集成 *dianzi fodian jicheng*—CBETA Chinese Electronic Tripitaka Collection. Taipei: Zhonghua dianzi fodian xiehui.

QISONG AND OTHER PRIMARY SOURCES INCLUDED IN CHINESE TRIPITAKA

Collected Works of Qisong, Qisong's *Fujiao bian* (Essays on assisting the teaching), the anthology of early Chinese Buddhism *Hongming ji*, *Platform Sutra of the Dharma Treasure of the Great Master, the Sixth Patriarch, Brahma's Net Sutra, Heart Sutra, Bodhisattva Syama Sutra, Ullambana Sutra, Sutra in Forty-Two Sections,* Fazang's *Huayan fa putixin zhang* (Essay on the arousal of the bodhi mind in the Huayan), and Zanning's *Song gaoseng zhuan* (Biographies of eminent monks of the Song).

These texts are cited according to standard numbers in the Chinese Electronic Tripitaka Collection Version June 2016. The latter includes the Taisho Edition Tripitaka (printed Japanese edition) and selected Buddhist materials not contained in the Japanese Tripitaka: Buddhist texts not contained in the Tripitaka, passages concerning Buddhism from the Chinese Official Histories, selections of Buddhist stone rubbings from the Chinese Northern dynasties (386–581), a supplement to the *Dazangjing*, and Chinese Buddhist Temple Gazetteers (www.cbeta.org).

For example, Qisong's articles included in the anthology *Fujiao bian* (*Essays on Assisting the Teaching*) are shown as follows:

Qisong, "Yuanjiao," CBETA T52n2115_001, 0648c25
Qisong, "Guang yuanjiao," CBETA T52n2115_002, 0654b07–0660a03
Qisong, "Quanshu," CBETA T52n2115_001, 0651c21–0653c13
Qisong, "Xiaolun," CBETA T52n2115_003, 0660a25–0662b11
Qisong, "Tanjing zan," CBETA T52n2115_003, 0662c06

The following abbreviations are used for cited titles of Qisong's essays, Confucian works, and Buddhist works (full information can be found in the bibliography).

(NEO-)CONFUCIAN WORKS

JSL	*Jinsilu* 近思錄 (*Reflections on Things at Hand*)
ZY	*Zhongyong* 中庸
ZYZJ	*Zhongyong zhangju* 中庸章句 (see Arghiresco/u 2013)
ZZQS	*Zhuzi quan shu* 朱子全書 (*The Collected Works of Master Zhu*; see Zhu 2002)

(CHAN) BUDDHIST WORKS

FJB	*Fujiao bian* 輔教編 (*Essays on Assisting the Teaching*)
ZYJ	*Zhongyong jie* 中庸解 (*Exegesis of the Mean*)
"YJ"	"Yuanjiao" 原教 ("Inquiry into the Teachings")
"GYJ"	"Guang yuanjiao" 廣原教 ("Extensive Inquiry into the Teachings")
"QS"	"Quanshu" 勸書 ("Letter of Advice")
"XL"	"Xiaolun" 孝論 ("On Filial Devotion")
"TJZ"	"Tanjing zan" 壇經贊 ("Encomium of the Platform Sutra")

BUILDING BRIDGES BETWEEN CHAN BUDDHISM AND CONFUCIANISM

INTRODUCTION

1. QISONG 契嵩 (1007–1072), HIS YUNMEN CHAN LINEAGE AND THE *ESSAYS ON ASSISTING THE TEACHING* (*FUJIAO BIAN* 輔教編)

The Song dynasty is the historical period when a significant philosophical dialogue was initiated between Buddhism and Confucianism. It represents a pivotal moment not only for Buddhism but also for Confucianism. This work argues that the Chan scholar-monk Qisong 契嵩 (1007–1072)[1] is an important Northern-Song originator of this kind of philosophical dialogue on the Buddhist side. The first Confucian philosophical response to the interpretative challenges he issued during the Northern Song came a generation after him, at the time of the founding of the Neo-Confucian school of principle.

This book translates and explores Qisong's *Fujiao bian* 輔教編 (*Essays on Assisting the Teaching*, hereafter *FJB*), an anthology composed during the 1050s,[2] in which he made substantial efforts to philosophically compare major dimensions of Confucian and Chan Buddhist traditions. It consists of several essays: "Inquiry into the Teachings" ("Yuanjiao" 原教), "Extensive Inquiry into the Teachings" ("Guang yuanjiao" 廣原教), "Letter of Advice" ("Quanshu" 勸書), "On Filial Devotion" ("Xiaolun" 孝論), and "Encomium of the Platform Sutra" ("Tanjing zan" 壇經贊).

The present study focuses on the dynamic process of mutual interaction between Chan Buddhist and Neo-Confucian doctrines and concepts that constitutes a salient feature of Song-dynasty culture. What is more, it argues that this movement is closely related to the individual development of different forms of Chan Buddhism during the Song dynasty—not only those that became

1

emblematic as Song-dynasty Chan but also those that disappeared. This investigation examines the particular perspective of an eleventh-century representative of a "nonorthodox" form of Song-dynasty Chan, which is described here as a "cohesive" and "Confucianized" (i.e., aimed at Confucian scholars and written not in Buddhist style but in Confucian *guwen* 古文 style) interpretation of Chan tradition: the thought of the abovementioned scholar-monk Qisong of the Yunmen 雲門 Chan subschool, one of the five major Song-dynasty Chan schools (Yunmen, Guiyang 潙仰, Linji 臨濟, Caodong 曹洞, and Fayan 法眼).

Huang Chi-chiang, in his overview of the monks of the Yunmen lineage during the Northern Song, argues that they were responsible for the consolidation of Chan Buddhism during the Song dynasty and developed a new form of Chan known as "literary Chan" (*wenzi* Chan 文字禪), which includes poetry and essays (Huang 1986, 115–140). Robert Gimello highlights the inherent polemical character of this term within the context of the Song-dynasty Chan history and advocates for the implicitly more assertive translation "lettered Chan." The latter suggests the combination of spiritual discipline with literacy and learning as the distinctive feature of this type of "conservative" Chan of the Yunmen school versus the "unlettered" or anti-intellectual Chan (Gimello 1992, 381). Gimello discusses its fate in the following terms: "In early Song, Yunmen was in close competition with Linji for the status of most influential Chan lineage. Its importance has been traditionally overlooked since then, perhaps because it did not last long (Yunmen was eventually absorbed or supplanted by Linji), but also perhaps because of bias against it, or ignorance of it, on the part of certain major chroniclers of Song Buddhism. Zanning 贊寧 (919–1001), for example, deliberately chose to exclude the very founder of the lineage from his *Song gaoseng zhuan* [宋高僧傳, Biographies of eminent monks of the Song]" (Gimello 1992, 420–421).

Qisong was a prominent Song-dynasty Chan scholar-monk who extensively wrote about the compatibility between Confucianism and Buddhism from a philosophical perspective.[3] His writings were well known by the Emperor Renzong of the Song 宋仁宗 (r. 1022–1063) and by the Confucian scholar-officials of his time. The scholar-official Chen Shunyu 陳舜俞 (1026–1076), in his book *Duguanji* 都官集 (Collected works of a town official), recorded that Qisong's essays had a positive impact on scholar-officials' perception of Buddhism as being compatible with Confucianism. In his article "Zhuzi dui fojiao de lijie ji qi xiangzhi" 朱子對佛教的理解及其限制 ("Zhu Xi's Grasp of Buddhism, and Its Limitations"; Tsai 2012, 177–213), Tsai Chen-feng notes,

> According to Chen Shunyu's (1026–1076) *Records of Qisong's Professions* (*Qisong Hangye Ji* 契嵩行業記), anti-Buddhist sentiments were widespread among Confucian scholars at the beginning of the Song dynasty, since they

"had studied and practiced the *guwen* style of the old texts, and admired Tui Zhi's [Han Yu 韓愈 (768–824)] rejection of Buddhism (學為古文, 慕退之之排佛)." However, after Qisong (1007–1072) published the "Inquiry into the Teachings" ("*Yuanjiao*" 原教) and "On Filial Devotion" ("*Xiaolun*" 孝論),[4] which included over ten articles that showcased many commonalities between Buddhist teachings and practices and the Confucian Way, those who had rejected Buddhism often read Qisong's texts and "were charmed by the eloquence of the writings and persuaded by his arguments. None could escape [Qisong's spell]; they all came around to his views" (Chen 1972: 16). Even though the words of Chen Shunyu may be slightly exaggerated, he made two serious points: First, the early Confucian criticisms of Buddhism were not persuasive because they were scattered and unsystematic; second, Qisong weakened the Confucian criticisms by pointing out commonalities between Buddhist teachings and practices and the Confucian Way. (Tsai 2012, 177–178)[5]

In the anthology *Fujiao bian* (*Essays on Assisting the Teaching*), he not only responds to the criticism expressed by the *guwen* movement promoted by the Tang Confucian Han Yu 韓愈 (768–825) and his heirs but, more importantly, initiates a philosophical Buddhist-Confucian dialogue concerning ethical and religious issues.

It is important to stress that Qisong wrote his work in the Confucian style known as *guwen*, clearly in order to better engage in a philosophical dialogue with the Confucians. To effectively highlight this style in his work, and the way he communicates Buddhist arguments and perspectives with a Confucian voice, I introduced in my translations the significant original phrases. Advocated by Han Yu, "*guwen* traces its origins to the language of the Zhou dynasty Confucian classics" (De Bary and Bloom 1999, 568). The Chan scholar-monk stressed that his goal was to introduce the essence of Chinese Buddhism to Confucians—obviously, in a language familiar to them. Indeed, the significant Confucian concepts that he uses in his new interpretation of Buddhism can be regarded as indicative of this intention. Understandably, he hopes that his work will have a stronger impact on Confucian readers if written in Confucian terms. "I wrote these two articles ["Yuanjiao" and "Guang yuanjiao"]," Qisong specifies at the beginning of his essay "Extensive Inquiry into the Teachings" 廣原教 ("Guang yuanjiao," 0654b18-1), "because I wanted to explain the great foundation (*datong* 大統) of the teaching created by the first sage [Buddha] (發明先聖設教之大統), and thus instruct contemporary Confucians who do not know Buddhism. Therefore, I wanted to write it in *guwen* and simplify the [Buddhist] theory (故其言欲文其理欲簡)." Chapter 2 focuses on this issue. Elizabeth Morrison also elicits, in a nuanced manner, Qisong's steadfast commitment to the ancient style, not for its utilitarian, intellectual, or apologetic value but as a life choice and quest for a profound nonduality between Buddhism and Confucianism beneath their apparently antagonistic ethical values and practices: "His use of *guwen* signaled his respect for Chinese culture as it existed before the rise of Daoism and the arrival of Buddhism. Nor does this seem to have been mere ploy or strategy" (Morrison 2010, 115).

In the moving testimony of Qisong himself, translated by Morrison in her book, the scholar-monk connects the idea of "stillness" with his capacity to be aware of the interdependence of the two traditions, of their profound nonduality. Despite his understanding of and being one with both traditions through stillness, he was perceived as "impure" by some of his contemporaries who still dwelt in the dualistic conceptualization of things and traditions—and therefore insisted on segregating "pure" Buddhists from Confucians. In an essay explaining his studio and literary name *Jizi* 寂子, Master Stillness, Morrison tells us, Qisong writes,

> *Jizi*, am one who studies Buddhism. Because the awakening it arouses is quiet and profound, call myself *Jizi*. *Jizi*, already study its teachings. I also delight in studying *ru* [儒, Confucianism]. I have made myself deeply familiar with *ru* books and take pleasure in [their] language. For this reason, scholars have argued. Those who study Buddhism say *Jizi* is definitely fickle. [He] cannot concentrate and keep his path pure; how can one make it mixed? Those who study *ru* say that *Jizi* is not truly a Buddhist. Such a one stays only temporarily in the dharma of the *Sakya* clan.... Because of this, I said to two guests, I enjoy *ru*. Therefore, I take [from it] that which harmonizes with my path and use it. (Collected Works, 686a11-18) (Morrison 2010, 115–116)

II. AIMS AND OBJECTIVES OF THIS BOOK

This study is a piece of comparative scholarship on the mutual influences between Song Buddhism and Song Confucianism. It is based on a philosophical translation and interpretation of Qisong's articles included in his *Fujiao bian* (*Essays on Assisting the Teaching*). Its main contribution is to elaborate in detail some of the similarities of Chan Buddhism and Confucianism. These similarities have long been recognized, but they have never been described at a persuasive level of specificity. The book makes a contribution in filling in the largely unexplored story of Buddhist/Confucian philosophical exchange in the Song period and provides an extensive analysis of the thought of Qisong.

In this research, I uncover and investigate two dimensions of the Chan scholar-monk's view. The first is his effort to efficiently identify specific weaknesses of the Confucian way and to propose a remedy based on his original Chan vision. Chapters 1–3 progressively explore this aspect by identifying the shortcomings to which he refers and then examining how he addresses these flaws using his cohesive Chan Buddhist interpretations. From this analysis gradually emerges a second core feature of his thought, intricately related to the first one: the monk's effort to bring to light the particularities of his "cohesive" Chan thought using an original and innovative comparative (Buddhist/Confucian) approach meant for his contemporary Confucian readers. Chapters 4–7 focus on this aspect while developing in this new light several themes already discussed in chapters 1–3.

The major goal of the *Fujiao bian* follows from this study: Qisong strives to bring Confucian and Buddhist traditions and practices closer, so as to promote together a united effort to restore the overall well-being of Song society and individuals. It is also important to observe that the Chan scholar-monk undertakes constructively his critical task of comparing these traditions, with a view to connecting and harmonizing them in a supportive way, which reflects Mahayana's major belief in the interdependency of all teachings and all human beings. The inference can be made here that Qisong's cohesive or nondual Chan perspective is faithful to the vision of the *Diamond Sutra* (*Vajra Prajna Paramita Sutra*) 金剛經,[6] a sutra to which his favorite *Platform Sutra*[7] explicitly refers several times (0348a07, 0349a17-3, and 0350c16-10). It can be said that his cohesive or nondual Chan constitutes his original interpretation and development of the *Diamond Sutra*'s perspective on the unity behind the complex diversity of teachings. According to this text, "all teachings [dharmas] are Buddhist (一切法皆是佛法)" (*Diamond Sutra*, 0751b2-2). The contemporary Chan master Hsuan Hua 宣化 (1918–1995) details this sutra's perspective on the Buddhist source of all teachings: "They [the teachings] do not go beyond the Buddha's teaching, because the Buddha's teaching contains all things. Buddhadharma is the totality of all dharmas. Buddhism is the totality of all other teachings. All schools and teachings are born from within the Buddha's teaching" (Hsuan 2002, 151).

The analysis of Qisong's ideas focuses on several key notions: universal principle (principle of coherence), authentic nature, heart-mind, emotions, behavior, sincerity, and filial devotion. All of them are equally important for his cohesive and Confucianized Chan Buddhism, as for the Neo-Confucian (Cheng-Zhu) school of the eleventh and twelfth centuries. Therefore, the examination of Qisong's line of reasoning is also relevant for the following reasons. On the one hand, it allows the reader to capture the differences between the Chan thought of the scholar-monk and (Neo-)Confucianism regarding the contextual meanings they assigned to these terms. On the other hand, it reveals the borrowings and mutual influences between the two traditions that occurred during the Song-dynasty eleventh and twelfth centuries. Their continuing contact stimulated the growth of special forms of Chan, such as Qisong's Confucianized one, and the philosophical Neo-Confucian development concerning the idea of principle and the practice of self-cultivation. The present study provides philosophical evidence that Qisong's eleventh-century work made a significant contribution to this transformation that took place within Confucianism during the Song dynasty.

III. MY ENCOUNTER WITH QISONG'S PHILOSOPHICAL WORK

This volume grew out of my long-standing interest in the peculiar features of the Song-dynasty culture and its specific philosophical roots. I come from the field of Song Neo-Confucian studies (the school of principle, *lixue* 理學) and have been trained in the Confucian texts and *guwen* style. The latter praises the Confucian values and makes ample references, both implicit and explicit, to the Confucian classics. In my research, I combine my perspectives as a sinologist and philosopher with my personal interest in ethical thought in examining the particularities of the Song-dynasty philosophical practice and identity.

I became captivated by Qisong's philosophy and by Song-dynasty Chan Buddhism more than a decade ago while working on my first book, a study of Zhu Xi's 朱熹 (1130–1200) Neo-Confucian ethical thought and his commentaries on the *Four Books* (Arghiresco/u 2013). At that time, I was completing a philosophical translation of the *Zhongyong* as well as of major sections of the *Lunyu* and the *Daxue* (original texts with Zhu Xi's commentaries) accompanied by a study of cultural presuppositions (fundamentals of Western ethics / fundamentals of Chinese ethics). On this basis, I was building a comparative, intertextual analysis as well as a philosophical hermeneutics of representative ancient Confucian ethical notions and their twelfth-century Neo-Confucian meanings. As I was pursuing this project, the presence of a subtle Chan Buddhist inspiration at the heart of Zhu's philosophy became increasingly palpable to me, despite his overt criticisms of Buddhism. After the completion of this Neo-Confucian project, the idea to embark on a study of a new topic related to my initial interest in Confucian ethical philosophy—identifying and explicating the Chan Buddhist threads woven into the Song-dynasty Confucian culture and into the Neo-Confucian (*lixue*) thought—had already germinated in my mind and begun to take root.

In the subsequent years, I familiarized myself with the Chan Buddhist style by translating several Chinese sutras that were popular in the Song dynasty, beginning with the mature version of the *Platform Sutra*, presumably edited by Qisong himself: *Platform Sutra of the Dharma Treasure of the Great Master, the Sixth Patriarch* (*Liuzu dashi fabao tanjing* 六祖大師法寶壇經). I also reflected more deeply on the philosophical connections between Chan and Neo-Confucian thought within the context of the Song-dynasty Confucian culture and in Zhu Xi's thought (Arghirescu 2020a, 2020b). The time was ripe for me to delve into the writings of the contemporary Chan scholar-monk Sheng-yen 聖嚴 (1931–2009), especially concerning his appreciation of the exchanges between Chan and Confucianism in China. During the last decade, I also had the opportunity to learn more about the Buddhist practice and scholarly research conducted at Sheng-yen's center Dharma Drum Mountain (Fagushan 法鼓山) near Taipei, Taiwan—a country that welcomed me most warmly. There I had the privilege to observe the oneness and interfusion between the texts and sincere practice. I am grateful for everything I learned there about contemporary, socially engaged Chan.

I commend as well the authors who have led me to better understand the life context and intellectual interests of the Song-dynasty Chan scholar-monk Qisong: Huang Chi-chiang 黃啟江 (1986), Elizabeth Morrison (2010), and others who have contributed to the understanding of the highly complex area of intellectual exchange between Confucianism and Buddhism in East Asia; Charles Muller (2015), who has examined fourteenth-century Korean interactions and their Chinese foundations; Uri Kaplan (2019) on eleventh-century China and fifteenth-century Korea; and Huang Chun-chieh (2020) on pre-Tang China, fourteenth- and fifteenth-century Korea, and seventeenth-century Japan, among others. In the following sections, I present how my study relates to and interacts with these previous works.

Clearly, the influences back and forth between the Confucian and Buddhist teachings incorporate a vast array of complementary features and purposes. The present study is especially dedicated to Qisong's philosophical/religious thought and his innovative understanding of the Confucian-Buddhist interaction and unity. It should be mentioned in passing that "philosophical thought" is a precise but limited concept invented by Western thought. The Western way of thinking calls on divisions and subdivisions, compartmentalization, and categories, in the same way that the Western alphabetic writing systems proceed. When applied to Chinese thought, whose coherence stems not from the abstract layout of alphabetic characters but from connecting Chinese logographs,[8] this Western form of identifier turns out to be reductionist. Too often, comfortably installed in our own Western cultural context based on categorical separation, we forget that in the Chinese context religion and philosophy inseparably belong together. Masao Abe clearly and strikingly describes this encompassing character of Eastern philosophy and the fusion between philosophy and religion: "In the West, philosophy and religion are generally understood as two different entities: the former is a human enterprise for understanding humans and the universe based on intelligence or reason, whereas the latter is faith in divine revelation.... In the East, especially in Buddhism, philosophy and religion are not two different entities. Since Buddhism is originally not a religion of faith in a transcendent deity but a religion of awakening to the true nature of self and others, *praxia* and *theoria*, to use Western terms, are interfused and undifferentiated" (Abe 1992, 11).

To investigate the "philosophical" dimension of Qisong's writings discussed in this study, I conventionally retain the imperfect characterization of religion/philosophy as "philosophical thought." However, one must not forget that, as Abe points out, when applied to the Eastern/Chinese sphere, this Western notion also implicitly includes a religious or spiritual dimension. Both aspects are analyzed in what I call a "philosophical hermeneutics" to be unfolded in the following chapters.

In addition, this work complements and engages with other research on Qisong and on the intellectual dimension of Confucian/Buddhist exchanges mentioned above, as well as with other analyses that explore different facets of these exchanges, such as by Yü Ying-shih, Bernard Faure, Koichi Shinohara, Albert Welter, and Mark Halperin, to name just a few. The next two sections articulate, first, the interrelation between this book and previous research on Qisong and, second, its correlation with earlier studies on Confucian/Buddhist exchanges.

IV. QISONG'S LIFE AND THOUGHT IN DIFFERENT RESEARCH CONTEXTS

For the reader who is interested in various facets of the life and thought of Qisong—the eminent Chan scholar-monk who lived in eleventh-century Northern Song China—and is open to various research approaches, the present project complements and dialogues with two earlier studies mentioned above: Huang's *Experiment in Syncretism* and Morrison's *The Power of Patriarchs*. Each of these studies is focused on a different aspect of Qisong's works and achievements and employs a distinctive approach, historical versus philosophical. It could be said that they are interrelated and develop the multidisciplinary (involving religious studies, history, and philosophy) comparative field of diverse inquiries into Qisong and his historical, intellectual, and religious context. Read together, they offer detailed knowledge and penetrating insight into this Chan scholar-monk and his age, as well as a complex and nuanced articulation of the religious, philosophical, and moral implications of his major studies. To illustrate their interrelatedness, let us first consider their respective approaches.

Basically, both Huang's and Morrison's books constitute exercises in the historical study of Chan Buddhism, focused on the life and accomplishments of Qisong in the context of Song-dynasty Chan Buddhism as well as on the interactions between Chan monks and Confucian scholar-officials. In the sphere of Chinese studies, Gimello distinguishes the particularities of this historical approach. He first defines this method comparatively as "distinct from the textual, systematic of philosophical investigation" (all these terms refer to the approach I adopt here) and then presents its essential elements: "By 'history' we mean not only a diachronic tracing of the internal evolution of Buddhist ideas and practices but also (and chiefly) a sustained investigation of the synchronic, multivalent, and densely circumstantial connections between Buddhism and the other values and events that comprise the full life experiences of particular Buddhists" (Gimello 1992, 373).

In Huang Chi-chiang's historical study, this diachronic tracing of the internal evolution of Northern Song Chan ideas and investigation of its circumstantial connections is articulated around two components: first, a history of Chan Buddhism—its rise to prominence in the Tang dynasty and its continuance as a major school of Song Buddhism (Chan Five Houses), which enjoyed a favorable intellectual climate and received imperial patronage during the early Song; second, a discussion of Qisong's life and writings, focusing on his ambitious plan to seek official patronage and imperial support as a way to institutionalize Chan Buddhism (Huang 1986, x), along with an evaluation of Qisong as a "syncretist of the three teachings" (according to Huang). The author offers insight into what he calls Qisong's "ambitious plan" and contextually elaborates it by conducting a historical review of the consolidation of Chan Buddhism by the monks of the Chan Yunmen lineage of Qisong and his dharma-brothers. In this specific perspective, Huang notes that Qisong's collection *Essays on Assisting the Teaching* was widely circulated due to both "Qisong's deliberate propaganda and the syncretic feature in his interpretations of Buddhist and Confucian teachings" (Huang 1986, 4). At the heart of Huang's detailed historical examination is what he defines as the "syncretic" nature of Qisong's works and his time: "The developmental process of historical growth within a religion by accretion and coalescence of different and often originally conflicting forms of belief and practice through the interaction with or supersession of other religions" (Huang 1986, 6). More recently, Timothy Brook has criticized the tendency among historians of Chinese thought "to let the concept of syncretism expand indiscriminately to cover all forms of interaction." He rightly argues that its "free application is not helpful because it prejudices our ability to appreciate the character of Chinese religious experience as distinct from European" (Brook 1993, 14). Nevertheless, Huang carried out a remarkable pioneering work in the somewhat neglected field of Northern Song Chan Buddhism. Without doubt, he deepened our understanding of this field, and his thorough work has guided subsequent researchers in this area, one that remains overshadowed by researchers' pervasive and persistent interest in Tang-dynasty medieval Chinese Buddhism.

Morrison's book, *The Power of Patriarchs: Qisong and Lineage in Chinese Buddhism*, offers a diachronic tracing of the internal evolution of the idea of lineage in general and of Chan lineage in particular—"and related issues, including conceptions of religious and intellectual authority, the growth of distinctive Chinese Buddhist traditions, Buddhist relations with the state, and Buddhist views of history—through attention to Mingjiao Qisong (1007–1072), a Chan monk and dharma heir who, in his writings on Chan lineage, lays bare his part in the inventing and imagining of his tradition" (Morrison 2010, 4). In the first part of her study, Morrison historically builds a comprehensive genealogy of lineage, from Buddhist notions of succession and transmission in India and pre-Han China based on early Chinese sources to mid-Tang transmission stories; next, she presents the emergence and development of the Chan lineage from Bodhidharma to the eleventh-century Song-dynasty *Jingde Record of the Transmission of the Lamp*. Part 2 of her book is dedicated to the life of Qisong—his early years in South China, the journey north, settling in Hangzhou, his successful mission to the capital Kaifeng, and the scholar-monk's rise to prominence in later life. In the last part of *The Power of Patriarchs*, the author details Qisong's vision of history and lineage through an annotated translation and close reading of two fascicles of his writings on Chan lineage, *Chuanfa zhengzong lun* 傳法正宗論 (*Critical Essay on the True Lineage of the Dharma Transmission*).

Morrison's and Huang's studies both present elaborate and complementary accounts of the monk's life, including his pilgrimages to prominent Chan sangha, his 1061 memorial submitted to Emperor Renzong 仁宗 (r. 1022–1063), and his reception of the purple robe presented in 1062 by the emperor. They are extremely useful to readers who are eager to learn about Qisong's life experiences and popularity as a scholar-monk who was highly regarded by the Confucian elites of his time.

Huang also offers insight into what he calls Qisong's efforts at "harmonizing the two teachings" (Huang 1986, 216). Morrison examines his writings on Chan lineage, his life as a dharma heir, and the interactions with Confucian officials. As she acknowledges, her book does "not address Qisong's so-called Confucian writings in depth, but takes them into account as a crucial part of the overall pattern of his intellectual career and inclinations. My focus is primarily on his writings on Chan lineage—and the spectacle they present of an intelligent man struggling with historical sources in the attempt to find a way to validate the existence and importance of the lineage in which he believes deeply and participates daily." Thus, Morrison innovatively paints a fresh and vital portrait: the Northern Song monk "as both a sophisticated historian and a committed Chan Buddhist unable to contemplate Buddhist history as anything but a matter of dharma transmission," as well as "a leader of a sectarian campaign, a seeker of commonalities, . . . and a creative traditionalist" (Morrison 2010, 6).

Building Bridges between Chan Buddhism and Confucianism interacts with these two previous studies. Each of these works took shape as a result of its author's research interests and intellectual sensibilities. The starting point for Huang's analysis is his feeling that Qisong's "religious activity and experience could broaden our understanding of early Song Buddhism" (Huang 1986, iv). Morrison reveals that she "came to this project with a persistent curiosity about religious authority" (Morrison 2010, 225). Beyond my interest in the exchanges between Chan Buddhist and Neo-Confucian philosophies within Song-dynasty culture (and therefore in the archaeology of concepts), I proceed from the idea that Qisong's interpretation of the subtle oneness of the teachings has broad contemporary implications beyond its religious significance: it broadens our understanding of our own relationships to others as well as with other cultures and religions. Therefore, this research could serve as the basis for building a richer sense of belonging in a multicultural world. It also represents an attempt to interculturally diversify the field of philosophy.

As noted, the present book offers a philosophical, textual, and systematic investigation of Qisong's *Fujiao bian* (*Essays on Assisting the Teaching*).[9] Accordingly, it develops a philosophical translation and a philosophical hermeneutics of this text that the Chan scholar-monk composed in Confucian *guwen* with the aim of "instructing his contemporary Confucians who do not know Buddhism." Accordingly, the comparative (Confucian/Buddhist) textual study of its connections with the Confucian classics and a comparative archaeology of its key concepts lie at the basis of this hermeneutics. I argue that Qisong's perspective is markedly different from that of mainstream medieval Chinese Buddhist thought, and I explain how he articulated a fusion of Confucianism and Buddhism and developed it in Confucian terms using philosophico-religious tools, achieving what I call an "inclusive" and "Confucianized" understanding of Chan. This special kind of fusion concerns not the perceptible aspect of teachings, which remain "different footprints," but a spiritual dimension that in Qisong's view constitutes the unique source of all teachings (Confucian, Buddhist, or other).

For him, this is the one common heart-mind (*xin* 心) possessed by every sage, which manifests itself by taking on different, specific, and perceptible forms or methods of teaching (footprints, *ji* 迹). Since Qisong's text is written in *guwen* Confucian style, I chose to translate his notion of *xin* 心 as heart-mind, which is common in Confucian studies. I explain this translation choice in detail in discussing the essays included in his volume *Essays on Assisting the Teaching*, which introduce and interpret this major notion from multiple perspectives. "Heart-mind" (*xin* 心) is a central term of his work, and the Chan monk progressively discusses several layers of its "Confucian-Buddhist" meaning in each of his essays and in different Confucian contexts—for example, *Analects of Confucius* 7:25 in Qisong's essay "Yuanjiao" (discussed in chap. 1), the *Great Learning* 7 (*Book of Rites*, 39) in his article "Guang yuanjiao" (examined in chap. 2), and the *Mencius* 2.A.6 in the essay "Xiaolun" (considered in chap. 4).

The choice of starting from these Confucian contexts is part of his interpretive strategy—an example of what I would call "infusing old Confucian concepts with new Buddhist meaning" or "establishing Chan within the Confucian context (culture)." *Building Bridges* argues that, in his volume *Fujiao bian*, Qisong progressively creates a new and original persuasive approach, not a mere strategy: he illustrates the complementarity between Confucian and Chan philosophical ideas by starting from Confucian classics and ideas. Consequently, the monk discusses Confucian concepts such as heart-mind and quotations from Confucian classics familiar to his eleventh-century interlocutors and uses them to address first what he implicitly sees as deficiencies of Confucianism, to be corrected by infusions of Buddhism. This viewpoint is helpful in two main ways: first, to show how Chan Buddhism could work together with Confucianism in the effort toward improving society; and second, to progressively interpret Chan Buddhist ideas in Confucian terms. In this process, he obviously not only infuses the meanings of these Confucian classic (pre-Song) terms with Buddhist resonances but also provides new, Song-dynasty meanings to major classical Buddhist terms. One of the dimensions of his thought that this book unveils and interprets in this way is what might be called a "Confucianized" Buddhist perspective—that is, an inclusive perspective that systematically connects specific Chan Buddhist and general Buddhist ideas with Confucian notions.

Let me return to the notion of heart-mind (*xin* 心). It is true that most Buddhological works simply use *mind* to translate this important concept. However, Qisong's *guwen* work falls within a different context: he did not write a Buddhist text intended for a general audience but wrote a study laced with Confucian resonances, offered specifically to Confucian readers. Therefore, I would suggest that his analysis does not fall into the category of Buddhological works sensu stricto. In section VII, I detail the theoretical elements that compose my philosophical approach.

In addition, due to its interest in the mutual shaping of Chinese Chan Buddhism and Neo-Confucianism in the Song dynasty, this book relates to the aforementioned research of Charles Muller, Huang Chun-chieh, and Uri Kaplan. The next section is dedicated to their dialogue.

V. CONFUCIAN/BUDDHIST EXCHANGES IN DIFFERENT RESEARCH CONTEXTS

In his book *Korea's Great Buddhist-Confucian Debate: The Treatises of Chong Tojon (Sambong) and Hamho Tuktong (Kihwa)*, Muller focuses on the specificities of the exchanges between Buddhism and Confucianism in fourteenth-century Chosŏn-period Korea: the debate between the Confucian statesman Chŏng Tojŏn (1342–1398) and the eminent Korean Sŏn (Chinese Chan) monk Kihwa (1376–1433). His study offers translations of two texts of the Korean scholar-official—*On Mind, Material Force and Principle* and *An Array of Critiques of Buddhism*—and *Exposition of Orthodoxy* by the monk Kihwa. In his comprehensive introduction to these translations, Muller traces the historical development of the interaction between Buddhist and Confucian traditions and their philosophical conversations. Starting from their initial meeting in China, he highlights the period of Buddhist preeminence during the early-to-mid Tang dynasty, the anti-Chan criticism of the Song-dynasty Neo-Confucian school of the Cheng brothers (Cheng Hao 程顥 (1032–1085) and Cheng Yi 程頤 (1033–1107)) and Zhu Xi 朱熹 (1130–1200), the development of Korean Neo-Confucian criticism, and its Korean Buddhist responses. The author stresses that the Cheng-Zhu school of Neo-Confucianism was accepted as orthodoxy in Korea, and he estimates that the fourteenth-century writings of the Korean Neo-Confucian Chŏng, whose translation he offers, are 80 to 90 percent based directly on the works of the Cheng-Zhu school (21).

Furthermore, Muller explains the particular resonance of those Neo-Confucian works in the fourteenth-century Korean context of exchanges between Confucianism and Buddhism. Note that the Korean climate was highly different from the Chinese context—that of Qisong and the Cheng brothers in the eleventh century and Zhu Xi in the twelfth:

> The ideological fervor with which Neo-Confucianism arose in Korea had a special dimension, with the venom of their rhetoric fueled not only by the earlier philosophical arguments of the Cheng brothers and Zhu but also by the extent of the observable degeneracy of the Buddhist establishment. Thus, in Korea the mostly philosophical arguments against Buddhism that had originated with the Cheng brothers became the ideology of a rising movement of resistance on the part of influential members of the intelligentsia determined to overthrow a decaying Koryŏ dynasty—along with the rotting Buddhist monastic system with which it was deeply entangled. Thus, the anti-Buddhist polemical dimension of the Neo-Confucianism that developed in Korea took on a focus, a vehemence, indeed an exclusivism not previously seen in China. (Muller 2015, 12)

The Korean circumstances and those of the Song dynasty were also fundamentally different. In the author's terms, "The most important difference between the two scenarios was the markedly greater degree to which the Korean Buddhist establishment was embedded in the state power structure as compared with the situation in the Song" (12).

Within Song Confucian culture, Buddhism was administered by the strong Confucian state. It was never a political force, a rival for the Confucian government, or on an equal footing with Confucianism. As detailed in this book, Qisong's eleventh-century anthology *Fujiao bian* is first and foremost a philosophical text. Its intent is not to open a confrontational debate per se; it does not put forward a defensive apologetics, nor is it meant to overthrow opposing arguments. Again, it does not argue for a viewpoint opposed to the Confucian viewpoint, but rather it philosophically demonstrates the harmony between the two teachings and the valuable assistance that Buddhism could provide to the Confucian government in its effort to maintain a morally good society and cordial social communion. *Building Bridges* also offers textual and conceptual evidence to articulate and support the interpretive claim that certain philosophical ideas of the Cheng-Zhu school found inspiration in Qisong's philosophical *Fujiao bian*.

Interestingly, as Muller also points out, the fourteenth-century Korean monk Kihwa shares Qisong's harmonizing perspective: the underlying unity of the teachings (24). In *Korea's Great Buddhist-Confucian Debate*, Muller identifies Kihwa as one of the leading exegetes in the Korean Buddhist tradition (17) and highlights the influence of the Tang-dynasty Chinese scholar-monk Zongmi 宗密 (780–841) and his *Inquiry into the Origin of Humanity* (*Yuanren lun* 原人論; see Gregory 1995) on Kihwa's text. Written in Buddhist style, Zongmi's ninth-century essay was, as Muller notes, "written for a broad audience, and typical of the writings of Chinese doctrinal Buddhist scholars of the sixth to eighth centuries, a hermeneutically oriented text that classifies the teachings of Buddhism into five levels" (2015, 15). Obviously, a comparative study of Zongmi's mid-Tang medieval text as an early response at the very outset of the Confucian anti-Buddhist polemic and Qisong's Song-dynasty work would be also interesting. A key difference between their perspectives is, as highlighted above, that, unlike Zongmi's work, Qisong's essays are written in *guwen* Confucian style for a very specific audience—the Confucian scholar-officials—and they discuss the Buddhist way only for lay practitioners.

It is possible that Qisong's writings influenced the Korean monk Kihwa. A comparative look at Qisong's essays "Inquiry into the Teachings" ("Yuanjiao" 原教, 0648c25) and "Extensive Inquiry into the Teachings" ("Guang yuanjiao" 廣原教, 0659b15) and Kihwa's *Exposition of Orthodoxy* (*Xianzheng lun* 顯正論), section 2, "Distinction in Levels of Teaching," and section 10, "Defense of the Doctrine of Karma and Rebirth," reveals that Kihwa uses certain arguments that were advanced by Qisong. Moreover, Kihwa reiterates some of Qisong's expressions and phrases verbatim, or almost verbatim (see also Arghirescu 2021). I suggest that this was a tribute to Qisong and manifests strong evidence that his philosophical development was known and appreciated by Kihwa. Besides, in his article "Uicheon's Pilgrimage and the Rising Prominence of the Korean Monastery in Hang-chou during the Sung and Yuan Periods," cited by Morrison, Huang Chi-chiang offers compelling arguments concerning Qisong's high scholarly reputation among eminent Korean Buddhists: "In time his [Qisong's] scholarly reputation was such that when Uicheon 義天 (1055–1101), the Koryo prince and great Buddhist scholar, was reckoning his own knowledge, he considered only his own teacher and 'perhaps' Qisong to surpass him" (Morrison 2010, 113).

Another significant illustration of the connection between Qisong's and Kihwa's works and what brings them together despite their different epochs and cultural contexts, is their abovementioned common dedication to harmonizing the Confucian and Buddhist teachings. I maintain that Muller's description of Kihwa's steadfast emphasis on the commonalities between the two teachings applies equally to the vision Qisong expressed three centuries earlier: "Kihwa is really not seeking to discredit the Confucian teaching but to show how, when properly understood, Confucian and Buddhist teachings can be applied together in harmonious fashion. This approach is reminiscent of that of the great Silla-period scholar Wonhyo (617–686), whose approach rarely pronounced a specific form of teaching to be entirely unuseful. He rather tended to see all kinds of teachings as expedients that could be fit into the larger whole and be understood properly in their particular contexts" (Muller 2015, 161n18).

In his introduction, Muller also treats the situation in China from a philosophical perspective. He traces the outlines of a highly interesting and relevant feature of the Buddhist texts composed in East Asia and recognizes it as a significant philosophical component of what is referred to as the "Sinification" of Buddhism: "A Buddhist view of human consciousness that had been contoured to indigenous Chinese understandings of the human mind as being something intrinsically pure, and that, although existing in a defiled, obscured state, could be perfected through training. The 'humaneness' articulated by Confucius and Mencius was transmuted to the 'originally enlightened mind' spoken of in these texts, and the structural paradigm for this transmutation, whether stated overtly or not, was that of essence and function, with the original pure mind being essence (K. *ch'e*, Ch. *Ti* 體) and good, enlightened, pure behavior being function (K., Ch. *Yong* 用)" (6). The author also dedicated two full-length studies (2000, 2016) to this topic of the essence-function paradigm, which he creatively characterizes as "the most pervasively-used hermeneutical framework in the interpretation of Chinese, Korean, and Japanese religious and philosophical works ranging from as early as the fifth century BCE up to premodern times" (2016, 151).

Huang Chun-chieh's 2020 book, *The Debate and Confluence between Confucianism and Buddhism in East Asia*, is another recent outstanding contribution to the development of three important but still incipient areas of research in intellectual history: the mutual influences between Confucianism and Buddhism in China, their mutual interchanges within the Sinicized Korean and Japanese cultures, and the instrumental role of this Confucian-Buddhist dialogue in the shaping of a common East Asian identity. This book is a translation in English of a part (chap. 5, sec. 2) of a large study devoted to the idea of "learning to be human" (仁學) in *Dongya rujia renxue shilun* 東亞儒家仁學史論 (Huang 2017).

The Debate and Confluence between Confucianism and Buddhism in East Asia is structured around three sections: a brief historical overview of East Asian (Chinese, Korean, and Japanese) Confucian-Buddhist debates, an examination of five common topics in these exchanges, and an identification of the main discursive strategies used in these dialogues by Confucianists and by Buddhists.

To illustrate the particularity of these discussions in the initial Chinese context, Huang chooses to focus on the period of five hundred years of polemics, from the Eastern Han dynasty through the Wei-Jin period and the Northern and Southern dynasties. This is epitomized in the collection *Hongming ji* 弘明集 compiled by the early medieval monk Sengyou (僧祐, 445–518). Like Muller, he calls attention to the fourteenth-century debates in Korea between the Confucian scholar Chŏng Tojŏn and the monk Kihwa, as well as to the seventeenth-century debate in Japan between Zhu Xi scholar Hayashi Razan (林羅山, 1583–1657) and the Buddhist Matsunaga Teitoku (松永貞德, 1570–1653). I have explored the content and scope of this book in a review essay (Arghirescu 2021).

Huang pertinently remarks that "all the debates that took place in China, Japan, and Korea . . . possess a high level of similarity" (2020, 28). He identifies five common topics (29) and examines each one in the three abovementioned East Asian areas and periods: family ethics (家庭倫理), political ethics (政治倫理), the distinction between Chinese and barbarians (華夷之辨), the relationship between soul (spiritual consciousness) and body (corporeal form) (神識與形體), and the concepts of karma and samsara (因果與輪迴).

An exploration of various illustrations of these five common topics allows the author to ascertain and enunciate two major discursive strategies of the East Asian Confucian attacks and of the Buddhists' defensive responses (84). The first Confucian strategy is the abovementioned "cultural nationalism of Confucians"—that is, the idea of Sino-barbaric difference (75). The second—which Huang calls the "monistic" (一元論) Confucian worldview (in which soul and body are one)—is based on the vital breath (*qi* 氣) (78). Huang also identifies two main strategies used by the East Asian Buddhists: "illustrating Buddhism by means of Confucianism" and "assimilating Confucianism into Buddhism" (78). In the author's view, the first strategy is best embodied in the debate on the issue of filial devotion, in what he calls a "recontextualization" of this notion (79). Huang explains the second strategy as the effort to demonstrate "the identity of Confucian and Buddhist teachings, through equating the values inherent in Confucian and Buddhist doctrines" (for example, the Five Precepts and Ten Good Deeds 五戒十善 and the Confucian Five Permanencies 五常) (79). Let us add that both approaches are creatively interpreted by Qisong in his essays "On Filial Devotion" (see chap. 4) and "Inquiry into the Teachings" (chap. 1).

Another recent book dedicated to these exchanges is Uri Kaplan's *Buddhist Apologetics in East Asia* (2019). He offers translations of two essays: the Northern Song scholar-official and devout Buddhist Zhang Shangying's (張商英, 1043–1121) "Defense of the Dharma" ("Hufa lun" 護法論), a Chinese Buddhist response to the Confucian critiques of Han Yu and Ouyang Xiu, and "Probing the Doubts and Concerns between Confucianism and Buddhism" ("Yusok chirui non" 儒釋質疑論), an anonymous fifteenth-century Korean text, possibly authored by the monk Kihwa or one of his disciples (Huang 2020, 23–24) as a direct response to the Neo-Confucian Chong Tojon (see also Muller 2015). According to Kaplan, the two essays elaborate in great detail the efficacy of Buddhism: the first discusses the supernatural personal benefits to be attained through spiritual resonance and enjoyed by those who practice Chan; the second "includes lengthy clarifications of Buddhist cosmology, history, and geography, . . . an attempt to use Sinitic numerology, extracted from the *Classic of Changes*, the Yellow River Diagram, and the Luo River Square, in order to explain and apologize for Shakyamuni's birth story, Buddhist mudras, Chan transmission, kalpas, Buddhist charity, and mantra practice" (2019, 2–3).

Kaplan contextualizes these translations by providing a historical introduction, "a survey—as preliminary as it may still be—of East Asian Buddhist apologetic literature from the tenth to the eighteenth centuries. In the following, I review some of the main Buddhist works written in Song, Yuan, and Ming China, in Chosŏn Korea, and in Tokugawa Japan, in order to defend the Buddhist tradition from the attacks by Han Yu, Zhu Xi, and their later supporters" (21).

It should be noted that, as the title of his research indicates, Kaplan is interested in identifying and examining the "apologetic" dimension of the Buddhist texts he presents: defensive and justificatory strategies, counterattacks against Confucians, arguments countering the Confucians' criticism and establishing the superiority of Buddhism, and so on (28). He thus includes the Buddhist/Confucian exchanges in a specific East Asian genre of apologetics. From this distinct angle, Kaplan discerns four general strategies and themes: "mocking Han Yu and Ouyang Xiu" (43–46)—note that, on the contrary, Qisong praises Han Yu in a subtle way, as having a "heart-mind sympathizing with Buddhism," see chapter 3, sec. IV.2; "defensive attempts to harmonize the three teachings" ("the idea that, although the three teachings may coexist in harmony, Buddhism remains in some way the superior teaching" [47–49]); "Buddhist-related historical analysis" (the life of the Buddha, historical counterexamples to Han Yu's criticism, the fates of particular historical individuals in relation to their sponsorship of the suppression of Buddhism [49–52], etc.), and "citing the classics to refute the Confucians" (52–55). The general conclusion of the author's analysis concerning this last point is that "a closer look at this prevalent polemic tactic reveals that it was used in two different ways: first, citing the classics in order to show that they did not contradict Buddhism; and second, citing the classics in order to criticize Confucianism and show the superiority of

Buddhism" (54). Again, this view is completely different from the Chan scholar-monk Qisong's perspective. Kaplan's apologetic approach identifies and highlights several methods and reasons for defending Buddhism. This is another way to address the issue of the dynamic interaction between Buddhism and Confucianism in East Asia and adds an additional dimension to this field of research.

It should also be noted that, while there are points of intersection between all of these works by virtue of their belonging to this common area of study, each provides perspective and insight on a particular topic. *Building Bridges*, a book about Qisong's philosophy and his central viewpoint—the oneness of the teachings (Confucianism and Buddhism included)—adopts a different view on these exchanges during the Northern Song eleventh century: using a comparative textual approach (Confucian classics and Qisong's *guwen* text), it builds an analysis of Qisong's philosophical hermeneutics of major Confucian concepts and virtues; next, it focuses on his idea of the profound nonduality of the teachings and of (Chan) Buddhism as organically integrated into the soil of Song-dynasty Confucian culture. I suggest that through his translation-interpretation of Chan and Confucian concepts embodied in the collection *Fujiao bian* written in *guwen*, Qisong builds a meaningful and compelling philosophico-spiritual and ethical bridge between Chan Buddhism (his inclusive interpretation of it) and the developing Cheng-Zhu school of Neo-Confucianism.

The present book offers a systematic and textual analysis of the nondogmatic approach taken by the scholar-monk in his commentaries on basic Confucian texts and concepts, from the ethical and practical to the most fundamental and philosophical, in a series of case studies of Qisong's essays. Without a doubt, the fact that these essays are written in Confucian style and not in a Buddhist format introduces in his writings a degree of intimacy and humility and an engaging quality. My conclusion is that even if, in the following centuries, the Confucian and Chan (the triumphant Linji school) traditions became more differentiated and focused on their distinct yet not mutually exclusive philosophico-religious identities (see also Brook 1993, 34), and Qisong's bridging efforts fell into oblivion, they produced some enduring results: the Buddhist strands that became woven into the texture of Confucian ethics and expanded its horizons, and the enrichment of the Chinese cultural value system as a whole. In all of this, I want to reiterate my broader objective, which is to demonstrate that Qisong's bridge not only fostered the formation of a philosophically deeper and ethically more compelling Neo-Confucianism but also contributed to a more socially and ethically engaged Song-dynasty Chan Buddhism.

The multiple dialogues among all these complementary books remind those studying this complex field of Confucian/Buddhist exchanges that this is a highly complex subject with deep roots in the East Asian cultural identity, which itself calls for reexamination in a variety of perspectives to tackle its various levels of meaning and implication. Indeed, a wide diversity of levels of interpretation and multiple approaches will be required to uncover the manifold facets of this phenomenon in all its richness.

The following sections are intended to address the distinct type of interpretation employed in the present book and to clarify its approach. In the next part, I explain in detail the starting point of my research on Qisong's thought: the exchanges between Confucianism and Buddhism in Song times.

VI. STARTING POINT: QISONG AND THE EXCHANGES BETWEEN CONFUCIANISM AND BUDDHISM IN SONG TIMES

Although Qisong's work was well known to the court and scholar-officials of Zhu Xi's 朱熹 (1130–1200) time, it is mentioned neither by him nor by the Northern Song Neo-Confucian masters that had influenced him most—the Cheng brothers, who were still in their twenties when Qisong wrote his essays. Yü Ying-shih affirms that the Cheng brothers strategically never mentioned Qisong in their writings. However, he argues that they certainly knew his essays. Yü Ying-shih's point is that during the 1070s, the "discussions on Chan" (*tanchan* 談禪), Qisong included, were a common topic of debate among members of the Luoyang school (the political adversaries of Wang Anshi) and that the young Cheng brothers attended these meetings organized by Han Wei 韓維 (1017–1098) and elder Confucian scholars. Yü Ying-shih quotes a comment by Cheng Yi from the book *Surviving Works of the Two Cheng Brothers* (*Er Cheng yishu* 二程遺書) about a meeting he attended in 1080: "During yesterday's meeting, the most discussed topic was Chan (大率談禪). I was not pleased with that. Upon returning [home], I felt bitterness for a long time" (Yü 2003, 1:108).

The author also highlights the existence of this two-way dialogue and interaction during the Song dynasty. He describes it as a bidirectional development: "The process of Confucianization of Northern Song Buddhism" (北宋佛教的儒學化)—in other words, "the process of becoming proficient as Confucian scholars undergone by Buddhist monks" (僧徒的士大夫化) (Qisong was one of them) and "the influence of Chan Buddhism on the Confucian literati" (士大夫中的禪風) (Yü 2003, 1:116).

The ongoing (Chan) Buddhist-Confucian interaction in the Tang-Song transition and Song times is well documented. Bernard Faure studied the dialectic relationship between "pluralistic or 'inclusive' Chan and sectarian or 'exclusive' Chan" (Faure 1991, 7). Koichi Shinohara (1994, 35–72) has explored the relationship between Confucianism and Buddhism as described by the tenth-century Buddhist monk Zhiyuan 智圓 (976–1022). Huang Chi-chiang has examined the "symbiotic nature" of the communications between Buddhist monks and Confucian literati in early Song times and their convergence of interests (Huang 1999, 297–410). Meanwhile, Albert Welter has investigated the role of literati in sanctioning the interpretation of Chan, the new style of Buddhism that was "more dependent on and subservient to the state" during the Five Dynasties and early Song period, and what he calls the "amalgamation of Chan and doctrinal Buddhism" in the thought of the tenth-century Buddhist Yanshou 延壽 (904–975). He also proposed a nuanced apprehension of early Song interpretations of *wen* 文 (see Welter 1993, 104, 161). Mark Halperin (2006) considered the lay perception of Buddhism, whereas Elizabeth Morrison (2010) discussed Qisong's writings on Chan history and lineage as a case study for the interactions of Buddhists, literati officials, and the imperial court.

The present analysis is complementary to these previous works. While the abovementioned works use the historical and religious studies approaches, this investigation introduces the new approach mentioned above in the collaborative dialogue among these various studies on Song-dynasty confluences between Buddhism and Confucianism: the philosophical method of hermeneutics. As already indicated, it covers a new type of material—Qisong's philosophical writings—and provides a new line of reasoning: hermeneutical arguments based on a comparative and interpretive understanding of the interaction between Buddhist and Confucian traditions as reflected in Qisong's essays. This type of evidence is adding a new perspective that joins the aforesaid historical and religious studies research. It stresses the inclusive, cohesive philosophical dimension of Northern Song-dynasty Buddhism. Moreover, as mentioned earlier, it presents Qisong's goal of reconciling and harmonizing Buddhist practices and doctrinal teachings with Confucianism and explores his interpretive strategies. In this way, it further contributes to understanding the specific features of eleventh-century Chan Buddhism. One may say that, during this period of powerful revival of Confucian learning, Qisong brought to a higher level the ongoing concern of the Buddhist community to promote the mediation between Buddhism and Confucianism. After the Huichang suppression in the 840s, this issue, as well as the related aspect of official patronage, influenced the Chan movement and became an important element of Buddhist rhetoric.[10]

This book is also correlative, in part, with the new philosophical scholarship on the Buddhist influence on Neo-Confucian thought, particularly with the recent study of the Buddhist roots of Zhu Xi's philosophical thought, edited by John Makeham (2018). However, the latter is a collection of essays and is focused on Zhu Xi. The Buddhists introduced there are mainly Huayan and Tiantai thinkers, who are interested neither in Confucianism nor in developing connections between Buddhism and Confucianism.

Qisong's "cohesive" Chan Buddhist thought is too complex to be simply labeled. For Huang Chi-chiang, let us recall, the originality of his thought lies in its "syncretic" quality (Huang 1986, x). In the present analysis, I highlight its "nondual" characteristic. Morrison notes in her research on Qisong's life and his contribution to the Chan lineage that "despite being a Chan dharma heir and a prolific writer, Qisong barely mentions meditation or dramatic awakening experiences. Nor does he appear to have had anything to do with the 'recorded sayings' or 'public case' genres. Indeed, aside from his historical writings, he wrote mainly on topics significant to the emerging Neo-Confucian movement.... His identity as an heir in the Yunmen 雲門 'house' of the Chan lineage seems to have meant relatively little for his religious and intellectual activities" (Morrison 2010, 8). The present philosophical investigation supports a different view. It aims to demonstrate that his identity as a Chan scholar-monk constitutes the very essence and core of the collection *Fujiao bian* 輔教編 (*Essays on Assisting the Teaching*).[11] Morrison's research on Qisong's historical works about Chan lineage also "challenges assumptions about the correlation of religious and intellectual affiliations to lineage and even sectarian identity, at least during the late eleventh century" (Morrison 2010, 8). Welter proposes to include Qisong in a group that he defines as "Buddhist with a serious interest in *guwen*, sometimes referred to as 'Confucian monks (*ruseng* 儒僧)'" (Welter 2011, 208). The Chan monk's writings certainly reflect an eleventh-century "new" style of Buddhism, an "inclusive" understanding of Chan—to use Faure's interpretation and Welter's description of the tenth-century thought of Yanshou 延壽 (904–975). As Welter noted in passing, "Qisong had close affinities with Yanshou's interpretation of Chan" (Welter 1993, 104, 175; 2011, 12, 26).

VII. APPROACH, METHODOLOGY, AND HERMENEUTICAL TRANSLATION

This philosophical research has two dimensions. First, it explores what I have called a "Confucianized" dimension of Qisong's thought, how he revisited and reinterpreted Confucian terminology in a special form of Chan aimed at his contemporary Confucian readers and auditors "who do not know Buddhism" (世儒之不知佛者; "Guang yuanjiao," 0654b19-5). Next, the study identifies another original feature, already mentioned above, of his singular form of eleventh-century Chan: its so-called cohesive or nondual perspective on Chinese Buddhist (under the aegis of Chan), Confucian, and other philosophical traditions, which considers all of them to be interdependent and to share a unique common root. The two integral elements of Qisong's thought, a cohesive/nondual Chan core and Confucian inspiration, are philosophically investigated. This involves philosophical (hermeneutical) translations from the *Fujiao bian* 輔教編 (*Essays on Assisting the Teaching*) and the *Zhongyong jie* 中庸解 (*Exegesis of the Mean*), as well as a purposeful and detailed interpretation that supports and explains these translations.

In this context, I use a broad concept of translation. Paul Ricoeur defines this notion as "synonymous with the interpretation of any meaningful whole within the same speech community" (2006, 11). The narrow notion, in contrast, is based on the theory of pure correspondence—that is, on the assumption that the translation embodies a total correspondence of meaning and therefore is sufficient to fully preserve the connotations of the original text. It has been consistently argued (Gadamer 2013, 547) that the theory of pure correspondence is false, especially in regard to philosophical texts, because it overlooks the central connection between language and thinking. Qisong's essays are philosophical works.

For this reason, the hermeneutical translation I am proposing here is based on a broader concept of translation—that is, as a restitution of the "complex of meanings" of the original. The underlying premise is that translation is already interpretation. It is for this reason that, in examining each of Qisong's essays, I choose essential paragraphs, translate them, and provide interpretations of these translations. In a sense, I would argue that every chapter of *Building Bridges* in its entirety constitutes an interpretive translation of a specific essay by Qisong—that is, of the essential themes the essay conveys and of the topics it treats. The interpretive translation in its entirety comprises the articulation of all these chapters as a coherent whole that involves two major extra- and intralayers. The extralayer sets the meaning of Qisong's paragraphs in the context of another language, culture, and time (contemporary English and Western culture) and expresses it in this new language-world—the emphasis here is on avoiding introducing in translation foreign cultural presuppositions that do not belong to the initial classic text and its culture. The intralayer of this interpretive translation uncovers Qisong's references to Confucian classics (Confucian concepts) and his progressive construction of an inclusive Chan Buddhist meaning of those classical Chinese concepts—the emphasis here is on Confucian and Chan Buddhist understandings connected through what may be called Qisong's own translation of Buddhist concepts into the Confucian *guwen* language and culture of his contemporary interlocutors.

This methodology is indebted in part to Ricoeur's theory of translation as a model of hermeneutics (i.e., the hermeneutic model of translation and its linguistic paradigm—namely, the two sides of translation, extra- and intralinguistic; Ricoeur 2006, 21–52), while remaining fully engaged with Qisong's own theoretical outlook made possible by his proficiency in both Confucian and Buddhist scholarly methods. The study is thus intended to provide a two-sided "hermeneutic translation" of the Chan scholar-monk's comparative, inclusive, and nondual perception of principal Confucian concepts and virtues (teaching, social virtues, filial devotion, human nature, emotions, principle, *zhongyong* [middle way], and so forth), including their interpretation within the context of the (Chan) Buddhist sphere of cultivations and ethical interrelationships. As noted above, the first dimension of this translation—extralinguistic—is embodied in the transfer of meaning from Qisong's Song-dynasty *guwen* language to the English language. It involves the author of this book, the translator in her philosophical role, and comprises all the interpretive passages located in the text before and after the de facto translations into English of Qisong's quotations. The extralinguistic facet of the hermeneutic translation focuses on the philosophical role of the translator and on the latter's effort to render explicitly and as accurately as possible the multiple layers of meaning and implicit resonances of Qisong's culturally different text. The translator's interpretations that form the chapters of this book therefore fulfill a mediating role. They mediate between the world of meaning of Qisong's Song-dynasty text and that of the contemporary Western reader.

I therefore occasionally appeal to several philosophical theories as interpretive tools by which I strengthen my interpretation and analysis. These conceptual instruments constitute an integral part of the extralinguistic facet of my hermeneutical approach. When relevant, I use them to fashion arguments that sustain my interpretation—for instance, in chapters 1, 3, and 4, I call on the theoretical structure proposed by Frederick Streng for understanding religion as a means to ultimate transformation and on his perceptions of "a natural universal order of life" and of "spiritual discipline"; in chapter 2, I draw on Paul Tillich's idea of religion as "ultimate concern"; chapters 3 and 6 bring into play Masao Abe's conceptions of "boundless solidarity of life" and "transvaluation of values"; chapter 4 mentions Felix Adler's ethics as religion as well as Akira Hirakawa's theory of "action"; chapters 4, 5, and 6 engage with Keiji Nishitani's interpretation religion, nothingness, field of emptiness, no-ego, and no-self; and chapter 7 appeals to Shin'ichi Hisamatsu's view on nonduality and

Charles Taylor's "sense of fullness." By bringing these theoretical perspectives to bear on the conceptuality of Qisong's and Zhu Xi's philosophic language, I attempt to carry across the Chinese Song-dynasty texts and the philosophy they embody into the context of Western language (English) and philosophy, suggesting intercultural comparisons without falsifying the original meaning of these writings.

Therefore, I am not using these theoretical devices to construct a "comparative discussion" that simply attempts to match non-Western content (Qisong's Chinese Confucianized Buddhist text) to Western philosophical terms, categories, and theories. As highlighted above, the theory and methodology used in this analysis are indebted in part to philosophical hermeneutics, while remaining engaged with Qisong's own theoretical outlook made possible by his proficiency in both Confucian and Buddhist scholarly methods. As such, this translation remains vigilant in not shifting the Chinese ideas into the Western system of thought and is committed to accurately reminding the reader of the cultural presuppositions involved in the Chinese (Chan Buddhist-Confucian) way of thinking.

The second side of the hermeneutic translation—intralinguistic—concerns Qisong himself in his translator or interpreter role, the comparative interpretation of the abovementioned concepts undertaken by Qisong, within the same linguistic community: the eleventh-century Song-dynasty culture of his Confucian and Buddhist interlocutors. This side focuses on Qisong as mediator, as intermediary between the Confucian and Buddhist communities of his time. One might say that Qisong realized this intralinguistic translation (reinterpretation) precisely through stepping into the fabric of Confucian *guwen* language and weaving into it the (Chan) Buddhist notions of the community to which he belonged. Furthermore, both facets of the two-sided hermeneutic translation that this book constructs around major Confucian and Buddhist concepts of the Song-dynasty thought embody my contemporary analysis of how Qisong conveys through his *guwen* translation the content of his Buddhist ideas. As pointed out, the hermeneutical interpretation proposed is composed of multiple overlapping layers, deployed in parallel fashion, which together provide the theoretical framework for the narrative development of this study.

To set the stage for what follows, I would like to try to further describe the extralinguistic aspect of my philosophical approach as an intercultural, "comparative hermeneutics." I use this term in the broadest sense. It bears repeating, it is not Western hermeneutics in the sense that it brings Western theories to investigate Chinese content; rather, it seeks to illustrate the theoretical developments that unfolded in Song-dynasty Chinese thought itself as the Buddhist and Confucian traditions came to accommodate each other within the Song culture. As stated above, the theory and methodology used in this analysis are indebted in part to hermeneutics and hermeneutic phenomenology, while remaining engaged with Qisong's own theoretical outlook made possible by his proficiency in both Confucian and Buddhist scholarly methods.

At the heart of this philosophical approach, concerned not to obscure or misrepresent the authentic Chinese presuppositions of Qisong's text, are what I call "philosophical/hermeneutical translations" of his writings into English. (Above, see the idea of the extralinguistic side of translation and the difference between the narrow and broad concepts of translation in Gadamer's and Ricoeur's theories of translation.) As such, these transcultural translations remain vigilant in not shifting the Chinese text and ideas into the Western system of language and into the Western thought and cultural presuppositions that dwell in the Western language. It is for this reason that the interpretations and explanations that precede or follow the English translation of a paragraph from classical Chinese are an integral component of the hermeneutical translation. They perform the role of better grounding the translated paragraph (now an English paragraph) in its original (Chinese) cultural context and of better connecting the two partners: the foreign (the semantic field of the original classical text and its author, Qisong) and the recipient of the translated work (the English reader) (on this theory, see Ricoeur 2006, 4).

This explains why, intentionally, I did not seek in any way to provide, above all, a translation that flows naturally and is easy to read in English. A translation is considered fluent and easy to digest—in other words, effortless—precisely because readers encounter in it familiar cultural presuppositions that they already understand, that spontaneously orient them toward particular culturally familiar meanings, existing within their own horizon of understanding. In this case, no hefty effort is necessary to apprehend the connotations of the translated text.

From a hermeneutical point of view, such translation obscures the original Chinese thought processes when transferring them into Western language and into the framework of Western thought (which is intrinsically related to the structure of Western language), distorts the Chinese presuppositions of the original text, and often replaces them with Western presuppositions. Let us not forget that this obscuration is the necessary and inevitable price to be paid in order to make the transcultural translation "natural" and "easy to read" in English.

In his essay "A Dialogue on Language: Between a Japanese and an Inquirer," Martin Heidegger charismatically unveils this danger. In that context, he illustrates that "the language of the dialogue constantly destroys the possibility of saying what the dialogue is about" (Heidegger 1971, 5). In the present case, the language of our dialogue with Qisong (i.e., the interpretive translation) is English. The challenge the interpreter and her reader face is the constant danger that English damages the possibility of explaining Qisong's arguments and their cultural roots by introducing Western presuppositions and preunderstandings through the translation and interpretation process. The hermeneutical translation and the comparative interpretation attached to it are the two interrelated tools of this study that overcome this menace, thus giving, hopefully, the English-language reader a less distorted access to Qisong's universe of thought.

In light of these considerations, the philosophical translations of Qisong's texts that I propose are committed to accurately reminding the Western-language reader of the culturally implicit presumptions involved in the Chinese way of thinking. The latter refers to Qisong's cohesive Chan Buddhist and (Neo-)Confucian traditions. This is the primary concern and premise of the philosophical translations proposed in this book, rather than to provide the reader with effortless, light, and fluid translations of the classical Chinese text. It is fair to point out that in this transcultural and cross-cultural context (i.e., the contemporary English translation of a classical Chinese text embedded in its own Song-dynasty culture), Western readers need to make an effort that brings them out of the comfort zone of their culturally conditioned understanding and orients them toward a discomfort zone, where they can first become aware of obstacles in understanding and unfamiliar cultural preconceptions, and then creatively and internally find their own way of adapting to the text, becoming aware of its own Chinese premises and embracing them.

Which text, precisely? The English translations are of passages from Qisong's Chinese collection of essays *Fujiao bian* dedicated to supporting Buddhist teaching in China, a Song-dynasty work written in the Confucian *guwen* style. Qisong realized a remarkable achievement with this sophisticated text and its approach, as in it, he not only explores connections and differences between notions shared by Confucianism and "cohesive" Chan Buddhism, which use the same Chinese characters to describe related though differently rooted meanings, but also finds a way to use, in a different context, Confucian *guwen*. This writing style, focused on the literary structures and Confucian meanings of the notions of the classics of Chinese antiquity, was strongly advocated during the Northern Song by the *guwen* movement and the heirs of Han Yu. This specific cultural tool, most familiar to Confucians, is highlighted above (sec. I) by the eleventh-century scholar-official Chen Shunyu, Qisong's friend and biographer, in his *Records of Qisong's Professions* ("Mingjiao dashi hangye ji" 都官集·明教大師行業記, see Chen 1972, Tsai 2012) as the core feature of the Song scholar-officials' education and training. Using his in-depth knowledge of this Confucian tool and of its contextual sensitivity—that is, the Confucian presuppositions embedded in it (discussed in this book) and centered on the horizon of meaning of the old texts of pre-imperial and early imperial China—Qisong adapts this Confucian device, infuses it with new meaning, and employs it to explain particularly difficult Chinese dimensions of Chan Buddhist ontology, psychology, and soteriology.

My starting point in this study is therefore Qisong's usage of Confucian *guwen*. As he himself stresses ("Guang yuanjiao," 0654b07), the Chan scholar-monk adopts it in order to explain Buddhism to his Confucian contemporaries. This constitutes for me the most powerful and original innovation of Qisong—his use of Confucian terms and references from Confucian classics, in order to persuasively interpret a special form of socially engaged Chan Buddhism and highlight its connections with Confucianism. His usage of this Confucian *guwen* device, how he implements it in order to explain in Confucian terms and within Confucian contexts the distinctive features of his cohesive Chan Buddhism, was my guiding line when clarifying textual issues and Qisong's interpretations of Confucian concepts. For this reason, as part of the hermeneutical approach, I first identify such key Confucian notions present in his argumentation and then explain their original and new meanings through introducing connected quotations from Confucian classics (the *Liji, Lunyu, Mengzi, Shijing*, etc.) and Qisong's essays. This interpretive strategy aims at broadening the reader's comprehension of his text as well as calling attention to the scholar-monk's innovations with regard to opening up the meanings of these original Confucian notions and extending them to the Song-dynasty Buddhist context.

The hermeneutical translation I propose takes the reader to such linguistical discomfort zones, preparing them not only to understand concepts rooted in a culturally different soil (Chinese) but also to penetrate the unique and unprecedented situation of using a Confucian literary and philosophical tool in order to expound complex Chan Buddhist features to a Confucian audience. When translating and interpreting Qisong, I therefore focus on uncovering and illustrating the implicit links between his text and Confucian terms and classics. This comparative Chinese Buddhist/Confucian hermeneutics thus represents an effort to, first, defuse the danger of relying on language (English) only and, second, to further stimulate a new understanding: that of Qisong's philosophical and religious arguments, situated at the interface between Confucianism and Chinese Buddhism.

VII.1. Overall Structure, Organization and Narrative of the Book: Articulation of the Themes to Be Addressed

As discussed, *Building Bridges* is intimately connected with the research discussed above and builds on those earlier studies while moving in a new direction. Those previous works introduce the reader to the universe of Qisong's life, lineage, and works; to the broader structure of the history of Chan (Buddhism); and to the exchanges between Buddhist and Confucian traditions in East Asia.

This book takes the reader through Qisong's *Fujiao bian* (*Essays on Assisting the Teaching*), its meanings, and its place within the philosophical context of Song-dynasty thought. The next seven chapters compose a unified philosophical hermeneutics and hermeneutical translation. They are organized in a sensible and progressive way, working up to the more philosophically intricate aspects of Qisong's thought by stages, chapter by chapter. Their sequence follows the path along which Qisong's Confucian scholarship unfolded in his *Essays on Assisting the Teaching*. Once again, I would like to recall that its five philosophically and deeply connected essays are written in the Confucian *guwen* style, for a Confucian audience. Each chapter focuses on a specific essay of Qisong's anthology and offers an analysis of its major ideas, based on essential paragraphs of the essay. This investigation consists of multiple layers as detailed above: it is based on translations and includes the interpretation of these translations, unveils the Confucian references that are implicitly present in Qisong's essays, and elucidates their meaning in the context of his Chan Buddhist thought. An earlier version of the last section, chapter 7, was published in the journal *Philosophy East and West*. After revision, I integrated it into the coherent structure formed by the other six chapters.

The organization of the book is thus inspired by the progressive order of difficulty according to which Qisong himself arranges his essays, from simpler issues such as the multiple meanings of the notion of teaching and the comparative features of Confucian and Buddhist social practice, to deeper, more complex dimensions and nondiscursive practices of Buddhist tradition, including Buddhist filial devotion, karma, retribution, seeing one's nature, the nondualities world/heart-mind,[12] suchness/completeness, and nature/emptiness. In the beginning of his essay "Guang yuanjiao" (0654b16-15), Qisong unveils the inspiration he found in the *Huayan Sutra*, which helped him organize his five articles: "By assimilating the branches, one returns to the root (攝末歸本門)." From the careful reading of his work, one understands that in the arrangement of essays collected in the *Fujiao bian*, the branches are the concrete topics exposed from simpler and tangible to complex and subtle, while the root is the spiritual Chan core of Qisong's thought. This examination also enabled me to discover and throw light on the connecting lines between his essays. The scholar-monk's first essay focuses on interdependency and transformative teaching; the second, on the meaning of the notion of teaching; the third offers his illustration of the deficiencies of Confucianism; the fourth discusses filial devotion; and the fifth focuses on Chan nothingness.

I therefore followed his articulation of branches/root when organizing the material of the seven chapters. Moreover, as he himself indicates ("Quanshu," 0651c21), Qisong wrote these five essays with the intention to illustrate and discuss major Confucian ideas and to explain their complementarity with Buddhist views. It is also with his goal in mind that I propose and construct the subjects examined in this book.

The articulation of the themes to be addressed has been organized under the following pillars: the notion of interdependent transformation of individuals, a process of fundamental change activated by social relationships and emotions/feelings; the concept of teaching and its multiple layers; the interface between external stimuli, names, and appropriate behaviors; the meaning of filial devotion; the junction of the heart-mind, emotions, and nature-emptiness; principle and nothingness; and spiritual discipline.

This specific, progressive organization of the themes I address forms the narrative of the present study. It can be defined as locating Chan within the Confucian context.[13] This narrative includes a sequence of topics that illustrate the abovementioned articulation of themes. They are detailed in the next section.

VII.2. *The Selection of Topics Addressed in the Book: Locating Chan within the Confucian Context*

In chapter 1, dedicated to Qisong's first essay, "Inquiry into the Teachings" ("Yuanjiao" 原教, included in *Fujiao bian shang* 輔教編上; see Bibliography), I highlight and interpret his perspective on the complementary roles of the Buddhist Five Precepts and Ten Goods and the Confucian norms of behavior identified as the Five Permanencies in the domain of everyday affairs, in cultivating social interdependency, and in making people good and transforming their heart-minds. In this context, I also build connections between the ideas of the "Yuanjiao" and Han Yu's article "Yuandao" 原道 and suggest that in this first essay, Qisong implicitly answers Han Yu's virulent criticism against Buddhism.

Chapter 2 focuses on Qisong's "Extensive Inquiry into the Teachings" ("Guan yuanjiao" 廣原教, included in *Fujiao bian zhong*; see Bibliography) and discusses the Confucianized and cohesive dimensions of his teaching as well as his interpretation of the notions of middle (*zhong* 中), sincerity (*cheng* 誠), and rectifying the heart-mind (*zheng xin* 正心), all in connection with the classics *Zhongyong* 中庸 and *Daxue* 大學.

Chapter 3 discusses the essay "Letter of Advice" ("Quanshu" 勸書, included in *Fujiao bian shang* 輔教編上; see Bibliography). It adds another layer of complexity to Qisong's demonstration of the complementarity between Buddhism and Confucianism through indirectly unveiling deficiencies of Confucian practice and highlighting Buddhist means of assisting Confucianism and correcting its failures. This chapter investigates the weaknesses of the Confucian notions of external stimuli (*gan* 感), ritual (*li* 禮), name/reputation (*ming* 名), rectification of names (*zheng ming* 正名), and appropriate behavior (*yi* 義). It also explores Qisong's view of the cohesive Chan concepts of authentic nature (*xing* 性), heart-mind (*xin* 心), and universal principle (*li* 理), on which he builds his original view on how the Chan Buddhist teaching is able to provide the assistance needed to remedy the Confucian flaws.

Chapter 4 examines the essay "On Filial Devotion" ("Xiaolun" 孝論, included in *Fujiao bian xia* 輔教篇下; see Bibliography), which introduces in Qisong's progressive argumentative architecture a new and essential notion and practice, the origin of which is, of course, Confucian: the Buddhist practice of filial devotion (*xiao* 孝). From this part to the end of the book, the study is centered on the differences between the Buddhist and Confucian teachings. Clearly, these are complementary to their similarities and arise from them. This time, the comparative topic of dissimilarities allows Qisong to unfold unique features of his cohesive Chan practice. This chapter makes reference to the Confucian *Classic of Filial Devotion* (*Xiaojing* 孝經), and to several Chinese sutras related to this subject: *Brahma's Net Sutra*, *Bodhisattva Syama Sutra*, and *Ullambana Sutra*. Compared to previous chapters, the fourth has a higher level of complexity, as Qisong introduces here more difficult dimensions of his Chan Buddhism: complete Buddhist filial devotion in relation with incomplete Confucian filial devotion, the interrelatedness of all sentient beings, karma, the rectification of feelings/emotions, and the interpretation of the Buddhist precepts as filial devotion.

The next section deepens Qisong's innovative interpretation of the spiritual dimension of Chan practice. Thus, chapter 5 further develops his specific understanding of the interdependent Chan concepts of heart-mind, causes, and fruits (因果) and its two associated correlatives—emotions (*qing* 情) and nature—while gathering and connecting elements of the analysis present in all essays discussed in the preceding chapters. The Chan scholar-monk outlines here the significance of the correlation emotions/nature as the core of what he distinguishes as the essential Buddhist interdependence—life, death, nature, and emotions.

The last two chapters deal with Qisong's "Encomium of the Platform Sutra" ("Tanjing zan" 壇經贊, included in *Fujiao bian xia* 輔教篇下; see Bibliography) and with his commentary on the classic *Zhongyong*, the *Exegesis of the Mean* (*Zhongyong jie* 中庸解; see Bibliography). They close the in-depth interpretation of key Chan notions (principle, nothingness, behavior, and emotions) while also building a transhistorical dialogue between the Chan scholar-monk and the well-known twelfth-century Neo-Confucian master Zhu Xi. These concepts are further comparatively explored, this time in the form of an encounter between the two prominent thinkers of the Song dynasty, and of Qisong's answer avant la lettre (one hundred years prior) to Zhu Xi's criticism against the Buddhist teaching.

ONE

CHAN SCHOLAR-MONK QISONG ON THE AFFINITIES AND DIFFERENCES BETWEEN CHAN BUDDHISM AND CONFUCIANISM IN "INQUIRY INTO THE TEACHINGS" ("YUANJIAO" 原教)

I. INTRODUCTION

The purpose of this chapter is to illustrate and analyze the significance of Qisong's particular contribution to the Song Chan Buddhist tradition[1] through his original and persuasive interpretation of the affinities and differences between Confucian and Chan traditions. The ideas of Qisong's Chan school (its inclusive character and Chan-specific characteristics are further detailed in the following chapters) are radically different from the previous Chan schools of the Tang dynasty[2]—namely, because it incorporates a Confucian dimension.

This exploration thus intends to highlight that in his writing "Inquiry into the Teachings" ("Yuanjiao" 原教),[3] the first essay of his collection *Fujiao bian* 輔教編 (*Essays on Assisting the Teaching* [of Buddhism]), the prominent Song-dynasty scholar-monk achieved two important goals. First, he responded convincingly to the criticism of his contemporaries, the Northern Song-dynasty Confucians,[4] and of their illustrious predecessor, Han Yu 韓愈 (768–824), who deemed the Buddhist tradition "heterodox" (*yiduan* 異端) and therefore harmful and incompatible with Chinese culture,[5] which they understood to be purely Confucian.[6] Second, this chapter intends to demonstrate that Qisong's most important achievement is to have identified and developed what might be called the Chineseness of the Song Chan tradition, thus initiating a genuinely intra-Chinese dialogue between the Buddhist and Confucian traditions during the Song dynasty. In other words, in his work, (Chan) Buddhist tradition is not a teaching of foreign origin anymore but a true Chinese one. Specifically, through elaborating his interpretation of the Chan Buddhist tradition by means of the classics of ancient China, Qisong explained it in authentically

Chinese terms—as being firmly rooted in the soil of Chinese culture, an eleventh-century expression of the enduring cultural unity of China.

Importantly, I suggest that the Song Chan / Song Confucianism encounter embodied in his work is no longer a transcultural debate but an exchange between two Chinese traditions of equal salience in the landscape of Chinese culture. Yü Ying-shih (1930-2021) also highlights the existence of this two-way dialogue and interaction during the Song dynasty. As already mentioned in section VI of the introduction, he describes it as a bidirectional development, "the process of Confucianization of Northern Song Buddhism (北宋佛教的儒學化)"—in other words, "the process of becoming proficient as Confucian scholars undergone by Buddhist monks (僧徒的士大夫化)" (Qisong was one of them) and "the influence of Chan Buddhism on the Confucian literati (士大夫中的禪風)" (Yü 2003, 1:116).

Accordingly, this chapter dedicated to the essay "Yuanjiao" explores the traditional Chinese terms Qisong uses to point out the manner in which he builds with them the core features of Song Chan Buddhism—that is, its Chineseness. His interpretation of Song Chan brings the latter in line with the prime concern of Chinese society and civilization throughout its history, emphasized by Confucianism since antiquity—namely, the building of good governance. Furthermore, as will be determined, Buddhism in his view is not merely a teaching compatible with Confucianism but an effective tool, a valuable assistant on which Confucianists can rely when performing their administrative duties.

That the unity between Song-dynasty Confucianism and Buddhism goes beyond their different methods is the central thesis defended by Qisong in his "Yuanjiao," and he builds all his arguments on this basic premise. To a lesser extent, he also touches on the essential differences between them.

The topic I address in this context is the idea, common to both teachings, of the interdependent transformation of individuals, a process of fundamental change activated by social relationships and emotions/feelings. Qisong further develops the themes from the "Yuanjiao" in another essay of the collection *Fujiao bian*, the "Guang yuanjiao" (Extensive Inquiry into the Teachings). This is the subject of the next chapter.

II. TEXTS, CONTEXTS, AND TEACHINGS OF THE SAGES

As stated above, the analysis focuses on Qisong's essay "Inquiry into the Teachings" ("Yuanjiao") and interprets its arguments in light of three sources: Han Yu's essay "Inquiry into the Dao" ("Yuandao" 原道; Han 1986, 12); the thirteenth chapter of the Neo-Confucian anthology *Reflections on Things at Hand*

(*Jinsilu* 近思錄; hereafter *JSL*), entitled "Distinguishing the Heterodox Doctrines" ("Bian bie yiduan" 辨別異端; *Zhuzi quan shu* 朱子全書 [hereafter *ZZQS*], 13:277–281); and Zhu Xi's 朱熹 (1130–1200) commentaries on the *Four Books*.

As noted, the "Yuanjiao" ("Inquiry into the Teachings") is the first essay of Qisong's book *Fujiao bian* 輔教編, a work composed during the 1050s and approved in 1062, by Emperor Renzong 仁宗 (r. 1022–1063), to be included in the Song Buddhist canon (Wang 2017, xxxiii, 108).

The aforementioned anthology *Reflections on Things at Hand*, compiled by Zhu Xi and Lü Zuqian 呂祖謙 (1137–1181) between 1175 and 1178,[7] contains the opinions of the Northern Song masters.[8] The Cheng brothers, founders of the Cheng-Zhu school, belong to the next generation after Qisong. Yü Ying-shih affirms that the Cheng brothers strategically never mentioned Qisong in their works. However, he argues that they certainly knew Qisong's work—the eminent representative of Song Chan, officially recognized by Emperor Renzong (Wang 2017, 195).[9] It can be said that their efforts to criticize Buddhism are also a response to Qisong's commitment to demonstrate the compatibility between Chan and Confucianism and their complementarity.

The parallel analysis of these texts is pertinent because the Neo-Confucian (Cheng-Zhu) school is the tradition that systematically brought forward criticism directed at Buddhist teachings after Qisong.[10] The condemnation of Buddhism in the thirteenth chapter of the *Jinsilu* anthology expresses Song Confucian views and constitutes a subtler continuation, at a philosophical and foundational level, of Han Yu's eighth-century socioeconomic criticism.[11] This parallel among Qisong's "Yuanjiao," Hanyu's "Yuandao," and the Neo-Confucian anthology is the analytical framework that enables us to develop a better understanding of the issues on which Qisong focuses in the "Yuanjiao" and the meaning of the specific concepts he uses within the context of the Northern Song debate between Buddhists and Confucians. Remember that Hanyu's fierce criticism is central to the Northern Song Confucian perception of Buddhism.

I suggest below that the title and topic of "Yuanjiao" are inspired by Han Yu's article "Inquiry into the Dao" ("Yuandao" 原道). The first connection between Qisong and Han Yu is their outstanding use of the "ancient style" (*guwen* 古文). Qisong is famous for his ability to write in this clear and simple Confucian style, lacking any spurious ornament, as can be seen from the citations provided in this study.[12]

Let us point out that the title "Yuanjiao" suggests that, in this essay, Qisong opens a dialogue with Han Yu's "Yuandao." The two titles are different in that Han Yu refers to the "way" (*dao* 道) and Qisong to the "teachings" (*jiao* 教; terms used in reference to both Buddhism and Confucianism). Qisong highlights the distinction between the way and the teachings in his commentary on the Confucian classic *Zhongyong*,[13] the *Zhongyong jie* 中庸解 (*Exegesis of the Mean*; hereafter *ZYJ*)[14]: "The way [*dao*] is that which flows in and out of the ten thousand things.... The teaching is what rectifies the ten thousand things [i.e., human affairs and behaviors] and corrects them (道也者, 出萬物也入萬物也.... 教也者, 正萬物直萬物也)" (Qisong, ZYJ 3, 0666b25-4). I would suggest that this contrast illustrates the manner in which Qisong intends to address Han Yu's criticism—that is, through dealing with it at a profound level, starting from the essential difference between the way as subtle environment and the teachings as functioning, daily practical awareness of the way.

In the above paragraph, he implicitly advances that the *dao* is a deep and higher level of reality, a perfect dynamic and living substrate pertaining to all realities (including human beings and their affairs), of which only the sages typically have awareness and mastery. Usually, ordinary people do not have access to it without instruction. It is the teaching, a form of concrete practice, through which the sages make people aware of the way and train them how to correct themselves and follow it. Most of the time, Qisong uses the term *sages* in a general way, without specifying to which teaching they belong, because he views these sages, Confucian and Buddhist alike, as the founders and leaders of Chinese culture. It is understood that Qisong refers here and in the other essays of his collection *Fujiao bian* to only one "way," one higher reality and subtle substrate that is possible to apprehend in many ways, and to different sages and teachings (Confucian and Buddhist), which are for him all equally worthy, universally valid, regardless of their birthplace identity: "The sage is one who has a great awareness and mastery of the way (聖人者, 蓋大有道者之稱也). How could the individual with great awareness and mastery of the way not be called a sage? How can there exist a way of the sage that cannot be followed everywhere (所至不可行乎)?" (Qisong, "Yuanjiao" [hereafter "YJ"], 651a10-5; 2016a). And also: "Thus the teachings provided by the sages unfold differently, but they are all adequate [to the way]" (Qisong, "YJ," 0649b24-4).

Through emphasizing this nondual unity, which for him arises from the way as highest level of reality and all-embracing spiritual environment, Qisong inherently offers his response to the narrow perspective of Han Yu and the Song Confucians that considers only Chinese-born teachings fit for the Chinese people. Indeed, Han Yu expresses this fear of deterioration of Chineseness as barbarization: "After not very long, all of us will become barbarian (幾何其不胥 而為夷也)" (Han 1986, 17).

Consequently, this is a major argument Qisong puts forward regarding the Chineseness of Song-dynasty Chan Buddhism: teachings are all adequate to the nondual *dao*. The next section explores the affinities between Song-dynasty Chan and Confucian teaching according to Qisong.

III. AFFINITIES BETWEEN SONG-DYNASTY CHAN BUDDHIST AND CONFUCIAN TEACHINGS: CULTIVATING INTERDEPENDENCY

III.1. A Common Goal

A noteworthy tactic that Qisong uses in a specific philosophical/spiritual context to give grounds for the commonality of Buddhist (on the interpretation given to it by Qisong) and Confucian teachings is to present the similarity of their ultimate goals across their different approaches.[15] He interprets with much originality their common objective as "making people good (*wei shan* 為善)": "The teachings [Confucianism and Buddhism] provided by the sages are different (不同); however, they are identical in that they make people good [stimulate good actions] (而同於為善也)" (Qisong, "YJ," 0649b28-10).

This idea sheds new light on the major goal of Confucianism, usually pointed out by Confucians themselves as "ensuring good governance"—that is, in the *Great Learning*'s terms, "governing one's country well" (*zhi qi guo* 治其國) and "making people live together peacefully" (*tianxia ping* 天下平; *Daxue* 大學, *jing*; ZZQS, 6:17). However, the opinion that making people good is also the intended aim of Confucianism, which Qisong implies, is not some artificial contrivance designed to further his cause but a valid interpretation, as the same classic, the *Great Learning*, also views "dwelling in the complete good" (*zhi yu zhishan* 止於至善) as an essential stage of learning and a preliminary basis for developing the capacity of good governance (see *Daxue*, *jing*). Thus, through this interpretation, and inspired by the *Great Learning*, Qisong effects an important interpretative change in the Song Confucian perception of those receiving the teaching: he brings to light the importance of the people as the intended final beneficiary of the teaching instead of emphasizing those responsible for governance—namely, the elite officials, exemplary persons (*junzi* 君子). It should also be noted that Neo-Confucians' vision is consistent with his. A century later, Zhu Xi in his commentary *Daxue zhangju*, *jing* also interprets the major objective of the great learning as the capacity to "renew people" (*xin min* 新民; Zhu, *Daxue zhangju*, *jing*, ZZQS, 6:17).

Furthermore, Qisong expresses even more clearly the connection he makes between this view of making people good, which is his understanding of the highest objective, common to Buddhist and Confucian teachings, and the standard Confucian ideal of good governance: "If all people were to cultivate each of the five Buddhist precepts (此各修),[16] even though they could not be reborn in a heaven (非生天), this would be sufficient for all people to become good individuals (人人足成善人). A world where all people are good and which is not well governed—there is no such thing! (人皆善而世不治, 未之有也)" (Qisong, "YJ," 0649b2-1).

Additionally, in this paragraph, Qisong implicitly expresses two ideas. The first is the fact that becoming good when following the Buddhist teaching means doing good on behalf of others, cultivating an interpersonal good and therefore interpersonal relationships (society is well governed). This perspective on the objective of Buddhist teaching thus addresses, as it will be discussed later, a major Confucian criticism that both Han Yu and the anthology *Jinsilu* emphasize. In the latter, Cheng Hao 程顥 (1032–1085) (*JSL*, 13.3) criticizes Buddhists for "damaging the human relationships" (*hui renlun* 毀人倫) when focusing on individual awakening. In the same paragraph, he points out that these human relationships and their corresponding feelings, which are destroyed by the Buddhists, are the inherent expression of the "real way" and the heart of the Confucian teaching: "The relation between father and son (父子) is founded on affection (親); the relation between ruler and official (君王) is founded on rigorousness (嚴); and all the other relations, between husband and wife (夫婦), between older and younger (長幼), between friends (朋友), they are all expressions of the natural way (無所為而非道)" (*JSL*, 13.3; *ZZQS*, 13:277).

This network of relationships could be regarded as the definition of the "Confucian way of life" and as the Confucian cultivation of interdependency. And Cheng Hao's view implicitly includes his Neo-Confucian interpretation of the "Buddhist way of life" as being opposed to the Chinese because it separates between cultivating correct social relationships in daily life affairs and cultivating enlightenment. It might be said that this assertion is true for the Mahayana Buddhism of the first centuries, for the Linji subschool of Chan mentioned earlier in the introduction. However, as Qisong demonstrates, this is not so for eleventh-century Chan Buddhism (in his interpretation).

Note that, through emphasizing the social relationships (interdependency) as the core of Buddhist teaching, the scholar-monk does not merely refute the Confucians' criticism but, more importantly, makes explicit the deep Chinese roots of Chan Buddhism. Scholars were already discussing the "strong secularizing tendencies" of Buddhism in the last decades of the Tang dynasty (see Zürcher 1989, 47). In what follows, I point out that in his essay "Yuanjiao" Qisong uses two forms of justification to successfully demonstrate that during the Northern Song dynasty, the focus of Chan Buddhism shifted definitively onto social relationships. First, he distinguishes between two types of Buddhist teachings—one for the laity[17] and one for the clergy, with the first type being the core topic of his work. Second, he establishes a certain equivalency between the Buddhist teachings for the laity and Confucian teachings, by relying on the abovementioned notion of social good and good actions (*shan* 善).

At the beginning of this introductory essay, "Yuanjiao," Qisong recalls the well-known five Buddhist "vehicles" (methods) laid down in the Buddhist tradition.[18] However, he clearly indicates that in his texts written in Confucian *guwen* style and intended for a Confucian audience, he deals only with the first two of the five vehicles, because these two concern Chan teachings for the laity (that is, members of the Confucian society): the so-called vehicles of man (*rencheng* 人乘) and of heaven (*tiancheng* 天乘). He briefly mentions the last three, which guide those who have detached themselves from the world, and focuses almost entirely on the first two vehicles for the use of ordinary people, the lay Buddhists (people and Confucian scholars), who are "considerably attached to emotions (以世情膠甚), and often cannot get rid of them; therefore, these two methods guide them through using their own emotions (就其情而制之)" (Qisong, "YJ," 0649a17-3, 0649a17-15). These practices include the constant observation of the Five Precepts (*wujie* 五戒) (i.e., the vehicle of man) or of the higher standard of the Ten Goods (*shishan* 十善)[19] (i.e., the vehicle of heaven). They form the structure not of simple instruction but of a "Buddhist way of life,"[20] which, in Qisong's view, is consistent with the "Confucian way of life" mentioned earlier. Clearly, concentration (*ding* 定) and wisdom (*hui* 惠) are the other specific dimensions of Chan Buddhism. Yet for the obvious reason that they are far less related to Confucianism, Qisong discusses them not in this comparative context but in his "Encomium of the Platform Sutra," and they are not included in the essay "Yuanjiao."

The Five Precepts are general and seek to restrain desires and evils (i.e., the desires to kill, to steal, to engage in illicit sex, to lie, and to drink intoxicating drinks). One realizes that Qisong's Ten Goods[21] have a lot in common with the Confucian Five Permanencies (*Wuchang* 五常)[22]: kindness (*ren* 仁), appropriate behavior (*yi* 義), spirit of ritual (*li* 禮), moral knowledge (discerning what is right and what is wrong; *zhi* 智), and fidelity to one's pledged word (*xin* 信). Note his powerful and persuasive argument that the Confucian virtues and Buddhist proscriptions are complementary. The Ten Goods include the Five Precepts and the following rules explained by Qisong in the subsequent terms: "speaking clearly, without unnecessary embellishments" (*bu qi yu* 不綺語), "not having two tongues" ("not talking behind another person's back"; *bu liang she* 不兩舌), "avoiding verbal abuse, as well as things that do not correspond to the sense of duty" (*bu e kou* 不惡口), "not being envious (jealous)" (*bu ji* 不嫉), "not reacting with anger" (*bu hui* 不恚), and "not being stupid" (not failing to distinguish good from evil; (*bu chi* 不癡) (Qisong, "YJ," 0649a25-14). Obviously, in his interpretation meant for Confucian readers, the Buddhist Ten Goods share quite an affinity with the Confucian Five Permanencies because, as shown below, they are sharply focused on building social cohesion, interdependence, and harmonious human relationships. Thus, Qisong's rule of "speaking clearly, without unnecessary embellishments" is reminiscent of the ancient and direct style of Confucius, known as *guwen*, and of Han Yu's Ancient Style movement,[23] oriented against the self-indulgent aestheticism of Tang literary culture. Clearly, this rule is geared toward cultivating social interdependency because a direct and concise style is a means to promote sincerity and fidelity to one's pledged word. "Never talking behind another person's back" also fosters social connection, trust, and the sense of duty. Forbidding "verbal abuse, as well as things that do not correspond to the sense of duty," obviously promotes the sense of responsibility, as well as kindness, social stability, and consensus. Cultivating the habits of "not being envious" and "not reacting with anger" evidently preserves social cohesion. And "not being stupid" is equivalent with cultivating Confucian moral knowledge—that is, being able to distinguish between right and wrong.

As illustrated further on, Qisong interprets these Buddhist precepts (*jie* 戒) in Confucian terms (see the Chinese terms in the next citation: (kind *ren* 仁), straight (*zheng* 正), faithful to their word (*xin* 信), and sincere (*cheng* 誠)). Notice that, in his view, all of these Five Precepts and Ten Goods perform the function of regulating emotions and behavior, which are both understood in their social dimension—that is, as performing the function of cultivating interdependency and social cohesion:

> When these [Five Precepts and Ten Goods] are completely cultivated (其修之至也), people do not kill and thus become kind (*ren* 仁); do not steal and thus become honest (*lian* 廉); are not licentious, therefore become straight (*zheng* 正); do not make comments that are false, so they become individuals faithful to their word (*xin* 信); do not get drunk, therefore their behavior is not chaotic (*bu luan* 不亂); do not uselessly embellish their speech, so they become sincere (*cheng* 誠); do not have two tongues, therefore are not slanderers (*chan* 讒); do not say evil things, thus do not fall into disgrace (*ru* 辱); they do not react with anger, thus do not make enemies (*chou* 讐); do not begrudge people, thus do not argue (*zheng* 爭); they are not stupid, thus not confused (*mei* 昧). Accomplishing only one of these is enough to become sincere towards oneself and to offer support to other people (足以誠於身而加於人), not to mention perfectly accomplishing all of the Five Precepts and Ten Goods. (Qisong, "YJ," 0650a4-7)

According to his perspective, the harmful emotions referred to above need regulation because they induce and stimulate perceptions of differences between individuals and reinforce individual interests, which come into conflict with the interests of others. As mentioned earlier, the Song Chan teachings focus on emotions because, Qisong explains, "People have long been confused by the emotions. Their considerable effect is that they have almost destroyed people and made them weak (人之惑於情久矣! 情之甚, 幾至乎敝薄)" (Qisong, "YJ," 0650a19-8). In his view, most emotions nurture friction and discord, whereas realizing the common nature of individuals—namely, buddha-nature (*foxing* 佛性)—nurtures understanding and peace. Qisong speaks here in universal terms, using the general term *nature* (*xing* 性; see the following quote).

From this perspective, "regulating (*zhi* 制) emotions" takes on a special meaning shared by both Chan Buddhists and Song Confucians: cultivating interdependent emotions (those sustaining interdependency) and eliminating individualistic emotions (those promoting personal interest, individualism, independency, and the ego, such as greed, pride, anger, and sadness). Here the Chan scholar-monk not only presents a Confucianized image of Buddhism but also offers a fresh vision of Confucianism as promoting good governance through adjusting and managing emotions/feelings. He introduces Confucian readers to an experience of Confucianism as seen through Buddhist eyes. In Qisong's terms, cultivating interdependency means "seeking sameness" (*tong* 同), which promotes good relations and peace (*an* 安), whereas "seeking difference" (*yi* 異) maintains rivalry (*jing* 競; see the next quotation). Thus, Qisong's Chan perspective resonates strongly with the abovementioned Confucian ideal of "the people living peacefully together," and from this point of view, the Buddhist sage (living buddha) as guide has much in common with the Confucian sage:

> The nature of all is the same, the emotions are different (性相同也, 情相異也). When seeking difference, rarely is there no rivalry among the people (天下鮮不競). When seeking sameness, few people do not live peacefully (天下鮮不安). The sage wishes to guide the people towards living peacefully together, therefore he promotes the fact that the nature of all individuals is the same (推性而同群生); the sage wishes to bring rivalry to an end, and therefore includes everyone into his bosom, and he is in all living beings (推懷而在萬物) [non-dual Buddhist perspective]. (Qisong, "YJ," 0649c19-14)

The Five Precepts, the Ten Goods, and their relationship with the Confucian moral qualities, as well as the articulation between emotions and behavior, are further developed in chapter 7, which focuses on Qisong's commentary *Zhongyong jie*.

Moreover, he stresses that these precepts or vows are understood in the Chan tradition not as rules imposed from the outside but as formless precepts (*wuxiang jie* 無相戒; *Platform Sutra*, 0346c10-3). In other words, they are not forms of pressure coming from the outside but inner dispositions present in the inner original nature or buddha-nature, that arise as a natural result of cultivating awareness of the buddha-nature (see also chap. 6, dedicated to Qisong's "Encomium of the Platform Sutra" ("Tanjing zan" 壇經贊), which is the last essay of his collection *Fujiao bian*). After Qisong, in Neo-Confucians' interpretation, the Five Permanencies (*wuchang* 五常), which preserve the interdependence and the harmony of social relationships, are also practical fruits of inner dispositions. According to Zhu Xi, who shares the opinion held by Master Cheng, *wuchang* 五常 are not external norms but innate moral capacities or natural dispositions (五性):

> Master Cheng said: The accumulation of the vital essence of heaven and earth, the accomplishment of the best in the five phases, this is the human being (天地儲精, 得五行之秀者為人). His own nature is authentic and untroubled (真而靜). When this nature is not yet in movement, the five natural dispositions, humaneness, sense of duty, spirit of ritual, moral knowledge and fidelity to one's pledged word, already exist within it (其未發也五性具焉, 曰仁, 義, 禮, 智, 信). (Zhu, *Lunyu jizhu* 6.2, ZZQS, 6:109–110)

In this regard also, the Neo-Confucian and Qisong's Chan Buddhist perspectives show clear affinities and mutual influences.

In this section, I have provided arguments in support of the idea that, in Qisong's interpretation, the teachings of both traditions have the same objective—making people good by encouraging good actions. The next section further examines the content of this common goal.

III.2. Making People Good

What does "making people good" mean, and what is the process to achieve this? The terms used by Qisong in his explanation of the practice of Song Chan further support his theory about the complementarity between the two teachings:

> If in a village of one hundred households (百家之鄉), ten people keep these five precepts (十人持五戒), then there will be ten honest and sincere (淳謹) people. If in a town of one thousand households (千室之邑), one hundred individuals follow the Ten Goods (百人修十善), then one hundred individuals live in harmony (百人和睦). If in this way the teaching [Chan] is practiced and spreads among the individuals of the whole district, and ten million households practice it, then there will be one million individuals endowed

with kindness (*ren* 仁). When one good can be practiced, then one evil is warded off (夫能行一善, 則去一惡). If one evil is warded off, then the need for one punishment (*xing* 刑) is removed (去一惡, 則息一刑). If the need for one punishment is removed in each family, then the need for ten thousand punishments is removed in the country (一刑息於家, 萬刑息於國). This is what your Majesty meant by "the ruler sits on his throne, and thus the people live peacefully (坐致太平是也太平)." (Qisong, "YJ," 0649b7-10)

According to Qisong, the Song (Chan) Buddhist teaching can be a useful, socially oriented tool for the Confucians, who exercise authority and bear the social responsibility of providing Confucian good governance, which is based on collective harmony and interdependence. In the next paragraph of the "Yuan-jiao," he provides a Confucian-Buddhist integrated perspective of a well-governed Song society, in which the five generic relationships are flourishing and further strengthened by the Buddhist practice:

If these precepts were really accomplished [Qisong asks rhetorically] how could there exist in the world younger brothers who do not obey their older brothers (人弟者而不悌其兄), children lacking filial piety towards their parents (人子者而不孝其親), families in which the women do not respect their husbands (人室者而不敬其夫), individuals who are not mutually kind to their friends (人友者而不以善相致), officials who are not loyal to their sovereign (人臣者而不忠其君), and sovereigns lacking kindness towards their people (人君者而不仁其民)? In the world, there would no longer be these kinds of people. (Qisong, "YJ," 0650a8-12)

For Qisong, the (Chan) Buddhist way of life is meant to preserve harmonious social relationships, a state of interdependence among the members of society that amplifies the social wholeness. In his view, the Confucian ideal of "making the people live together in peace" (*tianxia ping* 天下平; *Daxue, jing*) is also fostered by Chan Buddhist teaching and naturally stems from the focus on "making people good" (*wei shan* 為善). It is therefore important to concretely understand what exactly this common ideal (Buddhist and Confucian) means to him.

Interestingly enough, because he addresses the Confucian reader, the Chan scholar-monk defines this universal paragon of the "good individual" without drawing on any Buddhist literature but by using as examples important figures of the Three Dynasties (*Sandai* 三代) period—the founders and legendary rulers of ancient Chinese culture (i.e., Emperor Shun 舜 and Yu the Great 禹, founder of the ancient Xia dynasty) and ancient Confucian masters (i.e., Confucius, Master Yan [Confucius's disciple Yan Hui], and Mencius). He also uses other examples taken from Confucian classics (the *Zhongyong*, *Analects*, and *Mencius*) and Confucian terms, written in the *guwen* style (argumentative, explanatory text in dialogical form). I reiterate that these references denote not merely his profound familiarity with the Confucian teaching and classics[24] but also his understanding of Chinese Buddhism as completely Chinese—that is, sharing the same cultural sources as Confucianism[25] (i.e., its Chineseness, as suggested above). This is what could be referred to as "the Sandai heritage," the result of a natural germination of Buddhism within the soil of Chinese Confucian culture. In Qisong's view, Shun, Yu, Confucius, Mencius, and Yan Hui are "the five ancient exemplary men (*junzi* 君子) who most appreciated the good action" (此五君子者, 古之大樂善人也。; Qisong, "YJ," 0650b9-7).

Qisong cites paragraphs from the *Zhongyong* 6 and 8, the *Analects* 7:25 and 7:21, and *Mencius* 6B13 and 4A12 while describing the "good individual." These refer to the importance of cultivating and encouraging good words and good behaviors (*Zhongyong*) and of attentively preserving good habits within one's heart-mind and never losing them—that is, constantly performing new good deeds (*Analects*). In addition, Qisong does not forget the fact that understanding the good action is critical for ensuring good governance (*Mencius*). And he points out that the kind of goodness that these classics are speaking about is similar to the goodness advanced by Buddhism (以其善類固類於佛。; Qisong, "YJ," 0650b10-2).

It is essential to note the profoundly Confucian nature of two of his arguments in support of the close relation between (Chan) Buddhist and Confucian processes of "becoming good": the influence of role models and the holistic aspects of the way and of the capacities of sages. These are both explored more fully in the next section.

The first argument—namely, the importance of role models in teaching proper conduct—is a central aspect of the Chinese tradition in general. In the "Yuanjiao," Qisong states that the good Buddhist monk, like the Confucian good ruler, has this function in society: by the force of his example and words, he succeeds in transforming (that is, correcting) people, making them good.[26] To illustrate the functioning of the universally (whether Buddhist or Confucian) effective role model, Qisong refers to an ancient image—namely, the exemplary ruler who influences the people with his behavior—from the "Great Model" ("Hong Fan" 洪範)[27] chapter of the *Book of Documents* (*Shujing* 書經). According to Yü Ying-shih's study (2003, 2:536–538), this idea of the "ruler as a perfect example" (*huangji* 皇極) advocated in the "Hong Fan" was also a central issue discussed at length by the Northern Song Confucians. The interest in this topic shared by Chan Buddhists and Confucians illustrates that it was a common subject of debate during Qisong's time. At the core of this notion of role model, one can perceive interdependency as the principle of its functioning. In his commentary *Zhongyong jie* 中庸解 (*Exegesis of the Mean*), Qisong also cites the "Hong Fan" chapter. He equates the image of the "ruler as perfect example" with the perception of the sovereign as exemplary person and teacher, and the method of governing with the process of teaching: "The *Hong Fan* says: 'The ruler establishes himself as perfect example'" (洪範曰:「皇建其有極」; Qisong, *ZYJ*, 666b21-2). To describe the process of good governance, Qisong also adopts the ancient Confucian formulation of the "kingly way" (*wangdao* 王道) as "middle way" (*wupian wubei* 無偏無陂—i.e., neither inclined nor uneven) referred to in the "Hong Fan":

> The *Hong Fan* says: "The good sovereign is neither inclined, nor uneven: he follows the kingly behavior (無偏無陂遵王之義). He does not purposefully do good things (無有作好): he just follows the kingly way. Without doing bad things, he follows the kingly path. Free from bias, without taking sides (無偏無黨), the kingly way is wide (蕩蕩). Without taking sides, free from bias, the kingly way makes people live peacefully together (平平). Free of inconstancy and partiality, the kingly way rectifies and corrects all things (無反無側王道正). His example achieves perfection." How could this not rectify and correct all things (正直萬物)? (Qisong, *ZYJ*, 666c1-7)

According to the scholar-monk, good governance means that the rulers (sovereign and officials) are role models, and he points out the result of this "role-model teaching": people "rectify and correct" (*zhengzhi* 正直) themselves and therefore live peacefully together. Like the good ruler who possesses a transformative Confucian *dao*, the accomplished Chan follower, lay or ordained, also fulfills the function of a role model. Qisong refers in particular to the Song Confucian officials, many of them lay followers who were studying under the guidance of Buddhist masters (see chap. 3 and "Quanshu" 勸書, par. 2, the second article of Qisong's *Fujiao bian*). The (Chan) Buddhist follower is also able to touch the heart-minds and therefore transform the people, using his Chan Buddhist *dao*: "Like the Buddhist follower of today: when remaining silent, his heart-mind is sincere (默則誠); when talking, he influences the people to do good things (語則善). Thus, wherever he arrives, with his *dao*, he encourages people to give up all bad actions and orient towards good actions" (Qisong, "YJ," 0651a29-7).

Needless to say, following the Buddhist path is just as difficult as following the Confucian route. Qisong, like Confucian masters, admits that this method of teaching by example with role models hardly works. You may recall the well-known lamentation of Confucius that the way is not being followed (*Lunyu* 5.6). The scholar-monk notes that the Buddhist way faces a similar predicament, using perfectly Confucian terms to describe a Buddhist reality: "Alas! I cannot find people like me, so that we could together make our heart-minds sincere (同誠其心), together abstain from meat and wine (同齋戒其身), together stimulate people using our moral power (同推德于人), provide blessings to the members of our families (以福吾親) and help the sovereign to secure the well-being of the people (以資吾君之康天下也)" (Qisong, "YJ," 0651a20-5).

This calls to mind the monk's second justification, which concerns the holistic aspects of the *dao*. He reminds us that (Chan) Buddhist teaching has multiple dimensions, and it is only by following a holistic way (that is, a middle way, as the previous and following citations illustrate), not a unidimensional way, to understand and put Buddhist theory into practice, that it is possible to authentically bring this teaching to fruition. Regrettably, in his day, the scholar-monk remarks, the Buddhist path is understood unidimensionally; therefore, like the Confucian path, it is followed inappropriately. One also realizes the holistic feature of the practice that Qisong advocates. He leaves aside the differences between, for instance, Chan and general Buddhism, Buddhism and Confucianism, in order to further reinforce their partnership, their joint efforts and common goals:

> The Buddhist classics (佛之經)[28] have many dimensions [and layers of depth] (多方). The generations of followers after the Buddha have not been able to adequately teach them to the people. Those who believe, believe excessively [in a certain limited dimension] (*guo xin* 過信). Some rulers misunderstand what it means to do good and abandon their country to perform humble tasks. The people of the secular world, after having a superficial awakening (淺悟), rush to abandon the world and think that being a monk is the highest calling. This is not what is so-called "behaving by using one's Buddha's heart (用佛心而為道也)." The Buddhist classics say that the Buddha explains the Buddhist teachings according to different circumstances; their significance is difficult to understand. Therefore, for those following the Buddhist path it is not enough to wear black clothing and to cut their hair. The Buddha's heart is like this: it is very inclusive (然佛之為心也, 如此豈小通哉).[29] (Qisong, "YJ," 0650b16-5)

Once again, in this way Qisong implicitly reiterates that (Chan) Buddhism teaches, first and foremost, actively setting right social relationships and promoting communal harmony and that it is not unidimensional. When people abandon their social responsibilities to allegedly follow the Buddhist path, they actually do not follow it correctly (that is, holistically). I also suggest that the paragraphs cited above and below illustrate Qisong's new interpretation of "holism" as not only interconnection but, above all, inclusiveness.

He also invokes the emblematic holistic and unifying capacity of the sage. This idea is present in ancient Confucianism, embodied in the symbolic formula "for me, there is one, running through all my thinking" (*yi yi guan zhi* 一以貫之; *Analects* 15.3). It is worth noting that this notion can also be implicitly found in the weave of the following paragraph, in which Qisong refers to the five founders of Chinese culture who are most emblematic for him (Shun, Yu, Confucius, Mencius, and Yan Hui):

> If they weren't yet dead, when seeing the propagation of my [Buddhist] way, they would be very happy to follow it and promote it. Alas! It is unfortunate for the generations after them that these five didn't meet Buddha and didn't confirm to each other their common ideas. For this reason, until today, the disciples of the two schools continue to despise each other, and they do not trust each other. Alas! People's feelings concern only themselves and exclude others, confirm this side and disapprove of the other. Denial of others leads to contention; excessive self-affirmation, makes one's heart-mind narrow. The exemplary man understands everything holistically (君子通而已矣). Why should he limit himself to one thing? The exemplary man should think about what connects; he need not deny others. (Qisong, "YJ," 0650b10-10)

This reflection may also be interpreted as a direct reply to Han Yu's virulent criticism, as an implicit assessment of the narrowness and intolerance of Han Yu's perspective. The latter condemns the Buddhist teaching in his nonargumentative rhetoric, using the same image of a potential encounter between the exemplary men of the Three Dynasties and Buddhists:

> Nowadays the Buddhist teaching says: "One should abandon the relationship between ruler and officials, get rid of the relationship between father and son, and ban the way of mutual growth and nourishment," in order to seek purity and nirvana. Alas! It is fortunate that this Buddhist teaching appeared after the Three Dynasties epoch and was not rejected by Yu the founder of the Xia dynasty, Tang of Shang, King Wen of Zhou, King Wu of Zhou, the Duke of Zhou and Confucius. It is unfortunate that it didn't emerge before the Three Dynasties, so it was not corrected by Yu, Tang, Wen, Wu, Zhou Gong and Confucius. (Han 1986, 16)

In response, Qisong reaffirms the importance of inclusiveness as a quality of perfect teachings: "If one doesn't recognize the 'way' of a sage because of his barbarian (*yi* 夷) origins—while Shun was an Eastern barbarian, and Wen Wang was a Western barbarian, and their 'ways' connected with one another and were practiced in China; how can we reject the sage's 'way' because he's barbarian (可夷其人而拒其道乎)? Even more so, as the Buddha's origin is not barbarian [i.e., the Buddha's heart is within everyone]" (Qisong, "YJ," 0651a12-7).

This section has examined and developed the affinities between Buddhism and Confucianism as perceived by Qisong, arising from their common objective of cultivating interdependency. Nonetheless, he also highlights substantive differences between the two teachings. The next section analyzes them.

IV. DIFFERENCES BETWEEN SONG CHAN AND NEO-CONFUCIAN TEACHINGS: TRANSFORMING HEART-MINDS

As previously discussed, according to the scholar-monk, both Confucian and Buddhist teachings pursue the same objective—that is, making people into good individuals through transforming (*hua* 化) them. In the following period, after Qisong, Neo-Confucians are the ones who pay particular attention to the nature of this transformation. Therefore, this section provides a comparison between Song Chan Buddhism (according to his interpretation) and Neo-Confucian perspectives on this issue and argues that the natures of the transformations achieved through each of the teachings are different. The subsequent analysis begins from the premise that a transformation includes three dimensions:[30] a difficulty that needs to be overcome through transformation; the means to achieve the transformation; and a fundamental, higher reality that the individual has to realize as a precondition of achieving the transformation—namely, access to a state of higher being or higher capacity. The latter results from this awareness that the human has to reach in order to trigger the transformation. The difficulty that both teachings (Qisong's Chan Buddhist and Neo-Confucian) overcome through transformation is similar—namely a disharmonious social life resulting from the cultivation of overwhelming individual desires and personal interests. In what follows, I determine that their differences concern the last two dimensions: first, different conceptions of this state of higher being and, second, different means to obtain the transformation. Each of these elements will be examined in turn.

The Neo-Confucian theory of the awareness of a higher human dimension was developed especially by the Cheng brothers (Chan 1964, 140–141), one generation after Qisong argued for the compatibility between Confucianism and Chan and explained the differences between the two—and, it can be said, as a reaction to it (as noted already, Yü Ying-shih amply demonstrated that Chan was very popular among scholar-officials). This Neo-Confucian higher dimension present deep down in everyone is the principle of coherence *li* 理[31] (or, equivalently, the authentic nature *xing* 性; one could call it the potentiality in man as envisioned by Neo-Confucians), as masterfully laid out in the classic *Zhongyong* and its commentary by Zhu Xi, the *Zhongyong zhangju*, in reference to the "way of man" and the "way of heaven" (see *Zhongyong* 20). Remember that a century earlier, Qisong, a commentator and admirer of the *Zhongyong* (see chap. 7), explained the two ways of the Buddhist laity as the vehicles of man (*rencheng* 人乘) and of heaven (*tiancheng* 天乘; see sec. III.1). This is evidence that Qisong and the founders of the Neo-Confucian school mutually inspired each other in developing such a parallel vision of the practice. However, in the same essay, "Yuanjiao," Qisong presents the Buddhist higher dimension as the spirit (*jingshen* 精神), which has as reference the "way of spirit." Next, in Neo-Confucianism the major means of transformation consists of achieving a "complete understanding" (*zhizhi* 知至; Zhu, *Daxue zhangju, jing*) of the principle of coherence that naturally activates the transformation of the individual.[32] In Buddhism, according to Qisong's "Yuanjiao," the means of transformation consists of touching the heart-mind. The two issues are discussed in the next two subsections.

IV.1. The Highest Dimension

In both traditions, this highest dimension represents the ground or the subtle nature of all human beings. In each one, it involves a sense of the unity of reality. Let us first look at the Neo-Confucian vision to better identify the particularity of Qisong's Buddhist view, which is more complex.[33] In Neo-Confucianism this unity arises from a simultaneously organic and moral vision of reality. The transformation (change, *hua* 化) of individuals involves becoming aware of the higher reality of the way of heaven (*tiandao* 天道) as a spontaneous and universal (human and nonhuman) order of life, which is present in each reality as the principle of coherence *li*, or authentic nature (*xing* 性) (in humans). Neo-Confucians understand all these notions in moral terms: the universal and transcendental order is moral. The transcendence or the imperceptible "beyond form" (*xing er shang* 形而上) is here understood as, first, the subtle, constant animation of life in reality as a whole and, second, the profound moral quality that animates each of the individual realities of all the living beings. The latter arises from the former and could be defined as a form of self-transcendence—namely, the ability to look beyond one's individual self or reality, which is influenced by personal interests, and become aware of the unity of individuals. The unobstructed circulation of the breath of life within the real world is considered to be the highest good, and human social relationships are perceived as following the same subtle law. Harmoniously preserving this animation of the breath of life means in this optic harmoniously preserving interpersonal relationships. Therefore, this is a transcendence involving daily affairs.

The equivalence between physical nature and social life established in Neo-Confucianism also introduces a correspondence between natural growth (life) and morality. In his commentary to the thirty-second paragraph of the *Zhongyong*, Zhu Xi explains the moral nature of this transcendence (i.e., reaching beyond the faculties by which the body perceives and processes external stimuli), which is also a perfect "great moral quality" (*dade* 大德; see Zhu, *Zhongyong zhangju* 17, 30, 32) or a "perfect sincerity" (*zhicheng* 至誠; see Zhu, *Zhongyong zhangju* 23, 24, 26). It fulfills the role of source of the transformation-growth of reality (that is, the movement of the transformation-growth of the entity heaven-earth (*tiandi zhi huayu* 天地之化育)), or simply the functioning of the way (*dao zhi yong* 道之用) (see Zhu, *Zhongyong zhangju* 1) or the functioning of the entity heaven-earth (*tiandi zhi gongyong* 天地之功用; Zhu, *Zhongyong zhangju* 16). Zhu Xi explains that its presence in humans manifests itself as subtle and implicit knowledge, tacitly engraved (*moqi* 默契) within their heart-minds: "About understanding the movement of the transformation-growth of the entity heaven-earth (天地之化育): each form of reality endowed with this extreme and flawless sincerity (極誠無妄) possesses, tacitly engraved in itself, knowledge that cannot be explained, that does not rely on either hearing or sight (有默契焉, 非但聞見 之知而已). These relate to the complete and flawless sincerity and are part of the natural functioning (自然之功用)" (Zhu, *Zhongyong zhangju* 32). This explanation supports Wing-tsit Chan's remark that a major Neo-Confucian innovation was the interpretation of "change" and of the *Book of Changes* (*Yijing* 易經) in the "spirit of rationalism" and as an "intelligent" explanation of the evolution of the universe and of the principles of daily human affairs (Chan 1967, xviii, xxi).[34]

The transcendent source of the moral transformation is therefore the same as the natural source of harmonious natural organic growth. In the same way, the radical change of individuals emerges from immediate knowledge (i.e., intuition and instinctive feeling) already present within them. Therefore, the Neo-Confucian transformation is primarily a process of subtle moral knowledge. Equally, this process of individual transformation is considered as essentially a natural process (i.e., similar to the organic transformation-growth) through which the individual gradually understands the principles of coherence of things and affairs. This experience of comprehension induces in him an impalpable change. Zhu Xi's following passage describes this process: "'Sets them in motion' (動), means that sincerity can set realities in motion. 'Change'

(變), means that the realities change when they take their natural course. 'Transformation' (化), in this case there is a 'no-one knows how' that enables them to transform (有不知其所以然者)" (Zhu, *Zhongyong zhangju* 23).

Note that this renewal and the transcendence related to it are all about harmonious growth and evolution. There is nothing here about withering, decline, and death, which are also part of organic life. In contrast, as discussed below, this other facet is included in the Buddhist teaching. Given what one might call this "incomplete" Neo-Confucian view of transcendence, on closer inspection, the rhetorical criticism voiced by the Neo-Confucians against Buddhist teachings concerning transcendence (*JSL*, 13.8) lacks sufficient ground: "The Buddhists do not understand *yin* and *yang*, day and night, death and life, past and present. How can it be said that their transcendence (*xing er shang* 形而上) is the same as that of the Sage [Confucius]?" (Chan 1967, 285; ZZQS, 13:279).[35] The conclusion that can be drawn from the above analysis is that Neo-Confucians themselves have not dealt with the two inseparable aspects of the phenomenon of life. This is understandable, because good governance is connected with development and social harmony and not with death and loss.

Qisong believes that, in the Song Chan teaching, the higher reality that triggers human transformation through touching people's heart-minds is the spirit that subsists after death. One realizes the extended, complete meaning of the term *change* for Qisong, which doesn't include merely growth, flowering, increase, and expansion, as in the Neo-Confucian perception, but incorporates the articulation death-birth as the essential connector that links three lives (*san shi* 三世), three states of existence, which unfold as a continuum. This reality of spirit is grasped through religious apprehension. The Buddhist self-transcendence manifests as relatedness of all living beings in virtue of the spirit. Moreover, he also uses the term *transformation-change* to mean "death" (see below). The subsistence of the spirit links yesterday (one's last life and past relationships), today (one's present life and relationships), and tomorrow (one's future life and relationships) in a unity structured by the permanent interweaving of cause and effect. The awareness of the relatedness of things, which arises from this perception, fosters the cultivation of relationships based on compassion and solidarity.

If the Neo-Confucians develop the articulation "principle of coherence-vital breath" (*li-qi* 理-氣),[36] where the latter term is understood as emotions, Qisong connects "spirit-emotions" (*shen-qing* 神-情). Because the individual's spirit persists after death and is also attached to his or her actual life emotions and habits (*qing xi* 情習), the retribution continues after death. Consequently, a correction of people's emotions and habits enables them to shape their future retribution (*bao* 報): "When there is corporeal form [i.e., a life begins] (夫其形存) the results of good and bad deeds have already arisen. When the spirit leaves, how could the retribution of good and bad deeds (善惡之報) not be the same [continuing into the next life]?" (Qisong, "YJ," 0649c10-2).

If, for the Neo-Confucians, the organic growth segment of one life represents the continuity that naturally supports the transformation, the Chan Buddhists perceive the continuity between three lives as the natural support of the transformation. Accordingly, cultivating the spirit means performing corrections at the level of the emotions, thus improving future retributions: "The emotions [Qisong clarifies]—that means all that emerges within the authentic nature of humans. The emotions and habits are good and bad. When death-transformation (*hua* 化) occurs, good and bad actions resonate in the obscurity [i.e., the mystery of the passage-transformation between lives] with those of similar categories, and a fulfillment (成) in the future life results" (Qisong, "YJ," 0649a4-16). About this fulfillment, see the next section.

IV.2. *The Means of Transformation*

Qisong describes the Confucian teaching as the instruction where people are influenced from the outside (that is, transformed as a result of the perfect moral quality of the local elite and officials). In his view, the Buddhist teaching works from the inside out by moving or touching (*gan* 感) the heart-minds of the people. He thus makes a distinction between the "way of humans" (*rendao* 人道) and the "way of the spirit" (*shendao* 神道):

> If one wants to convince the people to accept and obey "the way" with all their hearts and cultivate themselves (人心服而自修), it is best to convince them from the inside (莫若感其內), through touching their heart-minds. If one wants only that the people say what he wants them to say and appear obedient (人言順而貌從), it is best to control their external behavior (莫若制其外). Control from the outside must follow the way of humans, otherwise it cannot succeed. What touches them inside must follow the way of the spirit, otherwise it cannot transform their heart-minds. Therefore, the Buddhist way must concentrate on the spirits of individuals first, and then on their behavior; this is what it means to touch the inside first, and then control the outside (感內而制外). (Qisong, "YJ," 0650b18-14)

In this context, "touching the inside" (感其內) has a religious connotation—namely, it provides the power necessary for achieving a transformation, which is not simply behavioral but soteriological. The basis of the process of transformation in the Neo-Confucian perspective is the accumulation of what I suggest translating in this context as "natural" knowledge (*zhi* 知)—namely, that which concerns the principles of coherence of things and affairs and whose source is an individual's principle of coherence bestowed by heaven (nature). In other words, individuals naturally get access to this knowledge when they make efforts to become aware of their self-centered perspective and strive to eliminate it. In the *Zhongyong*, this ultimate goal is explained as becoming as sincere as the heaven-earth. The *Great Learning* defines this method of "making one's natural knowledge complete" (*zhizhi* 至知) as the "investigation of things" (*gewu* 格物), and Zhu Xi explains it in Neo-Confucian terms as "fully developing the understanding of all principles of coherence of things" (物格者, 物理之極處無不到也; Zhu, *Daxue zhangju, ZZQS*, 6:17). About Zhu's understanding of the principle of coherence, see chapter 6, section III.2. This Neo-Confucian natural knowledge is not knowledge for the sake of knowledge but with a view to correcting behavior (i.e., choosing good actions and avoiding evil ones) to make it as harmonious as the life cycle, which is perceived as naturally harmonious—it is therefore naturally ethical knowledge. Zhu Xi explains that this understanding is gained from the experience of actions within society and of interpersonal relationships. He suggests that this knowledge is a cognitive and sensory operation fused with the innate ethical knowledge discussed earlier, which mediates conduct:

> Through fully understanding the principles of coherence of things and human affairs, he who studies wishes that his understanding becomes complete, capable of comprehending everything (窮至事物之理, 欲其極處無不到也) ... A complete understanding means that the heart-mind has a full understanding of every single thing (知至者, 吾心之所知無不盡也). When one's understanding becomes complete, he becomes able to make his thoughts sincere (意可得而實). When one's thoughts become sincere, he becomes able to rectify his heart-mind (心可得而正矣). (Zhu, *Daxue zhangju, jing, ZZQS*, 6:17)

In the anthology *Jinsilu* 3.8 (*ZZQS*, 13:194), Cheng Yi 程頤 (1033–1107) also makes clear that moral transformation, which he defines as "naturally and joyfully following the principle of coherence" (*ziran le xun li* 自然樂循理), results "naturally" from "clearly understanding this principle" (*zhu li ming* 燭理明). These "natural" Neo-Confucian means of transformation could be defined as rational as well as metaphysically reasoned means. In the next paragraph, Kirill Thompson vividly suggests the concrete meaning of the latter in Zhu Xi's thought:

> Zhu Xi sometimes regarded the investigation of things as proceeding in a step-by-step ascending process, culminating in a penetrating comprehension (*Great Learning* 大學, "Supplement" to chap. 5), a higher synthetic illumination, ultimately, of the *taiji* 太極 (supreme polarity).... Thus, while

he presented inquiry as a quest for ever higher patterns and truths in his "Supplement" to the *Great Learning*, the actual content of the process of inquiry was to stay focused on specifics. As one inquires into more and more specific situations, one becomes acquainted with deeper and more basic patterns (*li* 理) of change, structure, balance, and composition, which afford one a surer grasp of the new situations that one goes on to investigate. Zhu rationalized this position with the organic saying, "*Li* (pattern, patterning) is one, but its manifestations are myriad" (*liyi fenshu* 理一分殊). Again, like Confucius, he thought that one can penetrate the higher only by studying the lower, and criticized those who would study the Way or *li* in themselves, in abstraction from real situations or events. (Thompson 2007, 336)

In Chan Buddhist teaching, the means are philosophico-religious, as the spirit is a transwordly entity. According to Qisong, what moves people's heart-minds and triggers their transformation is the awareness of, or belief in, the subsistence of the spirit through the three lives, which generates the obligation to cultivate it:

> When one cultivates his spirit (人修其精神), he can engage in good behavior. During one's life, he receives rewards (生也則福應); after death, his spirit rises towards purity (死也則其神清昇). When one does not cultivate one's spirit, and engages in evil and aberrant things, then his life is not an occasion to celebrate, as after death his spirit is punished. Therefore, when ordinary people hear this teaching, their heart-minds are touched (心感動), they stop doing evil things and pursue good actions. Thus, they silently change. (Qisong, "YJ," 0650b24-12)

The change to which Qisong refers here is a transformation through good behavior and discipline that also continuously reshapes one's karma (the chain of spontaneous causes and results, rewards and punishments) and the abovementioned three lives. Chapter 5 (on heart-mind, emotions, and nature-emptiness in Qisong's thought) provides an in-depth analysis of his interpretation of karma. Qisong renders this indeterminate Buddhist notion of karma more precise and connected with determinable objectives when explaining it as the context of the three lives. In his view, karma becomes a force assisting the spirit in its process of purification. Qisong also notes that the idea of retribution is not completely new within the Chinese tradition. The argument he uses in the "Yuanjiao" is based on the "Hong Fan" mentioned earlier, a chapter of the *Book of Documents*, one of the texts that lie at the foundation of Chinese culture. It presents the Five Blessings (*wu fu* 五福) and Six Perils (*liu ji* 六極), respectively, as rewards and punishments spontaneously coming from heaven for the people who do and do not comply with the example set by the sage-ruler:

The *Five Blessings* [Qisong expounds here the view presented in the "Hong Fan"] are for those whose heart-minds conform to the model of perfection set up by the ruler (五福者, 謂人以其心合乎皇極). Heaven (天) uses the blessings to respond (應) to such people and encourage them to continue (應以嚮勸之). The *Six Perils* are for those whose heart-minds do not conform to the model of perfection set up by the ruler. Heaven uses the perils to answer (應) such people, and warn them to stop (應以威沮之). (Qisong, "YJ," 0649c7-6)

One may identify within this image the concept—shared by Qisong, the ancients, and the Confucians—of the existence of a resonance (answer; *ying* 應) between the inner and external worlds of the individual. This notion is further examined in chapter 3, which focuses on Qisong's essay "Quanshu." For Neo-Confucians, this resonance is a moral transcendence within the ordinary course of daily affairs, which manifests as moral understanding. Neo-Confucians believe that this understanding brings about a transformation of the individual. As explained above by Qisong, for Buddhists, this resonance is the result of the subsistence of the spirit within the three lives. They believe that this awareness touches individuals and activates their transformation.

Let us not forget that Neo-Confucian teaching concerns one life (*shi* 世), the present life, and the individual's interpersonal relationships, behavior, and heart-mind therein. The Neo-Confucian's major means of transformation is "rectifying human's heart-mind" (正其心) (a stage highlighted in the *Great Learning* and commented on by Zhu Xi; *Daxue zhangju* 1 and 7, *ZZQS*, 6:17, 22; *Lunyu jizhu* 6.2, *ZZQS*, 6:110), thus eliminating desires and correcting emotions, through extensive pursuit of "natural knowledge." The major reference of Neo-Confucianists is morality and the actual conduct of life in society, and they are interested neither in questions concerning the destiny of people before and after their actual life nor in the fears and hopelessness of individuals, which influence their conduct and feelings. This Neo-Confucian assurance follows from their full confidence in the principle of coherence, or authentic nature, which is perceived as the source of self-mastery, like a solid root, able to nourish an individual's life and correct its course of growth when firmly rooted in the soil. From this perspective, the anthology *Jinsilu* (13:4) condemns Buddhism: "It has been said: 'The different types of hell of the Buddhists are intended for people with a low root-nature (為下根之人), so they will be frightened into doing what is good'" (*ZZQS*, 13:278).

The Buddhist training also takes place in the actual life of the present, and Qisong too defines it as an effort to rectify (and therefore also in moral terms). Unlike Neo-Confucian education, it goes beyond the mere concerns of actual existence, focusing instead on "rectifying the individual's spirit" (*zheng qi ren shen* 正其人神; see below). This rectification influences not only one but three lives, the actual, the preceding, and the future: "Concerning the three lives, the spirit of the people should be rectified in order to show them the karmic causes, which are beyond life and death" (言乎三世也, 則當正其人神, 指緣業乎死生之外; Qisong, "YJ," 0649b25-16). This is a genuinely soteriological concern. The role of the Buddhist sage, in Qisong's view, is to unveil to practitioners (the Confucian laity, in particular, in the context of the "Yuanjiao") the connection among the trio of lives. Realization of this connection is the religious force necessary to trigger the initiation and pursuit of an individual's transformation. The connection is explained by Qisong as a simultaneous "fulfillment" or achievement (*cheng* 成), now and in the future life, resulting from one's deeds. See above: "When death-transformation occurs, good and bad actions resonate in the obscurity with those of similar categories, and a fulfillment (成) in the future life results" (Qisong, "YJ," 0649a4-16). The scholar-monk uses this notion of fulfillment to make explicit the interdependence among past, present, and future (the three lives)—that is, the fact that an actual deed is not actually fulfilled, not yet completed, and will be fulfilled in the future. This future fulfillment can be either good or bad depending on the actual deeds:

> Only sages with very wide and penetrating vision (大觀) understand the causes prior to this life (推其因於生之前) [and their effects on the present], instructing the people on what will come after death. They show them what "fulfillment" awaits them after death (指其成於死之後) and teach them what they should cultivate now (教其所以修也).... Life has a before and after, which have close ties with the actual life of the present (有前後而以今相與). Is this not what three lives means? If a good "fulfillment" (善成) during one's future life comes from what he cultivates now, then the fact that this human is able to perfectly understand this comes from his habits and practice during his past life (其已往之所習). (Qisong, "YJ," 0648c28-3)

The above comparison between the Buddhist (according to Qisong) and Neo-Confucian means of transformation illustrates their distinct natures.

The "Guang yuanjiao" is the continuation of the "Yuanjiao" and is discussed in chapter 2.

V. CONCLUSION

Starting from Qisong's essay "Yuanjiao," the present chapter determines and interprets the manner in which he demonstrates the Chineseness of Song Chan Buddhism: through its constant articulation with Confucianism within the Song-dynasty culture. Its framework is an analysis of the affinities and differences between Song Confucian and Song Chan Buddhist traditions as identified by the scholar-monk in the "Yuanjiao."

With this first article of his collection *Fujiao bian* (*Essays on Assisting the Teaching*), Qisong progressively starts building his interpretation of the connections between Buddhism and Confucianism. Gradually, he begins with evident and easier-to-understand articulations between the two teachings: those belonging to the domain of everyday affairs (Buddhist precepts and Confucian norms of behavior). As he explains later in the essay "Guang yuanjiao" ("Extensive Inquiry into the Teachings"), in this first article, "Yuanjiao" ("Inquiry into the Teachings"), he focuses on "the connection between the Buddhist Five Precepts and Ten Goods and the Confucian Five Permanencies; I ardently desired to dismiss the criticisms of contemporary Confucians against Buddhism. Regarding what the sage considers as the great root [foundations] of Buddhist teaching: I outlined it there but did not have time to present it completely" ("Guang yuanjiao," 0654b07).

In this chapter, I suggest that Qisong implicitly answers Han Yu's virulent criticism against Buddhism, which the latter considered a foreign teaching, destructive of the Chinese Confucian culture. I also argue that the Chan scholar-monk focuses first on similarities between Buddhist precepts and the Confucian norms of relationships with a view not only to answer Confucian criticism but as well to highlight in this way the Chineseness of Song Chan Buddhism, its belonging to the soil of Song culture, and its universal inclusiveness. In his view, what is cautiously called here "(Chan) Buddhism" is a universal and all-inclusive idea of Buddhism in which the reader nevertheless distinguishes the recognizable colors of Chan practice: heart-mind and emotional transformation. Next, he continues in the same direction, providing arguments in favor of the idea that the two Song teachings have the same goal: making people good by encouraging them to perform good actions—that is, transforming them to increase good fortune and reduce adversity. In this context, he further reestablishes a new connection with Confucianism through making reference to the classic text "Hong Fan."

Based on these well-argued primary resemblances, Qisong also introduces, at a simple level and starting from the central concept of emotions/feelings, the complex differences between Buddhism and Confucianism: the notion of spirit, the importance of cultivating the way of the spirit, and the interdependence among the three lives (present, past, and future). This first essay of the anthology *Fujiao bian* can be perceived as a simplified introduction that features the abovementioned major concepts. All of them are further detailed in his subsequent essays, starting from concrete similarities with tangible

Confucian tradition and progressively reaching religious and intangible core elements of Chan Buddhist practice.

I would highlight once again Qisong's interesting discussion on the interface between the basic Buddhist precepts and the basic Confucian moral qualities. While these precepts and virtues have correspondences, the precepts are basically proscriptions and negative, while the Confucian virtues are positive.[37] It would seem that through this articulation, the scholar-monk intends to bring out the Chinese nature of (Chan) Buddhism: its socially engaged dimension. In a sense, the original Buddhism appears to emphasize negative orientations—that is, a denial of tangibility and a progressive detachment from the world, thus disengaging oneself from actuality and from others. Qisong focuses on the positive orientation of (Chan) Buddhism, on practices and results, and on the self as profoundly interrelated with its social and cultural habitat. Finally, he envisages the nonduality of negative (prohibitions) and positive orientations as the achievement of a full engagement with others and life.

The next chapter explores the essay "Guang yuanjiao"("Extensive Inquiry into the Teachings") and reiterates these arguments in a new light, at a higher level of complexity. As mentioned in the introduction, section VII.1, the Chan scholar-monk explains in the beginning of this essay ("Guang yuanjiao," 0654b16-15) that while developing his own ideas, he took inspiration from the manner of presentation of the *Huayan Sutra* and its central principle: "By assimilating the branches, one returns to the root (攝末歸本門)." The branches that he examines in this extensive essay are the vehicle of heaven and the vehicle of humans: the practical Buddhism for his Confucian contemporaries, deeply ingrained in Song-dynasty Confucian culture and society.

After reading the end of his collection, one realizes that Qisong also followed this principle when assembling the structure of the book, arranging the articles and developing his gradual progression toward the essential and complex aspects of (Chan) Buddhism, presenting them in a way linked with Confucian themes. This comparative structure enables determination of his significant contribution not only to the Song Chan Buddhist tradition but to Chinese culture in general. His effort to highlight the symbiosis between these Song teachings and ways of life proves that, beyond the declared disagreements between them, they share at a profound level the same source of Chinese tradition and represent two complementary facets of its Chineseness.

TWO

AN ELEVENTH-CENTURY CONFUCIANIZED AND COHESIVE FORM OF CHAN

Qisong's Interpretation of "Teaching" (*Jiao* 教) in the "Extensive Inquiry into the Teachings" ("Guang yuanjiao" 廣原教)

I. INTRODUCTION

This chapter returns to questions raised in chapter 1 and puts the significance of the arguments presented there into a new, more complex perspective: it compares the ultimate concerns of Qisong and Confucian tradition in terms of the conception of reality and ultimate values through the Chan scholar-monk's study of Confucian teachings in the classics, the *Great Learning* and the *Zhongyong*.

Chapter 2 focuses on the concept of "teaching" (*jiao* 教) and its two major features—the subtle and perceptible dimensions—in Qisong's essay "Extensive Inquiry into the Teachings" ("Guang yuanjiao" 廣原教 [hereafter "GYJ"]; Qisong 2016c). Written in 1056, in his small residence Yongan shan 永安山 at the old and important Chan monastery Lingyin 靈隱 (Hangzhou, Zhejiang province),[1] "Extensive Inquiry into the Teachings" ("Guang yuanjiao") constitutes the core of his *Essays on Assisting the Teaching* (*Fujiao bian*), a work admired at the time by some Song-dynasty ministers and the emperor Renzong (r. 1022–1063). Impressed by this writing, the emperor bestowed Qisong the purple robe and the honorary title Mingjiao Dashi (Great Master of Illuminating Teaching 明教大師; see Wang 2017, 195; Morrison 2010, 122).

In the preface of the "Extensive Inquiry into the Teachings" ("Guang yuanjiao"), Qisong himself describes the context of writing this text and its goals—to discuss the foundations of the Buddhist teaching as compared to those of Confucian teaching and to further develop the themes from an earlier work, the

"Inquiry into the Teachings" ("Yuanjiao" 原教; discussed in chap. 1), in which he addressed Confucian criticism against Buddhism:

> In the past, I wrote "Yuanjiao" in order to show the connection between the Buddhist Five Precepts and Ten Goods and the Confucian Five Permanencies. I ardently desired to dismiss the criticisms of contemporary Confucians against Buddhism. Regarding what the sage considers as the great root [foundations] of Buddhist teaching: I outlined it there but did not have time to present it completely. I wished to write this essay in order to develop it further. "Yuanjiao" had been around for seven years when Zhangji from Danqiu sent me a letter encouraging me to fully develop this topic. The first version of this essay, I thought, was not well written and I burnt it. I just finished writing this version and I think it almost comes close to correctly expressing the heart-mind of the sage [Buddha]. ("GYJ," 0654b07-2)

In this quotation from Qisong's "Guang Yuanjiao" ("Extensive Inquiry into the Teachings"), the reference to the heart-mind of the sage (Buddha; 聖人之心) suggests his Chan approach and recalls the opening phrase of his "Encomium of the Platform Sutra" ("Tanjing zan" 壇經贊, Qisong 2016b, examined in chap. 6): "The *Platform Sutra* is the writing by which the complete man (至人) [Qisong refers to Huineng 惠能 (638–713), the Sixth Patriarch of Chan, presumed author of the *Platform Sutra*] communicate [disseminated] his heart-mind. What heart-mind? The marvelous heart-mind transmitted by the Buddha" (壇經者, 至人之所以宣其心也。何心邪? 佛所傳之妙心也。; *Platform Sutra*,[2] 0346a13-10). It is noteworthy that Qisong held in great esteem the *Platform Sutra of the Sixth Patriarch* (*Liuzu Tanjing* 六祖壇經), which is the major Chan text, attributed to Huineng. Qisong referred to his own Chan school as the Platform Sutra school (Huang 1986, 11) and, it is commonly presumed, prepared a more mature version of this Chan sutra, later edited by Zongbao 宗寶 in 1291 (Li and Ding 2010, 7–8). His "Encomium of the Platform Sutra" ("Tanjing zan" 壇經贊) is included in the *Fujiao bian*. As mentioned in the previous chapter, Qisong discusses Buddhism from an inclusive point of view; nevertheless, a close look at the key concepts he chooses (such as the heart-mind of the sage) enables one to distinguish his implicit dedication to Chan—let us call it inclusive and moral Chan Buddhism (for reasons set out below).

Like the previous article, this preface as well as the whole essay "Guang yuanjiao" ("Extensive Inquiry into the Teachings") clearly conveys Qisong's interest not only in answering Confucians' criticism but also in engaging and connecting with his Song-dynasty Confucian contemporaries through a philosophical development of the essence of his inclusive and moral Chan Buddhism written especially for them. No doubt, it is toward this goal that he decided to explain Buddhist teaching in the classical *guwen* language and in a way familiar and relevant to Confucians. I closely examine from this perspective the philosophical dimensions of Qisong's text and the pre-Song Confucian concepts that he reinfuses with new meaning in order to offer Confucians a persuasive and positive presentation of the key strengths of Chan Buddhism. Reference is made to the pre-Song Confucian school.

The present chapter, which focuses on the notion of teaching, has two dimensions. First, it explores a so-called Confucianized dimension of Qisong's teaching in the "Guang yuanjiao" ("Extensive Inquiry into the Teachings"): how he revisited and reinterpreted Confucian terminology in his special form of Chan aimed at his contemporary Confucian readers and auditors "who do not know Buddhism" (世儒之不知佛者; "GYJ," 0654b19-5). Next, this chapter identifies another original feature of his singular form of eleventh-century Chan teaching: its so-called cohesive or inclusive perspective on Chinese Buddhist (under the aegis of Chan), Confucian, and other philosophical traditions, which considers all of them to be interdependent and to share a unique common root. As noted above, key concepts of Chan are at the core of this cohesive interpretation of Buddhist teaching that he develops.

One could also say that this second, cohesive, feature is inspired by the previous work of the tenth-century Chan monk Yongming Yanshou 永明延壽 (904–975), who was the abbot of Lingyin, the same famous monastery where Qisong wrote "Guang yuanjiao" ("Extensive Inquiry into the Teachings"), for only one year, in 960, more than a century earlier (Shih 1992, 99). Yanshou's thought has been extensively examined by Albert Welter (1993, 2011, 2016) and Heng-ching Shih (1992). In a sense, Qisong follows Yanshou's perspective and further develops it in a new direction.[3]

The two integral dimensions of Qisong's idea of teaching, a cohesive Chan core and a Confucian inspiration, are philosophically investigated using the hermeneutical method. As already employed in the previous chapter, this method entails interpretive analyses of selected paragraphs from the "Guang yuanjiao." These investigations unveil and explore Qisong's systematic allusions to Confucian classics and the meanings of these allusions; they involve the translation and interpretation of the lengthy essay "Guang yuanjiao," which focuses on the notion of teaching and on his abovementioned goal to teach Buddhism to a Confucian audience in Confucian terms.

It will be recalled that Qisong's cohesive Chan Buddhist thought is too complex to be simply labeled (see the introduction, sec. VI). For Huang Chi-chiang, the originality of Qisong's thought lies in its "syncretic" quality (1986, x). Elizabeth Morrison notes in her study of Qisong's life and his contribution to the Chan lineage, "Despite being a Chan dharma heir and a prolific writer, Qisong barely mentions meditation or dramatic awakening experiences. Nor does he appear to have had anything to do with the 'recorded sayings' or 'public case' genres. Indeed, aside from his historical writings, he wrote mainly on topics significant to the emerging Neo-Confucian movement.... His identity as an heir in the Yunmen 雲門 'house' of the Chan lineage seems to have meant relatively little for his religious and intellectual activities" (Morrison 2010, 8). Douglas Skonicki (2011) has analyzed the political aspects of Qisong's thought and his refutation of the Ancient-style Learning movement's attacks against Buddhism.

As already mentioned, this chapter is complementary to these previous works. It attempts to unveil and explore the significant and profound presence of the Chan teaching in his *Fujiao bian* written for his Confucian contemporaries in the Confucian *guwen*, the classical style associated with Han Yu and his program for Confucian revival (see chap. 1). While the abovementioned studies use the historical and religious studies approaches, the investigation carried out in this chapter develops the aforesaid philosophical new approach in this collaborative dialogue among various studies aiming to shed new light on Song-dynasty confluences between Buddhism and Confucianism: the two-sided, intralinguistic and extralinguistic translation/interpretation (see the introduction, sec. VII). This includes several, gradual layers, from concrete and mundane (ethics of everyday social practice) to abstract and spiritual (nonduality and reverence). The previous chapter dealt with the affinities and differences between Confucian and Buddhist traditions exposed in the essay "Yuanjiao" ("Inquiry into the Teachings"). This chapter unfolds another level of Qisong's interpretation based on the notion of teaching. The analysis covers a specific type of material, a close reading of the "Guang yuanjiao" ("Extensive Inquiry into the Teachings") and it provides a specific line of reasoning—hermeneutical arguments based on a comparative and interpretive understanding of the two dimensions of Qisong's idea of teaching: a cohesive Chan core and a Confucianized dimension.

II. THE CONFUCIANIZED DIMENSION OF QISONG'S NOTION OF TEACHING

What this chapter calls a "Confucianized" dimension of Qisong's thought finds expression in two features. First, as already noted, Qisong wrote his work in the Confucian style known as *guwen*, manifestly to better engage in a philosophical dialogue with the Confucians. Advocated by Han Yu, "*guwen* traces its origins to the language of the Zhou dynasty Confucian classics" (De Bary and Bloom 1999, 568). The Chan monk stressed that his goal was to introduce the essence of Chinese Buddhism to Confucians—obviously, in a language familiar to them. Indeed, the significant Confucian concepts that he uses in his new interpretation of Buddhism can be regarded as indicative of this intention. Understandably, he hopes that if written in Confucian terms, his work will have a stronger impact on Confucian readers. "I wrote these two articles ["Yuanjiao" and "Guang yuanjiao"]," Qisong mentions at the beginning of the "Guang yuanjiao" (0654b18-1), "because I wanted to explain the great foundation (*datong* 大統) of the teaching created by the first sage [Buddha] (發明先聖設教之大統), and thus instruct contemporary Confucians who do not know Buddhism. Therefore, I wanted to write it in *guwen* and simplify the [Buddhist] theory (故其言欲文其理欲簡)."

Second, Qisong intends to point out what he sees as a shared feature of Buddhism and Confucianism—a harmonizing (和) influence on the sphere of human relations, maintaining mutual respect for each other (普敬), ensuring the order and well-being of society. "The Buddhist monks," Qisong stresses, "certainly can make people live in harmony and mutually respect each other" (能必和, 能普敬; "GYJ," 0658a18-8). Obviously, his description of the role of Buddhist practitioners (both lay and monastic) has much in common with the Confucian image of the eminent individual dedicated to the welfare of the community and capable of influencing and transforming people. Qisong highlights what he sees as the essence of Buddhist teaching (what I would call his "cohesive Chan," for the reasons set out below): it transforms people—that is, it orients them toward doing good. The previous chapter and the essay "Yuanjiao" present this idea as an essential link between Buddhism and Confucianism. The "Guang yuanjiao" further reiterates this issue and explores it in more depth. In the next paragraph, the Song scholar-monk explains how Buddhists could effectively assist Confucians and participate in governance. Qisong emphasizes that, even if this transformation that the Buddhist practice produces is subtle and therefore not directly perceptible and not readily ascertainable for everyone, it is an effective way to assist the sovereign in governing the world:

> By understanding good deeds, individuals come to admire them and are encouraged to do them (人慕而自勸). This transformation is within the individuals and is not palpable (化之, 故在人而不顯); other people are not able to see it in order to verify the meritorious actions of these individuals; they are not able to see it in order to evaluate its results. However, how do we know that a decrease of bad actions in the world is not caused by this transformation? (然天下鮮惡, 孰知非因是而損之?) How do we know that an increase of good actions in the world is not caused by this transformation? (天下多善, 孰知非因是而益之?) Those who say that Buddhist teaching does not give assistance to the sovereign in his endeavor to govern the world, say

that because they do not understand this thing [that the inner transformation is not directly perceptible but has efficient perceptible effects]. ("GYJ," 0657b12-6)

The transformation triggered by Buddhist practice religiously motivates people to perform kind acts, thus contributing to the preservation of social harmony. By addressing Confucians in *guwen*, Qisong aims to prove to them in the familiar language of their classics that Confucianism and Buddhism emerged from a common root and have a common goal (i.e., to inspire people to do good), even if they have different "footprints." In this sense, Qisong argues that all teachings have a subtle dimension (the root) and a perceptible dimension (the discourses adopted, specific texts, and the ideas, values, and representations that they convey). Qisong calls the latter the footprints (*ji* 迹) of teachings. He thus distinguishes between the conventional, ordinary perception of the teachings and the sage's insight. The first sees Buddhism and Confucianism as two different teachings because all that this approach is able to discern is their different perceptible footprints (methods). The second focuses on their identity at a profound, root level: "Buddhist monk or Confucian," Qisong writes, "this is an external difference [in footprints]. The sage no longer deals with the footprints in order to preserve the root" (僧, 儒者, 迹也. 聖人垂迹, 所以存本也; "GYJ," 0657a21-3).

At the same time, to highlight the effectiveness of the Buddhist teaching, Qisong also reveals a fundamental contrast. Unlike the Confucians, whose practice is limited to the concrete world and who do not have access to their spiritual unique and common root, the Buddhist monks perform efficiently in the tangible world exactly because they have the capacity to go beyond it and return to this source. Their greater efficiency in handling daily life affairs comes precisely from this ability. Therefore, the Buddhist quality of being a sage or eminent individual has a different nature than Confucian sageness and eminence:

> The monk is a complete man (人至) [Huineng, the presumed author of the *Platform Sutra*, is a complete man; see the introduction]. He has made his heart-mind broad (心溥), his moral behavior complete, and his way great (道大). He is an eminent person (賢), but it's not the type of eminence about which people of the world talk. He is a sage (聖), but not the type of sage about which people of the world talk. He is the special eminence and sage from beyond the world (出世殊勝之賢聖). He is like this; how can one not honor him? ("GYJ," 0658b04-5)

In what follows, Qisong's use of well-known Confucian terms is examined. With a view to having a positive impact on Confucian readers, he defines the teaching of Buddhism, the learning process, and the transformation it triggers (performing good deeds) using direct quotations from ancient Confucian classics, especially from the *Book of Rites* (*Liji* 禮記 [in his "GYJ," 0657c12, 0638a02, 0659c15]), but also the *Analects* (*Lunyu* 論語 ["GYJ," 0656a01]), and the *Book of Documents* (*Shangshu* 尙書, chapter "Hong Fan" 洪範 ["GYJ," 0657c12]). The next section demonstrates that in addition to direct quotations, he uses and reinterprets several significant Confucian terms in his special account of Buddhism: middle (*zhong* 中) and sincerity (*cheng* 誠)—terms that appear in the *Doctrine of the Mean* (*Zhongyong* 中庸), which was initially chapter 28 of the *Liji*; and rectifying the heart-mind (*zheng xin* 正心)—a term central to the *Great Learning* (*Daxue* 大學), initially chapter 39 of the *Liji*.

II.1. Infusing Old Confucian Concepts with New Buddhist Meaning: The Zhongyong

It is a known fact that the *Zhongyong* was a popular focus of study during the Northern Song among both monks and Confucian scholars (see, for example, Liu 1967, 96; Shinohara 1994, 38). Qisong himself wrote a commentary on it, the *Zhongyong jie*, which is examined in chapter 7 (see also Arghirescu 2020b). As already noted by Koichi Shinohara in his study on the Buddhist master Zhiyuan 智圓 (976–1022), the idea of the "mean" (middle; *zhong* 中) originated in Confucianism, and Buddhist masters have been acquainted with it only secondarily (Shinohara 1994, 38).[4]

The next section suggests that, starting from the ancient Confucian meanings of the "middle" and "sincerity" developed in the *Zhongyong* (hereafter ZY),[5] Qisong developed an original, Chan Buddhist interpretation of these terms. This Confucianized interpretation is proof that, during the eleventh-century Song dynasty, Chan Buddhism was taking a full and particularly active part in Song Confucian culture. The scholar-monk's implicit goal was to uncover and explain what he saw as the interdependency between Buddhism and Confucianism. I emphasize here that the meanings of the *Zhongyong* terms are "ancient," in order to clarify that I do not anachronistically rely on their twelfth-century well-known Neo-Confucian interpretation by Zhu Xi (1120–1200), which is a later addition to the classic, written a century after the Chan scholar-monk's text.

First, I identify the ancient Confucian notions directly related to Qisong's work. In the ancient *Zhongyong*, the term *middle* (中) belongs to the domain of ordinary human affairs, especially governance, and to the sphere of morality. It refers to a perfectly righteous standard of behavior—a capacity and efficacy exclusive to exemplary individuals, which is extremely difficult to reach and to constantly follow in ordinary life (see ZY 2, 3, 8, 9, 11).[6] This potency is described in the following converging ways: "a state in which the human personal emotions/feelings of happiness, anger, grief and enjoyment are not yet manifest" (ZY 1; see Arghiresco/u 2013, 86–89), and therefore the individual possessing it is immune to the distorting effects of the power of these emotions and able to be nonbiased; an exceptional quality of righteousness that the legendary predynastic sage ruler Shun 舜 possessed and with which he governed the people (ZY 6; see Arghiresco/u 2013, 141–153); and a high standard of impartiality—namely, not tending to either side (bu yi 不倚; ZY 10). The present study imperfectly translates this zhong 中 as "potency of the middle." Obviously, in the context of the Zhongyong, the potency is a moral/ethical potency.

Moreover, in conjunction with this notion of middle, the Zhongyong introduces the concept of sincerity (cheng 誠) as the way of heaven (tian zhi dao 天之道; ZY 20).[7] This is a natural, spontaneous sincerity, which is normally present and at work in the natural order (for example, the harmonious continuity and growth of the seasons and of the diversity of life may be considered as an illustration of sincerity at work in nature), and it manifests itself as effortlessly following the "middle" (i.e., as unbiased and nonpartisan as nature's workings). This innate capacity is solely reserved for the sage (誠者不勉而中 . . . 聖人也; ZY 20). To this Confucian way of heaven embodied in spontaneous sincerity corresponds a correlative way—namely, the way of humans, which is the process of making humans sincere (through teaching) (誠之者, 人之道也; ZY 20) What is the meaning of "being sincere" in this ancient Confucian context? Obviously, it is a moral meaning that entails choosing to do good deeds and firmly pursuing this endeavor (誠之者, 擇善而固執之者也; ZY 20).

Starting from this Confucian moral perspective, in the "Guang yuanjiao," Qisong goes beyond the simple moral connotation of the middle and sincerity to develop a spiritual (religious) understanding of their articulation. To that end, he introduces "middle" and "sincerity" in the sphere of two Buddhist concepts—the heart-mind (xin 心; the field of Chan practice) and the universal principle (li 理; the Huayan major notion that Qisong includes in his cohesive Chan). Qisong equates both of them with the cohesive Chan understanding of nature (xing 性) and the marvelous quality (miao 妙; see next quotation). Further evidence regarding the religious background of this vision is provided in the "Guang yuanjiao" (0655a26), where he stresses that the heart-mind is "this common spirit that all beings share" (萬物同靈之謂心). The notion of spirit (lingshen 靈神) embodies the religious viewpoint of his thought. Elsewhere ("Yuanjiao," 0650b23-12), Qisong stresses the clear distinction between his Buddhist meaning of spirit as the spiritual essence (jingshen 精神) of the heart-mind and the ancient Confucian meaning of spirit as imperceptible spirits and ghosts (*guishen* 鬼神).

Thus, he first suggests that the "potency of the middle" (middle) is to be found not in nature (i.e., the unity heaven-earth) but in every human heart-mind (Qisong's Chan perspective) and that it is a notion addressed in many teachings. On this basis, he proposes a new perspective about the middle: the teachings' approaches—or "footprints" in the scholar-monk's terms—discuss, explain, clarify, and discursively define the meaning of the middle in different ways. Therefore, in his interpretation, the middles (*zhong* 中) relating to different teachings, the teachings (*jiao* 教) themselves, and the ways (*dao* 道), the marvelous qualities (*miao* 妙), and the methods of self-cultivation (*xiu* 修) that are representative of different teachings are not monolithic concepts but of different types and qualities—that is, a distinction exists between lower, incomplete (i.e., ordinary) middles and higher, complete, great (spiritual, *da* 大) middles. Inspired by the nondual correlation of phenomena-universal principle (*shi-li* 事-理) espoused by the Huayan school of Buddhism, he distinguishes between an ordinary marvelous (*miao* 妙) that corresponds with a "potency of the middle" of ordinary affairs (*shi zhong* 事中) and a great marvelous (*damiao* 大妙) correlated with a "potency of the middle" of the universal principle (*li zhong* 理中; see in the introduction the reference to the *Platform Sutra*, the most important "footprint" of the Chan teaching, as the text that communicates the marvelous heart-mind of the Buddha). In Qisong's view, the ordinary level concerns just the span of one's life, without including anything before or after and without considering the connection between previous life, present life, and future life, how people previous life's deeds influence their present life, and how their present life's deeds affect their future life:

> Every individual has a heart-mind (何人無心), every individual has a marvelous quality (何人無妙). Each teaching embodies a way (何教無道), each one of these ways has its potency of the middle (何道無中). When he only briefly discusses the ordinary potency of the middle (中), no one in the world can achieve the most complete way (至道). When he only confusedly discusses the marvelous, no one in the world seeks to accomplish the complete heart-mind (至心). Those who cannot reach the complete way and the complete heart-mind are hypocritical, arrogant individuals, full of themselves and slow in thinking. These kinds of individual do not cultivate themselves. Ordinary people are born and die, and just follow the changes within this life cycle (因循變化). They are not vigilant with regard to the nature of these changes [the connections between life-death-life]. Regarding the marvelous, there is ordinary marvelous (妙) and great marvelous (大妙).

Regarding the middle, there is the middle of ordinary affairs (事中), and the middle of the universal principle (理中). The notion of the middle of ordinary affairs means grasping the middle criterion when dealing with each of the ten thousand ordinary things. The middle of the universal principle is the most complete and correct level of authentic nature and of the universal principle (性理之至正者). ("GYJ," 0656c21)

The scholar-monk thus reinterprets in a very original (cohesive) Chan manner the ancient Confucian idea of middle through introducing a correlation, which is ultimately nondual (this notion is also studied in depth in the following chapters), between two levels of the term *middle* (ordinary and marvelous). He defines the middle of ordinary affairs (i.e., for each affair, finding the middle or impartiality criterion applicable to that affair and handling that affair in a way that meets its specific middle criterion) and the middle of the principle (i.e., a unique spiritual criterion that requires becoming aware of the universal principle). Through this distinction, Qisong infuses Buddhist meanings into the notion of middle: as the highest moral and processual criterion, which concerns dealing with ordinary matters and is equivalent with the Buddhist method of expedient means (see next quotation) as well as with the Confucian approach (finding the moral criterion adapted to each ordinary affair); and as the highest nondual—therefore spiritual/religious—criterion that flows from gaining awareness of the Buddhist universal principle and makes reference to the way of the sage. In this manner, with his teaching, the Buddhist sage lays novel, spiritual foundations for the daily life morality of ordinary people. This religious basis simultaneously transcends and embraces the simple moral foundation of ordinary activities, initially overstepping these mundane affairs only in order to return to them and fulfill them in the kindest, most impartial (i.e., kind to all) way possible. Impartiality in this nondual sense is more than simple morality (being disinterested). It is what might be called kind impartiality, equally embracing everything with one's heart-mind (complete kindness). For this reason, the essence of teaching for Qisong is precisely explaining the middle. In addition, it is in this process of teaching that the sage reveals his heart-mind and conveys it to people:

> The sage uses the way (*dao* 道) when acting; he uses the expedient (*quan* 權) when adapting to circumstances (以權適宜); he uses his appearances when showing the footprints of teaching. The way is the sage's middle of the universal principle (聖人之理中). The expedient is the sage's middle of ordinary affairs (聖人之事中). His various appearances [methods] are that with which the sage instructs people about the middle. When the sage

instructs about the middle, one can understand his heart-mind (聖人之心可知). The middle of the universal principle (理中) means the most complete level of the way of the sage. The middle of ordinary affairs means that the individual [who follows the teaching] can handle ordinary affairs in the same way the sage does. ("GYJ," 0659b21-10)

In this paragraph, the notion of expedient (*quan* 權) has old Confucian resonances.[8] It seems that this term also came into Buddhism from Confucianism. Confucius introduced it as expediency or consideration (see, for example, *Analects* 9:30, 20:1). Kirill Thompson translates this notion as "expedient means" and "discretion" and discusses how it was further developed by Zhu Xi: "He noted several types of situations in which recourse to discretion and expedient means might be advisable: (1) extraordinary situations that cannot be covered by standard norms (in principle), (2) urgent situations that require a direct violation of the received norms to be resolved, and (3) situations in which it is prudent not to observe the relevant norms" (Thompson 2002, 54). Thompson also stresses that "Zhu insisted on the established probity and integrity of anyone who would venture to use discretion and exercise expedient means" and that "only those who have extensively 'investigated things to extend knowledge' and who are conversant with the subtle patternings of the human heart and human affairs would be qualified to consider exercising expedient means over simply following norms" (2002, 55–56).

Qisong's above paragraph indicates that through his teaching about the middle, the sage effectively transfers his heart-mind to other humans, extending the influences of his heart-mind (*xuan qi xin* 宣其心; see chap. 6 about the "Encomium of the Platform Sutra"),[9] so they can conduct ordinary dealings in the same way he does. This is the result of a transformation through teaching, and the heart-mind of the sage is what subtly triggers the transformation of those he teaches (let us recall Qisong's view of the *Platform Sutra* as the teaching that disseminates the Buddha's heart-mind). Obviously, this metaphor of the transfer or influence of the heart-mind belongs to the universe of Chan teaching (from heart-mind to heart-mind) and expresses the way in which Chan teaching operates inside oneself—that is, makes humans aware of their own heart-mind and nature, which they share with all sentient beings. As illustrated in the above quotation, the scholar-monk views the latter not only as the spiritual element of humans—namely, the repository of the marvelous dimension, of all the middles of the potency (ordinary affairs and universal principle)—but also as the embodiment of authentic nature (*xing* 性) and the way (*dao* 道). This brings us to the next old Confucian term of the *Zhongyong* that Qisong infuses with new meaning. Let's continue with the second term from the *Zhongyong* that he has a real interest in, the notion of sincerity (*cheng* 誠).

In this ancient Confucian text, the notion of sincerity refers to the spontaneous natural law of the natural order (heaven-earth; see ZY 23, 24, 25, 26), as well as to neutral impartiality, disinterestedness, or psychological distance—a mental state in which no emotions/feelings are developed (see ZY 32). Qisong puts the idea of sincerity in a new light. Through using the notion of heart-mind, he links sincerity with the notion of the middle. To that end, he stresses that becoming sincere is nothing other than becoming aware of one's heart-mind— that is, trusting it or having confidence in it. In his Chan interpretation, it is this particular sincerity or impartiality that leads to confidence in individuals' heart-minds and thus stimulates them to begin the process of rectifying these heart-minds (see below). The scholar-monk explicitly places emphasis on this dual inspiration (Chan and Confucian) in the next quotation. On one hand, he interprets Chan Buddhist ideas by means of Confucian notions. On the other hand, he demonstrates how practice of a Chan Buddhist nature (becoming aware of one's heart-mind, relying on it, and having confidence in it) not only enables one to acquire authentic moral Confucian virtues (which Qisong identifies below: filial devotion, loyalty, kindness, etc.) but also strengthens the practice of these moral virtues by providing them a spiritual, religious foundation:

> The heart-mind is the source of intelligence and wisdom (心也者, 聰明叡智之源也). If one cannot find this source, everything emanating from oneself is false. It is for this reason that the sage wishes that individuals trust their own heart-minds (人自信其心); it is through trusting their heart-minds that they rectify (*zheng* 正) themselves. This makes their constancy (*chang* 常) sincere, their good deeds (*shan* 善) sincere, their filial devotion for their parents (*xiao* 孝) sincere, their loyalty (*zhong* 忠) sincere, their kindness (*ren* 仁) sincere, their affection for their children (*ci* 慈) sincere, their spirit of concord (*he* 和) sincere, their conciliatory spirit (*shun* 順) sincere, their understanding (*ming* 明) sincere. When one's understanding is sincere, he has influence on heaven and earth (感天地), moves the ghosts and spirits (振鬼神) [note that the Confucian interpretation of sincerity is limited to these two levels], further comprehends the transformation death-life [the Buddhist interpretation of sincerity includes this level] and finally acquires [the way of the sage] (更死生變化而獨得). ("GYJ," 0656a16-6)

In this paragraph, Qisong aims to suggest that sincere moral practice mainly means heartfelt and effortless practice rooted in a religious foundation. If religion is human's "ultimate concern or unconditional concern" in Paul Tillich's terms (1990, 12), it is obvious that a religious premise provides one with the genuine urgency and motivation for uninterrupted moral practice. In making this assertion, Qisong elaborates from a Chan perspective on sincerity and its effects. At the same time, he implicitly warns about a very common deficiency of Confucianism: acting falsely, apparently in accordance with the norms of the Five Permanencies (filial devotion, kindness, loyalty, etc.) but purely out of self-interest. Hence, he significantly widens the nature of this old Confucian notion of sincerity and changes its ontological grounding from cosmological to religious. In his vision, sincerity is not a presupposed source of natural order and life, an external, impersonal, and remote one, as explained in *Zhongyong* 26, but one that comes from an individual's heart-mind and is spiritual, as it is a state of inner awareness about the intangible continuity between one's last, present, and future lives. The source of a person's moral motivations is not their apprehension of the natural and orderly continuity of the spontaneous changes in the lives that go on within nature (heaven-earth) but their realization of the unbroken continuity of their three lives as well as their interdependence with all other sentient beings. Confucian sincerity belongs to the sphere of morality, cosmology, and life—this present life—and its attendant natural vital changes, the development of which is obviously perceptible, except for its imperceptible beginning and end.

As mentioned above, sincerity in the ancient *Zhongyong* is a spontaneous natural law, rooted in earth and heaven (the natural world). Using the Chan Buddhist notion of the heart-mind, Qisong enriches with a new spiritual dimension the ancient Confucian vision of complete sincerity (*zhi cheng* 至誠). The latter is presented in the ancient *Zhongyong* 22 as a spontaneous moral quality possessed only by the sage (see Arghiresco/u 2013, 311), which gives him the power to completely employ or deploy his own moral nature (*dexing* 德性; ZY 27; Arghiresco/u 2013, 345–346) as well as the moral natures of ordinary humans and other beings. As a result, the Confucian sage is able to assist the natural movements of heaven and earth that constitute the spontaneous changes in this present life and in the growth of life (可以贊天地之 化育; ZY 22; Arghiresco/u 2013, 311). He thus joins nature (heaven-earth) and cooperates in an equal partnership (與天地參; ZY 22) meant to look after the transformation of the living beings within this life (Arghiresco/u 2013, 311).

The above quotation also illustrates that Qisong's Chan Buddhist sage goes deeper and beyond present-life changes and is able to elucidate and explain via long cycles of transformation and extensive chains of interdependence the causes that arise in one life and their effects that occur in another life. Hence, in comparison to Confucianism, Buddhist teaching fosters and conveys a stronger motivation for its followers to uninterruptedly practice morality both in society and in the broader world of sentient beings.

The next section analyzes the presence in his explanation of Chan Buddhist teaching of the term *rectifying the heart-mind* (*zheng xin* 正心), a term of great significance in the ancient *Daxue*, and the way the scholar-monk integrated and reinterpreted it in the context of his thought.

II.2. Infusing Old Confucian Concepts with New Buddhist Meaning: The Daxue

In the ancient *Daxue* (7 *zhang*), rectifying the heart-mind is explained in strictly moral terms, as something that the individual is prevented from achieving if his or her heart-mind is under the grip of certain emotions/feelings that make one biased: anger (*fenzhi* 忿懥), fear (*kongju* 恐懼), pleasure (*haole* 好樂), and suffering (*youhuan* 憂患). When one is affected by these emotions, stresses the same paragraph of the *Daxue*, one's heart-mind is no longer present (*xin bu zai* 心不在)—that is, humans' contact with their fundamental moral source is lost. In this pre-Song Confucian vision, cultivating oneself means learning to harmoniously channel and express these emotions through the external tool of ritual and thus render the heart-mind present in everyday affairs.

Qisong takes up this well-known Confucian idea and develops it in a new light, on a new footing. "The sages developed their teachings as the footprints of the way," he explains, "in order to explain in words this difficult to comprehend heart-mind, to define it, instruct the people and rectify their heart-minds (正之)" ("GYJ," 0655b12-14). The term *rectifying the heart-mind* that Qisong uses in his Chan Buddhist context requires special attention. The monk introduces from a Chan perspective this idea that has special significance for Confucians. In Qisong's view, when one's heart-mind is rectified through the sage's teaching, it results in one trusting one's heart-mind (正人心而與人信也; "GYJ," 0656a24-4) (this heart-mind that has nature (性) and spirit (神) as its foundations) and therefore following it of his or her own free will.

When incorporated into the Chan soil of Qisong's thought, where the heart-mind is the original root, rectifying the heart-mind becomes "rectifying the universal root" (*zheng ben* 正本): "In order to rectify the root of all beings (萬物)," notes Qisong, "nothing is better than practicing the teaching (教)" ("GYJ," 0654c04-14). What is more, within his vision, this also means rectifying one's nature (*zheng yu xing* 正於性). In his "Guang yuanjiao," he clarifies this by introducing the term "authentic (original) nature" (an important Chan Buddhist subject of interest) as correlative of the emotions/feelings (also a Confucian subject of interest): "The movements of the world arise from emotions. In order to eliminate the confusion of all sentient beings, one must rectify their nature" (天下之動, 生於情, 萬物之惑, 正於性; "GYJ," 0655b19-11). Nature and emotions/feelings are different terms that express the same abovementioned correlation between the universal principle and phenomena, between nondual awareness and processual differentiation. Qisong points out that, when the individuals are able to make good use of emotions, they become able to properly sort out negative emotions and finally to go beyond emotions and become aware of the true reality that dwells within emotional reality; that is, one is able to remain attached to one's original nature, not lose it, not stray far from this nature and the heart-mind, and therefore becomes a rectified human being. Unlike the rectifying process of ancient Confucian teaching achieved by following an external model (that is, the ritual), the rectifying process of Chan teaching is a completely inner affair, a bold exploit to move down to greater depths in oneself—to a marvelous (that is, rectified) heart-mind, thus becoming an enlightened individual, a Buddha. Again, as in the case of middle and sincerity, Qisong equally enriches the idea of rectifying and rectified with a spiritual (nondual) dimension: "What is the Buddha? The Buddha is the rectified (正) heart-mind of the human being. What is a human being? A human being is one who turns to this rectified heart-mind and undertakes to make every effort. The Buddha and the individual are one and the same (佛與人, 一而已矣)" ("GYJ," 0656c10).

Rectified is also the essential quality of the Rectifier of Buddhists, the highest official position of the Buddhist clergy within the Confucian administration (this function is discussed in sec. II.3). Qisong describes this distinctive attribute of the Rectifier through connecting it with the requirement of complete sincerity (discussed above) and with the Buddhist threefold practice of the precepts, concentration, and insight (*jie ding hui* 戒定慧): "A monk is one who manages to fulfill the precepts, to cultivate concentration and insight (出於戒定慧者也). Being a Rectifier (正) requires the qualities of being sincere (*cheng* 誠) and enlightened (*ming* 明). If the monk is not sincere and not enlightened, how can he sincerely fulfill the precepts, and sincerely cultivate concentration and insight? If someone is not sincere when fulfilling the precepts and cultivating concentration and insight, then he does not know how he should be when in the position of Rectifier (不知其所以為正也)" ("GYJ," 0658c17-11). In this paragraph, we again discern Qisong's nondual Buddhist perspective, here in the form of the correlation between being sincere and being enlightened. In its context, the nonduality involves the identity between morality (the quality of being sincere) and spirituality (being enlightened). That is, while being sincere evokes the utmost moral quality, the root of this quality is beyond morality; it is spiritual, as enlightened (i.e., being able to comprehend clearly) for the scholar-monk means being in the state of awakening while being fully present in the flow of ordinary or daily life (experiences and relationships; see below 生之常). Obviously, he sees the Rectifier as the teacher of the other monks. For the Rectifier to be efficient in his role, he must be himself awakened like the sage:

> One who is awakened (*jue* 覺) is enlightened (*ming* 明); one who is not awakened, is not enlightened. This is the difference between the sage and other sentient beings. The state of being awakened is not the ordinary gradual awakening, but the utmost awakening (*ji jue* 極覺). The utmost awakening is achieving the qualities of the sage (聖人之能事); this is all. The individual who becomes awakened is a Buddha (覺之之謂佛).... When examining the way in which one could awaken oneself and become a sage, he understands that the awakening occurs in the daily life of all sentient beings (在乎群生之常覺也). The people experience awakening in their quotidian life, but they are not aware of this awakening (眾生日覺而未始覺). ("GYJ," 0659b01-14)

Let's observe the philosophical strategy that Qisong uses to build an interpretation of the Buddhist teaching as targeted toward contemporary Confucian scholars: he explains to them the spiritual foundations of his cohesive Chan Buddhism through shedding new light on old Chinese terms, instrumental within Confucian culture. In this way, he recontextualizes these notions while also establishing them on a firm Chan Buddhist footing. First, his reappraisal suggests to Confucians a completely new spiritually based perspective on their major Confucian moral qualities and a new practical approach to achieving them. This approach judges the effectiveness of these qualities other than simply morally or cosmologically as is done in Confucianism. Second, in turn, his integrated Chan Buddhism inevitably takes inspiration from Confucianism and finds itself enriched with a Confucianized dimension that emphasizes the importance of the continuous and transformative engagement of the Chan Buddhists (both lay and ordained, especially Confucian scholar-officials studying Chan Buddhism) within society.

In light of the foregoing comparative hermeneutics and philosophical development, the next section examines sociopolitical issues, including Qisong's concrete response to anti-Buddhist criticism by his Confucian contemporaries. By considering the eleventh-century atmosphere of interaction between Confucians and Buddhists within which he wrote his essay "Guang yuanjiao," light is shed on how these exchanges directly motivated him to elaborate this particular interpretation of Buddhism in familiar Confucian terms. Welter (1993,

69) notes that, a century earlier, during the Chan monk Yanshou's life, the mediation between Buddhism and Confucianism had become a matter of concern to the Buddhist community. Qisong's interpretative effort is evidence that this was still an issue of great concern a century later.

II.3. Interactions with Contemporary Confucians: Sociopolitical Issues

Obviously, the scholar-monk interacted not only with Confucian concepts but also with his Northern Song Neo-Confucian contemporaries and their sociopolitical ideas. For instance, it is possible to perceive his philosophical commentary on the introduction of Buddhism in China (see below) as a direct philosophical response to the anti-Buddhist criticism voiced by Ouyang Xiu 歐陽修 (1007–1072), his "perfect" contemporary (both were born in the same year and died in the same year), in the essay "Ben lun" 本論 (On the root; Ouyang 2001). The latter was written during the 1040s, a decade earlier than Qisong's "Guang yuanjiao." Qisong met with Ouyang in 1061, when he traveled to the capital Kaifeng, to present his book Fujiao bian to Prime Minister Han Qi 韓琦 (1008–1075) and Vice Minister Ouyang Xiu (Huang 1997, 156).

In this essay, the Confucian scholar states that in the ancient times of Yao, Shun, and the Three Dynasties, rites and righteousness (li yi 禮義) flourished in the world and thus prevented Buddhism from entering into China (De Bary and Bloom 1999, 593). Ouyang Xiu takes note of the decay of rites and righteousness during the eleventh century and advocates their revival as the best method to eradicate the unwanted influence of Buddhism on Chinese society. It is clear that, like his Tang-dynasty orthodox Confucian predecessor Han Yu, he sees Chinese culture and society in a monolithic and unchanging manner—as a unified Confucian culture and society. His writing sets out a point of view and a feeling of animosity largely shared by the Northern Song Confucian scholars, who considered themselves as the guardians of this Confucian culture.[10] It can be said that their position regarding Buddhism is the authoritarian, exclusive, and nonaccommodating position of the centralized Confucian administration. Accordingly, Ouyang conveys their common perception of Buddhism as an intruder that has taken advantage of the decay of Confucian rites and righteousness and crept into Chinese Confucian society.

As already suggested, a decade later, Qisong advances in his essay "Guang yuanjiao" a different explanation of the introduction of Buddhism into China, which may well constitute a pertinent response to Ouyang's criticism. His position reflects the clear awareness of the Buddhists regarding the growing importance of their teaching within Chinese society (in 1056, exactly one hundred years later, after the last anti-Buddhist suppression in 955). Unlike Ouyang Xiu, the scholar-monk describes Buddhism as an integral component of Song culture, presents it as an efficient ally of Confucianism, and advocates for their cooperation in social affairs. Like Ouyang, Qisong acknowledges the degradation of Chinese culture after the ancient period, but contrary to the Confucian, he sees this process as an inevitable development caused by the departure and absence of the sages (Buddhist, Confucian, or other) from this world. And he makes clear that the Buddhists could help remedy this state of affairs: "After the ancient epoch, the world became seriously degraded. At that moment Buddhist teaching appeared in China and, together with all the other schools, greatly increased the number of people who did good acts (相資以廣天下之為善). Was the arrival of Buddhism the intention of heaven (天意)? Was it the result of the action of the sage [Buddha] (聖人之為)? It is difficult to tell" ("GYJ," 0660a07-13).

Qisong promotes Buddhism as an integrated element in what he sees not as a static and unidimensional Confucian culture but as a multifarious and dynamic Northern Song-dynasty cultural environment. Obviously, this viewpoint resonates with what the chapter calls his "cohesive" perspective of the unity of teachings. The monk highlights the abovementioned common social goal—of the well-being of the community—shared by Confucians and Buddhists, and the necessity of the cooperation between Buddhism, Confucianism, and all other philosophical schools. It is clear that Ouyang's criticism and Qisong's response are situated at different levels: the scholar's perspective is sociopolitical, while the Chan monk's is philosophical. Of note is the fact that there is something essentially new in the latter's description of the position of Buddhism compared with that of his predecessor Yanshou (see sec. I). Qisong explicitly stresses not only Buddhism's active involvement in the management of Chinese society but also the indispensability of Buddhist teaching within the Song-dynasty cultural landscape, with Buddhism contributing to Chinese culture to the same extent as Confucianism in both regards. And he invokes the Chan idea of the unique and common heart-mind of the sages when making this argument:

> If one says that the world cannot exist without Confucianism, without the philosophical schools, then one should also say that it cannot exist without Buddhism (方天下不可無儒, 無百家者, 不可無佛!). If a teaching is lost, then a method of doing good deeds is lost (虧一教, 則損天下之一善道), and consequently, the bad deeds increase in the world. The teachings consist of the footprints of the way of sages and have the sages' heart-mind within (聖人之心). If one sees the heart-mind of the sages (*jian qi xin* 見其心), then there

will be no more inappropriate conduct in the world. But if one only follows the footprints left by the sages, then bad deeds will remain in the world (天下無有不非). Therefore, in order to become an eminent (賢) person, the most important thing is to understand the heart-mind of the sages (貴知夫聖人之心). ("GYJ," 0660a10)

Note the cohesive dimension of Qisong's Chan thought (further explored in the next section) illustrated in the above quotation: the presence within the teachings of a heart-mind of the sages (Buddha, Confucius, etc.). Chan discusses one seeing or understanding one's heart-mind and original nature. He translates this idea of heart-mind into the physical and therefore "living" form (footprint) of the teachings. Exactly as the individual has a heart-mind, the teachings embody the heart-mind of the sages.

Another example of the distinctive character of the Confucianized dimension of Qisong's form of Chan and of his effort to connect what is called here a cohesive Chan with Confucian tradition is his new clarification on the status and role of Buddhist officials (*seng guan* 僧官) within the secular Confucian administration of his time as being "responsible for monitoring the numbers, qualifications and conduct of Buddhist monks and nuns" (Hucker 1985, 405). His evaluation is different from that of his other predecessor Zanning 贊寧 (919–1001), a monk who occupied the position of Buddhist Registrar (*senglu* 僧錄) in the Confucian administration during the tormented tenth century and witnessed the last anti-Buddhist suppression. Both Zanning and Qisong discuss the establishment during the Later Qin 後秦 (384–417) of the highest title—the Rectifier of Buddhists (*seng zheng* 僧正; in his *Dictionary of Official Titles in Imperial China*, Hucker translates this title as "Buddhist Chief"; Hucker 1985, 405). The emperor Wenhuan 文桓 (r. 394–416) selected the monk Daolüe 道䂮 as the first Rectifier, thus setting up this institution of Buddhist officials. Zanning mentions the process of transformation of the Buddhist monks, who became tainted by secular customs. Hence came the need for him to restrain and correct them by introducing a Buddhist clergy—namely, a Rectifier "famed for his virtue," appointed by the government. Welter explains that Zanning sees "imperial authority over Buddhism as enhancing rather than detracting from Buddhism as religion" and therefore emphasizes the success of the administrative subordination of Buddhism within the imperial bureaucratic structure (Welter 2016, 258). From within the community of Buddhist (religious) leadership, Zanning thus adds another layer of legitimacy and justification for the creation of this Buddhist official position by the Confucian administration.

In the "Guang yuanjiao," Qisong's opinion is far more nuanced and less subservient. First, like Zanning a century earlier, he acknowledges that the quality of Buddhist monks has deteriorated. And he considers this as a natural transformation that needs to be further controlled:

> At the time of my sage Buddha, the monks were administered using the law of the monks (以僧法治), and the secular people were administered using the law of the secular people (以俗法治). Each one was regulated using its own laws. I never heard of administering and restricting monks using secular law (未始聞以世法而檢僧也). It is because the sage disappeared from the world and his way has already declined that the Buddhists are all very stained. Is it still possible to govern the monks only with Buddhist law? ... Ancient things transform themselves; this is the natural tendency (物久乃變, 其勢之自然也). This already completed transformation [the monks' corrupted behavior] must be controlled (既變則不可不制也). The way to control it is through differentiation between good and evil, right and wrong. ... Highlight the merit of a single good behavior and all people will be encouraged to do good deeds (旌一善, 則天下勸善). Honor a single eminent man, and the whole world will respect eminent men (禮一賢, 則天下慕賢). ("GYJ," 0658b10-8)

By means of this interpretation, Qisong also suggests a positive dimension of the secular Confucian administration of Buddhists. It can be said that, in solidarity with Zanning, he concedes that this could be an additional way to control the behavior of the monks, meant to enhance the Buddhist law. However, this positive quality is for him only secondary, as first and foremost he strongly condemns the monetary dimension of this secular Confucian administration—namely, the awarding of ranks and salaries to the Buddhist monk officials. This is against the nature of Buddhist law, he reiterates, and the source of a major harm to Buddhists, because, exactly like in the case of Confucian officials, ranks and salaries stimulate personal interest, pursuit of power and control, and therefore corruption. Qisong is highly critical of the Buddhist monk Daolüe, who was the first to accept this title:

> Establishing a title of Rectifier of Buddhists is good, attaching to it the salary of a government official is not good (置秩不可). Monks are those who abandon privilege and profit (委榮利). They achieve excellence in morality and reach the highest level of morality while remaining among the people. How could a monk take an interest in the salary of a government official? If a monk is given the salary of a government official, isn't this a precedent which will make future monks compete for power? (與僧比秩, 不亦造端引後世之競勢乎)? The monk Daolüe was not enlightened. There has been a failure to stop this kind of tendency. This is Daolüe's fault. ("GYJ," 0658c14-6)

Qisong describes here the way in which an official post corrupts the individual holding it and the way in which a secular post deteriorates the moral quality of a religious Buddhist expected to be a model for all monks, their Rectifier. This issue was familiar to Confucians, as a similar problem preoccupied these Northern Song reformers: the power struggle and the corruption of Northern Song scholar-officials who were "shamelessly opportunistic" and did not give duty high priority (Liu 1988, 62).

III. THE "COHESIVE" DIMENSION OF QISONG'S NOTION OF TEACHING

The comparative hermeneutics unfolded in section I contributes to the mapping out of the conceptual milieu within which Qisong develops his notion of teaching. This first section examines the well-known Confucian vocabulary and patterns of Confucian moral thought that he exploits to build a new interpretation of Buddhist teaching with a Confucianized dimension (it bears repeating, written specifically for a Confucian audience) during the Northern Song dynasty.

Section II discusses the Chan Buddhist core of Qisong's thought, providing insight into his philosophico-religious understanding of the notion of teaching and the conceptual milieu attached to it. This exploration involves two different streams of focus. First, it recalls that the teaching has a soteriological purpose. In other words, it is equivalent with a practice of becoming, of transformation (an issue presented in the next subsection and fully developed in the next chapter). Second, it discovers that the originality of Qisong's ascription of a religious meaning to teaching as ultimate transformation resides in its "cohesive" feature: he leaves aside the sectarian aspect of various schools and perceives the cohesiveness of Buddhist teachings as a common spiritual root from which emerge all these different footprints or offspring (different Buddhist schools). In addition, he integrates Confucianism into this particular vision of teaching. In his view, a common root is entirely present in each footprint (concrete manifestation) of these only apparently different teachings. Both facets are addressed below.

III.1. The Religious/Soteriological Meaning of Qisong's Teaching: An Ultimate Transformation

The essay "Guang yuanjiao" presents teaching as an ultimate, powerful transformation (i.e., one whose effects extend over a span of at least three lives) of a person's heart-mind and consequently of their condition and circumstances. Moreover, Qisong defines the goal of this transformative practice as acquiring an imperceptible efficacy—"Doing good without leaving any footprints" (從善無迹之謂化; "GYJ," 0657b11-16)—and as an "ultimate" transformation (see next quotation). Thus, the scholar-monk perceives the heart-mind as engaged in a continuous process of change, eventually reaching its highest level (state) or maximum (*zhi* 至), at which the human becomes aware of the spiritual dimension of this heart-mind—that is, the Buddhist true reality (*ru* 如), the root of the marvelous (*miao zhi ben* 妙之本) in each thing (being). When this highest or complete state is achieved, the heart-mind does not transform anymore. Let's note that his view concerning the end of the transformation reveals a connection with a Confucian idea: the highest, complete, or maximum level of the individual cultivation depicted, for instance, in the *Daxue*; see *Daxue jing* (the complete good, *zhi shan* 至善) and *zhang* 5 (the most complete level of knowledge, *zhi zhi zhi* 知之至). It is arguable that this Confucian perspective is fused by Qisong into the Chan Buddhist end state of transformation (of the heart-mind), when the awareness of true reality is achieved and no further transformation is needed. Using the correlation of emotions and authentic nature mentioned above (see sec. II.2), he gives in the following paragraph a clear explanation of the requirements and outcomes of this ultimate transformation of the heart-mind:

> The heart-mind can certainly attain its highest state (心必至). When attaining its highest state, certainly it transforms itself (至必變). Transformation means the process of consciousness (變者, 識也). Attaining its highest state means reaching the state of ultimate reality (至者, 如也). The state of ultimate reality is a marvelous potentiality that all beings have (如者, 妙萬物者也). Perceiving entails making beings diversified [recognizing distinct individual beings] and considering them as different (紛萬物, 異萬物者也). Transformation is the set of imperceptible signs of movement (動之幾). The highest state is the root of the marvelous. In the world, there is no being without root, there is no being that does not move. It is for this reason that all beings emerge from the process of transformation and enter into the process of transformation. The beings rise from ultimate reality and return into ultimate reality. Their transformation is apparent in the human emotions (情); the ultimate reality of the world dwells in authentic nature (性). Through the emotions, one can perceive the transformation of beings (辨萬物之變化). Through authentic nature, the human can have sight of the great marvelousness of the world (觀天下之大妙). When the individual excels in both the sphere of the emotions and that of authentic nature, then he becomes able to discuss the way and the teaching of the sage. ("GYJ," 0655a19)

Aside from the soteriological feature of the teaching (i.e., Buddhist teaching) as transformation (that is, a process of change culminating in the ultimate transformative state evoked earlier), a second—and truly original—spiritual component of Qisong's understanding of Chan Buddhist teaching is what is called here its "cohesiveness." In other words, all teaching traditions share the same spiritual root or ground (are cohesive); however, it is by means of the Chan Buddhist teaching that one is able to reach this level—namely, to realize their original identity, the nonduality of Chan, other Buddhist schools, and Confucian tradition. This topic is explored in the next subsection.

III.2. The Spiritual Meaning of Qisong's Teaching: A Cohesive Instruction

To uncover this spiritual quality, particular attention needs to be paid to the distinct Chan Buddhist foundations of Qisong's notion of teaching. Starting from a specific conceptual content (way, heart-mind, sages, and sentient beings) that defines for him the sphere of training, the scholar-monk builds what is called here a "cohesive" Chan Buddhist view. Next, he also incorporates aspects of Confucianism and other philosophical schools. The following subsection considers first the conceptual content as foundations of the spiritual dimension of Qisong's notion of teaching, in order to subsequently develop the cohesive spiritual understanding of the term that he builds on these conceptual foundations.

III.2.1. The Conceptual Foundations of Qisong's Cohesive Teaching

As already argued, a particular notion of teaching (*jiao* 教) lies at the heart of his form of Chan. The analysis below reveals that the term, as it appears in the "Guang yuanjiao," does not have for him the usual Buddhist technical meaning of doctrinal Buddhism as opposed to Chan or practical Buddhism. Teaching denotes for him not sectarian differences but any kind of process of explaining or commenting on the way (*dao* 道) and all types of footprints, vestiges, or perceptible outer traces or methods (*ji* 迹) left by the sages (闡道之謂教。教也者, 聖人之垂迹也; "GYJ," 0654b24-5).

Clearly, the central concept related to his understanding of Buddhist teaching is the way. In the same paragraph, 0654b24, Qisong explains in Chan terms that "the way is the heart-mind (*xin* 心), which is the great root (*da ben* 大本) of all sentient beings, completely unknown to them because forgotten for a long time" (惟心之謂道,...道也者眾生之大本也. 甚乎群生之繆其本也久矣). This echoes the following passage from the *Platform Sutra* 0347b15-5: "That by which the ocean exists is the water; the fish and dragons die and live in the ocean, but do not see the water. That by which the way exists is the heart-mind; the humans speak of the way all the time, but do not see their heart-mind (海所以在水也, 魚龍死生在海而不見乎水; 道所以在心也, 其人終日說道, 而不見乎心。)."

The scholar-monk stresses that the way is the state of spiritual awareness from which arises the Buddhist consciousness that continues from life to life, the generator and beneficiary of karmic retribution: "The way is the deep content of the spirit (道也者, 神之蘊也), it is the origin from which arises the consciousness (*shi* 識). The consciousness is the source of great trouble (大患)" ("GYJ," 0659a04-5). And elsewhere ("GYJ," 0655a26-7), he defines the way as "the undertaking that the sages carry out in the world" (聖人所履之謂道). Thus, the first major interdependent concepts that Qisong uses in the "Guang yuanjiao" to build an integrated understanding of teaching are the way, the heart-mind, the sage, and all the sentient beings (i.e., "heaven, human beings, Asuras, ghosts and spirits, and the categories of animals with shells, with feathers, and those living under the earth"; "GYJ," 0655a19).

After presenting the nondual correlation way/heart-mind—that is, the way is the heart-mind, or the place of practicing the way is the heart-mind—he distinguishes the two notions according to another nondual correlation, sage/sentient beings, using "the way" as the prerogative of sages, while "the heart-mind" is the common, natural endowment of all sentient beings (see the next quotation). In Qisong's view, the way is the same unique resource that all sages possess, which makes them different from all other sentient beings precisely because it is they who develop teachings from this common resource in order to provide a transformative practice for all sentient beings. With his integrated vision of instruction, Qisong highlights the capacity to go beyond the apparent diversity of particular teachings and see their common foundation or essential sameness—that is, the unique manner in which each embodies the way in a different form. The original heart-mind is the common endowment shared by the multitude of sentient beings, sages included. "Nowadays," he explains, "in order to distinguish sages (聖人) from other sentient beings (群生), one discusses the way [of the sages], and one discusses the heart-mind [of the multitude of sentient beings]" ("GYJ," 0655b04-1). Indeed, all humans experience to a certain extent their heart-mind, while only sages experience the unique and common way. Moreover, as the *Platform Sutra* stresses, there is an intrinsic link between them, because the heart-mind is that by which the way exists.

This is a brief outline of the conceptual core of Qisong's interpretation of teaching. Starting from this conceptual core and from his specific definition of Chan Buddhist practice, he builds a so-called cohesive or nondual[11] meaning of this notion. This particular connotation of the concept of instruction is further developed below. In a vivid and straightforward explanation, the contemporary Chan East Asian teacher Thich Nhat Hanh specifies, "Non-duality means 'not two,' but not two also means 'not one.' That is why we say 'non-dual' instead of 'one.' Because if there is one, there are two. If you want to avoid two, you have to avoid one also" (Nhat Hahn 1987, 39).

III.2.2. The Cohesive and Nondual Chan Buddhist Essence of Qisong's Notion of Teaching

The abovementioned understanding of the way as a practice within the heart-mind and of teaching as aiming to help students acquire awareness of this long-forgotten heart-mind ("that cannot be seen" 不見乎心, in *Platform Sutra*'s terms), correct it, and gain confidence in it spotlights the Chan Buddhist essence of Qisong's thought and its deep connection with the *Platform Sutra*. (This connection is explored in chap. 6, dedicated to his "Encomium.") Further evidence regarding the nondual religious/spiritual background of this vision is provided in the paragraph "Guang yuanjiao" 0655a26, where he stresses that the heart-mind is "this common spirit that all beings have in common" (萬物同靈之謂心). The notion of spirit (*lingshen* 靈神) embodies the religious viewpoint of his thought. Elsewhere, in the essay "Yuanjiao," Qisong stresses the clear distinction between his Buddhist meaning of spirit as the quintessential spirit (*jingshen* 精神) of sentient beings and the ancient Confucian meaning of spirit as imperceptible spirits and ghosts (*guishen* 鬼神; see the following quotation). Through this distinction, the scholar-monk also points to the focus of Buddhist teaching on the cultivation of this "quintessential spirit":

> The spirit (神) means the quintessential spirit (人之精神) of humans; this is not something regarding the spirits and ghosts, who mislead people. That is, [Buddhism says] if the individual cultivates his quintessential spirit, then he can exhibit good behavior (謂人修其精神, 善其履行). During his life, one receives rewards (福應); at his death, his spirit rises up in purity (其神清昇). When one does not cultivate one's quintessential spirit, and practices evil and aberrant things (履行邪妄), life is not a time to celebrate (非慶); and after death, one's spirit is punished (其神受誅). When ordinary people hear this teaching, their heart is touched (其心感動); they stop doing evil things and follow good practices. Thus, they silently transform themselves. This type of transformation takes place for generations. (Qisong, "YJ," 0650b23-9)

As noted already, the bedrock and structure of his teaching is Chan as embodied in the *Platform Sutra*. However, his vision of the "teaching rooted in Chan" surpasses the limited sense of this term as being just one of various Buddhist schools. For the reasons set out below, we might call it a "cohesive" form of

Chan or "nondual Chan," as suggested earlier—a perception embracing all Chinese Buddhist teachings as one, including the doctrinal schools of Huayan and Tiantai, albeit a distinctly Chan-flavored one with its core concepts of the heart-mind and of the practice of seeing individual's nature (see chap. 5). In the opening section of his "Guang yuanjiao," Qisong also notes that he drew inspiration from the Huayan school: "In this essay ["Guang yuanjiao"], I first discuss the human and heavenly vehicles (*ren tian cheng* 人天乘) [obviously, this is an implicit reference to the Confucian way of humans and way of heaven, but expressed in Buddhist terms, as "vehicles"; in other words, he notes that he discusses aspects of Buddhism that are also found in Confucianism, in a Confucianized form, intended for a Confucian public] and I do this in accordance with what the *Huayan Sutra* calls [the practice of] 'assimilating the branches in order to return to the root' (攝末歸本門)" ("GYJ," 0654b16-15). Moreover, despite their diversity, he considers all Mahayana sutras of the various Buddhist teachings as interconnected (*guan* 貫) and permanent (*chang* 常) classics; that is, they contain the timeless words of ancient sages that convey through the ages a universal practice and way and keep alive the awareness of the universal principle (*li* 理). Qisong emphasizes that it is through their shared feature—the unique and common root—and not through their superficial differences that each of the different Buddhist schools contributes to bringing together sentient beings, to shedding light on their interconnectedness:

> What are the sutras of Mahayana Buddhism? They are classics and all they talk about corresponds to the universal principle (合理也, 經也). The classics embody what is continuous (常), connect everything together (貫), and provide guidance (攝) to people. In order to make apparent that the words of previous sages and the words of future sages are saying the same thing, there is nothing better than continuity (常). In order to understand the meaning of the universal principle and avoid losing it, there is nothing better than connecting everything together (貫). In order to gather all people and help them transform themselves through teaching, there is nothing better than providing guidance (攝). ("GYJ," 0656a27)

Historically speaking, starting from the Tang dynasty, all these Chinese schools evolved individually, as branches that, even if they grew out from the same trunk of Mahayana Buddhism, produced subschools, as in the case of Chan, and each of them claimed a distinct personality. It should also be noted that the antiscriptural tendency developed within certain Chan subschools (Linji and Caodong) expresses the same trend toward developing a specific individuality. In his study about the tenth-century monk Yanshou, Welter refers to his interest in "creating a syncretic harmony that encompassed a variety of philosophies and practices in the Buddhist tradition" while disregarding the "sectarian opposition which the teachings of different Buddhist schools had promoted" (Welter 1993, 92). It is to be noted that, in a sense, Qisong continues this approach that downplays particularism. However, he develops this view not from a "harmonizing differences" perspective but from a nondual or cohesive one, focusing on what he describes as the common spiritual root of the various teachings. After Qisong's death, the special cohesive form of Chan that he advocated would disappear, and the predisposition to develop and maintain sectarian identity, already prevailing during Yanshou's and Qisong's times, would become the Song-dynasty Chan orthodoxy (see, for example, the perspectives of the Linji and Caodong Chan subschools).

Note, once again, that in the context of continuous differentiation, divisiveness, and distancing of the Buddhist teachings from their common core, Qisong's eleventh-century effort is not to produce an organic synthesis of all of them but to highlight their original sameness as reflected in their common root, the way (*dao* 道), from which stem various methods only because they had to best fit the various qualities of individuals. He does not presuppose their separation and then work toward their unification but unveils their initial subtle identity, their nonduality. The Chan scholar-monk proposes a highly original interpretation of the teachings, which in his view are nondual. He stresses that it is only differences in the potential and karmic resources of people that make the teachings appear different:

> Teaching is the great tool of the sage, and he adapts it according to the circumstances and qualities (機) of the people; this is not something one could first conceive in the heart-mind and then make into reality. For the people who possess great qualities, he uses the method of sudden enlightenment (其機大者頓之). For those who have smaller qualities, he uses gradual enlightenment (機小者漸之). Gradual teaching (漸) uses expedient means (*quan* 權), sudden enlightenment (頓) uses real means (*shi* 實). The real means—relate to the teaching of the great vehicle. The expedient means—relate to the teaching of the small vehicle. By means of the great and small vehicles, the sage is able to include all the qualities of people, the full potencies of the hidden and the manifest. The sage promotes the sudden approach, but also knows the gradual approach (預頓而聞漸); he promotes the gradual, but also knows the sudden (預漸而聞頓). Thus, the marvelous and profound quality of the sage (聖人之妙) surpasses the unity heaven-human (天人), and the people cannot infer it by reasoning. If the sage shows the expedient means, it is in order to advance toward the real means

(聖人示權, 所以趣實也). If the sage shows the real means, it is because he relies on the expedient means (聖人顯實, 所以藉權也). Therefore, the expedient, the real, the partial and the whole are not unrelated (故權, 實, 偏, 圓, 而未始不相顧). ("GYJ," 0654c06-16)

Accordingly, rather than syncretic, or harmonizing, which means accommodating together schools of different natures, Qisong's perception of the teaching is cohesive or nondual in the sense that, he argues, all these schools share the same spiritual (i.e., beyond ordinary reasoning and perception, marvelous, *miao* 妙) origin, and all the sages who established the different methods have access to this common root or way. The scholar-monk emphasizes the existence of their connection point—a common nature—as a thread that connects the teachings at a "marvelous," nondual level. This is what this study calls the cohesive Chan meaning of his teaching.

Furthermore, he extends this connection beyond the Buddhist sphere and includes in the cohesive teaching the other native Chinese teachings. Yet, even if they all emerge from the same root, the outward forms of these teachings are not of the same quality and produce different results. In this broad area of the various teachings, he gives a new understanding to the correlative real-expedient means (*shi-quan* 實-權)—one that goes beyond the closed sphere of Buddhism. Let us recall that *expedient means* is an old Confucian term (see sec. II.1.). Like all the other correlatives used by Qisong and examined in the present study, for him, this one is equally a nondual correlative. The teachings that involve "real" means are those that provide access to fundamental, true reality (we implicitly recognize in this category the Buddhist schools Chan, Huayan, and Tiantai). Qisong includes in the group of those that employ "expedient" means all the Chinese philosophical schools (*bai jia* 白家), Confucianism included. Note that the scholar-monk describes cohesive Chan Buddhism as also including these doctrines. While only Buddhism can guide people to the highest level (that is, the one common root), Qisong acknowledges that the other expedient teachings also embrace all the worldly good deeds and therefore have soteriological implications and benefit people (救世濟物):

> The real means (實) involve attaining true reality (至實). When the individual has reached the level of true reality, all things and his self are nondual [are one and the same] (*wu wo yi* 物我一). When all things and his self are nondual, the sage is naturally with all sentient beings and he accomplishes what he needs to do (成之). Concerning the expedient method of the sage (聖人之權), this brings together all the good deeds of the world (周天下之善) and includes all the theories of the philosophical schools (遍百家之道). This is the great

expedient that saves the world and benefits all things (救世濟物之大權). As for the real method of the sage (聖人之實), this makes the phenomenal world unlimited (旁礴法界), and guides all sentient beings to reach the highest state (與萬物皆極). This method is the great way (大道) of the world to fully grasp the universal principle and become fully aware of authentic nature (窮理盡性). ("GYJ," 0654c18-13)

It must be recalled that Qisong considers the teachings as different only when regarded as observable footprints (i.e., distinct training methods and teaching materials) of different sages. In his view, this narrow perception of focusing only on the marks of a specific teaching is unidimensional, because it pays attention only to limited aspects of human life while considering them as representative of the whole (i.e., the spiritual, the human, the morality of ordinary human affairs, or the highest morality). To the contrary, the Song scholar-monk points to the interdependency of the teachings. He draws attention to a profound nondual reality—a common root of all teachings that is beyond their limited footprints and encompasses them. Therefore, he constantly advises against stopping at this level of the perceptible dissimilarities between the traces, which is a low-level quality of one's perception and training of one's heart-mind. The monk focuses on the need to refine the quality of humans' perceptions and heart-minds in order to become aware of the interdependency of the teachings. Huayan Buddhism highlights the interconnection between all things (phenomena). Chan Buddhism focuses on the interconnection between heart-minds. It can be said that Qisong transfers and adapts this core idea of interdependency to the specific context of teaching and learning: he sees all different sages who embody different teachings as sharing the same heart-mind. Therefore, all teachings emerge from this single heart-mind ("the marvelous heart-mind transmitted by the Buddha"; Qisong, "Encomium of the Platform Sutra," 0346a14-11). This view is another definition of what the present study means when referring to the construction of the "Guang yuanjiao" as a cohesive, nondual form of teaching based on Chan's central notion of the heart-mind:

> Among the sages' ways of teaching there are the way of the spirit (神道), the way of humans (人道), ordinary morality (常德), and the highest morality (奇德). We cannot consider only one of these dimensions and think that this is all, and we cannot examine them using popular opinion. The human acquires everything when his heart-mind fully understands and is connected with everything (得在於心通). He misses everything when he focuses on the differences between the footprints (失在於迹較). ("GYJ," 0654c26-1)

In his particular vision of all teachings as interdependent footprints, Qisong uses the concept of the common heart-mind of sages to highlight their fundamental connection. By placing emphasis on the common heart-mind, shared by all sages—Buddhist, Confucian, and other—the scholar-monk proposes a method to surpass the apparent differences between the teachings and to bring to light their interrelatedness (i.e., what he calls their common nature or root, mentioned earlier), which precedes and embraces their subsequent differentiation (i.e., the different individual tracks and signs as means of identifying the specificity of each approach, what renders it different from other perspectives):

> In ancient times, there were sages within the Buddhist school, Confucian school, and the philosophical schools. They shared the same heart-mind, but their footprints were different (心則一, 其迹則異). They shared the same heart-mind—they all wanted to encourage the people to do good deeds (其皆欲人為善者). Their footprints were different—each school was distinguishable from the others, and each one provided its own teaching (分家而各為其教者也). Each sage provided his own teaching—for this reason, the sages' methods of teaching people to do good deeds are different (其教人為善之方). There are superficial methods and profound methods; methods concerning what is near [this life] and methods concerning what is far [previous and future lives] (有淺有奧, 有近有遠). But when the people manage to give up bad deeds and harass each other no more—at this level, the moral influences of the teachings are all the same (其德同焉). ("GYJ," 0660a03)

From this paragraph, which gives prominence to the moral or ethical (*de* 德) influences of the teachings, one can understand that the most valuable dimension of each of the teachings highlighted by Qisong in the context of his Northern Song Confucian culture is not the spiritual, epistemic, or ontological one but the ethical one of nurturing and doing kindness. This is their manifest common denominator. The influence of Confucian culture on Qisong's thought is obvious here. Moreover, for the Chan scholar-monk, the most valuable teaching is cohesive teaching, which entails a heart-mind that fully understands and connects everything (*xin tong* 心通; "GYJ," 0654c28-2). It can be said that this is the Chan Buddhist core of his view. From this paragraph, it is also understandable that he advocates teaching and promoting all these dimensions with the explicit intention of transcending their individual limits and reaching the fundamental root that they all share at a profound level—that is, the heart-mind, buddha-nature, or authentic nature (*xing* 性).

The next section provides further evidence that the most important dimension of cohesive teaching is for Qisong its emphasis on active engagement with and contribution to society. With this criterion in mind, he establishes a hierarchy of the different Buddhist schools symbolized by the sages who established them: lesser sages, middle-level sages, and great sages. In the "Guang yuanjiao" 0654c29, the scholar-monk comments on different teachings and their different objectives (see below). It is important to note that one of the learnings mentioned is directed toward training Confucians in the sphere of governance. In this way, Qisong implicitly emphasizes their authority as administrators of society and stresses the concrete connection between Confucians and Buddhists—aiming, as this study frequently reiterates, to convincingly demonstrate that both work for the betterment of society. Accordingly, he suggests the Buddhist teaching of the Five Precepts and Ten Good Deeds (*wujie shishan* 五戒十善) as the best Buddhist teaching for those who govern. Obviously, this gives prominence to the ethical practice. I have already presented the way in which he connects this teaching with the Confucian Five Permanencies (*wuchang*五常; see chap. 1). Next, Qisong evaluates the Buddhist teachings of the Four Noble Truths (*si di* 四 諦) and of the Twelve Links of Conditioned Arising (*shier yuan* 十二緣) as the best training for those wishing to become the least of the lesser sages or a lesser sage. As regards the teachings of the Six Paramitas (perfections; *liu du* 六度) and the Ten Thousand Practices (*wan xing* 萬行)—that is, Ten Thousand Good Deeds (*wan shan* 萬善)—the monk sees them as the highest teachings, intended for those aspiring to become great sages and even striving to become the greatest of the great sages. This hierarchical perspective reflects his effort to develop a rather extroverted form of cohesive and nondual Chan Buddhism that puts a strong focus on morality, on building ethical interpersonal relationships in everyday life, on religious practice actively dedicated to cultivating interdependency and to serving and transforming communities—both of the abovementioned highest teachings stress compassionate human interaction, active deeds that benefit others. It is noticeable that the lower teachings mentioned first focus on individual introspection, as they provide solutions to the problems of individual suffering and attachment and revolve around personal transformation through individuals' contemplation of the noble truths and of causes and conditions. Moreover, it is worth noting that, according to Qisong's cohesive and Confucianized Chan, the focus of teaching, of engaging in learning, and of cultivating one's heart-mind is not escaping individual suffering but morally and actively committing to meeting the needs of the community. His cohesive form of Chan is therefore a socially engaged Chan. It is obviously of relevance that this dimension is the unmistakable stamp of Confucian culture on his perfectly Chinese Buddhist thought.

The scholar-monk's distinction between major (*da* 大) and minor (*xiao* 小) teachings derives from his hierarchical evaluation of the teachings (*jiao* 教) of the sages, of the ways (*dao* 道) or undertakings of the sages, and of the heart-minds of human beings. Hierarchical in Qisong's view means having different degrees, providing an ultimate (i.e., maximum or complete) transformation or partial (i.e., not yet complete) transformation. He focuses again on the ethical dimension of the transformation. According to the next paragraph, the objective of fully cultivating heart-minds eager to do good deeds is the objective that makes it possible to distinguish between major ways and minor ways:

> There are major ways of sages, and there are minor ways of sages. There are heart-minds eager to do good deeds and heart-minds eager to do evil deeds (心有善者焉, 有惡者焉). Eagerness to do good deeds and eagerness to do evil deeds are different qualities (厚薄) [generous and kind, ungenerous and unkind], the major and the minor ways have different degrees and different depths (漸奧). It is for this reason that among sages there are great sages (*da sheng* 大聖), middle-level sages (*ci sheng* 次聖) and lesser sages (*xiao sheng* 小聖). ("GYJ," 0655a26-14)

Consequently, the greatest sages and the major teachings are those able to produce an ultimate transformation, by means of which humans become completely aware of their heart-minds and thus able to interact with the world around according to the middle, with kindness and sincerity. The quotation is also an inspiring illustration of the nondual interdependence of the two dimensions of Qisong's cohesive meaning of teaching: a person's ultimate transformation, which involves awareness of their connection with all sentient beings (including an awareness of the interdependence between the disciple's own teaching and the teaching of others), and their traces in the world, the good deeds a human being does—at their highest level, all teachings are about encouraging good actions.

IV. CONCLUSION

This chapter discusses the "Guang yuanjiao"—the most developed essay of Qisong's collection *Fujiao bian*. The Chan scholar-monk continues and extends his advocacy of the complementarity and reciprocity between Buddhism and Confucianism. The "Guang yuanjiao" repeats a theme that appeared in his first essay, "Yuanjiao"—the meaning of the notion of teaching—and examines it at a higher level of depth, complexity, and abstractness. The present chapter identifies and explores the two essential features of his reasoning: a Confucianized dimension of Chan Buddhism and its cohesive, nondual perspective.

This thorough analysis of the "Guang yuanjiao's" line of argument intends to bring forth a threefold contribution in the area of the eleventh-century

Song-dynasty culture. Most importantly, it seeks to advance our understanding of the diversity of Chan subschools during Northern Song times through bringing attention to a special Chan subschool, represented by what I call the cohesive and Confucianized Chan vision of teaching of Qisong and the philosophical context from which it stemmed.

Second, it aims to shed additional light on the philosophical interaction between Chan Buddhists (Qisong) and Confucians (Ouyang Xiu) during the eleventh century, only a generation before the Neo-Confucian school of principle was founded by Cheng Yi 程頤 (1033–1107) and Cheng Hao 程顥 (1032–1085). One should not forget, for instance, that the Neo-Confucians Zhou Dunyi 周敦頤 (1017–1073)[12] and Zhang Zai 張載 (1020–1077)[13] are Qisong's contemporaries. The scholar-monk's interest in opening a philosophical dialogue between Confucians and Buddhists captures the zeitgeist of the Northern Song time. Specifically, this chapter provides new philosophical evidence (conceptual and comparative interpretation) concerning the Confucian influence on Qisong's thought and his cohesive and Confucianized view of Chan Buddhism. On this point, see, in sections II.1 and II.2, his new understanding of the key concepts of the classics *Zhongyong* and *Daxue*: middle 中, sincerity 誠, and rectifying the heart-mind 正心. Because he was the first to develop in Confucian terms a philosophical perspective on the complementarity between Chan and Confucianism, this analysis could also be useful for future research on the role of Qisong's Chan Buddhism in stimulating the development of the Neo-Confucian school of principle established a generation after him.

Chapter 3 investigates how he puts forward and sympathetically addresses in the essay "Quanshu" 勸書 ("Letter of Advice") specific deficiencies of Confucian tradition: its overemphasis on external stimuli (*gan* 感), name/reputation (*ming* 名), and appropriate behavior (*yi* 義). He uncovers these inefficiencies, no doubt with great sensitivity, and suggests how they can be addressed and corrected most effectively. Thus, it seems obvious that his Confucianized interpretation of Buddhism that speaks to Confucian scholars and his illustration of what dimensions Buddhism could bring to Confucianism in order to make more efficient the latter's administrative actions were meant to "assist both teachings" (*fujiao* 輔教) (let us recall the title of his work, *Fujiao bian* [*Essays on Assisting the Teaching*]): assist the teaching of Chan Buddhism by improving its connection with Confucianism within Chinese society, and assist the teaching of Confucianism by introducing cohesive Chan Buddhism to Confucians as an efficient companion in sociopolitical affairs. In other words, he was trying to convince Confucians about the utility of Buddhism in governing society and about the efficiency of a partnership between Confucianism and Buddhism.

These and a whole spectrum of related issues—his interpretations of the Confucian notions of external stimuli, name/reputation, and appropriate behavior in the context of his cohesive Chan—are the subject of chapter 3 and the "Quanshu." This essay thus continues from a new perspective, through exploring the new concepts mentioned above, Qisong's demonstration of the complementarity between Confucianism and cohesive Chan.

THREE

QISONG'S "LETTER OF ADVICE" ("QUANSHU" 勸書)

An Examination and Correction of the Deficiencies of Confucianism

I. INTRODUCTION

This chapter explores Qisong's essay "Quanshu" 勸書 ("Letter of Advice," hereafter "QS") and fully addresses the issues of cultivation, emotion, and human nature. In this article, the Song scholar-monk continues his demonstration of the complementarity between cohesive Buddhism and Confucianism from a different perspective—the transcendent perspective of the Chan Buddhist nature—and builds primarily on the findings of his essay "Yuanjiao" ("Inquiry into the Teachings" [see chap. 1]). Like in the other two essays previously examined ("Yuanjiao" and "Guang yuanjiao"), he starts from what he sees as their common objective, making people good, and proceeds to an assessment of the Confucian practice's effectiveness. Through a hermeneutic analysis of the "Quanshu" considered not in isolation but in direct connection with the "Yuanjiao," "Guang yuanjiao," and Qisong's commentary *Zhongyong jie* (*Exegesis of the Mean*), this chapter provides a new view on his comparative examination of Confucian thought and Chan Buddhism that includes two features.

First, it demonstrates that in his essay "Quanshu," which is also part of the *Fujiao bian* (*Essays on Assisting the Teaching*), Qisong made substantial efforts to compare, from a philosophical view, major aspects of the Confucian and Chan Buddhist traditions: the Confucian nature and the Chan Buddhist nature. The first is always bound up with the subject or person as embodied and in context. The second is free from dwelling—that is, free from the subjective and limiting perspective of the host.[1] Thus, just like in the previous essays, he not only responds to the criticism expressed by the *guwen* movement promoted by the Tang Confucian Han Yu 韓愈 but, more importantly, initiates a philosophical

Buddhist-Confucian dialogue[2] concerning the following ethical and religious issues: external stimuli (*gan* 感), name/reputation (*ming* 名), and appropriate behavior (*yi* 義). In this chapter, I suggest that his attempt to promote not only a "harmonizing" dialogue—to borrow a term from Huang Chi-chiang's and Albert Welter's studies (Huang 1986, 11; Welter 1993, 68)—but even more, a nondual exchange, allows Qisong to efficiently identify certain weaknesses of the Confucian way and to propose a remedy based on his cohesive Chan vision. In the "Quanshu," starting from the failings he perceives in the Confucian tradition, the scholar-monk highlights particular characteristics of his Chan Buddhist school that he reinterprets as (Buddhist) remedies for those (Confucian) flaws.

It is recalled that, in light of the analysis unfolded in chapter 2 and in the present chapter, this investigation loosely defines Qisong's work on the confluences between Buddhism and Neo-Confucianism as a form of cohesive and Confucianized Chan—cohesive, because Qisong harmonizes Chan with other doctrinal teachings, including Confucianism (see chap. 2); for example, he fully embraces the Huayan concept of universal principle (*li* 理; see sec. III.2). As the article "Guang yuanjiao" explored in the previous chapter, the essay "Quanshu" develops increasingly sophisticated arguments that his Chan school may be perceived as a form of Confucianized Chan. Let's reiterate that he wrote in *guwen* about reconciling, harmonizing, accommodating, and integrating Buddhism with Confucianism. In support of his rationale, which is Buddhist in nature, Qisong cited from major Confucian classics: the *Zhongyong*, *Analects*, and *Mencius*. His interest in commenting on a Confucian text dealing with the Confucian middle way (i.e., the *Zhongyong*; see chap. 2, sec. II.1) is a perfect illustration of the participation of scholar-monks in literati culture. The Tiantai Buddhist monk Zhiyuan also discussed the complementarity between Buddhism and Confucianism and commented on the classic *Zhongyong*. This perspective has been examined by Koichi Shinohara (1994), whereas I have studied Qisong's commentary *Zhongyong jie* in chapter 7 of this work.

Nevertheless, the Northern Song scholar-monk's affiliation to the Chan school is a major aspect of his religious identity, as can also be seen in Elizabeth Morrison's (2010) discussion of his activities as a Chan dharma heir. He held in great esteem the *Liuzu Tanjing* 六祖壇經 (*Platform Sutra of the Sixth Patriarch*), the major Chan text attributed to Huineng 惠能 (638–713). Chapter 6 explores his original interpretation of the key Chan notions highlighted in this sutra, including ethical discipline (*jie* 戒), concentration (*ding* 定), insight (*zhihui* 智慧), and nothing(ness) (*wu* 無). As Huang noted, Qisong identified his Chan school as the Platform Sutra school (Huang 1986, 11), and presumably, he prepared its mature version, edited by Zongbao 宗寶 in 1291.[3]

Again, the present interpretation of his rationale presented in the "Quanshu" starts from what he sees as a common objective shared by Confucianism and Buddhism—that is, the transformation of people, making them into good individuals (see this chapter, sec. II; chap. 1, sec. III.1; and chap. 2, sec. II). It can be said that this is a leitmotif running throughout Qisong's collection *Fujiao bian*, his major argument with respect to the interrelatedness between Buddhism and Confucianism. The identification of this goal allows him to observe that, up until his time, the Confucian tradition had not yet achieved this objective. It is in light of this awareness that he critically addresses what he sees as deficiencies of Confucianism. Understandably, nowhere does he clearly mention this idea of deficiencies.[4] This would have gone against his well-established reputation and his privileged relations with the scholar-officials and Emperor Renzong.[5] However, in the hermeneutical examination of his work unfolded below, this perspective emerges clearly.

II. THE COMMON OBJECTIVE OF MAKING PEOPLE GOOD IN CONFUCIAN AND QISONG'S COHESIVE CHAN TEACHINGS

As pointed out in the previous chapters, such an understanding of the work of the scholar-monk as endeavoring to demonstrate the complementarity of Confucianism and Buddhism is appropriate because, first of all, in his view, both traditions share a main objective of making people good[6] and educating for peace—a continuous concern about building, maintaining, and restoring ethical relationships and about cultivating a concrete righteousness that consists in being involved in social and political action within the community. One may say that, in Qisong's cohesive and Confucianized Chan view, both Confucian and Chan practices involve unconditionally pursuing the concrete concern of being present to others: treating each other with compassion and generosity, helping the most vulnerable and fragile among us, standing against indifference, engaging in public service, and striving to resolve unavoidable conflicts between the members of the community caused by differences between human beings.

Confucianism conveys this ultimate commitment toward serving others and building committed relationships in its own specific terms. Mencius formulates the concern as the "exercise of governance based on humaneness" (仁政; *Mengzi* 4.A.1, *ZZQS*, 6:336),[7] and the classic *Great Learning* (*Daxue* 大學) expresses it as insuring that "all the people live peacefully, which consists in governing one's country well" (平天下在治其國; *Daxue zhang* 10, *ZZQS*, 6:24). This is understood as a practice of governance focusing on harmonizing hierarchical relationships, ensuring that everyone receives their fair share, and thus eliminating conflict between the social groups: "Those in high positions respect the elders—in this way, the common people are encouraged to manifest their filial piety. Those of high position honor those superior in age—in this way, the common people are encouraged to manifest their respect and docility towards elderly persons. Those positioned above assume the care of orphans—in this way, the common people do not push them away" (*Daxue zhang* 10, ZZQS, 6:24).

In the following quotation from the "Yuanjiao," Qisong presents the objectives of the Chan practice in a way that resonates with all levels of Confucian practice—that is, the cultivation of the individual, the well-being of the family, and the well-being of the country (these stages of practice are discussed in the *Daxue jing* 大學經)—while remaining within the Chan universe: "I cannot find many people like me, so that we could together make our heart-minds sincere, together abstain from meat and wine, together stimulate people using our moral power, provide blessings to the members of our families and help the sovereign to secure the well-being of the people (同誠其心, 同齋戒其身, 同推德於人, 以福吾親, 以資吾君之康天下也)" (Qisong, "YJ," 0651a20-15).

Correspondingly, the element of Qisong's Chan practice—that is, "stimulate people using one's moral power (推德於人)"—resonates with the Confucian goal of "making radiant the luminous moral power of all the people (明明德於天下)" (*Daxue jing*). I suggest that the next element of "providing blessings to the members of one's family" through the transfer of merits constitutes a Chan religious interpretation of the Confucian ethical objective of "establishing order in one's family (*qiqijia* 齊其家)" (*Daxue jing*), the second stage of the *Great Learning*. To the third and highest stage of Confucian training—namely, "governing one's country well (*zhiqiguo* 治其國)"—corresponds the scholar-monk's inclusive and Confucianized Chan level of "helping the sovereign to secure the well-being of the people" (吾君之康天下).

It is arguable that in the "Yuanjiao," he reformulates the objective of Confucianism and cohesive Chan in a way that best singles out the existence of this common denominator of the two practices: "The teachings provided by the sages [Confucian and Buddhist] are different (聖人為教不同); however, they are identical (同) in that they make people good [stimulate good actions] (為善)" (Qisong, "YJ," 0649b28-10).

Furthermore, Qisong expresses even more clearly the connection he makes between this idea of making people good (which is his understanding of the highest objective, common to Buddhist and Confucian teachings), and the standard Confucian ideal of good governance. The following excerpt is another clear reference to the *Daxue*. It draws a parallel between Qisong's interpretation of the cohesive Chan ideal and the Confucian ideal: "If all people were to cultivate each of the precepts [of Chan Buddhist teaching], even though they could not be reborn in a heaven, this would be sufficient for all people to become good individuals (而人人足成善人). A world where all people are good and which is not well governed—there is no such thing (人皆善而世不治, 未之有也)!" (Qisong, "YJ," 0649b02-1). In the same essay, "Yuanjiao," Qisong notes that making people good is also an ancient Confucian objective and mentions, on this subject, Confucius's *Analects* 7.21, *Zhongyong* 8, *Mencius Gaozi xia* 6 B.13, and *Lilou shang* 4 A.12 (see chap. 1, sec. III.1).

Therefore, he astutely assesses the good in Confucianism as the adequacy of individuals' acts, emotions/feelings, or states of mind to align themselves with the perfect model of the ritual (*li* 禮), which emphasizes the common good, the harmony of community and of interpersonal relationships, uniformity, and conformity. Ouyang Xiu 歐陽修 (1007–1072), a prominent eleventh-century Neo-Confucianist and Qisong's contemporary, advocated for a fundamental renovation of social customs and therefore of ritual (see chap. 2, sec. II.3). He emphasizes that personal moral reform, like that recommended by the Buddhists, is not adequate to solve a social problem (see Liu 1967, 163). It can be said that the sort of critique of Buddhist self-cultivation made by Ouyang is what Qisong is responding to.

The Buddhist ideal is close in a sense to the Confucian because it also promotes interdependent relationships between humans, but starting from every individual's cultivation. As I have discussed elsewhere, awareness of the "interdependent self" (Arghirescu 2020b) results from transcending self-centeredness or, in Qisong's words, from focusing on shared sameness (同): "When seeking sameness, few people do not live peacefully" (同焉而天下鮮不安; "YJ," 0649c20-13). On the other hand, what constitutes evil in Confucianism as well as in the scholar-monk's cohesive Chan Buddhism is the prevalence of the separate ego or of the selfishness within selfhood—namely, egocentricity manifested in the form of desires, personal interest, and individual good, all of which generate social disharmony, rivalry, or competition (*jing* 競). This self-centeredness develops when focusing on difference. That is, in Qisong's view, "When seeking difference (異), rarely is there no rivalry among the people" ("YJ," 0649c20-5).

However, as this chapter shows, the Buddhist idea of goodness is significantly more inclusive, as it concerns all living beings—it interprets the interdependency of human relationships as reverence for life, as solidarity between humanity and nature, as linking of life with life (past, present, and future) through the religious notion of transmigration, which places an "emphasis on the boundless solidarity of life between persons and other beings" (Abe 1986, 141).

I offer that another main difference between the two practices, which are both defined by Qisong as practices of making the people good, is the fact that Buddhism strikes a balance between the community and the individual and thus begins the process of individual transformation from the inside, while pre-Song Confucianism (i.e., the Confucianism with which Qisong enters into dialogue) focuses on community, on the ruler seen as a role model, and thus on transformation from the outside. As scholars acknowledge, it is only after the encounter of Confucianism with Buddhism and after the transition from pre-Song Confucianism to Neo-Confucianism (from the twelfth century onward and Cheng-Zhu Neo-Confucianism) that Confucianism developed a spiritual dimension and a Neo-Confucian process of individual transformation from the inside (see De Bary and Chaffee 1989; Tu and Tucker 2003). As can be noted, the present study provides philosophical evidence that Qisong's eleventh-century work contributed to this transformation within Confucianism.

Furthermore, in this comparative context, I argue that in the scholar-monk's view, there is also a major distinction between the natures of Confucian and Chan practices of "making people good": the first is limited to an ethical meaning and to human relationships, with "good" being distinguished from "evil"; the second has an ethico-religious sense and refers to becoming aware of the complete relativity of good and evil as ethical terms, thus retrieving a "goodness" existing beyond this distinction as the original purity of one's nature and heart-mind. This does not mean abandoning ethics but means strengthening its basis, discerning the ethical duality good-evil in a new light, and realizing, it might be said, what Masao Abe calls "a transvaluation of values" (1986, 151). Obviously, when undertaking the task of rectifying the shortcomings of Confucian practice, Qisong recommends overcoming its limitations through adding to it a religious,[8] spiritual dimension.

His point of departure in the endeavor to connect Confucianism and Buddhism is a sincere regard for the effectiveness of Confucian teaching in governing Chinese society and preserving its harmony and also for the success of Buddhist teaching in transforming some individuals into "good people." I further suggest that he chooses a comparative approach, one that highlights and examines some evident weaknesses of Confucian practice as well as what he clearly sees as undeniable strengths of the Chan Buddhist practice, in order to support the appropriateness and reliability of his project to associate both teachings—to make them work together and support one another in the communal task of improving Chinese Song society.

Qisong also acknowledges the obvious primacy of Confucianism as a fundamental political practice and traditional social/ethical value system. And he refers to an ancient image—the good ruler who influences the people with his behavior, from "Hong Fan" 洪範 ("The Great Model")[9] chapter of the *Shujing* 書經 (*Book of Documents*). In his commentary *Zhongyong jie* 中庸解 (*Exegesis of the Mean*; hereafter *ZYJ*), the scholar-monk cites the "Hong Fan" chapter. He equates the image of the "ruler as perfect example" with the perception of the sovereign as exemplary person and teacher, and the method of governing with the process of teaching: "The *Hong Fan* says: 'The ruler establishes himself as perfect example'" (洪範曰:「皇建其有極」; *ZYJ*, 666b21). To discuss the idea of governance, Qisong also adopts the ancient Confucian formulation of the "kingly way" (*wangdao* 王道) as "middle way" (*wupian wubei* 無偏無陂) referred to in the "Hong Fan":

> The *Hong Fan* says: "The good sovereign is neither inclined, nor uneven (無偏無陂): he follows the kingly behavior (遵王之義). He does not purposefully do good things: he just follows the kingly way. Without doing bad things, he follows the kingly path. Free from bias, without taking sides, the kingly way is wide. Without taking sides, free from bias, the kingly way makes people live peacefully together (王道平平). Free of inconstancy and partiality, the kingly way rectifies and corrects all things (無反無側王道正直). His example achieves perfection." How could this not rectify and correct all things? (*ZYJ*, 666c01-7)

According to the scholar-monk and Confucian teaching, good governance means that the rulers (sovereign and officials) are role models, and he points out the result of this "role-model teaching": people "rectify and correct" (正直) themselves and therefore live peacefully together (平平). Undeniably, here Qisong refers to the ideal of good governance developed within the framework of the *Daxue jing*—people live peacefully together (天下平).

This section points out that the first step of his project is to identify weaknesses of Confucianism as opportunities for improvement, and the second is to correct them by means of his cohesive Chan practice. To this end, he puts forward two preliminary observations, the first being that Chinese society has made no progress toward becoming more harmonious during his lifetime and has greatly diminished in this regard in comparison with the past. This indicates that Confucian administrative methods are not working properly (see the following quote; his Confucian contemporaries also recognize this fact).[10] The second observation is that Buddhist practice has in his direct experience transformed a number of people, making them into good individuals. In his enterprise, one can also discern the presence of an idea expressed indirectly, which is the backbone of his project and connects the previously mentioned two steps of this project: the good governance and social harmony of the past have largely vanished because the originally pure heart-minds of individuals (rulers and ordinary people) have gradually deteriorated. The return to a complete state of social well-being, good governance, and peace depends on all people (elite and ordinary) making the effort to gain awareness of their original heart-minds and authentic natures. This is why Confucianism needs the support of Buddhism. In the essay "Quanshu," Qisong notes,

> Since the Three Dynasties, the country's governance has deteriorated, and the bad behaviors of ordinary people have increasingly worsened. The [Confucian] "ritual and the model of appropriate behavior (*li yi* 禮義)" were no longer sufficient to govern the people (不暇獨治). It is for this reason that Buddhist teaching has spread throughout China. Together, Buddhism and Confucianism advise the people, and due to them, the people harmoniously undergo transformation (遂與儒並勸, 而世亦翕然化之). There are people who have achieved positive change, and people who have moved away from bad behavior; and there are people who have been able to discover by themselves their own authentic nature and thus correct it (自得以正乎性命者). Therefore, until today, people have depended on Buddhism. It is for this reason that I think that Buddhist teaching provides a complementary support to Confucianism and makes society better (乃相資而善世也). ("QS" 2, 0653a02-3)

In what follows, sections III and IV distinguish what I identify as the two major deficiencies of the Confucian tradition implicitly singled out by Qisong in his closely intertwined works "Yuanjiao," *Zhongyong jie*, and "Quanshu": its overemphasis on external stimuli and thus failure of the ritual, status, and appropriate behavior. These are important aspects because his Confucian contemporaries such as Ouyang Xiu thought that the defeat of Buddhism depended on the restoration of the ritual (see Liu 1967, 163). The next two sections also interpret the way in which Qisong envisions cohesive and Confucianized Chan providing assistance in overcoming them, using the notions of human nature (*xing* 性), heart-mind (*xin* 心), and universal principle (*li* 理).[11]

III. THE INFLUENCE OF "EXTERNAL STIMULI" (GAN 感)

Confucianism uses ritual to inculcate appropriate behavior (*yi* 義) and operates through the regulation of human emotions. Thus, in chapter 9, "Liyun" 禮運, of the classic *Liji* 禮記 (*Record of Rites*), Confucius clearly states that ritual is the way in which "the first sovereigns carry on the way of heaven and govern people's feelings" (夫禮, 先王以承天之道, 以治人之情; Wang 1970, 291).

In the following quotation, Kirill Thompson examines the notion of appropriate behavior from a comparative and intercultural perspective:

> One cultivates discernment and self-discipline principally by developing one's native sense of appropriateness (*yi*). Unlike Western notions of justice, which are the product of rational consideration or of righteousness, which is an intuitive divine inspiration, *yi* is borne of one's native feelings of shame and aversion and emerges in elementary learning as the inner core of self. In advanced learning one develops this sense of *yi* into the cutting edge of a self-conscious, interpersonally reflective self. That is, as one investigates things and affairs and becomes able to discern their fine patterns, one's sense of *yi* sharpens into a locus of moral discretion. Because the investigation of things includes interpersonal practice and self-reflection, one moreover exercises as well as informs one's sense of *yi* thereby. Chu Hsi likens this to the apprenticeship of a skilled craftsman. (Thompson 1991, 502)

The major example of the influence of external stimuli on individuals in Qisong's Chan view also involves the activity of emotions/feelings (*qing* 情). They are perceived as arising from contact with the external environment and as reinforcing the external stimuli that produced them. In Qisong's cohesive Chan view, the abovementioned deterioration of society as a whole and of the individual human heart-minds that comprise it is the result of confusion (*huo* 惑) arising from these emotions/feelings. In his view, the negative impact of the emotional states originated in external stimuli that "wore out the people and made them unkind (*bi bo* 敝薄)": "For a long time, the people have been confused by the emotions. The significant impact of the emotions has almost worn out the people and made them unkind" (人之惑於情久矣! 情之甚, 幾至乎敝薄; Qisong, "YJ," 0650a19-8). In other words, certain emotions/feelings are perceived as the source of destruction of human relationships because of the ego-centered behavior they elicit, and thus they too are ultimately the reason why the Confucian ideal of "making people good" was finally abandoned. Why is this so? Because, Qisong explains, "the emotions of the people concern themselves, and exclude the others; they confirm this side, and deny the other. Excessively denying others leads to quarrels, excessively affirming oneself makes one obstinate" (人情莫不專己而略人, 是此而非彼, 非過則爭, 專過則拘; "YJ," 0650b13-4). This is a new and complex interpretation of the emotions that Qisong provides in order to build a completely new Buddhist understanding of Confucian ritual and of the weaknesses that its practice entails. This interpretation is analyzed in the next section.

III.1. The Confucian Overemphasis on External Stimuli: Qisong's Interpretation of "Ritual" (Li 禮)

In the following, I identify what I call an "overemphasis on the external" as the first deficiency that Qisong implicitly perceives in Confucianism, and I examine the way he suggests to correct it through using his cohesive Chan perspective. The subsequent analysis also connects the idea of external stimuli with the Confucian notion of ritual and argues that this link is also implied in his writing. As a matter of fact, the Chan scholar-monk considers ritual as a practice focusing on external stimuli—that is, emotions perceived as originating in the external stimuli. By means of his cohesive and Confucianized Chan perception of external stimuli he uncovers weak aspects of this essential tool (the ritual) used by Confucians to transform people.

In his commentary to the Confucian classic *Zhongyong*, Qisong explains the Confucian ideal of "universal and social order" as rooted in respecting and following what one would call an external model or ethical code—namely, Zhou ritual. This is how he describes its Confucian operation based on external stimuli. For the first time, Qisong implicitly establishes a connection between the five permanent relationships—the cornerstone of Confucian social and political organization, which can certainly be regarded as specific types of emotions/feelings fostering interrelatedness (respect, affection, differentiation, etc.)—and external stimuli:

> By means of ritual, the sage puts in order the positions of sovereign and official, establishes the affectionate relationship between father and son, the brotherly respect between elder and younger brothers, the differentiation between man's role and woman's role. Thus, the elders have food (老者有所養), the youngers are taught (少者有所教), the strong have work and the weak are safe (壯者有所事, 弱者有所安), weddings and funerals are always timely and appropriate, heaven-earth and the ten thousand things are in their right places (天地萬物莫不有其序). (ZYJ 4, 0667b06-11)

Obviously, all these relationships based on hierarchical distinctions are finally about ordering emotions/feelings. Thus, Qisong builds a new perspective on the Confucian ritual, one that highlights the emotions/feelings as simultaneously being external stimuli (liable, in the Buddhist view, to distorting reality) and the foundation of ritual (the rock on which social harmony relies; see sec. III.2 and the interpretation of the Buddhist authentic nature). This is different from the traditional unidimensional comprehension of Confucian ritual as the preeminent tool of statesmanship and as expression of emotions/feelings that stem from external stimuli—that is, using role models to set an example for people. However, it is noted that this new way of looking at ritual proposed by Qisong is not extravagant but quite reasonable because it resonates considerably with the following perception of ritual as focusing on emotions/feelings, which is found in the *Zhongyong* 20. This is a Confucian classic (which was initially chap. 28 of the *Liji*) that Qisong was interested in and on which he wrote a commentary:[12] "The hierarchical distinction that one fulfils when cherishing his loved ones, and when honoring men in distinct ways, according to each one's level of excellence: this is how ritual was born (親親之殺, 尊賢之等, 禮所生也)" (*Zhongyong* 20, *Zhuzi quan shu* 朱子全書 [hereafter ZZQS], 6:45).[13] One idea advocated by researchers (see Huang 2000, 316) is that members of what became known as the Cheng-Zhu school took interest in this ancient text a generation after Qisong, to the point where, over the next century (the twelfth century), it became one of the *Four Books* due to the influence of Zhu Xi 朱熹 (1130–1200).

By promoting a significance of ritual that resonates with the *Zhongyong*, Qisong clearly conveys that Confucian ritual provides an external ordering model. This model is taught to the people through the emotions/feelings, and individuals grasp and follow it through observation and imitation. Moreover, he notes that in the Confucian context, putting ritual into practice is understood as simultaneously correcting (*zheng* 正) the external or physical components of human behavior (i.e., seeing, hearing, speaking, and acting) and the internal or psychological ones (i.e., desires and inclinations): "Ritual is that which corrects seeing and hearing, corrects acting, corrects speaking, and guards against desires and inclinations" (禮者, 所以正視聽也, 正舉動也, 正言語也, 防嗜欲也; Qisong, *ZYJ* 5, 0667b29-3). Furthermore, when following the logic of this successive ordering of how ritual exerts its effect, one realizes that Qisong highlights here the fact that the internal effectiveness (acting, speaking, and guarding against desires and inclinations) of Confucian ritual is presupposed as spontaneously derived from its external effectiveness (correcting seeing and hearing). And it becomes clear that this reasoning follows from the implicit Confucian presupposition of the existence of an unbroken and consistent continuity between an individual's inner and outer life. The ancient text of the *Zhongyong* 1 thus illustrates the impact of this implied connection: "There is nothing more visible than the hidden, nothing more manifest than the extremely small; that is why the exemplary man remains cautious when alone (莫見乎隱, 莫顯乎微, 故君子慎其獨也)" (*Zhongyong* 1, ZZQS, 6:33). Qisong also pays particular attention to this Confucian presumption of the correlation between an initially external correction and a final internal correction that the first is supposed to produce: "When in seeing and hearing there are no wrongs, actions are not in disorder, speaking is not misleading, desires and inclinations do not rise up (視聽不邪, 舉動不亂, 言語不妄, 嗜欲不作)" (*ZYJ* 5, 0667c02-1). As an aside, it should be observed that the external and internal effectiveness of the imitation of an external model is actually not that automatic when this presupposed continuity is put aside. In the next section, I explain that neither does Qisong consider this connection to be as spontaneous as the Confucians presume; in other words, in his view, merely having an ethical code and making an effort to behave ethically is not enough to completely regulate and control human emotions. For this reason, Confucianism needs Buddhism's assistance.

In the next quotation, the scholar-monk also refers to other elements of the ideal of Confucian good governance through the education and transformation of the people, which are closely related to ritual and equally focus on transformation from the outside: the emotion/feeling of kindness (仁恩) that rulers are assumed to exhibit toward the ruled as the paradigm of good administration (治), and the paradigm that what constitutes appropriate behavior (義) varies according to one's status, as do the proper rewards (賞) given and punishments (罰) exacted for appropriate and inappropriate behavior. One must also add music (樂). In the "Yuanjiao," Qisong comments, "[The Confucian] sage governs through kindness (仁恩), through teaching appropriate behavior (義教); through rewards (賞) because he wants to encourage people to move towards doing good deeds (進其善), through punishments (*fa* 罰) in order to influence them to stop doing bad deeds (沮其惡). Even though the punishments were increasingly multiplied, as were the expenditures on rewards, the ordinary people's morals became increasingly degraded (世俗益薄)"(Qisong, "YJ," 0650a22-1). For this reason, he concludes that because the Confucian method is not effective enough, it is necessary to rectify it using a different method, one that is not based on external stimuli and yet could still be accepted by the Confucian sages (Yao and Shun): "If there were a method that needed to be used instead of rewards and punishments (有不以賞罰) to make the people move towards doing good deeds and turn away from doing bad deeds (而得民遷善而遠惡), then even sages such as Yao and Shun would be happy to accept it" (Qisong, "YJ," 0650a24-1). Let us look a little deeper into the way he understands as how best to address and redress this deficiency using Buddhist ideas and practice.

III.2. How Cohesive and Confucianized Chan Can Assist in Overcoming Confucianism's Weakness: Qisong's Vision of the "Authentic Nature" (Xing 性) and the "Universal Principle" (Li 理)

As suggested earlier, Qisong understands the practice of Confucian ritual as a transformation initiated from outside, rooted in the contact of an individual's self with external things, in what one experiences from outside (*gan* 感) and not embodied in one's self. The individual transformation and self-cultivation such as that promoted by Chan and the *Liuzu Tanjing* 六祖壇經 (*Platform Sutra*) were not a prominent presence in the Confucians' sphere of interest before the Song dynasty. Confucius conveys his absolute confidence in the power of will, seen as the master and principle of order of the heart-mind, through the following analogy: "A great army can be deprived of its commander, but no one may be deprived of his willpower" (三軍可奪帥也，匹夫不可奪志也; *Lunyu* 9.25, *Lunyu jizhu*, ZZQS, 6:146). Mencius only theoretically acknowledges the importance of self-cultivation (i.e., "preserving the heart-mind and nourishing nature" (存心養性); *Mencius* 7.A.1), without elaborating on how to achieve this in practice. In the twelfth century, Zhu Xi explicitly recognizes in his *Zhuzi yulei* 126 that Neo-Confucian scholars were attracted by the Chan training in self-cultivation (i.e., concentration) and that the Neo-Confucian master Cheng Yi 程頤 (Yichuan 伊川; 1033–1107) was the one who introduced the Chan practice in the Neo-Confucian instruction:

> From the Tang dynasty, the Sixth Patriarch [of Chan, Huineng, the presumed author of the *Platform Sutra*] started teaching people the method of training in self-cultivation [preserving and nourishing oneself] (存養工夫). Initially, before Cheng Yi started teaching people this method of bodily training, Confucian students only talked about it, they never personally engaged in this practice (只是說不曾就身上做工夫). This is why people say that Cheng Yi stole this training from the Buddhist teaching and he himself practiced it [and introduced it into the Neo-Confucian teaching]. (Zhu Xi, *Shishi* 釋氏, *Zhuzi yulei* 126 ZZQS, 18:3963–3964)

It can be argued that the nondevelopment of this theme of the self implicitly expresses the pre-Song Confucian self-assurance in the exemplary man, the conviction that the latter inherently knows what to change and how to change it in himself.

For Qisong, ritual-based transformation is not complete because it is grounded only in emotions/feelings and desires, which, in his Chan Buddhist perspective, are effects of environmental stimuli. He calls attention to the fact that "the emotions/feelings come from what one feels (*gan* 感)" (情感而有之也; *ZYJ* 3, 0666b21). Therefore, it becomes clear that Qisong doesn't agree with the Confucian presupposition of the natural continuity between the inner and outer worlds of the individual as an ordinary state. As explained below, "practice" is all about first restoring this connection, because understanding and agreeing with a moral model doesn't mean automatically putting it into practice, as Confucian ethics seems to suggest.

For Qisong, within each individual dwells something that goes beyond the ethico-moral sphere and that has a transcendent nature—a spiritual nature (*xing* 性), originally clean and not clouded by contact with external stimuli. In his commentary *Zhongyong jie*, Qisong equates one's universal principle (*li* 理) with one's authentic nature (*xing* 性), which he considers as spiritual (*xing ling* 性靈; see ZYJ 3, 666b21).

Becoming aware of its presence triggers a full and profound transformation, motivating and driving people from within to change and become good; in other words, it reestablishes from within the continuity described above. I further argue that to address this deficiency in the foundation of the Confucian practice of ritual, Qisong advocates a preliminary inner transformation involving self-awareness of one's spiritual nature as grounds for the practice of ritual. In his essay "Yuanjiao" (0648c25), he stresses the difference between ethical practice (ritual can be included in this category), which concerns only one life (*shi* 世, the individual's present life), and spiritual practice, which simultaneously engages three lives (*san shi* 三世, the individual's past, present, and future lives). In light of this difference, I imply that in Qisong's Chan Buddhist view, the capacity to transcend emotions means overcoming the negative repercussions of actual (life) emotions through making people aware of two spiritual interdependencies, an emotional one and an experiential one: first, the karmic causes that determine humans' emotional experiences during the present life; and second, the fact that actual life transformation has an impact on humans' emotional experiences during their next life.

Again, this doesn't mean that the emotions are eliminated or that the five types of proper human relationships of Confucianism are dissolved, criticisms that Confucians routinely lodged against Buddhist practice.[14] Because they unfold within the heart-mind in response to external influences, the emotions/feelings, including those underlying the five permanent relationships (常情, see next quotation), become distorted and develop incorrectly in impure hearts. In Buddhism's view, ordinarily, they are conditioned by ignorance and karma. To circumvent this, Qisong's Chan perspective deployed in the "Quanshu" recommends temporarily suspending the emotions—that is, the five types of proper human relationships—but only for the time one needs to purify one's heart-mind, so all these emotions can reemerge soundly, undeformed by one's prejudices and stereotypes: "The feelings between father and son, husband and wife are part of the five permanent relationships [of heaven] (天常). Nowadays, Buddhism guides the people to cut these permanent feelings (今佛導人割常情), and dedicate their efforts to cultivating and cleaning (*xiu jie* 修潔) their heart-mind, so they can return to these relationships in accordance with the way (反常而合道)" (Qisong, "QS" 2, 0653a17-3).

It should be noted that temporarily cutting the emotions means no less than reintegrating them otherwise. And elsewhere, Qisong clarifies that this effort to cultivate and clean oneself inevitably starts with the Buddhist practice of the Five Precepts and Ten Goods (see also chap. 1, sec. III.1).[15] This practice allows people to avoid definitively cutting off the above Confucian permanent relations and instead to purify and thus enhance their foundations of goodness, filial piety, concord, and so on:

> Those who inwardly cultivate themselves (陰自修者) benefit from the practice of the Five Precepts and Ten Goods (五戒十善). For fathers, the benefit (yi 益) is a further increase of their goodness (父益其善); for sons, the benefit is a further increase of their filial devotion (子益其孝); for couples, elder and younger brothers, the benefit is a further increase of the concord between them (夫婦兄弟益其和). Those who cultivate themselves in this way are many. (Qisong, "QS" 3, 0654a03)

These benefits (yi 益) resonate in one's future life, too. Being able to reinstate these relations on a pure and solid foundation and to perceive their true nature means considering them not as perfect reproductions of an external model but as a network of causal relationships rooted in dependent origination.

In consequence, unlike the externally grounded Confucian transformation, Qisong puts forward a different transformation, one based not on ephemeral emotions/feelings or desires but on something substantial, always present in the individual—namely, one's authentic nature (xing 性). Qisong envisages the latter as spiritual, as encompassing "present" emotions and going beyond them, simultaneously embracing one's feelings and not dwelling on them.[16] His specific meaning of "spiritual" is not limited to humans' actual lives and sentiments but concerns one's present, past, and future interconnected lives. In Qisong's comparative work (inclusive Chan Buddhism-Confucianism), spiritual nature represents exactly the restored awareness of this interdependence: "Today, I write this article because I want to give advice to people (必欲勸之者), not merely to promote Buddhism, but to let everybody know the most important thing is that all human beings are endowed with a 'spiritual nature (ling 靈),' which makes them humans (皆稟靈為人) and the most precious among all living beings (殊貴於萬物之中)" (Qisong, "QS" 2, 0653b21-10).

Moreover, this authentic spiritual nature is equivalent with the Huayan and Tiantai Buddhist universal principle li 理,[17] and subsists through the individual's consecutive lives, while the emotions, which are the fruit of external stimuli, are evanescent, continuously coming and going:

> What heaven endows with is "the dynamic ordering of the vital movements of heaven-earth" (*tiandi zhi shu* 天地之數)[18]; "authentic nature" is the spiritual authentic nature (性則性靈也). In other words, humans belong to this dynamic ordering of the vital movements of heaven-earth, and they fuse with the spiritual authentic nature. Authentic nature (性) is therefore the universal principle (*li* 理), which is always with us (素有之理). The emotions originate from what one experiences and feels (情感而有之). (Qisong, ZYJ 3, 0666c18-1)

From Qisong's perspective, unlike the Confucianism of his time (pre-Cheng-Zhu school Confucianism), no durable transformation can be rooted in the emotions/feelings; it must be rooted in this spiritual nature or universal principle[19] that not only permanently dwells within an individual's self but subsists from this life to the next as a "spiritual consciousness" (神明, 神識), which connects one's present, past, and future lives. It transmigrates (that is, preserves from one life to another), is constantly cultivated from one life to another, and can be used to address future life issues: "Today, what makes human beings human beings is the entry of a spiritual consciousness (*shen ming* 神明) into the corporeal form. The way the spiritual consciousness passes from individual [body and birth] to individual is much like the way a human changes residence [houses]" (Qisong, "QS" 2, 0653b13-14).

Thus, with his cohesive Chan interpretation of the notion of nature (about this notion, see also chap. 4), Qisong enacts a fundamental ontological change of the meaning of the notion of nature, the important term present in the opening phrase of the classic *Zhongyong* (paragraph ZYJ 3, 666b21, quoted above). As discussed, in this passage, he explains nature as spiritual (*xing ling* 性靈) and as the Huayan Buddhist "universal principle" (*li* 理)—that is, the emptiness-aspect (*wu* 無; the Chan full-fledged potentiality) dwelling within individuals and not a result of external stimuli like the emotions and desires. In his "Tanjing zan" 壇經贊 ("Encomium of the Platform Sutra"), Qisong interprets both in Chan terms and in Confucian terms the relationship between emptiness and spiritual nature: the spiritual nature is the state of not-dwelling (*wu zhu* 無住). In his view, the latter is neither a state detached from reality nor a passive one as the *Platform Sutra* might suggest, but an active practice required, the scholar-monk emphasizes, "to grasp all knowledge" (通一切智): "In order to grasp all knowledge, the best way is to focus on not-dwelling" (通一切智, 莫至乎無住; Qisong, "Tanjing zan," 0347a11-10). In other words, as elements of reality, the various forms of knowledge are context bound and exist in relation with specific things and affairs—time, place, and human relations. Humans' ability to grasp all knowledge relies on their capacity to not remain attached and therefore limited to a particular, fixed position (time, place, and human relation), confined to a particular condition, to what they already know.

It is worth noting that this term *li* 理, which is also discussed in the next section, was taken up by the Neo-Confucians of the Cheng-Zhu school a generation later.[20] As is well known, they reconstructed its meaning according to their Confucian view and created a Neo-Confucian school of principle.

With his cohesive Chan perspective on authentic nature, Qisong also operates a fundamental change of the pre-Song meaning of the notion of *xing* 性. As further detailed below, he makes a distinction between its traditional Confucian sense focusing on the external stimuli of sentiments (according to Qisong) and his Chan spiritual sense, which focuses on seeing one's nature (見性[21]; see also chap. 5; "Guang yuanjiao" 0659a08-10; *Platform Sutra* 0350c08-16): the interdependence between human beings and between each one's past, present, and future lives. In this Chan-Confucian comparative context, he insists on the meaning of spiritual (i.e., spirit 神) as the continuity between three lives. He finds here inspiration in Nagarjuna's well-known image of the fire (see also Nagarjuna, *Fundamentals of the Middle Way* 10, *An Analysis of Fire and Kindling*; Streng 1967, 194–196): "Once I said that after the individual's death, his spirit does not die (人死而其神不死). This is the proof that there are three lives. The spirit exists in the human being, as the fire exists in firewood (火之在薪). Even if the firewood of yesterday has disappeared [become ashes] with the fire, does this mean that the firewood of today which supports the fire has also disappeared [become ashes]?" (Qisong, "YJ," 0649c01-8).

He equally explains the importance of this change in the meaning of the term *nature*. In ancient Confucianism, Qisong points out, this term connotes the "manifestation of human nature in the form of desires" (性之所欲), and, in this respect, he refers to *Lunyu* 17.2 and *Mencius* 6A.3 (see next quotation). He makes a clear distinction between the ancient Confucian concept of human nature, in which human nature is perceived as desires that everyone possesses, and his abovementioned spiritual understanding of this notion. Although it is the same Chinese term *nature* (*xing* 性) that he uses, the Chan scholar-monk stresses that the change in meaning he has effected introduces a completely new perspective on the "individual self" intended to value the latter more. He interprets that, in fact, Confucius views nature as negative desires that contaminate the will and therefore should be eliminated through constant practice. Confucius notes that all people have them (see *Lunyu* 17.2: "By nature, human beings are near to one another; it is through their practice that they differ widely"). In the next quotation, Qisong sees the same meaning in Mencius. Unlike the latter, in his cohesive Chan view, human nature is valued as spiritual:

> When Mengzi says that the nature of the dog is the same as the nature of the ox (犬之性猶牛之性), and the nature of the ox is the same as the nature of man (牛之性猶人之性) [see Mencius, *Gaozi shang* 6A.3], what Mengzi describes is the manifestation of human nature (*xing* 性) in the form of desires (性之所欲也); this is not the same thing [as that which I discuss]. What I am talking about is authentic nature (*xing* 性); what others are talking about is the emotions (情). (Qisong, *ZYJ* 4, 0667a23-10)

The scholar-monk stresses that his understanding of nature is different not only from ancient Confucianism but also from Han Confucianism, which also focuses on external stimuli. In fact, the latter confirms the ancient meaning of the term that focuses on outside incitements, but it does so through the new theory of the five elements. In his commentary *Zhongyong jie* to the classic *Zhongyong*, written in the form of a dialogue between the monk and a student, the latter asks Qisong a question:

> Regarding Mister Zheng's[22] commentary on the phrase "what heaven endues with (*tianming* 天命) is what is called authentic nature"[23]: He says that this is what heaven assigns to an individual at his birth; it is for this reason that it is called assigned authentic nature (性命). The spirit of wood is humaneness (木神則仁); the spirit of metal is appropriate behavior (金神則義); the spirit of fire is ritual behavior (火神則禮); the spirit of water is wisdom (水神則智); the spirit of earth is fidelity to one's pledged word (土神則信). When examining Mister Zheng's doubtful explanation, it follows that if *tianming* gives birth to the individual, then his authentic nature comes from what one experiences [a response to an external stimulus] (感). When the spirit of wood affects him, this produces the nature of humaneness; when the spirits of metal, water, fire and earth affect him, this produces the natures of appropriate behavior, ritual behavior, wisdom and fidelity to one's pledged word. In other words, the individual can acquire them without any practice (似非習而得之也). This is different from what Confucius says, that in order to acquire and perfect the natures of humaneness [being humane] (仁), appropriate behavior (義), ritual behavior (禮), [ethical] wisdom (智), and fidelity to one's pledged word (信), one needs the teaching (必教). I respectfully ask: What does this mean?

Qisong answers,

> How can we say that authentic nature comes from what the individual experiences as outside influences (感而得)? When things don't yet have a

concrete form (物之未形), then they do not have an authentic nature, nor do they have life; how can they experience an outside influence? When the human is born, why wait until he experiences the outside influence of things and of spirits, in order to have his authentic nature? Metal, wood, water, fire and earth make things without having any knowledge about this process; why repeatedly talk about this? Mister Zheng's explanation is flawed, he didn't fully think it through. If what he said were true, why would the sage need to teach (聖人者何用教為)? (ZYJ 3, 0666c08-1)

I express appreciation and gratitude for the insight that Kirill Thompson has provided about Zheng Xuan's abovementioned materialistic misreading of the notion of authentic nature (*xing* 性) in the first paragraph of the *Zhongyong*. He suggests a captivating connection between Zheng Xuan's perception (loudly criticized by Qisong in this paragraph) and the lost "Confucian" text *Wuxingpian* 五行篇 (*The Five Aspects of Conduct*)[24]—a late Warring States–period text, associated with Zisi's 子思 (c. 481–402 BCE) school, a second-generation disciple of Confucius and the presumed author of the *Zhongyong*. As is well known, the first paragraph of the *Zhongyong* focuses on the concept of authentic nature. *Wuxingpian* was no longer extant by Zheng's time. This text was found in 1973, in the excavated early Han Mawangdui tomb (and in 1993 in Guodian). According to Thompson (2012, 314), *Wuxingpian* appears to be an early manual or codification of Confucius's core ideas—especially humanity, righteousness, ritual conduct, and wisdom—that discusses how they are best to be cultivated, manifested, and expressed. He observes that it is possible that Zheng Xuan had heard that these two theories were associated (i.e., the authentic nature of the *Zhongyong* and the theory of the five aspects of conduct of the *Wuxingpian*). As Qisong stresses, Zheng misreads the authentic nature as embodying the five material elements. Thompson recalls that, in the *Wuxingpian*, the five aspects of conduct *wuxing* are associated not with material elements but with five forms of moral practice thematized around the basic Confucian virtues. Zheng Xuan was therefore right in seeing a link between the notion of nature (*xing*) contained in paragraph 1 of the *Zhongyong* and these five aspects of conduct *wuxing*. However, as Qisong explicitly corrects Zheng's erroneous reading, the *wuxing* were not five basic elements (or phases) (metal, wood, water, fire, and earth) but five forms of moral practice (in *Wuxingpian*, humanity *ren* 仁, appropriate behavior *yi* 義, ritual behavior *li* 禮, ethical wisdom *zhi* 智 and sagacity [sagehood] *sheng* 聖)—formed and cultivated within and simultaneously manifested in an individual's ethical conduct.[25] One might say that Qisong's criticism of the Han Confucian scholar's interpretation is consistent with the newly discovered *Wuxingpian* text.

Note as well that Qisong cites above the usual list of five virtues highlighted by Confucius (仁義禮智信), while the list of the lost *Wuxingpian* (仁義禮智聖) includes as the last element not *xin* 信 (fidelity to one's pledged word, reliability, or honesty) but *sheng* 聖 (sagacity or sagehood). Thompson also offers a fascinating explanation for this incongruity:

> Whereas Confucius sometimes rounded off his list of four virtues with *xin* (reliability, honesty), the authors of the *Wuxingpian* rounded off the list with *sheng* (sagacity, sagehood). Why this difference? Does it suggest a doctrinal difference? Confucius was mainly in dialogue with students and adepts. By adding *xin*, he was stressing to them that in cultivating, manifesting, and expressing these four virtues it was necessary to be honest and forthright. By contrast, the *Wuxingpian* was addressed more to the ruling elite. By adding *sheng*, the authors of the text were confirming the aim and reward of cultivating, manifesting, and expressing these four virtues: sagehood. The ruler could become like the sage-kings of antiquity if he were just to devote himself to cultivating and realizing Confucius' virtues! (2012, 314–315)

Let us resume our reading of Qisong's paragraph quoted above: it can also be said that Qisong rightly perceives this overemphasis of Confucianism on reactions to the outside world as a method focusing on "controlling people's external behavior" (制其外). He proposes to correct this standpoint using the Buddhist approach, which "touches people's inner-selves" (感其內), focusing first not on emotions/feelings but on cultivating the enduring spirit that dwells in their heart-minds:

> If one wants to convince the people to accept and obey from the heart "the way" and to cultivate themselves (人心服而自修), it is best to convince them from the inside (感其內), through touching their heart-minds. If one wants only that the people say what one wants and appear obedient (人言順而貌從), it is best to control their external behavior (制其外). Control from the outside must be done using the teaching of the way of humans (人道設教), otherwise it cannot succeed. What touches them inside must be done using the teaching of the way of the spirit (神道設教), otherwise it cannot transform their heart-minds. Therefore, the Buddhist way must concentrate on the spirit of the individual first, and then on their behavior; this is what it means to touch the inside first, and then control the outside. (Qisong, "YJ," 0650b18-14)

At this point it is also necessary to present another new dimension of Qisong's specific perspective—namely, the "spirit/spiritual" (*shen* 神). At issue is how his cohesive Chan perception is different from the traditional meaning of "spirit" as "ghosts/spirits" (鬼神)—that is, the Confucian understanding of this imperceptible dimension of reality. As previously stated, the spiritual as authentic nature and universal principle is the major component of his correction of the Confucian weakness addressed in this section. The scholar-monk distinguishes his Chan idea of spirit from the traditional Confucian meaning of the term:

> The spirit means the spiritual quintessence (*jingshen* 精神) of humans; this is not something regarding the spirits and ghosts who mislead people. That is, if the individual cultivates his spiritual quintessence, then he can exhibit good behavior (謂人修其精神, 善其履行). During his life, this individual receives rewards (福); at his death, his spirit rises up in purity (其神清昇). When one does not cultivate one's spiritual quintessence, and practices evil and aberrant things, life is not a time to celebrate; and after death, his spirit is punished (其神受誅). When ordinary people hear this teaching, their heart-mind is touched (其心感動); they stop doing evil things, and follow good practices. Thus, they silently transform themselves (默化). This type of transformation takes place for generations. (Qisong, "YJ," 0650b23-9)

Unlike the Confucian practice of ritual, which focuses on the perfect adequacy of adhering to an external model, Qisong's Confucianized and cohesive Chan practice emphasizes an inner transformation that pays particular attention to the inner self, to becoming aware of the presence of one's spiritual nature through first pinpointing the specific emotions/feelings and desires that burden and obscure it, and then by becoming able to overcome or transcend them while fully embracing them. Qisong calls this practice "a marvelous way (*miaodao* 妙道)," so as to distinguish it from the perceptible and concrete socio-ethical Confucian practice (i.e., of ensuring peace and order in the exemplary man's family and country by cultivating respect for ritual, music, rewards and punishments, etc.). Also, unlike Confucian practice, which is limited to community and society—that is, to an individual's present life—the scholar-monk's interpretation of Chan practice concerns the three interconnected lives, as mentioned earlier. Therefore, the practice he proposes to improve the Confucian ritual is not merely a means of transforming one's relations with others during one's life. It presupposes that relations in this life depend on a person's connections during their past life and perceives the person's present practice as influencing the exchanges in their future life. He also explains the process of becoming aware of this interdependence as a purification of one's original nature and perceives it as an "extinction" (*mie* 滅) or removal of the burden of unacceptable emotions and desires. Qisong calls attention to his positive and active meaning of this Chan extinction, which is valued as a vigorous effort of constant purification and is completely different from the general Confucian understanding of Buddhist extinction[26] as renouncing the human relationships regulated by ritual: "What is called one's extinction, means to detach oneself of the many burdens (滅盡眾累), to purify one's original pure and tranquil nature; this is not extinguishing the individual's vitality (非謂死其生), nor looking for an empty and desolate extinction (取乎空荒滅絕之謂). When the individual reaches this level, he attains the sage's spirit (聖神) and goes beyond the limits of his present life" (Qisong, "YJ," 0650c06-10).

As an aside, note his effort to first distinguish between the different practices of many Buddhist schools, including Confucianism, only to better harmonize them and uncover their common root within the larger context of what might be called his cohesive and Confucianized Chan teaching. Confucians put forward a criticism of Buddhism in general. Undoubtedly, the scholar-monk's writings also aim to make his contemporaries more sensitive to the differences between the practices of the abovementioned five Chan Buddhist schools (i.e., a cohesive Chan [Qisong's school] or factional Chan [Linji 臨濟 and Caodong 曹洞]) and to point out the complementarity existent between Confucian practice and the focus on moral practice of his cohesive Chan school. It is also important to observe that he undertakes constructively this critical task of comparing Buddhist and Confucian tradition, with a view to nondually harmonizing them in a supportive way, which reflects Mahayana's major belief in the interdependency of all human beings and its inclusive and accommodating spirit that arises from this belief.

The scholar-monk constantly finds creative Chan ways to highlight the complementarity between Confucianism and Buddhism, their ability to work together and conduct a common mission. For instance, in the following paragraph from the "Quanshu," Qisong presents as a shortcoming of Confucianism the absence in its teaching of the spiritual dimension of the notions of "authentic nature" (*xing* 性) and "what heaven bestows" (*ming* 命). But he sympathetically adds that this absence occurs not because Confucians weren't aware of this spiritual dimension but rather as a provisory decision dictated by their conviction that ordinary people's heart-minds were insufficiently cultivated to benefit from such teaching:

> The Confucians of ancient times (先儒) did not promote the notions of "authentic nature" (性) and "what heaven bestows" (命) when educating people because these are profound and hidden ideas (幽奧), difficult to understand, which cannot be easily comprehended, and which cannot save them from bad things happening. They used ritual and the model of

appropriate behavior (禮義) provisionally, in order to govern the general feelings of the people and to rule them (統乎人情而制之). With regard to authentic nature (性) and the way of the spirit (神道), I think we can reserve them solely for the eminent individuals who can understand them (恐獨待乎賢者耳). (Qisong, "QS" 3, 0654a09-4)

His interpretation also reflects the specific way in which his cohesive school endorses somehow, in the politico-administrative context, the Confucian idea of moral and political elite. This quote also serves to introduce the other major dimension of Confucian teaching: the emphasis on hierarchy and status. To better perceive his specific understanding of it, the next section first provides an outline of this topic that directly relates to key issues identified by the scholar-monk in his essay "Quanshu."

IV. "STATUS/REPUTATION" (MING 名) AND "APPROPRIATE BEHAVIOR" (YI 義)

In Confucianism, the harmonization of society results from transforming all members of society through education (i.e., in a very broad sense). The foundation of this practice is hierarchical—in other words, the elite have a duty to morally cultivate themselves and thus provide a good example for people to follow. In the early period of Confucianism, cultivation of the people (*min* 民) was based on their imitation of the behavior of the sage (*shengren* 聖人) and, later on, of the eminent man (*xianren* 賢人) and exemplary man (*junzi* 君子). This is the main topic of a particularly popular text during the eleventh century—the "Hong Fan" chapter of the *Shujing* 書經 (*Book of Documents*) (Nylan 1992, 63). Qisong's interest in this text is evident throughout his collection of essays (see sec. II; chap. 1, sec. III.2). From this hierarchical perception of society stems the importance in Confucianism of social status or position—in other words, of one's name, title, or reputation (*ming* 名)—and of the appropriate behavior (*yi* 義) that corresponds to each position and type of relationship.

In a well-known passage from *Analects* (13.3), Confucius stresses that the first thing to do in order to ensure good governance is to "rectify the names" (*zhengming* 正名). As this remark concerns the historical context of the life of the prince of Wei 衛, Chugong Zhe 出公輒 (r. 492–481 BC), who did not recognize the authority of his father (see Zhu Xi, *Lunyu jizhu*, ZZQS, 6:179), it is understood that rectifying the names in Confucius's view refers to ensuring the adequate alignment of one's behavior with one's status (for instance, of sovereign, official, father, or son). A filial son must obey and respect his father.

Thereby, the term *name* in ancient Confucianism concerns mainly the individual's position within the sphere of the five relationships, and "rectifying names" designates rectifying one's behavior, which has to exactly correspond to one's role (one's relationships) in accordance with established ritual, as discussed in the previous section.

In other words, rectifying the names implies perfectly fulfilling all the specific duties that (Zhou) ritual designates to a human's particular role. It becomes clear that in this context, the sphere of the notion of "names" involves first adopting an external model. This is also obviously illustrated in *Lunyu* 12.11, where Confucius explains that good governance means that those in the position of sovereign (official, father, or son) have to act like a sovereign (official, father, or son)—that is, in accordance with the model of sovereign (official, father, or son) set down in ritual. The classic *Zhongyong* conveys the same idea of the primacy of status using the term *position/situation* (*wei* 位): "The exemplary man complies with his present situation and behaves in a way that corresponds to this place; he does not look for what is outside his condition.... Thus, the exemplary man simply remains in his position, and awaits what heaven bestows to him (君子素其位而行, 不願乎其外.... 故君子居易以俟命)" (*Zhongyong* 14, ZZQS, 6:40).

IV.1 The Confucian Overemphasis on Name/Reputation and Appropriate Behavior: Qisong's Interpretation

Qisong refers to this Confucian notion of "name/position/reputation," which is emblematic of hierarchy, in his "Quanshu" 勸書 ("Letter of Advice"). The notions of name and appropriate behavior are intimately connected with the idea of ritual discussed in the previous section. Therefore, one clearly understands why Qisong perceives the Confucian teaching as overemphasizing these two dimensions.

As illustrated earlier, he considers that a mere adequacy in imitating an external model transmitted by legendary sages (e.g., with regard to Confucian ritual, name, and appropriate behavior) without a profound inner transformation is problematic and most likely only partially successful. In his Chan terms, the Confucian perspective of name—that is, of the appropriate behavior that corresponds to this title—is only a preparatory or expedient means tailored to the capacities of the unenlightened people and is different from the ultimate means of practice focused on the heart-mind: "The heart-mind (心) is the root of the way and of the appropriate behavior of the sage (聖人道義之本). Name/reputation (名也者) is only the temporary [expedient] means (*quan* 權) by which the sage encourages the people to do good. When paying attention only to the temporary means without being aware of the root, are good deeds really good? Is the way of appropriate behavior really appropriate?" (Qisong, "QS," 0652a13-11). In this passage, Qisong clearly expresses his doubt as to whether the Confucian method of focusing on following the rules of an external model of appropriate behavior (*yi* 義) according to name/status (*ming* 名) is fully efficient.

IV.2. Cohesive and Confucianized Chan's Assistance in Overcoming This Weakness: Qisong's Vision of the "Heart-Mind" (Xin 心) and the "Universal Principle" (Li 理)

In what follows, I argue that in his essay "Quanshu," the scholar-monk implicitly indicates this deficiency in the practice that emphasizes name by urging ordinary people (as well as exemplary men) to consider their heart-minds (*xin* 心) first instead of their status. In his view, only when one's appropriate behavior is rooted in the heart-mind does one's behavior come from responsive commitment rather than mere compliance. Therefore, Qisong suggests rooting appropriate behavior differently—not in abiding by ritual nor in caring for name/reputation but in becoming aware of this heart-mind and rectifying it.

He amends the Confucian ideal of the rectification of names through proposing a different kind of rectification, of a higher order, and in line with the Chan vision of the rectification of heart-minds as conveyed by the Buddha. This higher-order rectification must precede the rectification of names and provide it with a spiritual foundation: "There was an ancient sage, he was called the Buddha, who firstly rectified completely his own human heart-mind (人心之至正); then, he wanted to extend (推) this practice [required to achieve the rectification of the heart-mind] and its result [a rectified heart-mind] to all people (推此與天下), so that all would be the same (同之)" (Qisong, "QS" 1, 0652a08-12). The Buddhist ethical message presented here by Qisong is founded on the conviction that there is a transmoral nature in every human heart-mind, the buddha-nature (*foxing* 佛性) or the authentic nature, previously referred to. Spiritually, humans are all the same—they all participate in a system of interdependence. Rectifying the heart-mind refers to one's ethical and spiritual development.

Unlike the elitist Confucian vision, which arises from a hierarchical perception of life and emphasizes social development and governance, the Buddhist conception of life is egalitarian and emphasizes being as a living entity; its practice concerns and transforms all people, irrespective of their social status. In the scholar-monk's words, "What is known as life has no high or low social status, no eminent and no humble people. The Buddha treats them as equals and guides them all, so that all can seek [for their original nature] by themselves" (謂生也, 無貴賤, 無賢鄙. 佛皆一而導之, 使自求之; Qisong, "YJ," 0648c25). The Five

Precepts and Ten Goods (*Wujie Shishan* 五戒十善) with which the sage guides and influences individuals in an all-inclusive way transform people of every status: "From village to town, from town to whole province, from province to whole country, from scholar-official of the court to people in the emperor's palace, all feel this influence [to fully cultivate themselves]" (自鄉之邑, 自邑之州, 自州之國, 朝廷之士, 天子之宮掖. 其修之至也; Qisong, "YJ," 0649c24-4).

He does not question in this way the appropriateness of the Confucian hierarchical structure of Chinese society but intends to improve its overall harmony and order through introducing a practice that is the same for everyone and a spiritual foundation to the social practice of the hierarchy. In doing so, it might be said that he intends to soften to some extent the inevitable compartmentalization of Confucian society and thus improve the connections between different social categories.

When explaining the importance of this significant shift in perspective, from an ethics emphasizing the cultivation of appropriate behavior in accordance with name and title to one emphasizing the development of the common heart-mind in all, he also uses the terms *way* (*dao* 道) and *universal principle* (*li* 理). Qisong makes an ontological distinction between the two kinds of rectification: the heart-mind, which harbors the spiritual authentic nature (that is, the principle) and therefore belongs to the sphere of the foundation, the essential, and the enduring and permanent "root"; and the category of name/reputation and appropriate behavior, which, in his Buddhist view, pertains to the domain of the "temporary means" (*quan* 權; see above), the provisional and transient "shoots." Moreover, one observes that his distinction implicitly brings to light a weak point of the Confucian practice and at the same time suggests a way to overcome it through bringing together Confucianism and Buddhism. In the scholar-monk's words,

> Those who study nowadays [i.e., Confucians] think that conformity with the model of appropriate behavior (*shi yi* 適義) is the principle (*li* 理), and that following the model of appropriate behavior (*xing yi* 行義) is the way (*dao* 道). But these are only the external dimensions of the way and the principle, that is, conduct within the specified limits on behavior (*zhongjie* 中節).[27] They do not grasp the great way and the great principle of the sages (未預乎聖人之大道也, 大理也). The great principle (大理)[28] is primarily the foundation (*zhu* 主) of the permanent way (*changdao* 常道). If all affairs are dealt with without taking into consideration their foundations, then are they dealt with how they really should be? (Qisong, "QS" 1, 0652a16-2)

Qisong points here to the fundamental difference between these terms (*way* and *principle*) in the Confucianism up until his time and in his cohesive and

Confucianized Chan school. The first envisages them as ethical notions, the second, as ethico-spiritual. As for the notion of nature (*xing* 性; see sec. III.2), Qisong also dwells on the change in the meaning of the term *principle* (*li* 理). In his Buddhist school's view, the universal principle is the enduring essential aspect (vacuity and therefore interdependence) of human beings and things, their common foundation, which is different from their multiple concrete and expedient embodiments or "phenomena" (*shi* 事). He also explains, in another context, this ontological difference between the expedient appropriate behavior (*yi* 義) and its essential foundation—namely, the universal principle. The issue here is not a critical perspective on Confucianism, as has been addressed previously, but the intention to argue the complementarity between Confucianism and Buddhism at the universal level of the principle:

> Kindness and appropriate behavior (*renyi* 仁義) [i.e., Confucian practice] are footprints of the method of good governance over a single lifetime (一世之治迹) left by the first kings. If one discusses their practices starting from these footprints, their practices are different (異). If one discusses them starting from the universal principle (理), their practices are the same (同). The footprints stem from the universal principle, and the universal principle is the origin of the footprints. The footprints are "the shoots" (末), the universal principle is their "root" (本). (Qisong, "YJ," 0649b13-16)

He endorses here the Huayan Buddhist school's idea of the universal and real principle (*zhen li* 真理)[29] that exists in all phenomena (*shi* 事) and is inseparable from them, along with the practice of becoming aware of this interdependence, as a way to comprehend the connection between Confucian (identified by him as being at the level of the phenomena) and cohesive Chan practice (identified by him as being at the level of the principle).

Starting from a well-known phrase from the classic *Liji* 禮記 that embodies the central ideal of the Confucian ritual, the Northern Song scholar-monk implicitly expresses the idea of overcoming this limitation of Confucianism to the ethical and phenomenal sphere through advocating the study of the principle: "Eating and drinking and the married life (飲食男女) [Qisong quotes here from the *Liji*, chapter "Liyun" 禮運 (see Zhang 1996, 35), without naming his source; in the same chapter, Confucius defines ritual as the tool for governing the people's feelings]—these are things the people consider precious and think they understand (能知貴). But for the exemplary man, these are not precious; what he considers as precious is being able to know the way and being aware of the principle (能知道而識理)" (Qisong, "YJ," 0650b15-14).

It is worth noting that this passage and his exhortation introduce, already, the emphasis on the principle (a specific, Buddhist meaning of it). The principle became the focus of the Neo-Confucian Cheng-Zhu school a generation later. It is useful to remember that Qisong composed his *Fujiao bian* during the 1050s at a time when Cheng Yi (1033–1107) and Cheng Hao (1032–1085) were still young, in their twenties, and obviously had not yet developed a clear vision of their school but were participating in Confucian discussions on Chan (*tan chan* 談禪)[30] and were certainly aware of the work of the well-known Chan scholar-monk Qisong. In addition, the principle was a term in common usage among both Confucians and Buddhists since the Tang dynasty. According to Wing-tsit Chan (1964, 123–149), this notion of *li* as moral principle is originally a Mohist notion. From the fourth century on, many of its philosophical aspects were fully developed in Buddhism, and only in the eleventh century did it become a central concept in Neo-Confucianism. Under the influence of Buddhism, it started to gradually be adopted and interpreted by Neo-Confucians in their practice. Thus, Qisong notes that even Han Yu (1986, 212), the well-known Tang dynasty Confucian who virulently criticized Buddhism, valued a practice focusing on principle. He attentively read Han Yu's works, and in his "Quanshu," he illustrates with quotes from the Tang scholar's writings that the latter was actually interested in Buddhism and praised certain Buddhist monks.

In the next paragraph, for example, the scholar-monk quotes Han Yu (as usual, without providing references). Han Yu's quotation is found in his letter addressed to the Minister Meng *Yu Meng shangshu shu* 與孟尚書書, volume 3, *Shu* (*Correspondence*), *Han Changli wenji jiaozhu* (Han 1986, 212). This provides an image of Han Yu as someone who appreciates eminent Buddhist monks and is interested in Buddhist ideas—completely different from his portrayal handed down by the Confucian tradition, which comes out of his well-known article "Yuandao" (see chap. 1), his official fierce criticism against Buddhists as destroyers of Chinese culture. Note that this difference, as interpreted by Qisong, echoes precisely his distinction between name/status and heart-mind: while Han Yu's criticism arises from his position as scholar-official, guardian of a culture highly unified around Confucianism, his admiration for the Chan monk Da Dian originates in his heart-mind. He writes,

> He [Han Yu] praises the monk Da Dian [大顛 (732–824)] by saying that "he is intelligent and sage, and he is conscious of the way and the principle" (頗聰明, 識道理). And he also says: "He was really able to master himself using the principle, from beyond his corporeal form. He didn't let things and affairs invade and confuse him" (實能外形骸以理自勝。不為事物侵亂). Wasn't Han Yu's heart-mind sympathizing with Buddhism? In his Chan writings (禪書), Da Dian also notes that Han Yu once inquired him about Buddhist teaching. This must be true. (Qisong, "QS" 1, 0652b16-15)

In this context, the Northern Song scholar-monk explicitly reiterates that the emotions/feelings are those responsible for invading and confusing individuals. He presents gaining awareness of the principle as the ability to leave behind—that is, to go beyond the emotions perceived as expedient and fully embrace them from the perspective of the principle. "When someone behaves starting from emotions," Qisong elaborates, "this method is close to an expedient type of approach. When one behaves starting from beyond emotions [and within emotions (in his daily life)], this method is close to the principle type of approach" (情而為之, 而其勢近權. 不情而為之, 而其勢近理; Qisong, "YJ," 0649c18-12). Manifestly, his perception of "beyond emotions" (不情) doesn't mean cutting them off but implies reaching the reality of the principle that the emotions reductively and distortedly embody at the expedient level: "Everything that has image and form carries emotions. How could the Buddhist way not include emotions? The Buddhist way follows the emotions and goes beyond emotions" (曰形象者舉有情, 佛獨無情邪? 佛行情而不情耳; Qisong, "YJ," 0649c13-10).

Thus, through building the correlation "(name, appropriate behavior, feelings)/(heart-mind, universal principle, beyond feelings)" (*ming* 名, *yi* 義, *qing* 情/*xin* 心, *li* 理, *buqing* 不情), Qisong implicitly proposes remedying this flaw through first becoming aware of and focusing on one's heart-mind and the universal principle embodied in it, instead of starting from one's position and corresponding appropriate behavior. Again, in his view, the terms of the pair name and appropriate behavior (that is, feelings) are external and transitory in comparison with the pair heart-mind and principle (in other words, beyond feelings) and therefore insufficient to initiate a profound transformation. Qisong straightforwardly encourages the people to replace in their life and personal decisions their status (name and position) with their heart-mind—in other words, to go beyond emotions first and then fully undertake them (in their daily lives): "I advise the exemplary man to trust his heart-mind, and after, to assume whatever position/name he fills" (勸夫君子者自信其心, 然後事其名為然也; Qisong, "QS" 1, 0652a07-11). Qisong thus advises that a real transformation starts when people take into account their heart-mind (their interdependent individuality, it can be said) and not merely their position (i.e., the community profile or status as determining the standard for their correct relations with others).

As noted already, in his view, becoming aware of one's heart-mind constitutes a form of ethico-religious practice in everyday life. It means realizing one's original heart-mind—an original heart-mind that is unchanging, tranquil, and pure—and preserving its purity in day-to-day actions and interactions. Chan understands the latter as completely undisturbed by personal desires (see chap. 6, dedicated to Qisong's "Encomium of the Platform Sutra"). In the particular case of the scholar-official, a member of the elite, these personal desires emerge as strong needs to satisfy what is expected of one's personal name with regard to power and ego fulfillment. All these needs make concrete what the Confucian scholar-official perceives as the positive social evaluation of reputation, recognition, and respect that are the basic elements of his elite status.

These constitute self-centered dimensions that inevitably conflict with the interrelated nature of his commitment, which is pursuing the common good. Qisong also refers to the emergence of this conflict at the expedient or ethical level. Quoting a scholar-official, he describes it as a "feeling of being suffocated," which disappears only when the heart-mind becomes tranquil and pure through ethico-religious practice in everyday relationships. At the end of the day, in Qisong's view, the cohesive Chan practice allows the individual to have full access to the Confucian qualities most valued in political practice, such as kindness (*ren* 仁) and worthiness (*xian* 賢). Qisong recalls,

> I once read an article by Yang Yi 楊億 (974–1020)[31] of this dynasty. He says that in his youth, he was a very hard-working official, that he looked disappointed and constantly experienced something in his chest that suffocated him. After studying Buddhism, this reverberated out and dissipated, no longer stifling or obstructing him, and his heart-mind became calm. So, Yang relied on Buddhism, he finally became a good scholar-official, a filial son (為良臣孝子), and all the people called him a man of great moral integrity. I have also heard about the Edict attendants Xie Mi 謝泌 (950–1013) and Cha Dao 查道 (955–1018) who both knew very well the Buddhist way. Therefore, they were able to become worthy people, endowed with kindness (仁賢). They had a high regard for dealing calmly with political affairs (為政尚清靜), and they were famous and appreciated by the greatest number of people for their good governance (所治皆有名迹). (Qisong, "QS" 3, 0653c13)

V. CONCLUSION

In this chapter, I uncover and analyze two main dimensions of Qisong's article "Quanshu" 勸書 ("Letter of Advice"). The first is his effort to efficiently identify specific weaknesses of the Confucian way and to propose a remedy based on his Chan vision. I explore this dimension by first identifying the shortcomings to which he refers—the overemphasis on external stimuli in the Confucian ritual context and on rectifying one's name with the appropriate behavior for someone in one's particular position—and by subsequently examining how the Chan scholar-monk believes that these flaws can be corrected using his cohesive Chan school notions of heart-mind and universal principle.

As in the previous chapters, I identify as a second dimension of this essay his effort to bring to light the particularities of his own cohesive Buddhist school. The most distinct feature of his thought that permeates each essay of the collection *Fujiao bian* 輔教編 (*Essays on Assisting the Teaching*), and in large part is the justification for it, is its objective of combining the Confucian and Buddhist traditions and practices to promote a united effort to restore the overall well-being of Song society and individuals.

Furthermore, Qisong's analysis focuses on three major (Chan) Buddhist notions: principle, authentic nature, and heart-mind. All of them are as important for Qisong's cohesive and Confucianized Chan Buddhism as for Neo-Confucian (Cheng-Zhu) thought. Therefore, Qisong's reasoning is also relevant for the following reasons. On the one hand, it allows the examiner to capture the differences between Qisong and Cheng-Zhu Neo-Confucianism regarding the contextual meanings they assigned to the terms *principle, authentic nature*, and *heart-mind*. On the other hand, it reveals the borrowings and mutual influences between the two traditions during the Song-dynasty eleventh and twelfth centuries. Their continuing contact stimulated the development of special forms of Chan, such as Qisong's Confucianized one, and the philosophical Neo-Confucian development concerning the idea of principle and the practice of self-cultivation.

The next two essays in Qisong's collection, "Guang yuanjiao" 廣原教 ("Extensive Inquiry into the Teachings"; chap. 2) and "Quanshu" 勸書 ("Letter of Advice"; chap. 3), are both tightly connected with "Yuanjiao" 原教 ("Inquiry into the Teachings"; chap. 1) and progressively elaborate and detail issues presented in his opening essay. Chapter 2 examines the way in which Qisong depicts in "Guang yuanjiao" the Confucianized dimension of his meaning of the teaching—through infusing old Confucian concepts from the *Zhongyong* and *Daxue* with new meaning (middle (*zhong* 中), sincerity (*cheng* 誠), and rectifying the heart-mind (*zheng xin* 正心)), as well as the cohesive, nondual, or spiritual feature of his conception of the teaching. Chapter 3 adds another layer of complexity to his demonstration of the complementarity between Buddhism and Confucianism, through indirectly unveiling deficiencies of Confucian practice and highlighting Buddhist means of assisting Confucianism and correcting its failures. Again, the idea of Buddhist proscriptions as complements to Confucian virtues is captivating and emphasizes the cohesion of Song culture and the nonduality of Confucian and Buddhist practices. This chapter investigates the weaknesses of the Confucian notions of external stimuli (*gan* 感), ritual (*li* 禮), name/reputation (*ming* 名), rectification of names (*zheng ming* 正名), and appropriate behavior (*yi* 義). Starting from his interpretation of these insufficiencies, Qisong's analysis introduces and expounds complex Chan Buddhist notions: permanent way (*chang dao* 常道), universal principle (*li* 理), authentic nature (*xing* 性), rectification of the heart-mind (*zheng xin* 正心), and "expedient" (*quan* 權) means as well as "principle" (*li* 理) means of transformation. It should also be noted that the notion "permanent way" has a Daoist resonance (Laozi, par. 1). The Chan scholar-monk's anthology focuses on the exchanges between Buddhist and Confucian traditions in the broader context of the discussion and dialogues among the schools of thought in Song China. He thus implicitly and consistently emphasizes the Chinese cultural oneness along with the complementarity of the three teachings within Chinese culture.[32]

The next chapter examines a fundamental practice of Confucianism and of Chinese culture in general—filial devotion. Qisong dedicates a whole essay to this concept: "Xiaolun" 孝論 ("On Filial Devotion"). In his preface to the "Xiaolun" (0660a25), the scholar-monk explains that he wrote it in 1053 as a response from the bottom of his heart to the constantly renewed Confucian criticism that Buddhism lacks filial devotion. In a comparative way (Buddhist-Confucian), he introduces in this article the Buddhist version of filial devotion.

FOUR

QISONG ON BUDDHIST FILIAL DEVOTION (*XIAO* 孝)
A Buddhist-Confucian Comparative Perspective

I. INTRODUCTION

The purpose of this chapter is to examine Qisong's essay "On Filial Devotion" ("Xiaolun" 孝論;[1] hereafter "XL"), which comprises twelve sections—plus a preface—and is part of the *Fujiao bian* 輔教編.[2] Kenneth Ch'en acknowledges that this is probably the sole Buddhist treatise devoted entirely to the discussion of filiality (Ch'en 1973, 48), a core value of Confucianism and of traditional Chinese culture. In his preface to the "Xiaolun" (0660a25), the Chan scholar-monk explains that he wrote the twelve sections in 1053 as a response from the bottom of his heart to the constantly renewed Confucian criticism that Buddhism lacks filial devotion. In this opening part of the "Xiaolun," he once again (as in the essays "Yuanjiao" and "Guang yuanjiao" examined in the previous chapters) clearly sets out the peculiar and innovative method that he has chosen so that his explanation of Buddhist filial devotion will have a real impact on his Confucian readers. Writing in the *guwen* style of the Confucian tradition, Qisong begins the essay with the Confucian meaning of the notion of filial devotion and thereafter broadens its foundation and scope, adding new dimensions to it and making it more inclusive and encompassing. The author considers that the best way to draw scholars' attention to his interpretation of the Buddhist "great filial devotion"—a concept that he considers as concealed and difficult to grasp—is to explain it in well-known Confucian terms: "[This essay] clarifies the abstruse principle and secret meaning of the great filial devotion (*daxiao* 大孝) of my sage [Buddha] through associating it with Confucian instructions (儒者之說). In this way, the elucidation of Buddhist filial devotion becomes almost complete. The practicing Buddhists of future generations can also learn from this essay (吾徒之後學。亦可以視之也。)" ("XL," 0660b09-14).[3]

Even if his interpretation is intended primarily for Confucian scholars, this introductory paragraph equally states that the work also constitutes a meaningful learning tool for Buddhist followers—in other words, that filial devotion is an important aspect of their practice, too. This analysis suggests that, consequently, the Chan scholar-monk did not merely provide a strong philosophical refutation of the widespread Confucian opinion that Buddhists lack filial devotion but also expanded the meaning of this originally Confucian practice and rebuilt it on a new Buddhist religious foundation. For this reason, his account of filial devotion is equally a training tool for the instruction of Buddhist practitioners, and he highlights this specific aim. From his exposition, it becomes clear that, within the Chinese Buddhist community, this issue was not understood well enough and not constantly practiced. Qisong's essay thus further develops the significance of the Chinese Buddhist practice of filial devotion in the larger sphere of Song-dynasty Confucian culture. As detailed below, this practice was only partially recognized in Buddhist circles, often poorly carried out, and with meager results. Regarding this matter, at the opening of the first section, he addresses the ignorance of some young monks who do not understand the importance of filial devotion in Buddhism for lack of sufficient practical training: "Certain people, just after having their hair cut and entering the Buddhist path, no longer come when their parents call them, because they consider themselves Buddha's children (逮其父母命之, 以佛子辭而不往)" ("XL" 1, 0660b13). A similar admonition can be found in the fifth section: "There are people nowadays who, precisely when they become disciples of the sage but have not come far along the road of studying, do not want to engage in the practice of filial devotion (乃欲不務為孝). They say: 'I have left my family to focus on the [Buddhist] way, how dare I get stuck in this [family relationships]?' What do those who say such things understand about the heart-mind of one who leaves his family (是豈見出家之心乎)?" ("XL" 5, 0661a24-15). Manifestly, Qisong had a key role to play not only in advancing the Song-dynasty philosophical debate on filial devotion between Buddhists and Confucians but also in developing "great" filial devotion as a Buddhist practice with Confucian roots. It can be said that a major role of Buddhist filial devotion in his interpretation is to strongly connect within Chinese culture two only apparently separated communities: the religious and lay disciples. He brings out their mutual interdependence.

Furthermore, it is arguable that his Buddhist philosophical interpretation, which retains the traditional Confucian structure of this term and expands it, vouches for the intense mutual exchanges between Confucianism and Chan

Buddhism during the Northern Song period. The examination undertaken in this chapter suggests that his work on filial devotion is also a valuable source of data for a specific type of research. I am referring to the growing interest in demonstrating that these eleventh-century Buddhist-Confucian interchanges—which immediately preceded the foundation of the Neo-Confucian school of principle by the Four Masters,[4] who were Qisong's younger contemporaries (a generation younger in the case of the brothers Cheng Yi and Cheng Hao)—philosophically influenced and stimulated the establishment of the Song-dynasty institution that produced a major reinterpretation of Confucianism. Later to be known as Neo-Confucianism, this school is grounded in practices of self-cultivation.

The first part of this comparative study explores the different foundations of the Confucian and Buddhist practices of filial devotion according to the scholar-monk. The second part focuses on the scholar-monk's original contribution in recognizing and developing two major areas of commonality between Buddhism and Confucianism where their seemingly opposing perspectives concerning filial devotion merge. These involve the issues of filial devotion as emotions/feelings and as precepts/moral qualities.

II. THE DIFFERENT FOUNDATIONS OF THE CONFUCIAN AND BUDDHIST PRACTICES OF FILIAL DEVOTION: QISONG'S COMPARATIVE PERSPECTIVE

The practice of filial devotion (*xiao* 孝) represents the core of Confucian culture. A systematic investigation of the ancient Confucian classics *Liji* 禮記 (*Book of Rites*), *Lunyu* 論語 (*Analects*), and *Xiaojing* 孝經 (*Classic of Filial Devotion*) shows that its ancient religious and moral meanings emerged from the paramount importance of ancestral worship and family relationships and that they are closely linked to the Zhou (1025–256 BCE) ritual (see *Zhongyong* 28; Arghiresco/u 2013, 353–355). As Mugitani Kunio stresses, the debate between Confucianism and Buddhism first arose in early medieval China concerning the practice of filial devotion (Mugitani 2004, 115; Guang 2010, 249). The lack of filial devotion (in other words, disinterest in starting a family and in family relationships, and disrespect to ancestors[5]) was the first major criticism addressed to Buddhists by Confucians starting from the earliest record of this debate—the *Mouzi lihuo lun* 牟子理惑論 (*How Master Mou Removes Our Doubts*), written in the second century CE[6] (see also Jan 1991, 30). In an already classic text, "Ethical Life," Ch'en gives a review of different responses by the Buddhists to the criticism that their religious practice is unfilial (Ch'en 1973,

14–50). For instance, one of the topics concerning filial devotion in *Mouzi* was Buddhist celibacy, and, as presented below, Qisong provides a philosophical and religious argument in this sense.

To better understand how he extended and developed the traditional Confucian meaning of filial devotion, thereby answering Confucian criticism, the first subsection (II.1) introduces the philosophico-religious foundation of Confucian filial devotion and its functioning, as it emerges in the Confucian classics. Based on the Confucian terminology and ideas examined in the first subsection, the second (II.2) investigates the manner in which the scholar-monk, using his Buddhist view, simultaneously embraces and goes beyond this initial indigenous Chinese Confucian foundation. The theoretical framework employed is intercultural and inspired by the writings in the philosophy of religion of Felix Adler (1851–1933) on ethics as religion (Adler 1929), of Frederick J. Streng (1933–1993) on understanding religious life (Streng 1985), and of Keiji Nishitani (1900–1990) on religion and nothingness (Nishitani 1982).

II.1. Confucian Filial Devotion: Religious and Moral Foundations

This subsection studies the ancient foundation of Confucian filial devotion. It suggests that this bedrock includes two major elements: filial devotion as an expression of the continuity between the transcendent moral law of life and concrete community life, and filial devotion as an expression of reverence and sincerity. Both elements are thoroughly addressed below.

II.1.1. CONFUCIAN FILIAL DEVOTION AS AN EXPRESSION OF CONTINUITY

Confucian filial devotion has a moral and religious meaning deriving from the ancient religious practice of ancestor worship. Obviously, no reference is made in the context of this study to the spiritual and religious dimension of Neo-Confucianism, which was a subsequent development resulting from Buddhist influence (among other factors) and did not take place until the epoch immediately after Qisong. The foundation of Confucian filial devotion, and of the ancestor worship out of which it arose, consists of two beliefs. First, it refers to the existence of an already-mentioned transcendent law of life or of nature—heaven or the way of heaven (*tian dao* 天道)—which provides a universal moral order.[7] The ultimate dimension that is the way of heaven is the metaphysical depth of the tangible reality and expresses itself in the human world as an individual's moral quality or the power that fuels one's moral growth. The latter is perceived as extending everywhere, in all directions, as unbeatable and unstoppable as the course of life and nature. This idea lies at the core of the *Yijing* 易經 (*Classic of Changes*). Second is the belief in the existence of an ethico-moral and natural element in each human individual's nature—the moral quality (*de* 德). This is the trace of the presence of universal ethico-moral law within humans and what makes them capable of following and fulfilling this naturally ethico-moral law of life in their everyday behavior. One should observe that this ethico-moral quality embodies the belief in the existence within individuals of a motivation to behave ethically that is natural—in other words, it does not come from the free will as in Western culture. In this subsection, I argue that the connection between these two beliefs of ancient Confucianism is enabled by the religious and moral practice of filial devotion. To that end, reference is made to the *Zhongyong* chapter of the *Liji*. In his "Xiaolun," when discussing filial devotion in a comparative, Buddhist-Confucian perspective, Qisong himself often calls attention to the *Liji* (chapters "Ji Yi" 祭義, "Zhongyong" 中庸, "Li Qi" 禮器, "Guan Yi" 冠義, and "Qu li shang" 曲禮上; see Zhang 1996, 163–199, reference notes). This issue of the religious and moral practice of filial devotion has been analyzed particularly in the context of the *Xiaojing* 孝經 (*Classic of Filial Devotion*), the *Lunyu* 論語 (*Analects*), and the *Mengzi* 孟子 (*Mencius*) ; see Chan and Tan 2004; Rosemont 2008; Rosemont and Ames 2009.

Paragraph 17 of the *Zhongyong* (hereafter ZY, chapter 28 of the *Liji* in the time of Qisong) offers a masterful illustration of this Confucian relationship between the law of life, moral order, and filial devotion. First, it explains the efficient operation (ensuring the growth and continuity of life) and the nurturing role of the law or way of heaven: "Thus, heaven-nature gives birth to and makes grow all living things, and according to their different characteristics, takes care of each one of them in a different way. The young plants, those that can take root in the earth—heaven-nature supports them. Those that tilt—it lets them wither (故天之生物, 必因其材而篤 焉。故栽者培之, 傾者覆之。)" (ZY 17, *Zhuzi quan shu* [hereafter ZZQS], 6:42).[8] It is noted that this paragraph describes what Streng would call "a natural universal order of life" (1985, 64). The plant that can take root in the earth, and therefore its growth, is supported by heaven-nature. This is the concrete, organic expression of the natural harmony (harmonious growth) that results when the law of life is followed. The plant that tilts (a direct allusion to morality can be seen here, as upstanding is a metaphor of ethical conduct) and, because of that, is left to dry up represents the metaphor of what happens when this law of heaven is not followed: disharmony, infirmity, poor health, and disaster. Second, as just stated, in the Confucian context, this law of heaven provides not only the order of life but also an omnipresent ethico-moral order. The latter is the highest expression of the spontaneous, harmonious, and permanent functioning of life, and it includes, at the community level, harmonious social relationships as a result of the people's moral conduct, and for eminent, exemplary persons (*junzi* 君子), not only status in conformity with their high moral quality but also good health (longevity) and good fortune (fame and dignified rank). Thus, physical nature (i.e., the plant's growth) corresponds to social life (i.e., moral conduct). The same paragraph of the *Zhongyong* describes this universal ethico-moral order as a direct expression of the previously evoked natural universal order of life: "Those who possess a great moral quality are able to naturally achieve a status congruent with their quality, dignified honors, customary fame and long life (故大德必得其位, 必得其祿, 必得其名, 必得其壽。)" (*ZY* 17, *ZZQS*, 6:42). According to Streng (1985, 2), religion is a means to ultimate transformation. In this Chinese context, the religious dimension of the Confucian life connotes the ability to realize an ultimate transformation as the capacity for ethico-moral change. Simply put, this makes it possible for one to go from behaving in accordance with one's own selfishness and desires (which carry the mark of disorder, disharmony, and eventually damage) to becoming an exemplary person, an individual who cultivates harmonious social relationships, embraces service to community, and is committed to the common good. This Confucian change can be activated by building and maintaining harmonious social relationships. As ultimate transformation, it not only allows individuals to grow through life in harmony with the natural law of heaven and hence to achieve longevity and social status (like the plant that takes root in the earth and is supported by heaven), but equally, it ensures harmonious social relationships, a healthy society, and moral growth for the entire community. As shown below, it presumes a continuity or resonance between an individual and his or her milieu. The following excerpt from the *Zhongyong* 30 illustrates the living connection between the "organic harmony" that results from the functioning of the law (order) of nature and the "ethico-moral harmony" that results from the functioning of the law (order) of humans. It uses the metaphor of a river flowing—big rivers (great moral qualities, which are transformative) and small rivers (small moral qualities, weakened and dried up by selfishness and desires). Ethico-moral law and law of life are thus two inseparable dimensions of the Confucian reality: "The myriad things grow together without harming each other. Together, each one continues on its own path without getting in another's way. The small moral qualities are like the rivers digging their riverbed and flowing into it. The great moral quality is what multiplies the continuous transformations of reality [individual realities]. This is what makes heaven-earth big (萬物並育而不相害, 道並行而不相悖, 小德川流, 大 德敦化, 此天地之所以為大也。)" (*ZY* 30, *ZZQS*, 6:55).[9]

The *Zhongyong* alludes to a moral order embodied in a broad moral quality (*de* 德) that embraces the whole set of specified moral qualities. In its seventh chapter, the *Xiaojing* 孝經 (*Classic of Filial Devotion*;[10] hereafter XJ) selects one quality as the emblematic symbol of all, namely, filial devotion, and recognizes it as the expression of the natural law of heaven (*tian* 天) and of its correlative—that is, the earthly (*di* 地) law of moral conduct (see the following quotation). The following paragraph from the *Xiaojing* 7 thus confirms and endorses the interrelated (life-moral) organic nature of reality, the identity between natural organic relationships and human moral relationships, as well as the possibility of the ultimate moral transformation of people through following the heavenly-earthly natural law of filial devotion. Qisong quotes it in his "Xiaolun": "Filial devotion is the constant law of heaven and the behavioral rectitude [righteousness] of earth; the people's conduct must follow it (夫孝, 天之經也, 地之義也, 民之行也)" ("XL" 3, 0660c13-3).

This excerpt also shows that filial devotion, as the constant natural law embodied in the concrete flawless filial devotion of the sovereign within his family, resonates and propagates uniformly in all directions, in all families. As already noted, this Confucian ethico-religious perception of the existence of a cosmic law is reflected in awareness of the existence of a state of perfect continuity, without the slightest discontinuity, between filial devotion as universal principle of heaven-earth, the concrete filial devotion of the sovereign within the daily life of his own family, and that of each individual within his or her own family. The realization of the moral universal law of filial devotion in the sovereign's and people's daily conduct thus represents the ethico-religious dimension of Confucianism. It is understood that this particular feature lies in the system of social relationships. In consequence, the core of Confucian spirituality is to be found in Confucian ethics—that is, in the way in which individuals ought to behave toward one another. Confucian religion might be referred to as an "ethics as religion" that has filial devotion as a paradigm.

Moreover, because this ethics or morality of filial devotion follows from the law of life, it could also be argued that this ethics as religion has an organic nature—that is, individuals within society are interdependent just as the interdependent cells, which vary in their function and structure, compose an organism. Individuals are seen as growing together within the community as cells grow together within the organism. The *Zhongyong* 17 illustrates this moral growth as attaining the great moral quality (*da de* 大德) by calling upon Emperor Shun, the mythical figure who embodies the ideal of great filial devotion (*da xiao* 大孝): "Confucius said: 'Shun is considered as one who has demonstrated great filial devotion. His moral quality was that of a sage; he was honored, obtained the status of Heaven's Son, and had all the riches of the four seas. He is thus honored in the Ancestors' temple and each generation of his descendants continues to hold memorial ceremonies for him' (子曰:「舜其大孝也與!德為聖人, 尊為天子, 富有四海 之內。宗廟饗之, 子孫保之。)" (ZY 17, ZZQS, 6:42). As will become clear, Shun's "great" filial devotion means "complete" and is different from the Buddhist "great" filial devotion. This paragraph reveals its Confucian meaning—a practice addressed to living parents, to the spirits of the ancestors, and to Shun's salient trait—as embodying both the law of the harmonious continuity of life (generation after generation, his descendants remember him as their ancestor) and the moral law (because Shun's great moral quality was exemplary, he obtained the highest status and reverence among his people). Hence, ancient Confucianism recognizes filial devotion as a simultaneously moral and spiritual practice. Performing it thus confirms the cosmic order.

The *Zhongyong* 19 defines ethico-religious filial devotion as the highest expression of the ideal of organic continuity between generations: "What is called 'filial devotion' can be defined as the effort to continue in a good way the goals of the Ancestors, and to complete in a good way their work (夫孝者:善繼人之志, 善述人之事者也。)" (ZY 19, ZZQS, 6:43). The same belief in organic, intergenerational continuity that is embodied in filial devotion is expressed in a more concrete way in the same paragraph: "To firmly establish oneself in the place of one's Ancestor means to observe the Ancestor's ritual and play his music, revere what he respected, appreciate what he cherished, serve the deceased [those no longer alive and already buried] as serving those alive, serve the dead [those no longer present who have already departed but are yet to be buried] as serving those present. This is what complete filial devotion is all about (踐其位, 行其禮, 奏其樂, 敬其所尊, 愛其所親, 事死如事生, 事亡如事存, 孝之至也。)" (ZY 19, ZZQS, 6:44). The core belief of this Confucian ethics as religion is therefore the idea of continuity or interdependence: between the natural law of life and concrete things, between the law of life and the moral law, between living individuals, and between successive generations. The main source of this specific pattern of ethico-religious thinking is the principle of the continuity of life. Filial devotion as the expression of this continuity or interdependence, conceived as "natural," translates into one's duty to continue and accomplish the work and aspirations of one's living and deceased parents. This act confirms the cosmic order.

In the next subsection, I argue that from this conviction in continuity (without interruption) stems the Confucian religious dimension of reverence, which infuses the relationship of individuals with the spirits of their ancestors (as part of the spirits (*guishen* 鬼神)) as well as their relationships with parents and all other members of society. Furthermore, I also suggest that, in reality, this Confucian reverence is expressed as sincerity (*cheng* 誠).

II.1.2. CONFUCIAN FILIAL DEVOTION AS EXPRESSION OF REVERENCE AND SINCERITY

The next quotation, from the *Zhongyong* 16, illustrates the feeling of reverence, which is the religious element that sustains the abovementioned Confucian continuity. Here, the archetype of this continuity is the reverent feeling that emerges when performing rituals addressed to the omnipresent spirits of ancestors and thereafter to the living parents:

> It is the spirits (*guishen* 鬼神) that make people put themselves in proper order, purify themselves, put on ceremonial vestments as a sign of respect when presenting offerings to ancestral spirits (*jisi* 祭祀). In permanent movement, the spirits can be everywhere in space, above one, on his right or left. The *Classic of Poetry* (*Shijing* 詩經) says: "Oh, the moment when the spirit arrives is that which cannot be predicted. Oh, how can one relax in showing his respect while waiting for the spirit to come?" (使天下之人齊明盛服, 以承祭祀。洋 洋乎!如在其上, 如在其左右。詩曰:『神之格思, 不可 度思!矧可射思!』). (ZY 16, ZZQS, 6:41)

Filial devotion, the paragraph explains, emerges from the feeling of reverence of the individual who waits for the spirits' arrival, knowing that they are omnipresent. The excerpt from the *Classic of Poetry* incorporated in this paragraph of the *Zhongyong* originates from the poem *Yi* 抑 (section *Daya* 大雅). The same poem further clarifies the nature of this feeling of reverence: "Do not say: 'This place is closed. Nobody can see me.'" In other words, the slightest lack of respect existing in the heart-minds of those who are waiting for the spirits to arrive cannot be hidden. It can be immediately seen and detected. This awareness of the existence of an intangible continuity between humans and spirits is the source of the feeling of reverence. The same religious origin is illustrated in the excerpt from the poem *Lie zu* 烈祖 (*Classic of Poetry*, section *Song* 頌) quoted in the *Zhongyong* 33: "At the time when the spirit is called [to accept the offerings], nobody speaks and nobody argues" (奏假無言, 時靡有爭。; ZY 33, ZZQS, 6:58). A similar feeling of reverence is expressed when serving one's living parents. It stems from the initial religious reverence felt toward the ancestors' spirits that occurs during ancestor worship. However, this reverence that permeates the practice of serving living parents no longer has as its religious foundation the reverence that living descendants exhibit toward their ancestors' spirits, but a derivative of it—that is, the reverence of children toward living parents. The latter anchors the Confucian religious dimension within the sphere of everyday social relationships, the so-called domain of the way of humans (人道). In this particular sphere, reverence takes the form of a deep sincerity (誠). The translation of this religious foundation of ancient Confucianism from "reverence" during ancestor worship to reverence expressed as "sincerity" in everyday familial relations is important. Nevertheless, its nature remains religious, as one of its major beliefs is in the continuity between religious and social, between the law of heaven-nature and moral social law.

As already mentioned, Confucianism is founded on the belief in the existence of a perfect continuity (i.e., without any discontinuity (無息); see below) between the law of life and moral law, between humans and spirits, and between inner respect (reverence and sincerity) and external behavior (service to ancestors, parents, and community). This assumption takes the form of confidence in the presence of a feeling of reverence in the world of social relationships, which becomes confidence in the natural presence within every human being of a quality of being sincere (誠), free from deceit and hypocrisy, which, as the *Zhongyong* 16 highlights, "even though it is intangible, it is evident, and cannot be hidden" (夫微之顯, 誠之不可揜如此夫。; ZY 16, ZZQS, 6:41). Confucians consider that it cannot be concealed because they see this quality of sincerity as a projection within humans of the way of heaven and therefore proof of the continuity between life and morality, the way of heaven (天之道) as model for the way of humans (人之道). Through this presupposition of continuity, the way of heaven or the law of life becomes synonymous with the law of sincerity that people have to follow as a model. This idea is clearly illustrated in this paragraph of the *Zhongyong* 20:

> Sincerity is the way of heaven. To conform with sincerity is the way of humans. So-called sincerity means to conform without any effort, to know what is natural without thinking and to exhibit behavior that naturally corresponds to the way. Only the sage can be like this. To conform to sincerity is to choose to do good deeds and to be firmly attached to this decision (誠者, 天之道也; 誠之者, 人之 道也。誠者不勉而中, 不思而得, 從容中道, 聖人也。誠 之者, 擇善而固執之者也。). (ZY 20, ZZQS, 6:48)[11]

Note the ancient Confucian definition of sincerity as "choosing to do good deeds" (擇善). This idea echoes Qisong's perception of the common goal of the two teachings—that is, "making people good" (為善) (Qisong, "Yuanjiao," hereafter "YJ," 0648c25). As shown below, the scholar-monk also incorporates this concept of sincerity in his interpretation of filial devotion (see sec. II.2.2). Moreover, the *Zhongyong* text makes clear that the quality of sincerity in each human being is different: more or less complete or continuous, depending on the overall quality of the individual. Only the sage has complete sincerity, which is identical with that of heaven-nature, identical with the continuity of life, without the slightest discontinuity, omnipresent, permeating everything, and, above all, transforming everything:

> Complete sincerity (*zhicheng* 至誠) is without discontinuity (*wu xi* 無息). Being without discontinuity, it is durable (*jiu* 久). Being durable, it extends far in all directions. Extending far in all directions in a visible way, it is durably manifest. As durably manifest, it possesses extent and density; extensive and dense, it is high and clear. Because complete, sincerity is extensive and dense, it carries all realities. Because it is high and clear, it covers them. Long-lasting, it forms and completes them. Extensive and dense, sincerity is like the earth (博厚配地). High and clear, it is like heaven (高明配天). Long-lasting, in other words, endless and limitless. Sincerity is like this: without showing itself, it is manifest; without moving itself, it transforms all things; without acting, it completes the transformations of all realities (不見而章, 不動而變, 無為而成。). (*ZY* 26, *ZZQS*, 6:51–52)

Confucianism establishes a deep connection between filial devotion and sincerity—a quality believed to be naturally existing within oneself but that needs to be activated and cultivated through learning. Sincerity is the power that enables one to serve one's parents with filial devotion, stresses the *Zhongyong* 20: "Here is the path to follow in order to behave with filial compliance towards one's parents: if, when turning in on himself, the individual sees that sincerity is lacking, he will not be able to conduct himself toward his parents in a filial way (順乎親有道: 反諸身不誠, 不順乎親矣)" (*ZY* 20, *ZZQS*, 6:48). In conclusion, Confucian filial devotion is based on the abovementioned belief in continuity and manifests itself as the expression of this continuity as well as an expression of two feelings presumed to be natural: reverence and sincerity. This sketch of the ethico-religious foundation of Confucian filial devotion provides the context within which Qisong's Buddhist view of filial devotion will be examined. It consequently serves as a reference for comparison between the different meanings of this notion in the two teachings.

II.2. *Buddhist Filial Devotion in Qisong's View: Religious and Ethico-moral Foundations*

This section elaborates the Buddhist religious and ethico-moral foundation of filial devotion and points out two major dimensions: its completeness and its spiritual nature. The analytical framework is comparative

(Buddhism-Confucianism) and is built around two correlative articulations: complete-partial (sec. II.2.1) and spiritual-organic (sec. II.2.2).

II.2.1. The Buddhist Completeness of Filial Devotion: A Comparative Perspective

Before going further with the analysis, let us recall the Confucian ethico-religious belief in the continuity between the universal law of filial devotion (governing the cosmic organism) and the moral duty of filial devotion (governing the social organism) in the sovereign's and ordinary people's concrete daily life. This is the foundation of the Confucian "ethical and spiritual ideal"—to use Felix Adler's term.[12] It brings forward the possibility of an ultimate moral transformation, ethico-religious in nature, of the people through following the sovereign's filial devotion as a model example, while the sovereign in turn follows the principle of filial piety of the natural moral law.

One may ask why Qisong proposed to expand Confucian filial devotion and whether, in his view, this Confucian ideal was comprehensive and powerful enough to help people adequately regulate their ethical conduct and preserve it, not only within the family but also outside, within their communities. In this subsection, I suggest that, from a careful reading of the scholar-monk's work, one understands that for him, the foundation of this Confucian ethico-religious ideal was not spiritual or powerful enough to effectively generate and maintain the continuity of ethical transformation generation after generation, nor could it uphold the belief in the ideal continuity between inner life, family, and others (this ideal continuity is expressed in the classic *Daxue* 大學, *Great Learning*; see Arghirescu 2012, 272–289). The idea that Confucian teaching is not effective enough to sustain an individual's moral transformation and behavior, which entails firmly holding the conviction of this continuity between inner life, family, and others—that is, the expansion of the same ethical standard in each domain of the individual's life—is clearly expressed in the final paragraph of his essay "Yuanjiao," where Qisong distinguishes between Confucianism as limited to the sociopolitical management of society (present life) and Buddhism as going beyond this life and dealing with the management of three lives (past, present, and future):

> Buddhism is my way. I also personally have some knowledge of Confucianism and have leafed a little bit through the books of Laozi and of the Daoist school. If asked to comment, I would say that all the teachings are like bridges crossing over a river (諸教也, 亦猶同水以涉). It is the same crossing, but the river has deep regions and shallow ones. In Confucianism, the sage governs one world [the present life, the present world] (儒者, 聖人之

治世者也). In Buddhism, the sage governs what extends beyond the present world [goes beyond the present life to include past and future lives] (佛者, 聖人之治出世者也). ("YJ," 0651c16-10)

In Qisong's words, elsewhere in the same essay, Confucianism emphasizes community life and is driven by a concern for community, to the disadvantage of individual lives and concerns. In a conversation with a Confucian student who asks questions to better understand the works of Buddhism, the scholar-monk responds, "You think about the concerns of society in an excessive way, and you pay too little attention to the individual" (子亦為世之憂太過, 為人之計太約; "YJ," 0651b11-5).

Inevitably, a teaching such as Confucianism that focuses on society, on governing the masses or aggregates of people, is less mindful of the worries and specific lives of the separate individuals; therefore, one could say, it cannot trigger a veritable transformation of the latter. In his view, Buddhism with its focus on the members of society and their interrelation can address and overcome this deficiency of Confucianism, and cooperation between the two, Qisong thinks, would improve the management of the community in general. To illustrate the possibility of such cooperation, in his interpretation of Buddhism, the scholar-monk focuses on the interrelationship of individual members of society, on their capacity to do individual good deeds and thus to advance the spirit of social harmony. It might be said that this Buddhist perspective would later come to constitute—after Qisong—an incentive for the Northern Song Confucian masters to overcome this deficiency of pre-Song Confucianism through building the Neo-Confucian perspective of self-cultivation.

Because its ethico-religious foundation is different from that of Confucianism, the teaching of Buddhism, in Qisong's view, embraces the teaching of Confucianism and goes beyond it, thus extending its scope and outreach. Thus, in his "Xiaolun," not only does he interpret Buddhist filial devotion in language familiar to his Confucian readers, but he also carries out what might be called a reconstruction of this traditional Chinese moral ideal on new Buddhist foundations. The Buddhist ethico-religious foundations of filial devotion as interpreted in the "Xiaolun" are explored further below. In the third chapter of this essay of his, the scholar-monk notes, "Buddha said: 'Filial devotion and compliance is the method to achieve the complete way' (佛曰: 「孝順至道之法.」)" ("XL" 3, 0660c11-1). Roughly speaking, the "complete way" (*zhi dao* 至道) in Qisong's thought means a way whose completion entails a perfect spiritual transformation and the achievement of enlightenment (see chap. 5, sec. III.2). According to the Chan scholar-monk, and in Nishitani's words (1982, 62), to realize the complete way or enlightenment implies, above all, that the individual has opened a breach in the field of his self, is able to go deeper within himself, and has access to the field of no-self. In this sphere, a human sees things as they really are, and, in daily life activities, they live their interrelatedness with all sentient beings. Inspired by the work of Streng, in what follows, I refer to this vigorous and constant endeavor in which one is engaged, to open that breach and enter the inner field of no-self and interrelatedness, as "spiritual discipline."[13] From this perspective, it becomes clear that Qisong's complete way is not an external natural law such as the Confucian way of heaven but a path of inner spiritual discipline that the person has to walk constantly in their daily life. His Buddhist perspective emphasizes an individual journey through which one becomes aware of one's interrelatedness with all sentient beings, and this interrelatedness becomes the individual's moral, ethical, and spiritual guidance for everyday living.

In the reference above ("Buddha said"), in fact, Qisong quotes the *Brahma's Net Sutra* (*Fanwang jing* 梵網經) 1004a25-1, without naming his source. This is an apocryphal text composed in China during the middle of the fifth century, which explains the major precepts from a Mahayana perspective, for everyone—monks, nuns, laymen, and laywomen.[14] Qisong endorses the perspective of this sutra on the primordial importance of filial devotion as the major method to achieve the complete way for all Buddhists, ordained and laypeople. This view is similar to that of the Confucian *Classic of Filial Devotion*, which also considers filial devotion as primordial but as natural law. While in both cases the emphasis is on filial devotion (as natural law in Confucianism and as privileged method in Buddhism), the nature of the Buddhist practice is fundamentally different from that of the Confucian. It does not follow an external law of heaven, assimilating and internalizing it by virtue of an ethico-religious awareness of its universal and obligatory character. Instead, Qisong presents Buddhist filial devotion as a method of overcoming the usual limitation of humans to the field of the self. The latter causes individuals to act in a dualistic, selfish way—that is, with an eye to the personal interests, desires, hopes, and expectations fabricated by the self. He highlights the capacity of the practice of filial devotion to help one rise from the state of self-attachment and actualize the human spiritual potential, to allow breaching of the field of ego that sees things as fundamentally separated from one another, and to become aware of the togetherness of things and able to live in this state of interconnectedness. As Streng notes, "People often cannot make use of their potential because they are attached to their anxieties; and they are attached to their anxieties because they are bound by superficial goals, values, and self-images" (1985, 99).

In the scholar-monk's view, filial devotion constitutes a spiritual discipline (i.e., nourishing filial devotion toward not only parents but all sentient beings), which enables one to break out of self-centeredness. Streng's theoretical account of spiritual discipline appropriately illustrates the scholar-monk's perception of this Buddhist filial devotion: "This process [spiritual discipline] is not primarily a struggle to attain higher knowledge.... Rather spiritual discipline focuses on letting go of false value" (1985, 92). In the following paragraph of the ninth chapter of the "Xiaolun," in the context of the practice of filial devotion, Qisong highlights the difference between the Confucian and Buddhist notions of the complete moral quality (德) and the complete way (至道) of the individual. The Buddhist complete moral quality (至德) goes beyond merely performing acts of gratitude (good deeds) toward one's parents and instead addresses them to all sentient beings. It has a soteriological grounding: salvation of all (including one's parents). The Buddhist complete way comprises awareness of the karmic causes and results of these good deeds. The practice of filial devotion guided by a complete moral quality and way is the most adequate means to ensure that individuals appropriately repay the debt of gratitude they have toward their parents (報父母) and toward all sentient beings, as they are aware of the interrelatedness of all:

> Nurturing parents with food or physical care *yang* (養)[15] is not enough to repay the debt of gratitude one has towards one's parents for their benevolence. So, the sage repays it through putting into action his moral quality (聖人以德報之). Putting into action one's moral quality is not enough to repay one's parents. To accomplish this, the sage cultivates the way (聖人以道達之). The so-called way (道) is not what the common people call the way, but rather the complete way of the sage; more marvelous than the spirits, it goes beyond the cycle of birth and death (妙神明, 出死生, 聖人之至道者也). The moral quality (德) is not what the common people call the moral way; it is the complete moral quality of the sage, which includes all the myriad good deeds, those that are clear and those obscure (備萬善, 被幽, 被明, 聖人之至德者也). ("XL" 9, 0661c16)

Qisong thus stresses the completeness of Buddhist filial devotion as a method to achieve the complete way and the complete moral quality as well as to completely repay the benevolence of parents and of all sentient beings. It can be said that his notion of completeness (至) very clearly and specifically refers to having access to the inner field of no-self. When entering it, one is enabled to live one's interrelatedness with all sentient beings and sees them all as parents. This practice or way of living translates not into accomplishing certain limited good deeds (as expressions of filial devotion) for relatives and people who are important to us but rather into doing all myriad good deeds for all sentient beings. Acting in everyday life is then guided not by the perspective of the individual's self but by the vision of this inner field of emptiness/interrelatedness, which Qisong calls completeness. Nishitani admirably describes this state as "a standpoint where one sees one's own self in all things, in living things, in hills and rivers, towns and hamlets, tiles and stones, and loves all these things 'as oneself'" (1982, 281).

The "complete" quality of Buddhist filial devotion, the spiritual way, and the moral quality is what makes all three of them powerful, as explained in this passage from the *Brahma's Net Sutra*, one of the apocryphal scriptures that the Northern Song scholar-monk mentions:

> All men have been our fathers, and all women our mothers. In our numerous past lives, there is no one who has not been our mother or father. Therefore, sentient beings in all six destinies (*liu dao* 六道)[16] have all been our fathers and mothers (一切男子是我父、一切女人是我母, 我生生無不從之受生, 故六道眾生皆是我父母。). (*Brahma's Net Sutra*, 1006b09-11)[17]

This is how the Chinese sutra and Qisong explain complete filial devotion as having a soteriological purpose, which includes the myriad good deeds for the benefit (salvation) of all sentient beings from all six destinies. Furthermore, the scholar-monk explains this Buddhist spiritual perspective of the way, of moral quality, and of filial devotion through referring to the quintessential spirit (*jing shen* 精神) as the fundamental nature of all sentient beings, humans included. It is possible that all sentient beings have been our fathers and mothers precisely because they all have a quintessential spirit that carries on existing after their death. This is what Qisong calls the vehicle of spiritual transformation (乘變化; see next quotation), which continuously connects past, present, and future lives. These connections are causal, emerging from the moral and karmic forces (causes and results) of the actions of sentient beings. Transformation (變化) in his view means spiritual and not organic transformation. He describes one's ancestors as quintessential spirits, having done good and evil actions and therefore continuing to exist in various forms, in all the six good and evil worlds or destinies (heavenly dwellers, humans, asuras, animals, hungry ghosts, and hell dwellers). Through this interpretation, he establishes and strengthens a link between the Confucian ancestor cult and the Buddhist precept to abstain from taking life. This gives a new spiritual basis to filial devotion. The scholar-monk describes the observance of this foundational precept as demonstrating one's true commitment (篤) to think about one's ancestors and parents and keep them in one's heart—that is, to honor and pay respect to them (篤於懷親):

> The sage [Buddha] grasps that spiritual quintessence is the vehicle that carries transformation (精神乘變化). Living beings move unceasingly and

become humans or animals. Since ancient times and down to our time, this transformation continues in an indiscernible way; people are not able to notice it. Nowadays people are not aware of this transformation, only the sage knows it. When he sees today's animals [cattle and sheep], he thinks that they likely originate from the spiritual quintessence of [people's] ancestral parents (故其視今牛羊, 唯恐其是昔之父母精神之所來也). Consequently, he establishes the precept to abstain from killing (戒於殺). Not to hurt the tiniest being is one's committed way to think about one's parents-ancestors (不使暴一微物, 篤於懷親也). ("XL" 4, 0660c23)

This paragraph could also be seen as his particular reading of a view expressed in the *Brahma's Net Sutra* (1006b27).[18] The filial devotion to which he refers here includes the future lives of the parents (i.e., parents today, ancestors tomorrow) and envisages them as continuing to exist and transform. It is not merely an honorable and uplifting memory of the defunct parents embodied in feelings (underlying memories) and rituals. Insofar as individuals continue to do good deeds for all sentient beings, to transfer the merits to their parents, this filial devotion Qisong refers to continues to be active and determine the parents' (ancestors') future lives: "When doing things for the parents, one should consider what has not yet happened, and therefore reach farther, up to their future life (為父母慮其未然, 則逮乎更生。)" ("XL" 4, 0660c28-11).

This is because, in his Buddhist view, parents (like all sentient beings) are quintessential spirits in transformation. It is clear, however, that filial devotion toward one's own parents is fundamental as the source of one's filial devotion toward all sentient beings. The cultivation of the latter is conditioned on the practice of the first. Elsewhere, in the *Sutra in Forty-Two Sections* (*Si shi er zhang jing* 四十二章經),[19] another probably apocryphal scripture that Qisong also tacitly cites in his essay, this idea is expressed clearly: "The two parents are the most spiritual" (二親最神也。; 0722c09-13). To highlight the meaning of Buddhist filial devotion as compassion toward all sentient beings, in the next paragraph, Qisong implicitly adopts from the *Brahma's Net Sutra* (1004b16) the notion of "heart-mind of filial devotion and compliance" (孝順心): "A Sutra [*Brahma's Net Sutra*] says: 'One should nurture a heart-mind of filial devotion and compliance, be affectionate towards and protect all living beings.' This is the meaning of filial devotion (經曰: 「應生孝順心, 愛護一切眾生。」斯之謂也。)" ("XL" 4, 0661a06-14). This practice is, in fact, nurturing a "heart-mind of compassion and empathic caring" (慈悲心; see the *Brahma's Net Sutra*, 1004b19-2), which helps one think ahead to the future lives of one's parents and be aware that their quintessential spirit could become imprisoned in a bad destiny, such as being reincarnated as an animal. With this heart-mind, humans continue to do good deeds for their parents—that is, to be affectionate toward and protect all living beings. I find that this interpretation of the scholar-monk is a particularly creative and inspiring fusion of the Confucian emphasis on reverence toward parents and the Buddhist prominence of the interrelatedness of all. Qisong thus makes implicit reference to the story of the mother of Buddha's disciple Mulian (Mahamaudgalyayana, *Da Muqianlian* 大目乾連),[20] from the mid-sixth-century Chinese apocryphal scripture the *Ullambana Sutra* (*Yulanpen jing* 盂蘭盆經),[21] which also focuses on filial devotion. At the same time, in his "Xiaolun" 4, he uses a well-known Confucian definition of filial devotion from the Confucian *Analects* 1.9 ("with all [his] heart-mind, [he] performs the funeral rites for the parents and the posthumous memorial ceremonies for them" (慎終追遠): "When the people who want to do things for their parents think of the imprisoned spirits [in a bad destiny] of their father and mother, they are able to broaden their filial devotion and their heart-mind, with which they perform the funeral rites for their parents and the posthumous memorial ceremonies for them (天下苟以其陷神為父母慮，猶可以廣乎孝子慎終追遠之心也。)" ("XL" 4, 0661a02-5). The above paragraph is also a perfect expression of the harmonious fusion that Qisong realizes between the two teachings. In this context, he connects the Buddhist broad heart-mind of filial devotion, which is concerned with the future lives of the parents, with the well-known Confucian definition of filial devotion (*Analects* 1.9), which focuses on performing funeral rites and memorial ceremonies. Thus, it is arguable that, in a perfectly coherent way, he implicitly links the *Ullambana Sutra* with the *Analects* using the concept of filial devotion as a connection point.

In the same section, the scholar-monk further develops a relevant comparison between the Buddhist complete or universal filial devotion and the Confucian concept of filial devotion, limited to one's present life, parents, and ancestors. After presenting the unlimited Buddhist filial devotion, way, and moral quality (see above), Qisong indirectly quotes, for comparative purposes, the following two paragraphs from the *Book of Rites, Liji*, chapter "Ji yi" 祭義. He concludes that, even if Buddhists and Confucians seem to refer to the same idea (*yi* 意) of filial devotion, the significance (*yi* 義) of this notion in the two teachings is different. The difference is that the Buddhist meaning implies globality, all-inclusiveness, interrelatedness, and limitless time (beyond the present life) as ethico-religious foundations of filial devotion, whereas the Confucian meaning is restricted to human community, to the governing sphere, and to one's present life relationships with parents, ancestors, sovereign, and country:

> The Confucians say: "What the exemplary person calls filial devotion means first, to discern the desires of the parents, realize their aspirations, and

guide the parents towards the way (先意承志, 諭父母於道). I, Zengzi [Zeng Shen 曾參 (505–435 BC), Confucius's disciple, presumed author of the *Great Learning*, one of the Four Sages of Confucianism—Confucius, Zengzi, Zisi, and Mencius], can only nurture them with food and physical care (養). How can I be considered someone who performs filial devotion?" And they also say: "What the exemplary person (君子) calls filial devotion, is that of someone who all the people of the country would like to have as son (國人稱願), and of whom they say: 'Blessed are the parents who have such a son!' (幸哉有子如此)! Such is one who is considered a model of filial devotion." Even if it seems that Buddhists and Confucians refer to the same idea (意同) of filial devotion, their significations are different (義異). ("XL" 9, 0661c20-7)

In the fourth section, he further develops the differences between the two views on filial devotion, through the idea of "heart-mind of filial devotion and obedience" (孝順心) mentioned earlier: "What ordinary people call filial devotion refers to the things of this present life, and they are unable to examine what is hidden, the profound things. They refer to the human and do not refer to the spirit (世之謂孝者, 局一世而闇玄覽, 求於人而不求於神。)" ("XL" 4, 0661a04-10).

However, in spite of highlighting the differences between the ethico-religious natures of the two practices of filial devotion, the scholar-monk finally focuses rather on the similarity of their purposes—the importance for those who engage in cultivating their moral quality to constantly continue it until achieving its highest and complete level. This is because, for Confucians as for Buddhists, Qisong stresses, all other lower levels of moral quality are just imperfect and intermediary stages that do not allow access to the complete way (Buddhist or Confucian). Hence, he calls attention to two aspects that both teachings share. First, they focus on cultivating individuals' moral quality—that is, the power that adequately controls their behavior, the way in which they ought to behave toward each other. Second, in his view, Buddhism and Confucianism also share a common goal—developing harmonious relations within the community as a result of the high moral quality of the individuals. Undeniably, when interpreting the Buddhist practice, the scholar-monk focuses on the importance of actively engaging and participating in society. This idea is reflected throughout the whole study. The first abovementioned common aspect is illustrated in his "Xiaolun" 8 through the following quote from the twenty-seventh chapter of the *Zhongyong*.[22] Obviously, this choice demonstrates Qisong's interest in this Confucian classic and in developing the resemblances between the two teachings rather than in emphasizing their different natures: "The *Zhongyong* says: 'If one does not have a complete moral quality, one will not accomplish one's complete way.' This meaning of the

Zhongyong is what I want to convey (中庸曰:「苟不至德至道不凝焉。」如此之謂也。)" ("XL" 8, 0661c14).

Nevertheless, for Qisong, the magnitude and scope of Buddhist filial devotion are broader than those of its Confucian counterpart. Because of their essential similarities, the Buddhist practice of filial devotion may support and considerably extend the Confucian one. He therefore stresses the perfect possibility and viability of their joint effort. His perception is clearly illustrated in the following quotation from the "Xiaolun" 6. As it is based on the spirit, Buddhist filial devotion governs the spiritual dimension of the human. Thus, it embraces and goes beyond Confucian filial devotion, which is rooted in human affairs and behavior in the present life. In his view, the two are inseparable. The Buddhist perspective could be an efficient governing tool for ruling and harmonizing society, as, due to its emphasis on spiritual discipline, it could enhance the efficiency of the Confucian practice. Qisong illustrates the affinity between Confucianism and Buddhism using powerful images: the indissoluble link between water and the network of canals that help move, control, and tame it, and between the fire and the bellows that assist, guide, and keep the fire going in the forge:

> People believe that only Confucianism promotes filial devotion, and they do not think that Buddhism also promotes it. They say: "If there is already [Confucian] filial devotion, what else is there to add?" Oh! This means only understanding Confucianism and not understanding Buddhism (見儒而未見佛). Buddhism also reaches to the highest level (佛也極焉). With Confucianism, the individual obeys the behavioral norms of this life; with Buddhism, he broadens this practice (以儒守之, 以佛廣之). With Confucianism he manages human affairs; with Buddhism he governs the spirit (以儒人之, 以佛神之). Filial devotion is an essential dimension in Buddhism, too. Inherently, water moves downward (水固趣下也) [allusion to the Confucian practice]. If canals are made to guide it [allusion to the Buddhist practice], the water reaches its destination faster, right (洫而決之, 其所至不亦速乎)? Inherently, the fire burns upward (火固炎上也) [Confucian practice]. If one uses a bellows to blow air into it [Buddhist practice], the flames raise up even higher. Is this not so (噓而鼓之, 其所舉不亦遠乎)? ("XL" 6, 0661b05)

In this subsection, I have examined the "completeness" of Buddhist filial devotion as presented by Qisong in a comparative perspective (with Confucianism as its frame of reference). Buddhist filial devotion is considered as complete and universal compared with the Confucian conception, which is depicted as partial and local. The all-embracing nature of the first is for him the concrete proof that it can complement and enrich the Confucian practice of filial devotion with beneficial effects for the harmony of society and its interconnected environment (all sentient beings on which human society depends). The next subsection further develops this Buddhist perception of filial devotion as embracing and expanding its Confucian counterpart. Concretely, it takes up the Confucian ideas illustrated in section II.1—life and sincerity—but this time from the Buddhist perspective of the "Xiaolun." If in this subsection the theoretical articulation used was complete/partial, the next subsection is built on a new articulation: organic/spiritual.

II.2.2. Buddhist Sincerity in the Practice of
Filial Devotion: A Comparative Perspective

This subsection argues that in his "Xiaolun," Qisong extends the major foundation of ancient Confucian filial devotion—sincerity—from the sphere of organic life to that of spiritual life. As shown in section II.1, Confucian thought anchored ethico-morality in the law or order of life—ideally, nurturing an ethical attitude means sustaining life, or longevity; an unethical behavior means harming life, or misery. In this context, filial devotion is a duty toward one's parents, who are considered the root or the fundamental source of life (of the individual and of the family). The scholar-monk expands the scope of filial devotion as well as the meaning of the notion of life—from organism-focused life and the continuity of life to spirit-focused life and the continuity between life and spirit. Once again, it becomes clear that, by building this expansion, Qisong's goal is not to contrast Confucianism and Buddhism through articulating them in opposition but to highlight the overarching and all-embracing nature of Buddhist teaching, to illustrate how the latter integrates and goes beyond Confucianism, and to suggest the need for a fruitful cooperation between the two realms of practice, within Confucian culture. Moreover, one also understands his clear intention to connect organic life and spiritual life in a nondual structure.

The first theme presented in this context is the meaning of filial devotion as root. For the author of the "Xiaolun," the world has three fundamental roots instead of only one; therefore, the complete practice of filial devotion should honor all three: the parents, the master and the monk, and the way (*dao* 道; see "XL" 2). Parents are the root of life, by which the birth of a particular individual occurs. Obviously, it is a necessary root. The master, usually associated with the monk, is—the Northern Song scholar-monk suggests—the root of the teaching focusing on the moral quality (*de* 德) and of the encouragement to practice spiritual discipline. This transforms the individuals, thus giving them a new birth. The way is the most important root according to Qisong; namely, it is the root of spiritual practice (神用; see below), by which humans transform themselves and are "born" anew, becoming aware of the connections between their current, past, and future lives and of their interrelatedness with all sentient beings. People realize that to the spontaneous and continuous flow of life (highlighted by the Confucian tradition) must be added karmic causes and conditions in order to deeply understand the roots and consequences of one's actions:

> It is my parents who gave me life, so I put parents in the first place. For those who want to make clear their moral quality, nothing is better than the teaching (天下之明德者, 莫善於教也). It is the master who gave me the teaching, so I put the master in the first place. Among the marvelous things of the world, the most marvelous is the way (天下之妙事者, 莫妙於道也). It is the way upon which I rely to live, so I put the way in the first place. The way is the root of the spiritual practice (夫道也者, 神用之本也). The master is the root of the teaching and encouragement (師也者, 教誥之本也). Parents are the root of the life which takes shape (父母也者, 形生之本也). These three roots are the most important roots of the world (是三本者, 天下之大本也). ("XL" 2, 0660b22-11)

This paragraph introduces a major distinction between organic life (emblematic of Confucianism and the classic *Zhongyong*) and spiritual life (representative of Buddhism), which is developed throughout the "Xiaolun." This contrast is his second major tool (the first is the articulation partial/complete; see the subsection above) for comparing the two teachings and for arguing that Buddhism embraces and transcends the Confucian perspective. He states that filial devotion has not one but three roots. In this paragraph, the scholar-monk expands filial devotion as a practice oriented not only toward parents, the source of biological life, but also toward the master-monk and beyond the human world, toward the way.

In what follows, I explain how he further broadens the meaning of the traditional Confucian concept of filial devotion, with his innovative perspective that embraces all three of these roots, and within the context of the nonduality organic life–spiritual life or, as will be further interpreted, functionality (behavior, 行)–inner essence (principle, 理).[23] In the "Xiaolun" 3, Qisong describes the ethico-moral quality of filial devotion as having two dimensions. The first one is visible to the eye—concrete behavior (行) that carries out or puts into effect filial devotion through manifest actions. It may be argued that this is included in the sphere of organic life, sentient beings (present parents and teachers included), and manifest phenomena. The other dimension is invisible—the inner essence of principle (理). In other words, it is the source, inner potential, or power (the way) from which stem the acts that are a direct expression of filial devotion. This essence belongs to the inner world of the individual, the heart-mind. It may be observed that this is an interesting and original way to interpret filial devotion—the very core of Confucian culture—using Buddhist tools, such as karma, "action," and the imperceptible force or fruit that continues to exist after the perceptible action has ended. The scholar-monk uses here the Buddhist understanding of "action" or karma.[24] He identifies and analyzes the notion of filial devotion as "action":

> Filial devotion has a visible dimension (可見) [behavior] and an invisible one (不可) [the heart-mind]. Its invisible dimension is the inner essence of filial devotion (孝之理也). Its visible dimension is the practice of filial devotion (孝之行也) [expressed in one's behavior]. The inner essence is the source from which filial devotion emerges (孝之所以出也). The practice is that by which filial devotion takes on its appearance (孝之所以形容也). If the human cultivates (修) only this appearance, without cultivating his heart-mind [inner source], then serving his parents lacks commitment (不篤), and doing acts of charity for others lacks sincerity (不誠). If one cultivates one's heart-mind and, at the same time, cultivates the appearance of filial devotion, then one not only serves one's parents with commitment and does acts of charity for others with sincerity, but also assists heaven-earth and makes the ghosts and spirits (*guishen* 鬼神) respond (豈惟事父母而惠人, 是亦振天地而感鬼神也). ("XL" 3, 0660c04)

In other words, this paragraph suggests that cultivating the inner dimension of filial devotion means becoming aware through spiritual/religious practice of the existence of the imperceptible karmic and moral force that continues and matures as a result of filial actions, long after these have ended. According to Hirakawa Akira's theory of "action" (1990, 185–196), one could equate this resulting power with the volition or essence of karma. The functioning of volition or inner essence could also be considered as unmanifested karma that generates manifest acts of filial devotion and continues to produce karmic results. This inner essence of filial devotion represents the force or power within individuals that encourages them to act with filial devotion and also produces as a result, or through the transfer of merits, good karma and good birth (within the realms of humans and heavenly beings) for their parents. In language familiar to Confucians, Qisong equates this inner essence with sincerity (*cheng* 誠). And he highlights the nonduality between inner essence–sincerity and filial behavior in a concrete way, through stressing the necessity to cultivate both—that is, a real or karmically derived and driven sincerity. This is another explanation of why, in his Buddhist view, the practice of real sincerity and of real filial behavior means not only to fully serve one's parents, or in Keith N. Knapp's (2004) words, provide them with "reverent caring,"[25] but also to treat equally all sentient beings when responsible for practicing charity toward others and for assisting and protecting all. Thus, like the Confucians, the scholar-monk also emphasizes the importance of sincerity when practicing not only filial devotion (service to parents) but also charity (service to others). Confucian culture perceives charity as perturbing the hierarchical social order and does not encourage it. It should be highlighted that in Qisong's view, the practice of filial devotion is inseparable from the practice of charity, as the enlightened Buddhists perceive every sentient being as their parent and therefore serve and protect them all. Note that the notion of treating equally all sentient beings clearly refers here to gaining awareness of the so-called field of emptiness, no-ego and no-self (see Nishitani 1982), already discussed in the context of his perspective on one's nature and emotions. Moreover, treating all equally is nothing other than the result of individual's awareness concerning the interdependence of all sentient beings, parents and all others:

> Putting into practice filial devotion means nurturing parents [with food or physical care] (孝行者, 養親之謂也).[26] If this practice is not sincere, then nurturing parents is at times deficient (行不以誠, 則其養有時而匱也). If the filial devotion comes from one's sincere heart-mind, then one's service to parents is complete (全), and when one is doing charity among others and assisting sentient beings, one treats them all on an equal basis (其惠人卹物也均). ("XL" 3, 0660c16-1)

It can be said that, when one's practice of filial devotion is driven by sincerity, one's filial devotion, spirit of charity, and assistance to sentient beings are all complete (全). This is equivalent to treating each and every one on an equal basis (均; see quote above). In other words, things are all part of individual's no-self, not as external, objective, different things but as nonobjective, inwardly present ones, as they really are in themselves. It could also be noted that equality (均) here is equivalent to having achieved awareness of the nonduality between one and all sentient beings and thus being able to deal with things based on the awareness of a person of their interrelatedness with all other sentient beings. Through the practice of filial devotion based on sincerity, the scholar-monk suggests, people are able to become completely devoted (效) and to accomplish

(成) their way (see the following quotation)—that is, to become enlightened. Astonishingly, in this way he considerably expands the meanings of two well-known Confucian concepts, filial devotion and sincerity, while also connecting them into a nondual relationship as manifest and unmanifest intrinsic features of the same reality—filial devotion as "karma," as action having a good karmic effect. Through transfer, the latter positively influences the future lives of one's parents and of all sentient beings, as one's self is interrelated with them all. These Buddhist aspects of filial devotion are suggested in the next passage through the notion of "accomplishment (achievement, becoming) (成)"—that is, the enlightened way (see *Platform Sutra*, 0345c08, 0347c28, 0350b29; the way of becoming a buddha 成佛道). While expressly extending the meaning of filial devotion and sincerity as "effective action" and "accomplishment," the scholar-monk addresses his Confucian auditors; therefore, he does not directly refer to the implicit Buddhist karmic resonances of his interpretation, articulated above. Instead, he equates the action of filial devotion (孝) or the manifest dimension of filial devotion with "effective action" (效), and he considers "sincerity" (誠), or the unmanifest and continuing (from one life to another) moral force of the action of filial devotion, as equivalent to "accomplishment (becoming)" (成):

> The action of filial devotion (*xiao* 孝) means effective action (*xiao* 效). To be sincere (*cheng* 誠) means to be accomplished (*cheng* 成). To be accomplished means to accomplish one's way (成其道). Effective action (效) means to effectively practice filial devotion (效其孝). When the individual practices filial devotion but without being effective, this is not, in fact, filial devotion (為孝而無效, 非孝也). When one is sincere but without having accomplished his way, one is not, in fact, sincere (為誠而無成, 非誠也). ("XL" 3, 0660c18-5)

It is apparent that his intention here is mainly to expand the meaning of the traditional Confucian notion of sincerity in the context of the "filial devotion practiced by the sage" (聖人之孝; whether a Confucian or Buddhist sage) and to develop it in a new direction, comprehensible and acceptable to the scholar-officials. This new path is implicitly Buddhist in its essence; however, it is formulated in terms suited to Confucian scholars, with the aim of making an immediate impact on their understanding of this specific topic. He directly acknowledges this fact immediately after this hermeneutical analysis, indirectly quoting a phrase that is found in the twenty-fifth paragraph of the classic *Zhongyong*: "Thus, the filial devotion practiced by the sage has sincerity as its most valuable aspect. This is what the Confucians also say: 'The exemplary person considers sincerity as the most valuable' (是故聖人之孝, 以誠為貴也。儒不曰乎: 君子誠之為貴)" ("XL" 3,

0660c20-9). Suggestive enough, in this view, enlightenment, which is completely accomplishing one's way, does not mean awareness or knowledge of something individual-oriented, such as the presence of the buddha-nature within oneself, but first and foremost, practice of the interrelatedness of all sentient beings and engagement in the world. This is how he highlights the importance of living and working togetherness: through constantly practicing sincere and effective filial devotion within the broad family consisting of all sentient beings. However, Qisong also advances a Buddhist dimension of filial devotion essentially different from its Confucian meaning: practicing filial devotion with sincerity is precisely doing charity to sentient beings and protecting them all. This is a nonhierarchical family, where all are treated on an equal basis, where charity is not only encouraged but considered a responsibility.

The scholar-monk philosophically brings out the differences between the ethico-religious foundations of filial devotion in the Confucian and Buddhist teachings, here in a new perspective, using the nondual articulations organic/spiritual, essence/functioning, committed/with sincerity, and effective/accomplished. This section analyzes the connotations of the notion of sincerity in both schools (i.e., Confucian practice and Qisong's interpretation of Buddhist practice). The author's constant emphasis in the essay "Xiaolun" on the similarities between the social objectives and practices of Buddhist filial devotion and of its Confucian equivalent cannot go unnoticed. The section III, develops this issue in detail.

III. THE AFFINITIES BETWEEN THE CONFUCIAN AND BUDDHIST PRACTICES OF FILIAL DEVOTION: QISONG'S COMPARATIVE PERSPECTIVE

In what follows, I suggest that a careful reading of the "Xiaolun" reveals two particular topics to which Qisong attaches special importance when illustrating the essential identity of the two practices of filial devotion: first, he discusses it as an expression of one's feelings/emotions; second, as a source of moral values (Buddhist precepts and Confucian moral qualities). This part also addresses an issue mentioned in section I: the neglect of the practice of filial devotion by the young, newly ordained Buddhist monks.

III.1. Filial Devotion as Expression of Feelings/Emotions

In the scholar-monk's strategical comparison between Confucian and Buddhist filial devotion, the dimension of feelings/emotions is an essential starting point, as one of the major accusations addressed by Confucians to Buddhists is their apparent absence of emotions/feelings in general, and in particular their lack of filial sentiments toward parents, of attachment and helping behaviors in relations with parents. In Confucian culture, attachment and helping behaviors include living near the parents, regularly visiting with them, and actively providing caregiving. Confucians frequently blame Buddhists for no longer nourishing these kinds of feelings and behaviors after leaving their families (see, for instance, article fifteen about the primacy of the family in the *Mouzi lihuo lun*; Keenan 1994, 105). With the force of philosophical and historical arguments—stories about filial monks of the Tang dynasty recorded in Dao Xuan's 道宣 (596–667) *Xu gaoseng zhuan* 續高僧傳 (Continuation of biographies of eminent monks) and Zanning's 贊寧 (919–1001) *Song gaoseng zhuan* 宋高僧傳 (Biographies of eminent monks of the Song)—Qisong demonstrates that this Confucian criticism is unjustified.

Furthermore, he warns the young Buddhist monks who have left their families that they need to rectify their feelings/emotions (情可正), but they should not leave behind their parents (親不可遺) and ought to continue to help and serve them, as, for a monk, this is obligatory in order to quickly achieve the complete and correct way [enlightenment] (無上正真之道). The analysis developed in the previous sections makes clear why Qisong stresses this. In support of his opinion, he further cites a Buddhist text: "This is why the sutra says: 'The moral quality of filial devotion enables people to rapidly achieve the ultimate, correct and real way'" (故經曰:「使我疾成於無上正真之道者, 由孝德也。」; "XL" 1, 0660b19-12). The scholar-monk quotes here, without naming his source, paragraph 0438a24-12 of the *Pusa shanzi jing* 菩薩睒子經 (*Bodhisattva Syama Sutra*),[27] which recounts stories about former lives of the Buddha that encourage the practice of filial devotion. As argued below, the reason for this emphasis is that filial devotion is considered by the Chinese Buddhists as the real origin not only of all Buddhist precepts but also of all good deeds.

In the fifth section of his "Xiaolun," the author defines Buddhist practice as the "way of universal good deeds" (道之溥善). He rightly argues that for an authentic Buddhist's good actions to be universal—that is, complete and all embracing—they should naturally include their parents as recipients. Obviously, if a person excludes their parents from the recipients of their good actions, these actions are not universal (complete) anymore. In other words, the practice of filial devotion within one's family (even when one has left home to enter the Buddhist path), through their relationships with their own parents, is the necessary beginning of the Buddhist training to accomplish universal good deeds, which should be directed toward all sentient beings. In his view, leaving one's home (family) does not mean giving up on one's parents:

> The sage's [Buddha's] practice (*yong* 用) of the way (*dao* 道) consists of doing good deeds (*shan* 善). According to the sage, the commencement (*duan* 端) of doing good deeds is the practice of filial devotion. When one is [apparently] doing good deeds but without starting with their commencement, then no good deeds are done (為善而不先其端, 無善也). If one wants to follow the way, but without putting it into practice, then there is no way (為道而不在其用, 無道也). The practice (*yong* 用) serves to evaluate the effectiveness (*yan* 驗) of the way. The commencement launches the good deeds. Doing good actions which do not include the parents: can it be said that such good deeds are universal? Evaluating the effectiveness of the way, but without doing universal good deeds with this way: in this case, how can the effectiveness of the way be evaluated in practice? For this reason, the sage puts the way into operation through doing only good deeds (是故聖人之為道也, 無所不善). The sage does good deeds, starting with never giving up on his parents (聖人之為善也, 未始遺親). ("XL" 5, 0661a09)

In support of this interpretation, Qisong mentions as evidence the story of Buddha's life. Even after he had transcended the cycle of life and death, the scholar-monk relates in the same section ("XL" 5), Buddha still "responded to things" (應物) by following the way of humans (順乎人道). He forgot neither his dead mother nor his father's demands. After enlightenment, he returned to his country, discussed with his father the way that he had discovered, and promoted the transformation of all the people in his community; and at his father's funeral, he himself carried the coffin with his disciples. Because the Buddhist way is about doing universal good actions after leaving one's family, he adds, this practice begins with doing good deeds for one's parents, being involved in their care, and cultivating a sense of duty toward them and feelings of concern for their welfare.

In section 11 (0662a21), he presents several monks whose filial devotion is recorded in the *Chen shi lun* 成實論 (Treatise of establishing reality) and in the *Song gaoseng zhuan* 宋高僧傳 (Biographies of eminent monks of the Song; see Zhang 1996, 193–194, reference notes), completed at the end of the tenth century by the Buddhist scholar-official Zanning 贊寧 (919–1001). Qisong mentions the monk Daoji 道紀 from the Northern Qi dynasty (circa 550–577), who served his mother and carried her on his back (*Cheng shi lun*). He also recounts the story of Huineng 惠能 (638–713), the sixth Chan patriarch, presumed author of the *Platform Sutra*, who sold firewood to support his mother (*Platform Sutra of the*

Sixth Patriarch). The monk Daopi 道丕 (889–955), the scholar-monk narrates, lived during turbulent times, carried his mom on his back to escape war, and begged for food to feed her (Song gaoseng zhuan, quan 17). And the monk Zhizang 智藏 (458–522) served his master as if serving his own parents (Cheng shi lun).

In a very original way, most familiar to Confucian scholars, the scholar-monk interprets the reason for leaving one's family as proof of filial devotion. Thus, he presents the undertaking to leave one's family in order to accomplish the Buddhist way as a Buddhist counterpart of the Confucian duty to make one's parents illustrious (顯其親). Qisong takes up this idea highlighted in the *Xiaojing* 孝經 (*Classic of Filial Devotion*). Its first chapter defines "the highest level of filial devotion as fully cultivating oneself through following the [Confucian] way, gaining a reputation with future generations and making one's parents illustrious" (立身行道, 揚名於後世, 以顯父母, 孝之終也).

From his Buddhist perspective, the author of the essay "On Filial Devotion" conveys a similar meaning: "In order to make one's parents illustrious, the best way is to put into practice one's moral qualities" (顯其親德為優。; "XL" 10, 0662a02-6). He suggests in this manner that leaving one's family in order to achieve enlightenment and the Buddhist complete way is also a way to honor one's parents. Moreover, in the following excerpt, Qisong argues that this is a better way to fully cultivate oneself and bring one's parents wide recognition than "reporting to parents" (告)—in other words, than being in constant contact with one's parents, living with them, or visiting them regularly (i.e., that which is considered preeminent in Confucian family relationships). It is understood that "reporting to parents" designates an individual's full engagement in social relationships or the "way of humans," a Confucian form of filial devotion, focusing on what has been called "nurturing parents with food or physical care" (養). And he stresses that this is a limited form of filial devotion that does not permit one to achieve a complete way and a complete moral quality. It is understood that the Chan monk implies that Confucian social relationships do not leave any time for completing humans' cultivation. To achieve this goal, Qisong points out in the following paragraph, one has to detach temporarily from social relationships and go beyond them while in solitude (that is, purify oneself) to be able to return to them in a different way, transformed, with a broad, all-encompassing perspective:

> When only reporting to parents [being in regular contact] (告) the individual is unable to accomplish his way and moral quality (告則不得其道德). When not reporting [not in regular contact], one is able to accomplish one's way and one's complete moral quality. It is for this reason that the sage hides

himself in the forest (是故聖人輒遁于山林). After achieving the complete way, the sage returns to the world, propagates his moral quality throughout the whole society (逮其以道而返也, 德被乎上下), and people praise his moral quality by saying: "To have a son like this is a good fortune." And they honor his parents (尊其父母) by saying: "These are the parents of the great sage." It can therefore be said that the sage places less emphasis on the beginning [retreat from society and solitude] and that he focuses on results, on doing good deeds according to concrete circumstances (聖人可謂略始而圖終, 善行權也。). The exemplary men of Antiquity did this. Wu Taibo (吳泰伯)[28] was one example. Great determination (*da zhi* 大志) is required in order to develop substantial good behavior (*da yi* 大義). Great cleanliness (*da jie* 大潔) is required in order to uphold great righteousness (*da zheng* 大正). ("XL" 10, 0662a02-12)

The author highlights in this quotation the need to temporarily leave family and society not in order to abandon the sentiments concerning society and family, which express interrelatedness, but to clean oneself of self-absorbing emoting, nourish determination and firmness of purpose, and restrain one's impulses. In his view, all these qualities and skills can be acquired only through transformative retreat training. Once they are acquired, those who possess them can come back to community and family differently, with perfect moral qualities and clean sentiments. The latter have as defining characteristics their distinct emotive and behavioral states. In the next paragraph, he explains this in concrete terms by invoking positive emotions/feelings (i.e., emotive and behavioral states) familiar to Confucians, such as peacefulness and gentleness (*heping* 和平), symbolic of social unity and concord, as well as negative ones, such as angriness and quarrelsomeness or contentiousness (*fen zheng* 忿爭): "Relying upon filial devotion when living in the world (資其孝而處世) means to peacefully live with others, forgetting one's anger and quarrels (資其孝而處世, 則與世和平, 而亡忿爭也). Relying upon good actions when leaving the world (資其善而出世) means to be greatly compassionate (大慈) to the people and encourage them to do good deeds" ("XL" 8, 0661c10-14).

Here Qisong equally describes the moral efficiency of the true Buddhists, who, through each of their good deeds, promote the universal good. In this sense, he draws a parallel with the Confucian exemplary individuals of Chinese Antiquity such as the legendary Wu Taibo 吳泰伯, considered by Confucius a model of moral quality because he demonstrated filial devotion. Out of respect for his father's wishes, Wu Taibo renounced the throne three times and exiled himself far away, as a hermit, in an unknown land where he founded the Zhou state of Wu (see *Analects* 8.1). Obviously, it can be said that both Confucian and Buddhist approaches to filial devotion, to ethics and morality, are holistic. However, their natures are fundamentally different. The enlightened Buddhists feel the presence of all sentient beings within themselves, and this inner feeling of interrelatedness and no-self is the source of their good deeds. Qisong suggests this profound identity by stating that "the sage does not take into consideration his own direct descendants." Clearly, this is because all sentient beings are already his descendants. The Confucian holistically extends his moral quality and his self through putting himself in the position of others. In the following paragraph, after illustrating their different natures, Qisong emphasizes their similarities through drawing a parallel that is arguably striking and familiar to his contemporary Confucians:

> The sage aims to extend the wonderful moral quality to all the people and to heaven (聖人推勝德於人天), to make the complete and right moral quality manifest everywhere in the world (顯至正於九嚮). It is for this reason that the law of the sage does not consider his own direct descendants. The exemplary persons of Antiquity (古之君子) were able to show this example. For instance, the brothers Boyi and Shuqi 伯夷叔齊[29] were this kind of people. ("XL" 10, 0662a08-15)

When developing his particular view on Buddhist filial devotion, he infuses special meaning into the idea of leaving the family, leaving the world: this does not mean abandoning family and society but just leaving them temporarily in order to reenter them in a better state (morally and spiritually)—in other words, leaving them only for the duration of a training in retreat, which enables an individual to break the field of self-attachment, the ego, and the duality self-things and then reenter from the field of no-self, suchness, and nonduality. Symbolically, it can be said that "leaving the world" acquires in Qisong's thought the connotation of leaving the superficial field of self-attachment and, after the necessary retreat, embracing the world from the field of no-self. To realize this transformation, it takes the power to leave the world and the power to reenter it.

The question arises: if, as he mentions above, "achieving enlightenment and purifying one's feelings/emotions" is the Buddhist equivalent of the Confucian "cultivating oneself and gaining a reputation with future generations"—that is, accomplished filial devotion—how do the Buddhists concretely come back home to honor their parents ("make their parents illustrious") after achieving enlightenment and purifying their sentiments? In the next quotation, the scholar-monk provides his answer to this question by invoking an already existing Buddhist rule: "The Buddhist law teaches disciples that they can reduce part of the amount of money that should be remitted to the temple and instead give it to their parents and nurture them (養其父母). If one's parents are Buddhist believers, one can give them what one wants to give. If they are not believers, he should still give a bit. This rule already exists" ("XL" 5, 0661b01-9).

And again, he answers the same question ("What does it mean to reenter the world differently?") through giving an account of the story of the sixth patriarch, Huineng, the presumed author of the *Platform Sutra*, a scripture Qisong highly valued and for which he wrote a well-known encomium (discussed in chap. 6). One understands from the way in which the scholar-monk tells this story that Buddhist filial devotion implies a different way of practicing moral quality (異德; see next paragraph), one that presupposes this special training of leaving and reentering the world and is not accessible to ordinary people who have never left the world or the field of self-attachment. His story features another major sentiment, that of sadness or regret (*kai* 慨). It is worth noting the existence of a direct relation between it and the feelings of grief, sorrow, and mourning (哀戚; see *Xiaojing* 孝經 18), which are an expression of Confucian filial duty and of humans' moral quality:

> Huineng was selling firewood to support his mother (養其母). Before he finally decided to leave home to follow a master and practice, being afraid that his mother would not have food, he worked as a servant to earn money and gave it to her. When he finished his practice, his mother had already died. Full of sadness because it was too late to show her his way (慨不得以道見之), he transformed the place where his family lived into a temple, so he could do good deeds there (遂寺其家以善之) for the spirit of his deceased mother. Finally, he died in this place. It is for this reason that it is said that he was the falling leaf which returned to its root (葉落歸根). Master Huineng was someone who had achieved the complete way (became a complete individual) (能公, 至人也); how can ordinary people understand the distinctive [different] way in which he practiced the moral quality (其異德)? One could say that he showed people that he did not forget his root (猶示人而不忘其本也). ("XL" 11, 0662a23-16)

This story appears in the 1004 Song compilation *Jingde chuandeng lu* 景德傳燈錄上 (*Jingde Era Record of the Transmission of the Lamp*) juan 5, chapter "Di sanshisan zu Huineng dashi" 第三十三祖慧能大師 (Gu 2009, 249–254). The paragraph emphasizes a significant feeling—an individual's sadness and grief at his parents' death (慨). Qisong discusses it in the Buddhist context. His objective is to demonstrate that the common view is completely wrong when it considers Buddhists to lack emotions in general and this kind of feeling of grief as an expression of filial devotion in particular. The latter is considered a filial duty by the Confucians, and the classic *Xiaojing* 18 describes it as an integral part of the highest level (終) of filial reverence: "When their parents are alive they are served with love and respect and when they are deceased they are served with grief and sorrow" (生事愛敬, 死事哀戚).³⁰

The scholar-monk acknowledges that, as a matter of principle, the Buddhist teaching does not encourage the expression of one's feelings of grief and loss: "Shedding tears during the period of mourning is something that my teaching does not encourage. It wishes that people detach from feelings of love and hate, so that they rapidly find peace and tranquility (然喪制哭泣, 雖我教略之, 蓋欲其泯愛惡, 而趣清淨也。)" ("XL" 12, 0662b27). However, he makes a distinction between such kind sentiments generated by the attachment of the self to things and the grief over the loss of parents emerging from the fundamental connection between parents and children. He sees the latter as the archetype of the interdependence that links all sentient beings. It is arguable that Qisong wishes to point out the existence of a fundamental difference between the feeling of attachment to parents, from which emerges sorrow and bereavement and which is expressed and respected not only by Confucians but also by Buddhists, and the attachment to things, which arises from craving, from a contaminated, impure self, and is denounced by Buddhists.

In the next quotation, he finds another ingenious and efficient way, again familiar to Confucians, to defend the Buddhist position about showing pain when losing one's parents, arguing that Buddhism considers it just as important to acknowledge this expression of sorrow in a compassionate manner and pay due regard to it. To that end, he indirectly refers to the famous Mencian phrase (2 A.6) "everyone has a heart-mind which cannot bear the suffering of others" (人皆有不忍人之心)³¹:

> If one does not forget the feelings of love and hate, his heart-mind is still attached to things (苟愛惡未忘, 遊心於物). How can one feel at ease and bear to force such an individual [who has not yet forgotten the sentiments] to refrain from showing pain when mourning his parents (臨喪而弗哀, 亦人之安忍也)? [Qisong refutes here the Confucian criticism against Buddhist teaching that views it as forcing individual Buddhists to refrain from showing their pain.] It is for this reason that, when Buddha left for Nirvana, all his disciples beat their chests and lamented greatly. Their blood appeared like flowers of the flame tree. This [the appearance of the bloodlike flowers] is the reaction of a heart-mind [Buddha's] which cannot bear the suffering of others (蓋其不忍也). The School of Discipline (Vinaya) (律宗) says: "The heart-mind which does not manifest grief, for both religious and secular people, should be considered disgraceful" (不展哀苦者, 亦道俗之同恥也). Therefore, how could Buddhist followers not express their grief during the mourning period? ("XL" 12, 0662b28-4)

In the same section, Qisong also invokes as an argument the image of Mulian, Buddha's disciple Mahamaudgalyayana, stricken with grief and crying loudly when he could not feed his mother because she was reborn in the realm of hungry ghosts. The *Ullambana Sutra* says, "Before the rice reached her mouth it turned into a piece of burning charcoal, and she could not eat it at all" (0779a28).³² Mulian's story could equally be perceived as a challenge of the abovementioned Confucian presumption of the spontaneous continuity between generations during the performance of the ancestor cult ritual, when the spirits of the ancestors "naturally" arrive to receive offerings (i.e., no one questions the arrival of the spirits). If, due to a karmic result—the Buddhists warn—the ancestor is reborn as a hungry ghost, they are simply not able to receive the Confucians' food offerings.³³

The scholar-monk provides all these arguments as proof that the Buddhist followers also carry the feeling of sorrow and grief in their heart-mind for their deceased parents and teachers. His discussion of this emotion starts from recalling that the Confucians have reproached the Buddhists for not having this sentiment or for suppressing it. Next, he provides philosophical arguments and proof from the Chinese Buddhist scriptures that everyone naturally possesses this feeling and that nobody could justifiably ask one to repress it, as Confucians claim the Buddhists do. Qisong argues that nobody would do this because everyone has a heart-mind that cannot bear the suffering of others, as Mencius said as early as in the ancient times. Therefore, nobody (especially not the Buddhist master), when seeing another suffering, would add to it by insisting that she or he hide the suffering.

This subsection explored Qisong's argument that despite what Confucians say, Buddhists also nourish and express grief and sorrow as concrete manifestations of filial devotion, and it also examined his interpretation of the nature and depth of these emotions. The next part analyzes a parallel idea, which also proves the aforementioned similarity between the two teachings—his demonstration that filial devotion is a source of moral quality not only for Confucians but also for Buddhists. To that end, he points out that the Buddhist precepts essentially involve moral qualities and argues that the practice of filial devotion equates with the practice of the Buddhist precepts.

III.2. Filial Devotion as the Root of Moral Qualities/Precepts

In the opening of the *Xiaojing* 孝經 (*Classic of Filial Devotion*; hereafter *XJ*), Confucius stresses that filial devotion is "the root of all moral qualities" (夫孝, 德之本也) and that "out of it emerges education (teaching)" (教之所由生也; *XJ* 1). In other words, its constant cultivation forms the basis to completely acquire all moral qualities necessary for "ordering all of society, those above and those below" (上下治; XJ 16). As discussed earlier, the foundation of this Confucian inference is the belief in the resonance (感應; XJ 16) or extension (移; XJ 14) of familial harmony to the whole society, an assumption that the *Xiaojing* acknowledges. As discussed previously (see sec. II.1), the archetype for this extension is the dynamics of organic life, which spreads wider and multiplies, assuming new forms. For instance, the *Xiaojing* indicates that filial devotion within the family is the source of specific moral qualities, such as serving the sovereign with loyalty (忠) and elders with compliance (順; XJ 5), not being arrogant when in a high position (上不驕; XJ 10), not being mutinous when in a low position (下不亂; XJ 10), and not sending in the army to preserve reputation when humiliated (在醜不爭; XJ 10).

In reality, as already stressed, this Confucian belief in the extension of moral qualities from the inner circle (individual relationships with people one knows and appreciates, notably family members) to the outer (relationships with others, such as officials and members of the community) embodies a tension that Confucianism erases. In all epochs, outwardly putting into effect inward moral qualities (i.e., a good, kind, and loving husband, father, and son who is equally renowned for being a good, kind, and loving scholar-official, administrator, leader, etc.) as a means of assisting in the betterment of society was not as spontaneous as the spread of organic life—not even for an eminent person. Let's also recall the situation of the corrupt officials and factionalism during the eleventh-century Song dynasty, Qisong's epoch, as reported by Ouyang Xiu 歐陽脩 (1007–1072) in his memorial "On Factions" (see Liu 1967, 52–64). That many were focused on honors for themselves and their families and not on the common good was a well-known fact. In the twentieth-century context of Western culture, Felix Adler (1851–1933), founder of the Ethical Culture movement, clearly identified this difficulty of outwardly extending one's moral and supportive qualities expressed within one's family. He suggests that individual conscience is "divided," and therefore, to reconstruct a society, it is necessary to spiritually reconstruct its moral ideal. "By the divided conscience," Adler explains,

> I do not mean what is sometimes called the departmentalized conscience, or the arrangement, so to speak, of water-tight compartments in the inner life. Of that indeed we may see many examples, as in the case of persons who are fine and even exquisite in their private relations, but are hard as nails in business, unscrupulous partisans in politics, or lying diplomatists for their country's supposed good. But the intolerable strain of the divided conscience of which I speak is felt by men who are eagerly desirous to make their life

whole, all of a piece, of achieving consistence in their conduct throughout, and who do not see how to do it because they find that the ethical standard which they acknowledge in their private relations, and which they would like to expand so as to cover their business and professional relations, their conduct as citizens, is incapable of such expansion. (1929, 24)

And he acknowledges that "the same ethical principle must run like a golden thread through all human relations" (24–27). It is understood that this is what the Confucian ideal suggests. Confucius sought the spontaneously continuous, all-encompassing, and one-and-only moral ideal: "My way," he says, "is the one which connects everything" (吾道一以貫之。; *Lunyu* 4.15). Adler certainly would agree with this ideal; however, he would stress that for this to be possible, society would have to become a "commonwealth of spiritual beings" connected not by "social relations" but by "ethical relations." Adler defines the social relations as exchanges of egotisms, as "mutual dependence on the principle of Do ut des—I satisfy a certain want of yours on condition that you satisfy a certain want of mine" (1929, 65). "But the ethical relations," he elaborates, "in contradistinction to the social, is that in which the supreme interest of each individual is achieved in complete harmony with that of all the others. And let us be clear upon the point that such harmony has never been realized, that it is an ideal. No social relation has ever become a completely ethical relation, no social institution is worthy of being dignified as entirely ethical institution" (67). So he calls for discovering a new spiritual principle as a foundation for ethical relations. In a sense, this is exactly what Buddhism brought to Confucianism during the Song dynasty.

Qisong's Buddhist thought also values this unique moral ideal and the building of ethical relations through Buddhist precepts. In Adler's and Nishitani's terms, practice means for Qisong to break the field of the "divided conscience" and gain access to the field of no-self. For the scholar-monk, as for Confucians, the unique moral ideal and ethical relations have their source within filial devotion. Moreover, in the next paragraph, his perspective goes beyond seeing filial devotion merely as a source of ethico-moral practice. The scholar-monk describes it not as one of the Buddhist "great precepts" (大戒) but as their fountainhead, as their expression. The notion of precept, as will become clear below, implies a lot more than simply moral practice:

> You must have already heard that when the first Buddhist sage started to lay down the great precepts, he called filial devotion "the precepts" (即曰孝名為戒). He established filial devotion as the beginning *duan* (端) of these great precepts. The young followers [seemingly] obey them, but they ignore filial

devotion: in fact, in this case, they do not obey the precepts (子與戒而欲亡孝, 非戒也). Filial devotion is the source out of which emerge the great precepts (夫孝也者, 大戒之所先也). ("XL" 1, 0660b15-5)

Clearly, at the beginning of the above quotation, Qisong incorporates the following idea of the apocryphal *Brahma's Net Sutra*: "Sakyamuni Buddha first sat beneath the bodhi tree and achieved peerless enlightenment. [After this] his first act was to establish the Pratimoksa [encouraging his followers] to practice filial devotion and compliance (孝順) to parents, monk-teachers and the Three Treasures. Filial devotion and compliance is the law of the complete way, filial devotion means the precepts (戒), and also means restraint (孝名為戒, 亦名制止)" (1004a23-7).[34] One learns that in the context of Chinese Buddhism, Buddha laid down the great precepts with filial devotion as their source and encouraged the disciples to practice filial devotion. This is the archetype of ordaining an individual with the precepts—that is, with filial devotion. The precepts are transmitted through a lineage of teachers (see Groner 1990, 269). As established by the Buddha, these precepts have a nonperceptible dimension, as a force individuals receive from their masters at the time of their ordination with the precepts (monks, nuns, and lay practitioners; see the transmission of the precepts in the *Platform Sutra*, 0353b29). Another dimension of this strength is the vow from which it emerges. As Hirakawa Akira (1990, 191) notes, the precepts include a subtle essence (*jie ti* 戒體), which resembles unmanifested activity of karma as the force that joins actions with their karmic results but is different in certain ways. According to Qisong's interpretation of filial devotion, the observance of the precepts means the practice of filial devotion, and "filial devotion as [root of] the precepts" is essential to Buddhist practice and spiritual development. Hirakawa explains the essence-dimension of the precepts as a power that helps the individual ordained with the precepts refrain from doing wrong. In his Chinese cultural context, the Northern Song scholar-monk operates a major transformation to this traditional (Indian) Buddhist perspective that formulates a precept negatively, as a prohibition or restraint. In the next paragraph, he describes the precepts in a fundamentally positive way, formulating them not as restraining from doing evil but as karmic forces to perform good deeds and as karmic causes of those good deeds. In his view, the precepts are not a prohibition but constitute a positive power stimulating engagement in the world, which multiplies good deeds—with the practice of filial devotion as its source: "By following the precepts—this is how all good deeds are generated (眾善之所以生也). If one wants to do good deeds but without following the precepts—then, from where do the good deeds arise (為善微戒, 善何生邪)? If one wants to follow the precepts but without practicing filial devotion—then, from where do the precepts arise (為戒微孝, 戒何自邪)?" ("XL" 1, 0660b18-3).

It can be said, again, that this particular perspective operates a perfect fusion between Confucian and Buddhist practices. In the tenth section of the "Xiaolun," Qisong explains that doing good actions arises from following the precepts, which have as their source the practice of filial devotion. In other words, as already suggested, (the practice of) filial devotion means (the practice of) the precepts; when one practices filial devotion, one practices the precepts. Practice of the precepts is, in fact, expedient practice (善行權也; "XL" 10, 0662a06-12). The precepts are intended to benefit sentient beings, through the karmic potency they embody. Moreover, these good deeds stemming from (the practice of) "filial devotion as the precepts" are intended to benefit those to whom the follower owes debts of gratitude, starting with the parents and ending, obviously, with all sentient beings. The author of the "Xiaolun" presents this innovative argument to justify why good works begin with the parents: because not only are they "the root from which the living form is born, but also the embodiment, within the way of humans, of great kindness" (親也者, 形生之大本也, 人道之大恩也。; "XL" 5, 0661a14-13). Therefore, he adds in the same passage of section 5, "only the sage [Buddha] is able to attach due importance to this great root and repay the debt of gratitude for their great kindness" (唯大聖人為能重其大本也, 報其大恩也。; "XL" 5, 0661a15-11). It is comprehensible that to repay this debt means serving parents with a "great" filial devotion—in other words, in the author's Buddhist view, performing good works that benefit all. What exactly does performing Buddhist great filial devotion mean? Qisong answers this through making obvious allusion to the *Brahma's Net Sutra* (1007b27), the apocryphal scripture that presents the bodhisattva precepts or the great precepts: "The great precepts say: One should give parents, monks and teachers filial devotion and compliance. Giving filial devotion and compliance is the method to achieve the complete way (大戒曰: 孝順父母師僧, 孝順至道之法。)" ("XL" 2, 0660b01-2). Remember that he refers to the Buddhist "great precepts," the ones based on filial devotion expressed toward all sentient beings and on repaying a debt of gratitude toward parents and all sentient beings. The scholar-monk thus highlights the precepts as the embodiment of filial devotion expressed, first, toward parents and, second, toward all sentient beings. The practice of the precepts in his thought has a particular meaning. It is not merely observing a set of prohibitions against immoral behavior but the expression of repaying a debt of gratitude to parents and sentient beings. In addition, as mentioned above, the scholar-monk highlights the precepts not as restrictive but in a positive light as a karmic force that constantly guides individuals' conduct (physical, verbal, and mental), therefore providing continuity of their good actions.

But this is not the only perception of the precepts in Qisong's thought. The next paragraph presents another dimension of them that he builds within the context of his Confucian culture: interpreting the precepts as practice aimed at "making one's parents illustrious" (*xian* 顯). In this perspective, he intimately connects Buddhist precepts with Confucian moral qualities in a way particularly appealing to the scholar-officials. To this end, he associates the Five Precepts (*wu jie* 五戒) for lay followers with the five Confucian moral qualities. The correlation appears in several different sources before the Song dynasty (see Ch'en 1973, 55–60). This strategy allows him to set aside the traditionally conceived prohibitive nature of the Buddhist precepts and reconstruct them as facilitative of active engagement within society and of the expression of filial devotion:

> The Five Precepts begin with the first which is "do not kill," followed by the second which is "do not steal," the third—"do not engage in licentious behavior," the fourth—"do not make comments that are false," the fifth—"do not drink intoxicating drinks" (五戒, 始一曰不殺, 次二曰不盜, 次三曰不邪淫, 次四曰不妄言, 次五曰不飲酒). Not killing is the moral quality of kindness (*ren* 仁); not stealing is the moral quality of fostering appropriate behavior (*yi* 義); not engaging in licentious behavior is the moral quality of ritual propriety (*li* 禮); not being intoxicated is the moral quality of knowledge [discerning what is right and what is wrong] (*zhi* 智); not making comments that are false is the moral quality of fidelity to one's pledged word (*xin* 信). When the individual cultivates the five precepts, he becomes an accomplished individual and makes his parents illustrious (是五者修, 則成其人, 顯其親). Is this not filial devotion? ("XL" 7, 0661b21)

Qisong's school of Chan stresses the spiritual importance of the practice of the precepts. This emphasis on moral and ethical practice is a significant dimension of his thought and one that was not preserved in what became the surviving Chan schools (Linji and Caodong). Contrary to his nonfactional perspective embracing all teachings, the members of the Linji school, which gained predominance, were looking to cement their own unique and separate identity, which did not focus on this major feature of Chinese culture—interrelational ethico-moral practice.

As seen above, the scholar-monk concentrates on the interpretation of the precepts as filial devotion. That is to say, a person practices the latter not only to take care of and protect their parents and all sentient beings but also to honor their parents. It is easy to see how Qisong weaves together Buddhist and Confucian moral values in this coherent articulation of the precepts as filial devotion. The result is a Song-dynasty Buddhist texture imbued with Confucian moral values, a Buddhist voice with Confucian tonalities. What is particularly striking in his philosophical development is his consistent extension of the Confucian notion of filial devotion ("great filial devotion") and of the Buddhist moral concept of the precepts ("great precepts"). It may be said that his strategy really calls on Confucian scholars, addresses them in their own language on how Confucianism could be made broader, more encompassing, and enriched with new perspectives, and thus induces them to think more deeply about the shortcomings of their own tradition and how to address them from within, as well as about a possible conciliation with Buddhism.

IV. CONCLUSION

In the following autobiographical passage found in the preface, the scholar-monk confesses that in this essay "Xiaolun" 孝論 ("On Filial Devotion") he shows his own heart-mind (示其心; see his vision of the heart-mind in chap. 3, sec. III.2, and chap. 5). That is to say, the essay is not simply a theoretical, philosophical, emotionless argumentation but is based on his own feelings and experiences and the events of his time. He writes that it was his dying father's wish that he become a monk. Qisong was seven years old at that time, and his mother supported this wish and his Buddhist way, even when other members of his family wanted him to abandon it and embrace a Confucian education and career. He was grateful his mother had encouraged him to pursue the Buddhist path. Through recounting significant episodes of his life and sharing his story, he concretely illustrates with his own personal experiences all the salient dimensions of his interpretation of a Buddhist filial devotion possessing all the essential Confucian resonances—his desire to return home, take care of his parents' grave, and conduct commemorative ceremonies for them; his feelings of grief that Buddhist duties were keeping him away from home; and the decision to replace these unfulfilled fundamental duties with the writing of this piece, thus expressing his filial devotion and honoring his parents through his essay:

> Twenty-seven years have passed since I left my old village. Every moment I wanted to return south to clean the tomb of my parents and perform commemorative ceremonies for their spirits. I could not fulfill my wish. In

1051, because of the fact that I was developing Buddhism, I was faced with misfortune. The next year, my village was stormed by bandits. How could my parents' tomb not have suffered from this robbery? When I look to the south, I could not stop my tears from falling. Still, a year after, more things have happened. All this has deeply touched my heart. Thus, I wrote the twelve sections of the "Xiaolun" to show my heart. ("XL" 0660b04-11)

This fourth chapter continues the analysis of his novel Chan Buddhist interpretation of major Confucian terms. It exposes not only Qisong's particular way of demonstrating the complementarity between Confucianism and Buddhism and advocating the efficient assistance that the latter can provide Confucians to help them preserve the peace and order of society, but also his explicit intention of explaining the subtleties of his cohesive Chan Buddhist practice to his Song Confucian interlocutors.

As discussed above, this chapter focuses on the "Xiaolun." This essay introduces in his progressive argumentative architecture a new and essential notion and practice, the origin of which is, of course, Confucian: the Buddhist practice of filial devotion. It comprises a higher level of complexity than the previous chapters because the exposition of the differences between Confucian and Buddhist filial devotion (he argues that the first is partial, while the latter is complete; the first is limited to the ethico-organic level, while the latter is ethico-spiritual) constitutes the context that enables Qisong to present and focus in depth on complex Chan Buddhist notions such as the Buddhist interrelatedness of all sentient beings, karma, the rectification of feelings/emotions, the interpretation of the Buddhist precepts as filial devotion, and their practice as connected with the five Confucian moral qualities.

The focus changes radically in this chapter from Confucian practice and meanings to Chan Buddhist training and signification, and this in the context of a major Confucian concept: filial devotion. In Buddhism this is a less understood and developed practice, and a matter on which concentrates the Confucians' criticism aimed at Buddhism as destructive of traditional familial relations. By explaining the Buddhist understanding of filial devotion, Qisong efficiently refutes Confucian disapproval and, even more importantly, contributes to developing its comprehension and practice within Buddhism.

After having built a concrete proximity—several bridges between Buddhism and Confucianism, starting from specific Confucian concepts, filial devotion included—the next chapter further explores the scholar-monk's cohesive Buddhist interpretation of major Chan topics, destined for his Confucian interlocutors: the interdependence life-death, heart-mind (心), emotions/feelings (情),

and nature-emptiness (性). Chapter 5 further develops Qisong's presentation of complex Chan notions intended for Confucian scholars and constructs the scholar-monk's cohesive perspective, through gathering and interpreting together paragraphs from "Yuanjiao," "Guan yuanjiao," and "Quanshu," which all address these major Chan "technical" terms.

FIVE

HEART-MIND (*XIN* 心), EMOTIONS (*QING* 情), AND NATURE-EMPTINESS (*XING* 性) IN QISONG'S THOUGHT

A Song-Dynasty Interpretation of Cohesive Chan Practice Intended for Confucian Scholars

THIS CHAPTER PRESENTS AND FURTHER analyzes Qisong's innovative interpretation of the meaning and dimensions of Chan practice, for which he relies on the interdependent concepts of heart-mind (*xin* 心) and its two associated correlatives—emotions (*qing* 情) and nature (*xing* 性). It is worth repeating that he gradually expounded this interdependence as the main expression of the distinctive character of Chan Buddhism in his *Fujiao bian* 輔教編 (*Essays on Assisting the Teaching*).

In Confucian tradition, the nature is regarded in human, interrelational perspective, while in the scholar-monk's Confucianized Chan, it is regarded simultaneously in social and transcendent perspectives. This chapter focuses on his understanding of the spiritual, transcendent, not self-centered core of the nature. Within the nature, the emotions are distorted by the arousal of self-centered personal desires. When individuals are able to crack the wall that limits their self-consciousness and thus experience their own "nature-emptiness" and "no-self" (i.e., the self connected with everything), a profound transformation occurs: one's emotions become not contaminated and nondistorted; one is spontaneously pure not only at the social level of everyday ethical interactions but also at the spiritual/religious level of the interconnection between one's past, present, and future lives, of the karmic causes and fruits.

I. INTRODUCTION: AN INTERPRETATION OF CHAN BUDDHISM INTENDED FOR CONFUCIAN SCHOLARS

Qisong outlines the significance of the correlation emotions/nature as the core of what he distinguishes as the essential Buddhist interdependence—life, death, nature, and sentiments. It is arguable that he chooses to put forward this peculiar association not only to highlight the functioning of the Buddhist karmic law, of karmic causes and fruits, but also to build a link between (Chan) Buddhism and Confucianism. And he uses the latter as a pedagogical method intended to help Confucians understand Buddhism. The terms in which he presents the spirit of his teaching in the following quotation—namely, the importance of people's lives as matrices of relating, of their emotions as derived from the relationships between them, and of the sage who founds the teaching in order to educate them—also convey significant topics of interest for Confucians. In fact, all the concepts he refers to are woven into the fabric of human relationships, which is the material society is made of:

> All the myriad things have their nature and emotions (萬物有性情). From early times right up to the present day, there is death and there is life. However, since the beginning, death, life, nature and emotions have existed in interdependence (相因而有之). Death is certainly caused by life, life is certainly caused by emotions, the emotions are certainly caused by nature (死固因於生, 生固因於情, 情固因於性). The reason the myriad things are continuously submerged within the cycle life-death is because of the emotions. Only the sage with his penetrating vision (大觀) sees the causes from before the present life, advises people about what happens after death, shows them what they will become after death (乃推其因於生之前, 示其所以來也, 指其成於死之後), and teaches them what they should cultivate now. ("Yuanjiao" [hereafter "YJ"], 0648c25)

In the essay "Quanshu," the scholar-monk implicitly reveals that his objective is to tackle and challenge a common view, widespread during the Northern Song dynasty and after. According to it, Confucianism is a comprehensive doctrine, able to provide answers to all questions, regardless of their different political, social, psychological, or spiritual natures:

> People say: "I have read for quite some time now the books of our Confucians and I have understood for quite some time their concept of heart-mind (心). I also read Li Ao's 李翱 (772–841) essay *Fuxing shu* 復性書 [On returning to nature][1] and I also grasped its meaning. So, I do not need to seek these things in Buddhism." I answer: "To quench one's thirst, one does not need to choose a particular well to drink from. To appease one's hunger, one does not need to select a specific kitchen to eat in. When the individual is really aware of his heart-mind, he is doing good deeds and is not confused. That is a good thing. (得子審其心, 為善不亂可也.) Why push people to follow my way? It is not necessary." ("Quanshu" [hereafter "QS"] 1, 0652c10-16)

By drawing on what is universally human—the sense of hunger and thirst, wanting to cease suffering from hunger or thirst, and eating or drinking—processes vital to sustaining or maintaining life, he stresses that, as long as a particular teaching leads people to do good deeds, this teaching is valuable; therefore, all methods (Confucian, Buddhist, or other) that lead to this result are equally beneficial. His stance may be understood as an effort to promote the integration of Buddhism within the context of the centralized and homogenizing Confucian culture, through emphasizing that the two practices, although different, achieve the same result of making people good.

His statement also offers evidence that, beyond this official uniformizing view that required the general adoption of Confucian practices at all levels of society, Confucian scholars such as Li Ao, who studied Buddhism with the Tang-dynasty Chan monk Yaoshan Weiyan 藥山惟儼 (745–827),[2] had a deep knowledge of Chan Buddhist teaching. Thus, the scholar-monk aims to effectively demonstrate the complementarity between the two teachings, the fact that Confucianism needs the assistance of Buddhist teaching to the same extent as Buddhism needs the support of Confucian scholars. His essays focus on the first aspect—that is, the usefulness of Chan Buddhist practice for assisting Confucians in the ordering of society. The second aspect of this complementarity—namely, what Confucians can offer to Buddhist practice—is best embodied according to Qisong in the ninth-century work of the Confucian scholar Li Ao: "When I obtained Mr. Li's article, I read it attentively. Its profound meaning truly resembles the Buddhist sutras (其微旨誠若得於佛經), but the concrete form of the article and of the citations is different (文字與援引為異). It seems that Buddhism also needs to be promoted by the Confucian exemplary man's (jun 君) explanations" ("QS" 1, 0652c17-5). It is therefore arguable that Li Ao's work was a source of inspiration for him. The Tang-dynasty Confucian scholar emphasized the divergence between nature and emotions, and, as discussed in this chapter, Qisong in his own work also takes over this articulation already relevant for Confucians and develops it from a cohesive Chan perspective.

Undoubtedly, through this interpretive strategy that sheds light on the Chan Buddhist view using familiar Confucian concepts, he succeeded in advancing (that is, "assisting" (fu 輔), as the title of his collection Fujiao bian suggests) his own teaching, which was flourishing in the Confucian environment some one hundred years after the last Buddhist persecution. The latter had taken place in 955 during the short reign of the Later Zhou–dynasty emperor Shizong 世宗 (r. 954–959). Moreover, this chapter further argues that, in doing so, Qisong not only supported Chan practice within this Song-dynasty Confucian culture but also reinterpreted Chan Buddhism in the light of the distinctive feature of

Confucian society: a focus on interpersonal relationships and duty or responsibility to others, family, and community at large. He uses this framework in an original way to detail in concrete terms the Mahayana ideal of the bodhisattva's practice. It should also be noted that, as examined elsewhere (see chap. 2), the scholar-monk undertakes the specific task of presenting the unitary essence of Buddhism, or its root, in a nonsectarian (i.e., cohesive) way. The next section examines the particular context within which he builds his cohesive Chan perspective on emotions and nature: the spiritual feature of human beings.

II. THE SPIRITUAL DIMENSION OF HUMAN BEINGS

The Chan scholar-monk points out that the core intention of his account of cohesive Chan is to "warn people" about the existence of a spiritual dimension of the world and to provide evidence of it. Thus, in the "Quanshu," he advises about the presence within every human being of a spiritual consciousness (神明) that subsists through successive lives and of a spiritual quintessence (靈) that is not merely human but shared by all sentient beings. Qisong spells out the reasons for his warning about the presence, indestructibility, and functioning of this aspect—first, it befits one to respect and cultivate this dimension, as it influences one's future lives; and second, it is incumbent on one to value and assist all other humans, as everyone is endowed with this spiritual quintessence:

> Today, what makes human beings human beings, is the entry of a spiritual consciousness [awareness] (神明) into the corporeal form. The way the spiritual consciousness passes from individual [body and birth] to individual is much like the way a human changes residence [houses] (亦猶人之移易其屋廬).... I have written these essays because I want to warn people (今為書而必欲勸之者). I do not merely promote Buddhism, but I warn every Confucian exemplary man (*jun* 君) that all humans are endowed with a spiritual quintessence (稟靈為人), and that humans are the most important among sentient beings. ("QS" 2, 0653b13-14)

Moreover, his warning also implies that Confucian teaching does not possess a religious (spiritual) dimension comparable to that of Buddhism, hence the importance of explaining this feature to Confucians. The Buddhist perception of life is based on a spiritual foundation, subsistent from one life to another—in other words, connecting past, present, and future lives and affecting them through the functioning of an "infra-memory," a consciousness that stores "hidden merits" (陰德; see below), whereas the Confucian view is a morality-centered one that focuses on the present life. This ethico-moral feature is mainly expressed through Confucian mores, beliefs, and traditions—that is, ritual. In this way, Qisong exposes issues familiar to Confucians, such as emotions and human nature, in a spiritual light.

To that end, he describes the purpose of his writings in connection with this religious dimension based on trust in the continuity of lives and karmic causality: warning and persuading people of their continuous existence amounts for him to convincing them to accomplish good deeds and avoid evil ones in order to ensure now an improvement in their future lives. Because he addresses a Confucian audience that officially avoids discussion of obscure things such as passing from death to life and supernatural beings (死生鬼神; see the following quotation) and focuses on concrete human relationships, he labels the issues that form part of the spiritual dimension as "indistinct" (惚恍) and chooses not to discuss them directly in abstract, metaphysical language but within the context of ordinary human affairs (人事), in terms of people's good fortune and merit. Obviously, he proceeds in this way in order to have a stronger impact on his Confucian auditors and connect with them. As a result, Qisong's Chan viewpoint focuses on human affairs understood in terms of social interaction, emotional states, and good and evil deeds. He considers the latter from the Chan perspective as the complex processes associated with the triad of physical actions, words, and thoughts.

Thus, in his hermeneutical explanation of cohesive Chan Buddhism intended for Confucians, the scholar-monk innovatively and pertinently connects the Confucian notions of daily human affairs and social interaction with the Buddhist concept of deeds assessed at three different levels, each of them carrying karmic imprints: physical actions, words, and thoughts (see his explanation of the Five Precepts and Ten Goods in chap. 1, sec. III.1). To that effect, he provides a striking example of adverse effects concerning a specific issue that was regularly on the agenda of Confucians—their criticism against Buddhism. In the light of this spiritual dimension, people's correct and incorrect appraisals of others' acts, as well as of other schools of thought and other practices, may influence (diminish) the appraisers' "hidden merits and good fortune." In the case of Confucians, he comments, their appraisal is fraught with more serious consequences than those of ordinary people. Evidently, this is so since it is they who govern and influence people to follow their example. Thus, he warns,

> Supernatural beings and the passing from death to life are indistinct things (死生鬼神之惚恍). I am not myself expert enough to talk about them. Further on I will discuss them starting from the issue of human affairs (ren shi 人事),

hoping that this will help you a little bit to understand these indistinct things. Concerning the words you use, they must encourage people to behave well and to avoid evil conduct (所以勸善而沮惡). It can be said that some people do good deeds and some evil deeds. Whether your evaluative comments [about people's deeds] are accurate or not—this in the end will change your hidden merits (則損益歸乎陰德) [one has to read "change" as "diminish," as he implicitly refers here to Confucians' criticism against Buddhism, which he considers as partisan and unjustified]. Nowadays, when people want to insult others (辱人) with their words, they should think this way: This individual has good fortune and merit (彼福德人也). I must not insult him, because if I do so, I destroy my good fortune (折吾福矣). Therefore, Buddha, even if he is not on equal footing with all sages and eminent individuals of this world, is he less than equal with the ordinary people who have good fortune [happiness] and merit? Now, if you insult Buddha, all people after you will follow your example (百世效之). Look how this diminishes your hidden merits. It is better to think a little more deeply about this. ("QS" 2, 0653b24-12)

This paragraph from the "Quanshu" states Qisong's intention to focus on explaining the spiritual in his interpretation of Chan Buddhism and suggests his method—to use topics familiar to the Confucians—but it also illustrates his, so to speak, bodhisattva goal. With his teaching and warnings, the Chan scholar-monk wishes to protect Confucians from diminishing their good fortune and merits, through making them understand that their criticism against Buddhism might be biased and all the more injurious because of their official position. In the long run, their actions—that is, this criticism—is not harmless or without consequences but wrong and detrimental to Buddhism. Such deeds oriented toward a school and its practical methods might decrease Confucians' good fortune and hidden merits as well.

All the abovementioned notions belonging to the sphere of the spiritual dimension of life in his Chan Buddhist view are further examined in detail. The theoretical structure of this philosophical investigation is inspired by the work of the Chan Buddhist philosopher Keiji Nishitani. His philosophy and its connection with the Northern Song scholar-monk's work are explored in the next section.

II.1. Applying Nishitani's Theoretical Structure to Address Qisong's Spiritual Dimension

In his work *Religion and Nothingness*, Nishitani focuses on the notion of "emptiness" and on the distinction between the "field of (self)consciousness" and the "field of emptiness" (1982, 105–112). This analysis first links his concept of "field of (self)consciousness" with Qisong's apprehension of "emotions." Second, it relates Nishitani's "emptiness" and "field of emptiness" to the scholar-monk's notions of nature and emptiness.

What the Japanese philosopher calls the "field of (self)consciousness" or the "field of reason" of the human is centered on the self. In Buddhist terms, the self is the set of experiential faculties—that is, the five skandhas of form (*se* 色), sensation (*shou* 受), perception (*xiang* 想), volition (*xing* 行), and consciousness (*shi* 識; see the *Heart Sutra*).[3] This independent self (reason) is therefore responsible for addressing phenomena and relating with them from the standpoint of the self and using itself (this collection of faculties) as a frame of reference and mediator between one's deeds and external reality. This mediation presupposes duality, separation, or opposition between subject or within (self) and object or without (phenomena). Usually, human beings are limited to this field. Nishitani argues that because in this sphere human reason is the absolute and independent authority, at this level the relationship between individual and external world is established by means of concepts and representations. This type of relationship regulates a person's actions and their building of discursive knowledge. The mediation work of the independent self presupposes attachment: the self constantly engages in making choices and showing preferences between likes and dislikes. Therefore, at this level, "things do not truly display their reality to us," in their suchness (Nishitani 1982, 9, 34, 60). In what follows, this area is connected with Qisong's understanding of the emotions.

Nishitani discusses the existence within each human being of another field—namely, the ground of the human being. The individual shares it with all other beings, human and nonhuman. On this ground, things are as they are in themselves and not as they seem to appear as objects of representation, as "objectivized external realities" (Nishitani 1982, 110) selected by the individual self. Here they stand together with the human being in a nondual way. Deep inside, as the foundation of the field of consciousness, this field is that of the "non-selective" non-ego, the state of emptiness or lack of selfishness, to which one normally cannot have direct access. Only after having breached the field of (self-)consciousness can one gain access to it, when "from ever deeper within the soul itself, the element of self is broken through again and again" (62). "Emptiness" (that is, being emptied of the individual self) as a description of the distinctive feature of the state individuals achieve when they reach down to this innermost level refers to the "non-selective non-ego," or the nondiscursive awareness that is different from representation and arises from direct experience of the original nonseparation or interrelatedness between subject and object, between humans and their external world. According to Nishitani, when a person is able to reach this inner field, they become awake to "the mode of being of things when they are what they are in themselves, on their own homeground, cut off from the sort of being reflected in the subject-object relation" (112). Emptiness therefore relates to a so-called nondual action or knowledge, the nature of which is different from that of the dualist (subject-object) and discursive ones. Nondual in this context means not two (no separation between subject and object) but also not one (no fusion of initially separated subject and object). Nishitani's field of emptiness is connected here with Qisong's explanation of the nature of human beings.

The analysis presented in the next section suggests that the main issue interpreted by the author in *Fujiao bian* is the spiritual dimension of Chan Buddhist practice, and it examines his arguments using Nishitani's philosophical theory of the field of emptiness defined in relation to the field of self-consciousness referred to above. First, it explores the scholar-monk's understanding of the notion of heart-mind (*xin* 心) as the repository of this spiritual dimension, the nourishing soil and place of practice of Chan. Second, it clarifies his perspective on the constant functioning of this spiritual element in the everyday life of ordinary people by illuminating his specific correlation between one's nature (*xing* 性) and emotions (*qing* 情) as the nondual correlation between the spiritual "field of emptiness" and the everyday "field of (self)consciousness." Lastly, out of this articulation nature/emotions, the analysis develops an interpretation of Qisong's conceptual milieu of the spiritual: the causal link (*ye* 業) between deeds (causes, *yin* 因) and their consequences (fruits, *guo* 果) and the related notion of retribution (*bao ying* 報應). In this hermeneutical process, the next section uncovers and explains the new inspiration he drew from the Confucian classics while working out a comparative method to persuasively demonstrate to his auditors the complementarity between Buddhism and Confucianism.

II.2. *The Inner Place of the Chan Way of the Spirit (神道): The Heart-Mind*

Qisong perceives the inner dimension (內) of the human being—that is, the heart-mind, a distinguishing feature of Chan Buddhism—as the soil that the individuals cultivate, the place where they sustain a spiritual practice or way (神道). In the next paragraph, he defines Chan as a "teaching based on the way of the spirit" (神道設教), which operates inside the human being by inducing inner stimuli (感內). The way of the spirit prompts one's heart-mind to move and therefore correct itself (心化) through inducing from inside the heart-mind what could be referred to as inner stimuli: "Controlling the outside (制其外) must follow the way [method] of humans (人道); otherwise, one cannot succeed. Inducing an inner stimulus (感其內) must follow the way of the spirit (神道); otherwise, one cannot change and correct one's heart-mind. Therefore, the Buddhist way (故佛之為道也) must first focus on human spirit (神), and only after, on human behavior (人). This means first inducing an inner stimulus and after controlling the outside (感內而制外)" ("YJ," 0650b20-5).

He highlights in this paragraph of the "Yuanjiao" the distinction between teaching based on the way of the spirit and teaching based on the way of humans (人道設教). The latter, the author notes, controls the human being from the outside, through regulating one's outer behavior. One implicitly recognizes in this "way of humans" a reference to Confucian teaching. The twentieth paragraph of the *Zhongyong*, for example, extensively discusses this way of humans. Qisong paid particular attention to this classic and dedicated to it a special commentary, the *Zhongyong jie*. Furthermore, in the passage above, he implicitly suggests that the two teachings are not separate but convergent and that the Buddhist one encompasses the "outer, individual's behavior," but from the perspective of his spirit. In the next citation, the scholar-monk explains what the spirit or spiritual quintessence (精神) is, how it is different from the ancient Chinese notion of "ghosts and spirits" (鬼神), and that Buddhist teaching is about cultivating this quintessence:

> The spirit (神) means the quintessential spirit (精神)[4] of the human being; this is not something concerning the ghosts and spirits (鬼神) who mislead the people. This means that, if one cultivates (修) one's quintessential spirit, then he can exhibit good behavior (人修其精神, 善其履行). During his life, the individual receives good fortune [happiness] (福); at his death, the spirit rises in purity. When one does not cultivate one's quintessential spirit (精神不修), one practices evil and aberrant things (履行邪妄); then, life is not a time to celebrate, and after death, his spirit is punished. When ordinary people hear this [teaching], their heart-minds are moved (心感動) to stop doing evil deeds and to pursue good deeds (惡者沮而善者如之). Thus, they transform/correct themselves silently (默化). This transformation has been present for generations. ("YJ," 0650b23-9)

In short, he teaches that Chan Buddhism is about changing and correcting the heart-mind and about cultivating the human spiritual essence (quintessential spirit). This spirit is obviously related to the heart-mind. He notes that the "way of the spirit" of Chan teaching focuses on cultivating the spirit, cultivating the heart-mind. In his view, the Chan Buddhist way of the spirit (神道) is not something different and separate from other ways but constitutes their common root. It therefore englobes the Confucian way of humans (人道), in the sense that becoming aware of a spiritual dimension makes the Confucian way deeper and more efficient. Through the idea that all the various teachings have a common root—the way of the spirit—not only does he teach inclusiveness (cohesiveness), in contrast to what could arguably be regarded as sectarian Buddhism and exclusive Confucianism, but he also provides a concrete manner for practicing any particular way or method at a deeper level—namely, the heart-mind level or the field of emptiness:

> Among the sages' different teachings (教) there are the way of the spirit (神道), the way of humans (人道), the ordinary morality (常德), and the highest morality (奇德). We cannot consider only one of these dimensions and think that this is all (不可以一概求), and we cannot evaluate them using popular opinion. One acquires everything when one's heart-mind fully understands and is connected with everything (得在於心通). One misses everything when one focuses on the differences between the footprints [of the different teachings] (失在於迹較). ("Guang yuanjiao" [hereafter "GYJ"], 0654c26-1)

Obviously, he seeks here to raise awareness among the Confucian rulers about the importance of governing using the "way of the spirit." He explains this as nothing else than taking the Confucian governance method of the "way of the human" regarded by Confucians as reflecting the natural "way of heaven" and instead considering it from the broader and complete perspective of the "way of the spirit." In Qisong's view, the latter is the profound, universal root of all teachings, including the Confucian way, which he perceives as deficient and narrow because it is limited to the Chinese (Han) human order. To that effect, he presents the following argument advocating good governance that is envisaged not merely from the limited human perspective but from the spirit, which embraces every other form of existence and is present in everything, all sentient beings, human as well as nonhuman, Chinese and non-Chinese. From his viewpoint, only in this way can the ruler be assured that he is taking care of all beings, human and nonhuman, that his governing is all-encompassing, and that he leaves no one outside the scope of his guiding. The scholar-monk evidently assumes that a Confucian will pay attention to such consideration, as it relates to the overall efficiency of ruling all the people of the empire (Han and non-Han):

> Those endowed with the spiritual quintessence (*ling* 靈) are dispersed everywhere in the sky and on the earth, in the dark and in the light, among foreigners in the East, the *Yi* (夷), and foreigners in the North, the *Di* (狄), among the birds and beasts (禽獸). If not governed using the way of the spirit, from the early days until now, there are probably sentient beings left abandoned (有棄物). The sage attaches great importance to the fact that all

things have the same spiritual quintessence (重同靈). Because he is afraid that he may lose some of them (懼遺物也), the sage carries out his work using the way of the spirit. ("GYJ," 0655a15-14)

Consequently, the topic of good governance based on the way of the spirit goes back to the question: What does this way of the spirit mean in practice, in the author's view? A close investigation of the essays of the *Fujiao bian* shows that for him, the starting point and core of this peculiar way is the notion of heart-mind. In the "Guang yuanjiao" (0654b24), speaking to Confucians, the scholar-monk explicitly describes the heart-mind—the central concept of the Chan universe—as intrinsically related to the way (道). While he defines the latter as intrinsic brightness or luminosity (that is, the most wide, extensive, and spiritual brightness (廣大靈明)), Qisong describes the heart-mind as the functioning or putting into practice of this spiritual brightness (that is, the most spiritual, moral, and marvelous functioning (神德妙用)). Therefore, in his view, the way and the heart-mind are one and the same; they are different manifestations—essential brightness (明) and functioning (用)—of the same entity, namely, the way/heart-mind or root of sentient beings.

In the following paragraph, it is noted that he describes the relationship between "heart-mind" (心), "way" (道), and "[Chan Buddhist] teaching" (教) (provided by the sage) through borrowing the structure of the first paragraph of the classic *Zhongyong* (天命之謂性, 率性之謂道, 修道之謂教。), where the ancient Confucians define the relationship between "nature" (性) (conferred by heaven), "the way" (道), and "[Confucian] teaching" (教):[5]

> Relying upon the heart-mind is the so-called way; explaining the way is the so-called teaching (惟心之謂道, 闡道之謂教). The teaching includes all the trails (footprints) left behind by the sage; the way is the great root of all sentient beings (教也者, 聖人之垂迹也; 道也者, 眾生之大本也). Sentient beings have long forgotten their root; the sage no longer appears [in the world] and all sentient beings have come to be ignorant (萬物終昧). What the sage did was to greatly enlighten all the myriad beings (萬物大明). ("GYJ," 0654b24)

Again, in the same paragraph of the "Guang yuanjiao," in Confucian *guwen* style, he strategically adopts the structure of the argumentation of the *Zhongyong* 1 and adapts it to the Chan Buddhist context (see below). Here, Qisong expresses his nondualistic idea that the way is the spiritual essence of the heart-mind and the heart-mind is the functioning of the way. In other words, because the heart-mind includes everything, nothing is outside of the way: "The heart-mind has no outside, the way is invariably inclusive; therefore, there is no thing isolated from the way" (心無有外, 道無不中, 故物無不預道). It is worth noting the correspondence between his idea of the all-encompassing heart-mind and the ancient Confucian conception of the all-inclusiveness of the way conveyed in the *Zhongyong* 1: "One cannot be separated from the way—never, even for a moment; that from which one can be separated is not the way" (道也者, 不可須臾離也, 可離非道也).[6] It is important to observe, however, that the scholar-monk specifies the correspondence way/heart-mind as a nondual reality—that is, as a unique way/heart-mind shared by everyone at a spiritual level—while Confucians make reference to a way that encompasses (manages) all the different and individualized paths corresponding to all the different individuals and their distinct positions within society.

According to him, finding the forgotten way is none other than becoming aware of the heart-mind—the great spiritual root of all sentient beings, including humans. In the next citation, he clearly focuses on the Chan religious meaning of this notion—namely, the abovementioned nondualistic understanding, which goes beyond the logic of mutual exclusion and conveys the common root of all seemingly opposite, logical dichotomies such as darkness/light, vast/minute, somethingness/emptiness, somethingness/non-somethingness, and so on. In addition, the universes evoked (ghosts and spirits, emptiness, and the reality beyond words) encapsulate the suggestion of a spiritual depth:

> The heart-mind is wide and reaches everywhere (大哉至也). The darkness (幽) of the heart-mind surpasses that of the ghosts and spirits, and its light (明) exceeds that of the sun and the moon. Its vast expanse (博大) incorporates the heaven and earth, its minute subtlety (精微) is very close to infinitesimal (隣虛). Its darkness cannot be perceived as darkness, therefore is the most complete darkness (至幽). Its light cannot be detected as light, therefore is the most complete light (至明). Its vast expanse (大) cannot be identified as vast, therefore is the most extreme vastness (絕大). Its imperceptibility (微) cannot be grasped, therefore is the most perfect imperceptibility (至微). Its quintessence (精) surpasses that of the sun and the moon; its spirit (靈) is higher than that of the ghosts and spirits; and its marvelous (妙) goes beyond that of the three cosmic substances (三才) [heaven, man, and earth]. Does the heart-mind belong to somethingness (*you* 有)? Does it belong to emptiness (*wu* 無)? Does it belong to non-somethingness (*bu you* 不有), or to non-emptiness (*bu wu* 不無)? To non-nonsomethingness (*bu buyou* 不不有) or to non-nonemptiness (*bu buwu* 不不無)? Can words be used to give it an appearance? One cannot expect to have it elucidated through mysterious explanations (玄解諭). ("GYJ," 0655b04-16)

It is understood that, because the initial trigger and core place of Chan practice is the undetectable depth of the heart-mind (an illustration of which Qisong presents above), he defines this practice carried out within the heart-mind as the way of the spirit. In the preceding paragraph, the Chan scholar-monk reiterates not only that the nature of the heart-mind is nondual (that is, not a set of distinctions and not a fusion of distinctions into a whole) but also that the knowledge coming from the practice of the way of the spirit is not merely discursive, conceptually dualistic knowledge arising from the constant interchange between what Nishitani calls the internal field of (self-)consciousness (of reason and intuition emerging from the self) and external reality. According to him, this is not some "mysterious" explanation (玄解) either, which might be translated as absurd and empty inventions meant to provide wordy descriptions of otherwise inexplicable things. What Qisong evokes here as the Chan practice of "relying upon the heart-mind" (惟心) is something different. As already mentioned, it is a nondualistic, religious/spiritual practice that involves becoming aware of one's heart-mind, listening to it, and speaking from it. It can be observed that his perception of the heart-mind—a field characterized in his view by quintessence (精), spirit (神), and marvelousness (妙), where one's perception of reality is able to go beyond the dualities darkness/light, vastness/imperceptibility, somethingness/emptiness, non-somethingness/non-emptiness, and non-nonsomethingness/non-nonemptiness—is adequately described by Nishitani's field of emptiness, the "non-selective non-ego" (1982, 60). One has complete access to the heart-mind only when reaching this level, after opening up the self-centered mode of being, which is ordinarily limited to the field of (self-)consciousness, and extending it inwardly, even more deeply, into the deeper level of the inner field of emptiness.

However, Qisong stresses that this practice of the way, defined in his essay "Yuanjiao" as "cultivating the heart-mind" (修心), though subtle, is not at all separated from the day-to-day relationships and emotions referred to generically as "human affairs (人事)": "This marvelous way (妙道), obscure power (冥權), also reaches farther into human affairs" (有妙道冥權，又至於人事者邪; "YJ," 0650c05-1). Moreover, in the next citation, he reiterates that perceiving the way of the spirit as "marvelous," as manifesting itself as an "obscure" power, does not suggest a supernormal character or lack of connectivity with ordinary, normal, and usual human activities. On the contrary, these features bring to light how powerfully and efficiently this practice contributes to the proper functioning of social life, as it purifies a person's heart-mind of emotions/burdens that distort their perception of reality and therefore make their behavior inappropriate. One could equate this proper functioning to what Nishitani describes as "a finitude of a higher order" (1982, 218). Similarly, in the following paragraph of the "Yuanjiao," the notion of "extinction" (滅) has nothing to do with losing contact with society or human relationships but suggests the effort to restore the initial calm and purity of one's heart-mind—in other words, to remove from it the emotions and attachment that make it troubled and agitated, enabling it once again to operate effectively and correctly in daily activities by embracing, integrating, and transcending emotions in daily life:

> The marvelous way (妙道) is the so-called state of purity and calm extinction (清淨寂滅) [of one's heart-mind]. What is called one's extinction means to detach oneself of the many burdens, to purify one's original pure and tranquil nature (本然); this is not extinguishing the individual's vitality (死其生), nor looking for the empty and desolate extinction (取乎空荒滅絕). When the human reaches this level, he attains the sage's spirit (成乎聖神) and goes beyond the limits of [transcends] his present life (超出其世). The obscure power (冥權) is a name that indicates the manner in which this way (道) functions without functioning (不用之用). This is the way to deliver all living beings from their dependence on emotions (出乎情溺). ("YJ," 0650c05-15)

This citation puts forward several key notions of the author's Confucianized presentation of the Chan Buddhist practice: "transcending (going beyond the limits of) this life" and the adjacent notion of "transformation"; "nature," its connection with the heart-mind, and the "emotions" as "movements" of the heart-mind; and the "causes and fruits" of these movements and their connection with the notions of "karma" and "retribution." The next section suggests that these notions—together with the central notion of heart-mind—provide the specific structure and dimensions of the scholar-monk's way of the spirit; and it examines them all in detail, as well as the connections between them.

II.3. Heart-Mind, Causes, and Fruits

First, let us have a closer look at Qisong's idea of "transcending this life" (超出其世; see quotation above). This constitutes a major dimension of Chan Buddhist practice and indicates the practice necessary to become aware that the consequences of one's actions, words, and thoughts go well beyond one's current life due to a connection between past, present, and future lives—the law of karma, of causes and effects that appear in and across lives. The author clarifies this using the notion of "transformation." His essay "Guang yuanjiao" makes clear that, unlike the Confucian way of man that follows the way of heaven and is limited to the present life, the way of cultivating the quintessential spirit goes beyond it. In the spirit of the *Classic of Changes* (*Yijing*), Qisong recalls that, generally speaking, the "way" means natural transformation or change (變化自然), a term certainly familiar to Confucians, and he distinguishes between becoming aware of the transformation as such (what he considers as the Confucian way of man) and becoming aware of that by which the transformation occurs (what he recognizes as the Buddhist way of the spirit)—that is, realizing the obscure causes and effects that influence the transformations occurring in the present life, and overcoming them while simultaneously embracing them. Indeed, one's knowledge of remote previous causes and future fruits can influence deeply, and from the inside, one's behavior in the present life:

> People everywhere think that the transformation of natural things (變化自然) is the way of the spirit (神道). But this means seeing only the transformation itself and failing to see that by which the transformation is made (不見其所以然). The transformation is what is perceptible (顯); that by which the transformation is made is something obscure (幽). It is for this reason that the sage teaches how the transformation occurs, and thus puts into stark relief the clear and obscure dimensions of the way of the spirit. The sage highlights that which is far (遠) [i.e., past or future lives] and no longer deals with that which is near (近) [i.e., the present life], in order to testify to the causes and fruits of the way of humans (人道之因果). ("GYJ," 0657c03-15)

This passage explains that the Confucian way of humans deals with correctly understanding, answering, and embracing in one's behavior the present life's perceptible and social transformations as well as their proximate (近) causes and fruits (因果)—that is, the cause-and-effect relationships immediately detectable in the context of one's present life. The author's Buddhist way of the spirit describes humans' behavior in accordance with their knowledge of the distant (遠) and therefore obscure causes and fruits of their present life transformations—that is, causes belonging to individuals' past life and fruits that will ripen in their future life. Thus, he introduces a pertinent and original distinction between behaving according to one's awareness of the development and course of present life transformations (the Confucian practice of the way of humans, which follows the way of heaven (天道)) and of that which causes present (and future) transformations to occur (the Buddhist practice of the way of the spirit (神道)). What purpose does this distinction serve? Through it, Qisong illustrates the difference between practicing in accordance with one's self-consciousness and self-centeredness (the Confucian way, as he sees it) and practicing through experiencing the no-self, in conformity with how things really are (his Buddhist way). In addition, as explicated below, by emphasizing this distinction, the scholar-monk introduces and articulates a clear rationale for the functioning of the concept of karma as the core of the way of the spirit.

Furthermore, whereas in the Confucian context the transformations referred to concern natural and social matters, in the Chan context of the practice of the heart-mind, the major transformations to which the scholar-monk calls attention primarily regard the inner heart-mind's movements. In the next citation, he emphasizes the gradual awareness (from incomplete to complete) over several consecutive stages of the awakening of the heart-mind (from a fragmentary to a full heart-mind). The heart-mind's transformation in his view implies reaching the level of complete awareness. One might say that this progression is reminiscent of Nishitani's abovementioned theory of the descent from an initial field of self-consciousness limited to human reason and apparent reality, to opening a breach in the self and thus gaining access to the deeper field of nonselective non-ego, emptiness, or reality as suchness, where things are present in the heart-mind as they really are and not obscured by the diverse attachments produced by the likes and dislikes of reason and self. In the following paragraph, Qisong also emphasizes the spiritual nature of the transformation as something that occurs only when one's awareness is "complete," when the individual surpasses all the many levels of ordinary perceptible transformations and just as many states of consciousness, until finally reaching complete awareness. This completeness is not merely the complete moral quality of a person who has entire moral awareness of their social reality—that is, full knowledge of rules of behavior appropriate for each and every circumstance, as in the Confucian completeness—but is the complete (and therefore marvelous (妙)) moral attribute of an individual who has entire awareness of true reality (如). In other words, this moral quality comes not from one's reasoning but from one's capacity to go beyond the field of reason, sense perception, and emotions and to reach a field of ultimate reality and of nature. In Nishitani's words, in this field, "things can be made to disclose their selfness" (1982, 119), and in Qisong's words ("Guang yuanjiao," the following paragraph), at this level "the ten thousand things are marvelous" (妙萬物):

> The heart-mind certainly can reach its completeness (*zhi* 至). When reaching its completeness, certainly it transforms itself (*bian* 變). Its state of transformation is consciousness (*shi* 識). Reaching its maximum (至者), this is the ultimate reality [when this state is achieved, there is no more transformation] (*ru* 如). In the state of ultimate reality, all sentient beings [ten thousand things] are marvelous (*miao* 妙). Consciousness makes the things diverse, considers them as different (紛萬物, 異萬物者). The transformation consists of the imperceptible signs of movement (*dong* 動). The state of the maximum (completeness) is the root of the marvelous (至也者, 妙之本也). There is no such thing as a thing without root in this world. There is no such

thing as a thing that does not move. It is for this reason that all sentient beings emerge from the process of transformation and enter into the process of transformation (故萬物出于變, 入于變). The beings arise from ultimate reality (completeness) and return into ultimate reality (萬物起于至, 復于至). The transformation of sentient beings is perceptible in their emotions (萬物之變見乎情); the ultimate reality of the world exists in their nature (天下之至存乎性). Through the emotions, one can recognize (辨) the transformation of sentient beings. Through one's nature, he can observe (觀) the great marvelous of the world. When one excels in the spheres of the emotions and of universal nature, then he can discuss the way and the teaching of the sage. ("GYJ," 0655a19)

It can be seen that, to explain how the individuals become aware of the spiritual dimension present in their heart-mind, Qisong uses several pairs of correlatives that describe different facets of the same undertaking—the process of transformation of the heart-mind through Chan practice and its different states: from the heart-mind in a state of constant transformation (that is, movement) to the heart-mind in a state of completeness (*bian* 變/*zhi* 至); from the state of consciousness to the state of ultimate reality (*shi* 識/*ru* 如, *miao* 妙); from diversity, difference, and movement to the common root (*fen* 紛, *yi* 異, *dong* 動/*ben* 本); and from emotions to universal nature (*qing* 情/*xing* 性). Clearly, in his thought, the last pair, emotions/universal nature, is the common denominator of all others, the fundamental correlation that describes the interdependence between the two levels (emotions and nature) of what is called here the heart-mind/reality. And in his view, the aim of Chan practice is to become aware of this interdependence. The latter constitutes the spiritual dimension of the human being. The next section expounds how the Chan scholar-monk expresses the nondual identity between the heart-mind and external reality and examines each of its two levels or fields—of the emotions and of nature.

III. INTERDEPENDENCE BETWEEN EMOTIONS AND NATURE

Each of the abovementioned correlations that Qisong brings to light may be understood as a dimension in which he builds a distinction between self-consciousness and emptiness—the two major states of the heart-mind identified above in the context of Nishitani's thought—and describes their different functioning and functions. It is noticeable that, in his thought, all these correlatives are interdependent; that is, they have a common source. Using them, he clearly develops a Chan nondual equivalence between phenomenal reality and the heart-mind, between the movements of the world (phenomenal reality;

天下之動) and the movements of the heart-mind (the emotions; 情)—in other words, relationships with others. Phenomenal reality is precisely the heart-mind, and the heart-mind is precisely phenomenal reality. Everything in reality is to be understood and managed through the heart-mind. Instead of choosing to directly explain to his Confucian interlocutors the well-known traditional Buddhist idea of the nonduality between form (phenomenal reality) and emptiness (see *Platform Sutra*), the Chan scholar-monk spotlights and develops, in a creative way, another nondual correlation—namely, between phenomenal reality (daily affairs) and the heart-mind. This seems easier to interpret by his intended audience, as both of these correlative terms have a strong connection with an individual's behavior and with being with others, more meaningful topics for Confucians than the abstract notion of emptiness.

As already mentioned, Qisong interprets the relationship between emotions and nature as a nondual interdependence. To that end, he first distinguishes each of them as paradigmatic of a different field of the heart-mind. Thus, the emotions belong to the field of the perceptible and intelligible and, of course, of the individual self—in his words, "the beginning of what is" (*you* 有; see sec. III.1). "What is" (in other words, what is perceived and experienced in one form or another) includes the individual self, as all emotions are self-conscious; that is, the subject personally experiences them. One may say that emotions shape the human's state of self-attachment, the ego. I adopt here Nishitani's definition of the "ego" as "self in a state of self-attachment" (1982, 14). According to the next paragraph from the "Guang yuanjiao," one's nature is the most complete state of emptiness (至無). This denotes the lack of selfishness of the field of nature, a state of non-ego. It is therefore appropriate to translate the author's Chan notion of authentic nature as "nature-emptiness." This is the translation of the notion of *xing* 性 that this chapter privileges. Note that the same idea of completeness examined earlier reappears, this time within the context of one's nature and its field of emptiness:

> One's nature is the most complete state of emptiness (無之至). The most complete state of emptiness: this does not mean that from the very beginning there is emptiness (則未始無). When one enters into the world: this is life. When he leaves the world: this is death. In reality, one's nature is not life, nor death (非死非生). It is for this reason that the way of the sage is implicit [silent] (寂), but also clear (明). His way is how one is able to perceive it. ("GYJ," 0655b28-14)

In this paragraph, to stress their nonduality, Qisong first observes the ontological difference between the essence of emotions and the essence of nature—that is, between "what is" or the "perceptible" (*you* 有) and "emptiness" (*wu* 無). He describes the emotions as the "beginning of what is" (i.e., manifest reality, ordinary human experience, feelings, and sentiments); in other words, emotions are the main feature of organic life, which has a beginning and an end. They thus evolve within perceptible temporality and structure the flow of organic time. Nature-emptiness has a different essence, beyond the limited organic time of life. This idea is best exemplified in his clarification that the state of emptiness does not follow the flow of an organic time that has a beginning, a starting point. In his own words, it cannot be said that there is a beginning of one's nature-emptiness, as the latter is beyond temporal life and death—neither life, nor death.

The scholar-monk observes that unlike emotions, which are the beginning of some "thing"—that is, of concrete and perceptible representations (of things that can be perceived by the self)—it cannot be said, as he stresses in the above citation, that nature-emptiness is the beginning of some "thing." Qisong's concept of nature-emptiness can be related to Nishitani's notion of emptiness: "Not an emptiness represented as some 'thing' outside of being and other than being. It is not simply an 'empty nothing' but rather an absolute emptiness, emptied even of these representations of emptiness. And for that reason, it is at bottom one with being, even as being is at bottom one with emptiness" (1982, 123). Thus, as the core of the way of the sage, nature as a complete state of emptiness does not mean one thing or another but for the Chan scholar-monk is empty of representations. It is therefore "silent," he notes in the citation above—that is, being implicit, it cannot be described by words, as a thing; but also, being "clear," it can be fully realized through experience of the no-self, the nonattachment to things and terms ascribed to things. "Neither life nor death," as the description of nature-emptiness indicates, it has a spiritual (sustaining and connecting life and death), nondual (forming the common ground of life and of death) identity. If the terms *life* and *death* are attached implicitly to a self or an ego (it is the self, a subject, who lives and dies), then nature-emptiness as neither life nor death suggests the state of no-self, or non-ego, which is the nonduality of self and other.

He further elucidates the ontological essence of nature-emptiness—namely, of the field of emptiness of the heart-mind. In his work, nature-emptiness is the great root from which emerges everything—human beings, heaven, and the sage (人者, 天者, 聖人者, 孰不自性而出也?; "GYJ," 0657b22-11). In other words, it is, to use Nishitani's term, a "horizon of intercommunication with the being of all things of the world," which everyone contains. "Within this horizon we are a sheer being-in-the-world as such, rid of all particular determinations" (Nishitani 1982, 248). Clearly, the sphere of human beings in conjunction with heaven (including earth) and the sage suggests in familiar Confucian terms (see *Zhongyong* 22, the unity heaven, earth, and sage) the world and sentient beings, including the sage who can grow and transform them. It is instructive to approach this definition of the state of nature-emptiness given by Qisong with the aid of Nishitani's figurative account of "the field of possibility of the world," or "home-ground," a field in which every "thing" (for instance, the humans, heaven, and sage to which the scholar-monk refers),

> while continuing to be itself, is in the home-ground of everything else. Figuratively speaking, its roots reach across into the ground of all other things and help to hold them up and keep them standing. It serves as a constitutive element of their being so that they can be what they are, and thus provides an ingredient of their being. That a thing is itself means that all other things, while continuing to be themselves, are in the home-ground of that thing; that precisely when a thing is on its own home-ground, everything else is there too; that the roots of every other thing spread across into its home-ground. (Nishitani 1982, 149–150)

Elsewhere ("GYJ," 0655b18), Qisong adds that nature-emptiness manifests itself as the real state of things (*shi* 實) or, equivalently, the state of suchness (*ru* 如). In other words, this is the common field or home-ground—in the words of Nishitani—of things, where they exist not objectively, as objects of representation, but non-objectively, as they are in themselves. The Chan-monk recognizes it as a state of completeness (至), a state of purity (清), calmness (靜), and without evil (無邪; "GYJ," 0655c05). And he warns that, when misused in the form of deception, cunning, ferocity, impertinence, greed, or desires, for instance, the movements of the emotions destroy nature-emptiness (see sec. III.1).

The Northern Song monk explains that the goal of practice is to come into contact with this field of nature-emptiness (the non-objective way of being, in Nishitani's sense), concealed by emotions and the objective way of being. "Concealed" in this context entails for him the character of the nonduality emotions/nature-emptiness. Therefore, the starting point of his practice is a particular exploration of emotions and interpersonal relations within which dwells nature-emptiness. Consequently, the idea of living in the social world—the favorite theme of Confucians—is equally an integral component of his Chan vision. This topic is obviously present in his interest in the emotions as movements of the heart-mind. The next section explores this noteworthy conception of the sentiments.

III.1. Emotions, Karmic Causes, and Fruits

"The movements of the world," Qisong specifies, "arise from emotions" (天下之動, 生於情; "GYJ," 0655b19-11). In the same paragraph, he interprets them as the very source of the reality heaven-earth: "The whole heaven-earth spreads to the farthest extent possible and arises from the emotions" (天地至逺, 而起於情; "GYJ," 0655b24-5). He thus builds this Chan nonduality "world/heart-mind" using the central notion of sentiments, a concept that is also at the heart of Confucian practice and extensively discussed in the classic *Liji* in terms of music and rituals. In fact, his section "Guang yuanjiao" 0658a02 directly refers to the *Liji*, chapter 17, "Yueji" 樂記 (without naming the source).

In the next citation, the scholar-monk describes the importance of focusing on the emotions in cohesive Chan practice in terms well-known to Confucians—namely, the order and harmony of human relationships (between relatives and nonrelatives) and moral practice. He also implicitly suggests the imperfection of practice centered on human emotions (such as Confucian music and rituals) by pointing out that when making adequate use of sentiments, one can still generate evil deeds and demonstrate indifference to others who are strangers and not relatives (see below). For this reason, even though Chan practice still focuses on human emotions, it first transcends them by reaching the full depth of the heart-mind to the field of the no-self and only then returning to the feelings in order to make use of them from a different perspective, not merely a moral one (i.e., the particular Confucian morality based on Confucian ritual tradition and self-consciousness) but in the spirit of the field of no-self. He notes this about emotions:

> The emotions can produce mistaken perceptions, as well as mistaken consciousness (*shi* 識). When one manages to make adequate use of emotions, one shows affection (*ai* 愛), serves others, cherishes his relatives, is distant with distant relatives, does good deeds and evil deeds (則為愛, 為惠, 為親親, 為疎疎, 為或善, 為或惡). When the individual fails to make adequate use of emotions, he resorts to deception; uses cunning; acts with ferocity, impertinence, greed; is submerged in desires: and the individual loses his heart-mind and extinguishes his nature (則為欺, 為狡, 為兇, 為不遜, 為貪, 為溺嗜欲, 為喪心, 為滅性). ("GYJ," 0655c02-1)

In this passage, Qisong emphasizes the different outcomes achieved whether or not the human makes adequate use of the sentiments from the perspective of the field of self-consciousness. The two states or fields of the heart-mind—self-consciousness and no-self—are further examined in detail in this part and in the next one. The first state of the heart-mind is its ordinary condition: in constant emotional agitation and therefore peaceless, troubled and therefore impure. The scholar-monk describes it variously as the permanent transformations at the level of distinguishable diversity, the difference between the forms of reality and the emotional movements of the heart-mind governed by the self, and the self's attachments.

In this context, one may notice that the author originally introduces the definition of this state as the (Chan) Buddhist field of consciousness (*shi* 識), which results from the movement of emotions. According to the Buddhist view, consciousness is not only part of the mentioned sphere of discursive reason but also part of the domain of karma, since consciousness produces the latter and is shaped by it. As is well-known, consciousness is the result of the interaction between form (*se* 色), sensation (*shou* 受), perception (*xiang* 想), and volition (*xing* 行); it is the recipient and originator of karma—that is, the result of past actions that occur in the present life or in future ones.[7] The eight consciousnesses continue from one life to another, connecting and influencing subsequent lives. Thus, when using the term of consciousness as generated by emotions and the recipient of karma, Qisong also tacitly suggests that the two fields of the heart-mind are not disconnected but rather connected in nondual interdependence and correlation, and that the level of emptiness and of the spirit is, in fact, the fundamental ground of the level of the consciousness of everyday life. In this regard, he notes that "the way is the deep content of the spirit, it is the origin from which the consciousness emerges. The consciousness is the source of troubles" (道也者, 神之蘊也, 識之所出也. 識也者, 大患之源也; "GYJ," 0659a04-5).

It is noteworthy that he establishes a correspondence between the fundamental Buddhist notion of consciousness as karma recipient and several core Confucian notions. When defining the emotions as the source of perceptible reality—the field of perceptible reality, "what is" (*you* 有; see next quotation)—the Northern Song monk places great emphasis on a moral image, also significant for the Confucians, of good and evil deeds. Another idea he takes up that matters a great deal in Confucian morality is that of affection (*ai* 愛) as love between members of a couple or fraternity between people, and therefore social harmony. In his Buddhist perspective, this is not only the socially positive emotion outlined above but also a source of attachment and desires that generates positive and negative causes and effects that continue to mature and develop from one life to another. Thus, he evokes the continuity and interdependence between actions: good ones generate subsequent good deeds, and evil ones produce ensuing evil acts. Using this moral image, he introduces a Buddhist view, the cause-and-effect chain that links subsequent lives and therefore extends the relevance of emotions beyond their limited domain of the present life in Confucian practice:

The emotions are the beginning of what is [perceptible] (有之初也). After there is what is, there is affection (有有, 則有愛); after there is affection, there is attachment to desires (則有嗜欲); after there is attachment to desires, there is the death and life of men, women and sentient beings. Death and life influence each other, and in the process good deeds and evil deeds occur, transforming themselves according to their category [good deeds generate good results; evil deeds generate evil results] (死生之感則善惡以類變).
Life begins, life comes to an end [death], death and life follow one another without ever stopping. ("GYJ," 0655b25-14)

Elsewhere ("GYJ," 0655c16), Qisong defines the meaning and functioning of feelings, as well as their connection with karmic law, starting from another ancient concept, well known to Confucians: the ancient cosmological principle of stimulus and response, action and reaction, or mutual influence (感應; see, for instance, *Yijing*, hexagram 31, *xian* 咸, mutual attraction). When following his explanation of the emotions, one can understand that, because in his view the heart-mind is equivalent with phenomenal reality, emotions are movements arising within the heart-mind, just as the movements of the myriad things emerge within natural reality. One also notes that he uses this notion of mutual influence within the context of sentiments in order to demonstrate, using traditional Chinese terms, the Buddhist ideas of the interdependence between things and of the karmic law.

First of all, he understands emotions as "stimuli" (感; see below). Thus, Qisong identifies them as stimuli-connectors that link the heart-mind with external reality. As shown in the citation below, he also uses the ideas of "stimulus" and "response" to introduce in his explanation of sentiments intended for Confucians the Buddhist idea of the accumulation of karma and of the karmic principle of cause and effect. In this way, he reconsiders this ancient concept of stimulus and further develops it in the Buddhist context. Unlike the ancient cosmic resonance, the emotions-stimuli and their responses no longer occur together within the limited time of one life, or within the *Yijing*'s cyclic process of life, but arise during successive and interconnected lives, which are not cyclic existences but interconnected, distinct lives. For this reason, he urges people to be vigilant about the movements of their heart-minds, which produce good and bad effects, disaster and good fortune:

The movements of the heart-mind (心動) are the so-called karmic acts (*ye* 業) [physical actions, words, or thoughts] that will produce a fruit or effect in the future. The accumulation of karmic acts (會業) is the so-called stimulus (*gan* 感). The stimulus is what connects the inner heart-mind with outer reality (通內外). There are no heart-minds in this world that do not move. There is no karmic act among the myriad things which is not the result of a stimulus. The principle of karmic acts is something obscure (業之為理也幽). The power of this stimulus manifests itself for a long time (遠) [i.e., in future lives], but the people do not see it, and therefore, they are not afraid (民不睹而不懼). ("GYJ," 0655c16)

In his persuasive examination of the emotions, the Chan scholar-monk reinterprets not only the ancient term of stimulus but also the second concept of the correlative articulation, which explains the stimulus's resonance within reality—the "response" (應). The "stimulus" is used to demonstrate the interdependence between different lives and between the heart-mind and external reality, while the "response" serves to suggest the different qualities of the emotions as well as the different natures of the future "karmic retributions" (*bao* 報) that they generate. Qisong differentiates sentiments as good or bad, superficial or deep, and understands them in terms of the type of response they generate within reality, either disaster or happiness [good fortune] (禍福):

> When the heart-mind moves, its movements are either with [nature] or against [nature] and thus arise the good and bad emotions. When good and bad emotions (善惡之情) develop, then in response arise disaster and happiness [good fortune] (禍福之應). Among the good and bad emotions, there are superficial and deep ones (淺深); therefore, their retribution in disaster and happiness is also either heavy or light (報之有輕重). Light retribution can be discharged, heavy retribution cannot be avoided. There is a before and an after good and bad emotions, the retribution in the form of disaster and happiness can be slow or fast, the mutual stimuli traverse ten lives, and ten thousand lives and cannot be avoided. They never appear during only one life. ("GYJ," 0655c21-12)

To demonstrate that this idea of karmic retribution (disaster and good fortune) as a spontaneous response to the movements of emotions-stimuli that take shape and become acts (behavior) is not a completely alien concept within Confucian culture, Qisong suggests a comparison between the Buddhist idea embodied in the previous citation and the Confucian notions of auspicious testimony (休證) and ominous testimony (咎證) sent by heaven in response to the acts of the sovereign and of the people: "Concerning retribution (*baoying* 報應), Confucians, too, speak about auspicious testimony (*xiu zheng* 休證) and ominous testimony (*jiu zheng* 咎證). When good deeds accumulate, favors from heaven come (積善有慶). When evil deeds accumulate, calamities come (積惡有殃). This is very clear" ("YJ," 0651b12-2).

In this paragraph of the "Yuanjiao," his terms "auspicious testimony" (*xiu zheng* 休證) and "ominous testimony" (*jiu zheng* 咎證) make an implicit reference to the "Great Model" ("Hong Fan" 洪範)[8] chapter of the Confucian classic *Book of Documents* (*Shujing* 書經). Indeed, "Hong Fan" is a text the scholar-monk appreciates and directly refers to elsewhere, in his commentary *Zhongyong jie* (see chap. 7). The exact terms used in the ancient Confucian context are "auspicious signs" (*xiu zheng* 休徵) and "ominous signs" (*jiu zheng* 咎徵). In this case, his purpose of connecting cohesive Chan thought with Confucian thought takes the form of an analogy that he builds between the principle of karmic retribution based on causes and effects and the Confucian conception of "retribution" coming from heaven. Concretely, as seen in this last citation, his analogy connects the Buddhist "testimony" (*zheng* 證) or "experienced fruit of retribution" (*zheng guo* 證果) with the Confucian "precursor sign" (*zheng* 徵). The latter means the early signs and evidence sent by heaven in the form of natural phenomena (their seasonableness or unseasonableness) to make known whether the administration is effective or not, whether or not those who govern are moral and capable men (see "Hong Fan").

To better understand Qisong's analogy and how he connects Buddhist and Confucian teachings in this specific context of "retribution," it is necessary to first look at how the Confucian notion is articulated in the "Hong Fan." The central issue around which that text revolves is the sovereign as Confucian model to be imitated by the people. The "Hong Fan" states that the ruler

> establishes himself as the most accomplished example, he gathers together the Five Happinesses or good fortunes (*wu fu* 五福) [long life (*shou* 壽), riches (*fu* 富), soundness of body and serenity of mind (*kang ning* 康寧), love of virtue (*hao de* 好德), and a crowning end of life (natural death at an advanced age; *lao zhong ming* 老終命)]. Through disseminating them, he bestows them to the multitudes of his people. The multitudes of people imitate his accomplished example and thus bestow to the sovereign the preservation of his accomplished example (皇建其有極, 斂時五福, 用敷錫厥庶民, 惟時厥庶民於汝極, 錫汝保極). ("Hong Fan" 3.5)

Otherwise, if the people do not follow the accomplished example, "Hong Fan" 3.9 warns, heaven sends its response in the form of the Six Exhaustions or calamities [*liu ji* 六極; early death (*xiong duan zhe* 凶短折), illness (*ji* 疾), sadness (*you* 憂), poverty (*pin* 貧), wickedness (*e* 惡), and weakness (*ruo* 弱)]. The "Hong Fan" highlights the importance for the sovereign to disseminate (*fu* 敷) his accomplished example and for the people to preserve it (through following it) (*bao* 保).

Unlike the Chan inner stimulus and response within the heart-mind depicted by Qisong, the "Hong Fan" describes external stimuli (provided by the accomplished example of the sovereign, the one responsible for the harmony of society) and external responses (of the people, expressed in their behavior; and of heaven, expressed in the natural phenomena referred to further). Thus, when all the affairs of government are in good order, including the appointment of valuable officers free of corruption, and the accomplished example is disseminated by the sovereign and followed by the people, the "Hong Fan" 3.8 stresses, heaven sends five auspicious signs or good fortunes—namely, seasonable rain (proof of the presence and functioning of solemnity within society and governance (su 肅)), seasonable sunshine (proof of the existence of order and effective control (yi 乂)), seasonable heat (proof of the perspicacity of the sovereign and his officials (zhe 哲)), seasonable cold (proof of proper deliberation within the political sphere (mou 謀)), and seasonable wind (proof of the sageness of rulers (sheng 聖)). Otherwise, the "Hong Fan" notes, heaven sends five ominous signs or calamities—namely, prolonged rainfall (proof of the rulers' violence (kuang 狂)), prolonged sunshine (proof of the presence of attempts at usurpation (jian 僭)), prolonged heat (proof of the rulers' apathy (yu 豫)), prolonged cold (proof of the rulers' impatience (ji 急)), and prolonged wind (proof of the rulers' ignorance (meng 蒙)). A synthesis of this perspective of the "Hong Fan," which connects precursor signs, natural phenomena, and human behavior, can also be found in the *Zhongyong* 24 (see Arghiresco/u 2013, 323–328).

Qisong interprets the Confucian sign or testimony (zheng 徵) of heaven—the unchanging or interrupted seasonableness of nature, socially translated as people's good fortune or calamity—as a form of retribution and as the correlation stimulus/response, thus justifying the functioning of the Buddhist doctrine of cause and effect as well as karmic retribution. In his view, Confucian political and moral acts produce an external future influence or retribution, which results in changes in natural seasonableness. One may say that the latter is a testimony (zheng 徵) within natural reality, exactly as the Buddhist testimony (zheng 證) is an inner one, within the individual's heart-mind. The natural precursor sign and inner testimony are one, because the external phenomenal world (society) and the heart-mind are one. Again, his analysis involves the identity between natural reality and the heart-mind, used as a way to demonstrate the nondual interdependence between inner and outer reality.

It is noteworthy that the scholar-monk's Chan conception of nondualistic thought (i.e., the heart-mind is phenomenal reality) reconciles two types of testimony, which although similar in goal (justifying disasters or blessings) have different natures. The Confucian precursor sign is an external testimony and response, confined to the cosmological and moral field of reason and self-consciousness, while the Buddhist fruit of retribution is an inner experience, an inner testimony, an experienced awareness that allows access to the profound level of emptiness and no-self, which, as presented below, is nothing other than the Chan universal nature (*xing* 性). In his view, this inner testimony or fruit or retribution is the best way to examine one's nature—that is, "to verify that one has 'seen' [i.e., realized, expressed, or manifested] one's nature"[9] (見性之驗; "GYJ," 0659a15-14). At this point, the Chan key concept of "nature" inevitably emerges in our analysis of "emotions." This is perfectly coherent in the scholar-monk's interdependent perspective (where emotions are indissociable from nature). The hermeneutics of the next section focuses on this notion of the individual's nature: on the Chan practice of "seeing/manifesting the nature" that all sentient beings (human and nonhuman) inherently share, on the identity between nature and emptiness, and on the connection between nature and karmic causes and fruits.

III.2. Nature, Karmic Causes, and Fruits

The Chan scholar-monk explains the nondual relationship between nature and emotions thus: "The emotions originate from nature, and nature is hidden in the emotions (情出乎性, 性隱乎情). If nature is hidden, then the way of complete reality (*zhi shi zhi dao* 至實之道) is lost. It is for this reason that the sage makes nature the content of his teaching and guides people [toward their nature] (是故聖人以性為教, 而教人)" ("GYJ," 0655b18).

The analysis elaborated above deals with Qisong's interpretation of the emotions as stimuli of karmic responses, arguing that it was clearly based on a comparative perspective intended for his Confucian audience. It suggests that this field of emotions is equivalent to the first of the two levels of the heart-mind identified by Nishitani. One observes that this development inevitably brings us to the notion of one's nature as nondual correlative of the emotions. This is a concept also discussed by Mengzi (see Mengzi 7A, 7B, *Jinxin shang, xia* 盡心上,下); therefore, it would be generally familiar to Confucians, as would the discussion of emotions in the *Liji*.

This part expresses the view that in Qisong's thought, the human's nature, which is hidden within the emotions, within the first field of the heart-mind, is accessible only when this shallow level of the emotions and self-consciousness is broken and one is able to become aware of the deeper, second level of non-consciousness, of suchness. In his words, this is the level of complete reality (至實), the field of nature. For this reason, Qisong—like the Chan sage-teacher he refers to in the abovementioned paragraph—finds it essential to focus his teaching on nature. If "seen" (*jian xing* 見性)—that is, experienced, not hidden in the emotions (性隱乎情)—the awareness of nature allows practicing Chan Buddhists to recover the way, not of incomplete and distorted reality, but of complete reality (reality as it is). As phenomenal reality is the heart-mind (a nondual relationship) according to him, it is clear that complete reality is the deep field of nature within the heart-mind.

This second level that the scholar-monk depicts using the abovementioned correlatives is the final ground and depth of the heart-mind: the field of emptiness or of true reality, where the process of transformation and differentiation ends, because when one reaches this level, one gains awareness of the common root of all phenomenal realities and of their interdependence. To describe the characteristics of this field, Qisong establishes another original parallel, between the description of this level of the heart-mind as true reality (*ru* 如) and as a state of completeness (*zhi* 至; see above, the description of this level as complete reality (*zhi shi* 至實)). In doing so, through describing the Chan notion of suchness or true reality using the well-known Confucian term of completeness (*zhi* 至), his interpretation again puts the two teachings in communication. Indeed, the state of completeness is a meaningful term for Confucians. The highest or complete level (*zhi* 至) of the way of the Confucian exemplary man (君子之道) is discussed in the *Zhongyong* 12 (about this subject, see Arghiresco/u 2013, 207–217); complete sincerity (至誠) is developed in the *Zhongyong* 22, 23, 24, 26, and 32 (Arghiresco/u 2013, 311–328, 337–343, 369–377); the complete way (至道), in the *Zhongyong* 27 (Arghiresco/u 2013, 345–352); the complete moral quality (*zhi de* 至德), in the *Zhongyong* 27 and 33 (Arghiresco/u 2013, 345–352, 379–390); and the most accomplished (complete) sage of the world (天下至聖), in the *Zhongyong* 31 (Arghiresco/u 2013, 367–368). The *Daxue jing* and *zhang* 3 develop the highest state of practice as the "complete good" (至善) and "complete knowledge" (知至). Let us look at how the scholar-monk interprets and further develops this concept of "complete knowledge" as equivalent to "seeing/realizing one's nature," expanding the old Confucian notion in a new Chan direction.

III.2.1. "Seeing/Realizing One's Nature" as Acquiring "Complete Knowledge"

To better perceive the meaning of Qisong's definition of Chan practice as "complete knowledge," let us look first at the ancient Confucian understanding of this term. The ancient Confucians consider their practice as focusing on acquiring "complete knowledge" (*zhi zhi* 知至) of things (see, for example, *Lunyu* 16.9; *Lunyu* 6.21; *Zhongyong* 6, 7, 20, 24, 25, 31) as a method of developing the necessary tools for perfectly governing society. According to the *Zhongyong*, this implies fully grasping each element of reality to be able to correctly observe the rituals (*Zhongyong* 27) and understand heaven and human beings (*Zhongyong* 29). Moreover, paragraph 32 of the *Zhongyong* specifies that complete knowledge in support of perfect governance ultimately means "understanding the movement of the transformation-growth of the whole heaven-earth" (知天地之化育; see Arghiresco/u 2013, 369–377).

Obviously, the scholar-monk indirectly recalls this Confucian view when highlighting that the Chan conception of complete knowledge goes beyond full comprehension of the "transformation-growth" of reality (see the next citation). The latter connotes an exclusive concern with the means of living, the maintenance of life, and the development and activities of different living organisms from the perspective of emotions and morality. From the following paragraph, it appears that in his view, this Confucian perspective translates into knowledge of the various good and evil deeds of living beings (知善惡) that emerge from emotions. Furthermore, in this context, it means being able to differentiate which actions are good (entail stimulation of organic growth and social harmony) and which are evil (trigger stagnation, decline in vitality, and social disorder). The complete knowledge of the Chan sage (聖人之至知), stresses Qisong, goes beyond the limited moral and organic development to which other teachings dealing with nature refer. It is not limited to distinguishing good actions from evil ones but goes beyond the moral angle, aiming to understand the karmic causes and effects of these actions or, in his terms, "knowing the end and the beginning of these good and evil deeds" (知夫善惡之終始; see next quotation). This does not depend on rationality and discursivity but rather is a realization that enlightens us from the inside, from the inner field of nature.

Hence, achieving this complete knowledge is possible only when the humans get access to the spiritual level of the heart-mind—that is, have an enlightening experience of their own nature. The scholar-monk describes this experience in well-known Chan terms as "seeing/realizing one's nature" (見性). In his view, this is equivalent to "rectifying one's nature" (正於性)—the nature hidden within emotions, the extraordinary and marvelous hidden within ordinary social interaction, in people's everyday behavior. Within this deep field of nature, the process called "seeing" or "rectifying" refers not to a moral knowledge, such as that acquired within the field of emotions, but to a spiritual enlightening. The latter implies the soteriological aspect of removing the state of delusion in which sentient beings usually live (萬物之惑). Because their nature is obscured, in this ordinary state they behave only according to their emotions. Qisong explains how it is possible for sentient beings to see their own nature using the notion of understanding or knowledge (知)—a concept familiar to Confucians. In the next paragraph from the "Guang yuanjiao," this understanding is for him becoming aware of one's nature—that is, of the karmic causes of one's actions, those prior to their concretization in causes-phenomena (appearances) and causes-forms:

> The state of delusion of the myriad sentient beings can be removed by rectifying their nature (萬物之惑, 正於性). In this case, how can one not pay attention to the fact that one's nature and emotions generate good and evil actions in the world (情性之善惡天下)? Knowing which are good deeds and which are evil deeds, and not knowing their end and beginning [their karmic effects and their karmic causes, connecting the present life with future and previous lives]: can this be considered a complete knowledge? (知善惡, 而不知夫善惡之終始, 其至知乎?) Knowing the end of these good and evil works, but not knowing their beginning: can this be considered a complete knowledge? (知其終, 而不知其始, 其至知乎?) Only the sage can make complete his knowledge (至知). Thus, he has the knowledge of the beginning (知始) and of the end (知終) of acts, of their subtle (知微) and of their extinguished (知亡) aspects. The sage sees what runs through and links together death and life (貫死生), the obscure and the clear (幽明), and sees the way this thing concretizes in the world of appearances and forms (成象成形). ("GYJ," 0655b20-1)

Elsewhere in his essay ("GYJ," 0659a08), the scholar-monk explains in more detail the notions "the end and beginning of acts" and "what runs through and links together death and life," which he thinks illustrate the complete knowledge of nature according to Chan teaching. He also clarifies what distinguishes this cohesive Chan Buddhist complete knowledge from the knowledge of nature sought and promoted by other schools. The next subsection shows that Qisong views this notion as comprising the following four particular aspects. The first consists in the individuals' realization of their acts (deeds) as causes (*yin* 因). The second involves seeing acts as fruits of retribution (*guo* 果). In other words, this apprehension concerns achieving awareness of the causal links connecting past, present, and future acts, and this complete knowledge is knowledge of the continuity between life and death and of the consequences of acts in the past, present, and future lives (the law of karma). Third, he specifies further that Chan practice intended to acquire this particular awareness about causes and fruits is based on "cultivating" (修) the individual—specifically, cultivating one's quintessential spirit, one's heart-mind (see above, "YJ," 0650b23-9), and one's nature ("GYJ," 0659a15-14). It can be seen that this Chan cultivation extends beyond the realm of ethical and moral practice and concerns precisely the spiritual feature of the human being. The fourth essential aspect of the Chan practice of acquiring complete knowledge highlighted by Qisong is experiencing the "inner testimony" (證) mentioned earlier. Obviously, his explanation of "cohesive Chan complete knowledge" refers to the full knowledge of nature. It constitutes an interpretation intended primarily for Confucians, of the central definition of the Chan practice—coming to "see one's nature" (見性)—that is, to experience the nature hidden within emotions.

Moreover, as the next citation shows, through these four features of his cohesive Chan practice, he further develops an original definition of the Chan concept of "seeing/manifesting one's nature" interpreted as achieving a specific complete knowledge. This angle certainly makes his audience think in terms of the Confucian theme of knowledge. In his view, the four components serve to ensure that nothing is omitted in the practice of seeing nature, so that the reader is able to distinguish between correct and incorrect ways to "see one's nature" (achieved by the realization of causes and fruits) and between completely and incompletely seeing it (achieved by the cultivation of one's nature and inner testimony). Once again, the Chan nature is a spiritual essence and not merely a moral essence. For this reason, the scholar-monk considers as superficial the way the other schools investigate the concept of nature compared to the Chan four-dimensional analysis of "seeing" it that he recommends:

> People have different ways of seeing. There are those who see all things as having a particular visible form (有見), those who see all things as without any visible form [empty] (無見), those who see all things as terminated [at the end of the visible life] (斷見), those who see all things as permanent (常見). All these rhetorics are vague and mixed together, and one cannot distinguish between them. Some say that the individual does not need to experience inner testimony (證), nor to examine it [see if it is reliable or unreliable]. So how will people distinguish between the right way to see one's nature and the wrong way to see one's nature (見性之正乎邪), and between when they completely see it and when they do not see it completely (至哉不至哉)? All the one hundred philosophical schools (百家) discuss nature, but they do not address acts envisaged as causes (*yin* 因), nor as fruits of retribution (*guo* 果); neither do they address the issue of cultivation (*xiu* 修), nor of inner testimony (*zheng* 證). In this case, how can their discourse about one's nature be effective? The sages of other schools all focus on one's nature, but without looking for causes, fruits, cultivation and inner testimony. Are they really able to have a complete knowledge of one's nature? It is for this reason that, within the way (*dao* 道) of my sage, this nature is considered as starting

from causes, fruits, cultivation and inner testimony (是故吾之聖人道性, 必先夫因果修證者也). This is admirable! People need to think about this. ("GYJ," 0659a21-15)

It may be said that the guiding thread throughout Qisong's thought is the Chan issue of "seeing/manifesting nature." Inspired by Nishitani's thought, one can translate this goal as managing to open cracks in the wall of the field of self-consciousness and reason that prevents individuals from seeing their own nature, encloses them, and impedes them from going deeper inside and reaching this inner level. By relying on the well-known Confucian theme of knowledge, he interprets the Chan practice necessary for achieving this goal as an endeavor to acquire complete knowledge—that is, the awareness and practice of causal law, which is embodied in the four abovementioned features, practice of which enables one to fracture one's enclosing wall. The next subsection is dedicated to the practice of seeing one's nature according to the scholar monk's abovementioned four features—karmic causes, fruits, cultivation of nature, and inner testimony. The focus is on the first two, by which Qisong also explains the last two and Chan practice in general.

III.2.2. "Seeing/Manifesting One's Nature": Karmic Causes and Fruits

This subsection explores the connection that Qisong establishes between nature and karmic causes and fruits. As already discussed (see sec. III.1), Qisong develops the explanation of the Buddhist notions of causes and fruits based on the concept of stimulus (*gan* 感). In the "Guang yuanjiao" (0655c16), he describes causes (*yin* 因) as inner stimuli (*nei gan* 內感) or triggers (*zhao* 召), and fruits (*guo* 果) as external stimuli (*wai gan* 外感) or responses (*ying* 應). The monk also stresses the universality of the relationship between cause and fruit within the phenomenal world: "All sentient beings that have an appearance participate in causes and fruits" (因果, 形象者皆預也). In other words, traces of acts carried out in previous lives do not disappear but rather subsist from one life to another within the most profound consciousness of the human heart-mind and become the inner stimuli for present acts. The present acts triggered by these accumulated causes, in turn, are external effects; that is, they take shape in elements of concrete conduct (physical actions, words, and thoughts). Obviously, the principle of interdependence (stimulus-response or cause-fruit) is intrinsically connected with one's behavior or acts, specifically with the moral quality of those acts (good or evil). As previously discussed, the moral quality of individuals' actions depends on their emotions. Therefore, according to Qisong's theory, becoming aware of the existence of stimuli as causes and of responses as fruits and understanding their functioning amounts to paying attention to the quality of the inner stimuli generated by good and evil emotions, which translate into external responses—namely, good or evil works. Moreover, he specifies in the next citation that good deeds promote life, while evil deeds destroy life. Confucian interest in organic life and growth and its association with harmonious social life and morality has been previously stressed. In the following paragraph of the "Guang yuanjiao," the Buddhist prohibition against the killing or harming of life is thus introduced by the author in a positive way (to love and nurture life) and in a moral context (good and evil actions and emotions), both familiar to Confucians. It is therefore arguable that his method of presenting Chan also assists in building bridges between Buddhism and Confucianism:

> Sentient beings love life and detest death (物好生, 物惡死); all the different categories of living beings are like this. It is for this reason that the sage puts forward life and does not promote destroying life (聖人所以欲生, 而不欲殺). Actions that preserve life as well as actions that destroy life have causes and fruits, the good and evil deeds have stimuli and responses (夫生殺有因果, 善惡有感應). Pursuing a good cause results in a good fruit. Pursuing an evil cause results in an evil fruit. The heart-mind that likes preserving life is good (好生之心善). The heart-mind that likes destroying life is evil (好殺之心惡). Therefore, how can one not pay attention to the stimuli generated by good and evil emotions (善惡之感)? ("GYJ," 0656a01-6)

Furthermore, Qisong interprets the notions of causes and fruits (the first two features of his conception of cohesive Chan training) in the light of the Buddhist notion of cultivating the individual (the third abovementioned feature), whose objective is to reach the level of completeness (至). From this point of view, the presence and functioning of causes indicate the way of ordinary people—his so-called "way of causes"—or intermediary levels, not yet accomplished, of the Chan practice. This is the way of being among all those who are ignorant because their nature is hidden, whose present behavior is motivated by past intentions that have become causes and therefore been shaped by the automatic functioning of the karmic imprints present in causal consciousness, which is the repository of the inner stimuli. What the scholar-monk calls the complete level of practice is that of those who have become Buddhas (enlightened individuals). He calls this "the way of fruits," because no causes are activated anymore by those who spontaneously make good acts. Their good deeds are "fruits" unblemished by tainted motivations:

> The way that humans follow is the so-called way of causes (因). The way that Buddhas [enlightened individuals] follow is the so-called way of fruits (果). The way of causes: this means that the level of completeness has not been reached (言乎未至也). The way of fruits: this means that the level of completeness has been reached (言乎至也). When the individual has reached the level of completeness (至), he is rectified [his acts are correct] (正). When one is rectified, one is at ease (自得) no matter the position he is in. ("GYJ," 0656c13-1)

In this passage, Qisong introduces the parallel between karmic causes/fruits and not-yet-enlightened (ignorant)/enlightened individuals. He describes the level of completeness reached by those enlightened, who have completed the cultivation of their nature, see it, and have reached the field of nature-emptiness of their heart-mind, as the way of fruits—the state in which their acts are fruits only, without causes—fruits no longer motivated by attachment and ignorance, no longer determined by the causes stored in causal consciousness. The latter functions automatically only in the case of those ignorant (non-enlightened), whose acts are caused by attachment and self-centeredness. The fruits of the acts of the enlightened individual are free of attachment and self-centeredness; they are spontaneous responses without self-involvement. In other words, they are not determined by the karmic force of the causes. These causes are therefore empty in the case of enlightened individuals because they have no attachment and their selves are empty, having become the abovementioned no-self, non-ego. It is significant that, while this is the highest spiritual level, the scholar-monk chooses to highlight it through focusing on the ordinary everyday life of such an enlightened individual, and this again in terms familiar to Confucians ("one's acts are correct (zheng 正)" and one is "at ease no matter the position one is in (無所居而不自得)"). In his view, the enlightened person—a Buddha (bodhisattva)—is not a spiritual individual cut off from the ordinary social world but an ordinary spiritual person whose conduct is correct or rectified and who is at ease no matter what position they are in. This is so because for such a human being, existence (i.e., one's position or specific role in society) is emptiness, and emptiness is existence (one's position). We can clearly see how the author admirably illustrates in concrete Confucian terms the Mahayana awareness that existence and emptiness are the same.

The first term with strong Confucian resonance that he uses in the above citation is the concept of to correct or rectify (zheng 正), which implicitly refers to one of the major stages of the Confucian practice discussed in the classic *Daxue*—that is, "to rectify one's heart-mind" (正其心; see *Daxue, jing* and *zhang* 7). Qisong infuses a spiritual meaning into this ancient moral term when he understands correctness or rectification of the individual as access to the way of Buddhas, where all acts performed become fruits free of any causes, of any karmic imprints.

In addition, note that the end of his citation is an unequivocal reference to paragraph 14 of the *Zhongyong*, which stresses that "there is no circumstance or position the exemplary man is not at ease in" (君子無入而不自得焉; see Arghiresco/u 2013, 213–241). Again, he completely opens up these Confucian terms, which have a limited moral meaning. The *Zhongyong* 14 explains that the exemplary man is at ease because "he complies with his present position and behaves in a manner that corresponds to it, without looking for something that is outside his situation" (君子素其位而行, 不願乎其外). Qisong's enlightened person is at ease everywhere not because they comply with an external model, such as the Confucian ritual, but because their karmic causes are empty; they are free of attachment, selfless, and aware of the nonduality "existence is emptiness and emptiness is existence"; the person is therefore mindful that there is no emptiness separated from ordinary existence. Once again, such an explanation of Chan Buddhist practice must have been meaningful and inspiring for Confucian scholars.

Qisong also explores the compatibility between Confucianism and Buddhism through interpreting the difference between the fundamental causes (*yin* 因) and the accessory causes (*yuan* 緣) as reflecting the distinction between the source of what he calls Buddhist happiness (*fu* 福) and the wellspring of Confucian happiness (see above, where this notion of happiness or good fortune is discussed from the perspective of the emotions). For this purpose, he refers to the *Liji* 禮記, chapter 22, "Ji tong" 祭統 (2), without naming his source (see reference note Zhang 1996, 35): "The Confucians [*Liji* 22 (2)] say: 'Happiness (福) means brought to completion (*bei* 備). Brought to completion means that everything follows the norms (corresponds to its name) (百順之名). When everywhere, everything follows the norms, this means brought to completion.' This is the accessory cause of the way (道其緣), and it is not its fundamental cause (不道其因). If people do not know the fundamental cause, then they do not know what it is that brings happiness" ("GYJ," 0657c22-14).

The fundamental causes have their roots in events of past occurrence, in remote past time and past lives, and they give birth to present effects—that is, the effects that follow the causes. The accessory causes or causal factors support and provide assistance to the effects that occur simultaneously with them. Qisong argues that Confucian happiness, which is the result of following norms within society, governance, and family, is a happiness or good fortune stemming from having knowledge of merely accessory conditions—namely, proximate, present life causes—without being aware of distant, past-life causes. Thus, Confucian happiness is only relative, still ignorant and motivated by self, compared with the complete Buddhist happiness, which arises from the awareness of the karmic force embodied in the fundamental causes, of the interconnection between causes and effects over past, present, and future lives. This experience gives a different meaning and depth to the perception of happiness, one that goes beyond merely emotions.

The Confucian happiness (*fu* 福) described in the *Liji* is limited to the field of morality, emotions, and human interrelationships; and it originates from completely internalizing a ritual norm, which is an outward restriction. Actually, the same paragraph of the *Liji*, chapter "Ji tong," from which the scholar-monk has quoted only the beginning, further explains this action of bringing duties to completion, called happiness, as a complete inward regulation of feelings and outward following of the way—that is, serving the sovereign with loyalty and serving the parents through fulfilling the duty of filial devotion (see also chap. 4). He uses another similar illustration to distinguish the fundamental or distant cause from the accessory or near cause (condition). Thus, the monk concretely defines the latter as embodied in the image of the parents and the married couple—namely, the sphere of the family and interpersonal hierarchical relationships: "The people recognize the relationship between father and son, and between husband and wife within the couple (父子, 夫婦), as the way of humans (人道); this means seeing only the accessory cause of the way of humans, and not seeing its fundamental cause (是見人道之緣而不見其因也)" ("GYJ," 0657c02).

Therefore, in the Chan scholar-monk's view, seeing (becoming aware of) one's nature in Confucian perspective is directly related to seeing (becoming aware of) only the accessory causes (this life), while seeing it from the Chan standpoint means discerning the fundamental causes (past, present, and future lives connected). The above paragraph from the "Guang yuanjiao" represents his interpretation of the notions of causes and fruits, explained using Confucian notions. To clearly understand how he effectively introduces these concepts in the practice of cultivating the Chan nature—namely, of "seeing/realizing one's nature"—the next step includes an examination of his viewpoint on the effective relationship between causes, fruits, and nature. His most original idea is establishing a perfect equation between causes and fruits on the one hand and nature on the other. In the next quotation, also from the "Guang yuanjiao,"

Qisong introduces a meaningful difference between "seeing" one's nature (this suggests the focus of Chan practice) and "talking about" it (this indicates the priority of Confucian teaching about cultivating nature). Interestingly enough, a century later, Zhu Xi described in exactly these terms the Confucianism before the emergence of the school of principle—see *On Buddhists* (*Shishi* 釋氏; Zhu Xi, *Zhuzi yulei* 朱子語類126, *Zhuzi quan shu*, 18:3924–3966) and chapter 6 of this book, dedicated to Qisong's "Encomium":

> People do not believe that nature is what the sage refers to as karmic causes (天下不信性為聖人之因). People do not believe that nature is also what the sage refers to as karmic fruits (天下不信性為聖人之果). People's nature is deluded (天下惑性), so they do not know how to cultivate it. People know to talk about nature, but they do not know how to see it (天下言性而不知見性). Not believing that the nature and the karmic cause the sage is talking about are one and the same thing: this means to make oneself ignorant (自昧). Not believing that the nature and the karmic fruits the sage is talking about are one and the same thing: this means to abandon oneself (自棄). When the individual's nature is not cultivated, it becomes submerged (不修性而性溺): this means to trouble oneself (惑). When one does not see one's nature but talks about nature (不見性而其言性): this means not being careful (非審). ("GYJ," 0659a08)

According to Qisong, nature is precisely karmic causes. In other words, nature is the state of the profound level of the heart-mind, in which the humans are able to realize the causal necessity embodied in the karmic causes that predetermine their acts. One who is not aware of these karmic causes is in an ignorant state and acting blindly. That is to say, in his view, to gain this awareness and reach the level of nature means that one has removed one's ignorance, and therefore one's actions do not emerge from incomprehension and do not produce infinite causal necessity anymore. This is because, as previously examined, the state of nature is also the field of emptiness, non-ego, and no-self. Nishitani explains the quality of the acts of one who has reached this level: "On this field doing is constant non-doing" (1982, 252). In this case, "our work," the Japanese philosopher adds, "does not arise from the darkness of ignorance (the root of self-centeredness)."

Nature is the karmic fruits too, as gaining awareness of the latter also occurs at this profound inner level. Nature and fruits are also one in the scholar-monk's view. This implies that cultivating their nature also allows individuals to empty their causes and to produce acts-fruits free of any ignorant motivations. In Nishitani's view, these fruits are the result of "a freedom altogether unbound" (1982, 249). In other words, the future acts occur spontaneously, no longer conditioned by previous karmic causes. Qisong calls this achievement "not abandoning oneself"—that is, taking care of oneself through improving one's future lives. The self (oneself; *zi* 自) involved in this field of nature as karmic fruits is the authentic self—the no-self or original self, free of all difference between self and other, and defined by the nonduality of self and other. Accordingly, he implicitly suggests here that, at this stage, one is not only not abandoning oneself but also not abandoning all sentient beings. The Japanese philosopher describes the production of such acts-fruits as doing things in a way that "implies a responsibility to every neighbor and every other . . . on the standpoint of non-ego," which is "the standpoint of the debt without debt toward all other beings" (Nishitani 1982, 255, 264). Indeed, Qisong's idea of "not abandoning" is used in the same sense as Nishitani's "responsibility" or "debt without debt."

In this manner, through building an intimate connection between nature, causes, and fruits, the Northern Song monk highlights the concrete future benefits that emerge from teaching people the notions of causes and fruits and their functioning. Teaching the causes is instrumental in showing people how they can concretely cultivate their nature—that is, govern their nature (修也者, 治性之具也)—and an incentive to stimulate them to continue cultivating it until completely unveiling their nature and becoming aware of the completeness of their nature (全性). Equally, teaching them the notion of fruits and its implications is important to allow them to understand what exactly the completion of practice is and how it affects the individual's life. Qisong's conception of nature as karmic causes and fruits is the original dimension of the *Fujiao bian*'s creative approach to explaining nature. It is easy to understand for Confucians because of its obvious connection with the ideas of good fortune and disaster. In the same section, "Guang yuanjiao" 0659a08, the Chan scholar-monk further develops his innovative interpretation of nature understood as causes and fruits. The latter provide not only a framework to assess disaster and build good fortune but also an impetus for cultivating one's nature. His interpretation thus connects the first two dimensions of the Chan practice (namely, causes and fruits) with the third—that is, the importance and the efficacy of cultivating one's nature.

Equally in the same section ("GYJ," 0659a08), Qisong describes the karmic causes (*yin* 因) as "the force coming from the outside that drives one to cultivate one's nature" (因也者, 修性之表也) and the karmic fruits (*guo* 果) as "the efficacy resulting from the accomplishment of the process of cultivating one's nature" (果也者, 成性之效也). In his view, it is essential to teach people about karmic causes. The first step of the teaching is persuading them that there are karmic causes and that they produce effects. When people are thus persuaded through teaching, these karmic causes become an external force, a serious incentive for them to cultivate their nature (修性之表). In other words, as a core part of the effort to cultivate one's nature through Chan teaching, a person becomes able to open a breach within the field of reason and self-consciousness, which is also the field limited to the present life consciousness, and thus becomes aware of their karmic causes imprinted in their causal consciousness. Qisong presents these causes as an external force that drives humans to keep cultivating their nature for the reason that their source is outside the present life and relates to past lives. The next step proposed by the author is to explain karmic fruits to people as the "efficacy" (*xiao* 效) resulting from "accomplished [accomplishing] nature" (成性), or, as discussed above, the ability to produce present acts empty of causes and free of any ignorant motivations as a result of the individual's nonattachment and enlightenment. Obviously, this efficacy is, for him, both the direct result of the fact that one has reached the completion of this process of cultivating the nature and the proof that one can achieve this final level.

In the "Guang yuanjiao," when defining the karmic causes as outside forces that urge people to cultivate their nature, Qisong advances the idea that to start this task is not something instinctual or simple, and people absolutely need a strong incentive to engage in this exercise of individual cultivation and transformation. The scholar-monk reflects, "Because people's heart-minds are not persuaded and are deluded (方疑之惑之), they do not take the decision to practice. They do not believe that there are fruits and are unaware of their efficacy (不必果而周其效者)" ("GYJ," 0659a18-4).

He highlights that people do not become involved easily and naturally in the activity of cultivating their nature; they need to be persuaded. For this reason, the teaching about causes is profitable because it shows them the positive effects of self-cultivation and thus provides an efficient incentive to motivate them to engage in cultivating themselves. Note that the idea that most people do not pursue their cultivation themselves is also expressed in ancient Confucianism (see *Zhongyong* 3; *Lunyu* 6:5); however, Confucians did not develop it or provide a specific method to correct this issue.

The fourth feature of the practice, inner testimony, is also clarified in the same context. If the process of cultivation is what keeps the individual's nature intact and prevents it from being submerged by emotions and ignorance, inner testimony—what one feels and experiences inwardly when practicing—is useful for examining whether or not the practice is efficient, whether one effectively and correctly sees one's nature (證也者, 見性之驗也, "GYJ," 0659a15-11; see sec. III.1).

IV. CONCLUSION

After discussing the complementarity between Confucianism and Buddhism from the perspective of Confucianism and Confucian concepts in the previous three chapters, this chapter examines a more complex, Chan dimension of Qisong's analysis: it calls attention to how his focus on the nondual character of the Chan practice is intended to have simultaneous impact on two interdependent levels—that of self-consciousness, everyday reason and logic, and emotions; and that of nature-emptiness. This nondual vision also allows him, when explaining Buddhist practice to a Confucian audience in terms familiar to them, to logically describe the indescribable, religious effects of Chan practice, which are beyond perceptible reality. Thus, the scholar-monk does not separate these effects from everyday ordinary reality but instead concretely anchors them in it. Arguably, the nonduality method provides him with a tool that builds a tangible explanation of the spiritual and its intangible features. This elucidation enables him to convincingly demonstrate that the spiritual is the root of ordinary activities, to a Confucian public that focuses on concrete, sociopolitical affairs. Qisong designates the latter as the proximity level (*jin* 近), which concerns all the perceptible facets of the everyday life of the present life, while designating the first as the distant level (*yuan* 遠), which deals with past and future lives and therefore surpasses present life ignorance, the cycle of death-life.

As a result of the nondual character of practice, he also describes (in the next paragraph from the "Guang yuanjiao") its highest level, the state of awakening (*jue* 覺), as having a nondual nature, occurring and unfolding simultaneously on both proximal and distant levels. In the quotation below, to illustrate their nonduality and interdependence, the scholar-monk describes each of the two fields examined in this chapter as having both types of attributes, proximity and remoteness. In other words, his description of each of these levels also nondually includes characteristics of the other one. For instance, at the level of proximity, one is able to "shed light on one's spirit," which is a remote attribute. And, at the level of remoteness, one "has a moral quality such as that of the sage." Obviously, the moral quality is a proximate feature. In this way, Qisong strategically and credibly stresses that awakening is simultaneously spiritual and mundane, transcendent (beyond life and death) and societal (anchored within society and governance). Undeniably, the tool of nonduality allows him to underpin the solid and visible presence of Buddhism in the everyday life of Song-dynasty society and thus promote the positive effects of the Buddhist practice of awakening when practiced in a community setting:

> The state of awakening (*jue* 覺) discussed based on a close point of view [current life, present experiences] (*jin* 近) entails ending troubles [caused by desires] that daily contaminate one (息塵勞), being peaceful, shedding light on one's spirit (靖神明), correcting the root [the essential dimension of existence] (正本) and cultivating the branches [secondary dimensions] (修末). The state of awakening discussed based on a distant point of view [past and future lives] (*yuan* 遠) entails having removed false views (了大偽), having surpassed the cycle of death-life (外死生), and having become completely untroubled [free of desires] (至寂); therefore, being constantly enlightened (常明), unattached and having a moral quality such as that of the sage's (聖人同德). The effect of the state of awakening is like this. The state of awakening is broad and complete. It cannot be completely expressed in words. Those who possess knowledge have not necessarily reached the state of awakening (不可以智得). The state of awakening persists (存) in those aware of their spirit and, therefore, enlightened (神而明之). ("GYJ," 0659b03-1)

In the same essay, the "Guang yuanjiao," another argument that suggests the subtle and nondiscursive interdependence between the two levels—their nonduality—is the author's description of them within one's heart-mind not as watertight compartments but as spheres in sporadic communication:

> When examining the way, the human experiences awakening and becomes a sage, and he understands that this permanent awakening (常覺) dwells within the daily life of all living beings. People experience the awakening in their day-to-day life, but they are not aware of it (眾生日覺而未始覺). Their awakening is like a dream; even when the sun rises, their sight is blurred. It is for this reason that the sage prods them and explains to them—because he wants them to continue their efforts towards awakening. He guides them so they aim at reaching awakening, because he wants them to reach complete awakening. ("GYJ," 0659b06-9)

In Qisong's words, all ordinary, ignorant people who are usually limited to the first level of awakening occasionally experience this profound level as flashbacks and without knowing it. This is instantaneously experiencing their own nature but not completely seeing, that is manifesting it.

This chapter explores several major dimensions of Chan—nonduality, knowledge, and karmic principles. Their nondiscursive realization and practice enable one to reach the level of complete awakening. Given the difficulty in discursively explaining these cohesive Chan features of the Northern Song scholar-monk's teaching, I have chosen Nishitani's Chan philosophical approach as an interpretative tool that gives the reader a theoretical device for understanding the distinctive facets of his doctrine and practice as compared to those of the Confucians. Two essential concepts of his specific Chan vision—the universal principle (理) and nothingness (無)—are further examined in chapter 6, dedicated to the last and most complex essay of Qisong's collection *Fujiao bian*, his "Tanjing zan" 壇經贊 ("Encomium of the Platform Sutra"). These themes appear a century later in Zhu Xi's 朱熹 (1130–1200) Neo-Confucian condemnation of Chan Buddhism. For this reason, the next chapter unfolds in the guise of a transhistorical conversation between two Song-dynasty thinkers: the Chan scholar-monk Qisong and the well-known Neo-Confucian master Zhu Xi. Chapter 6 argues that this dialogue not only represents the quintessence of the philosophical exchanges between Confucians and Buddhists during the Song dynasty but also provides essential conceptual evidence about the Chan Buddhist philosophical influence on Song Neo-Confucianism.

SIX

QISONG ON UNIVERSAL PRINCIPLE (*LI* 理), NOTHINGNESS (*WU* 無), AND THE "ENCOMIUM OF THE PLATFORM SUTRA" ("TANJING ZAN" 壇經贊)

Answers avant la Lettre to Zhu Xi's Twelfth-Century Criticism

I. INTRODUCTION

As already emphasized, the dynamic process of mutual interaction between Chan Buddhist and Neo-Confucian doctrines and concepts constitutes an important dimension of Song-dynasty culture. The present chapter argues that this process is closely related to the individual development of different forms of Chan Buddhism during the Song dynasty—not only those that became representative of Song-dynasty Chan (i.e., Linji) but also those that disappeared (Qisong's Yunmen Chan subschool). It examines the particular perspective of the Northern Song monk-scholar—the eleventh-century proponent of Yunmen Chan (see the introduction, sec. I)—described as a cohesive and Confucianized form of Chan practice (see chap. 5 and chap. 2). Specifically, this chapter offers a suggestive discussion of Qisong's and Zhu Xi's treatments of fundamental terms such as nothing(ness) (*wu* 無) and principle (*li* 理).

In this way, it contributes to the further analysis of the interaction that occurred in eleventh- and twelfth-century Song-dynasty China between Chan and Confucian approaches to the development of the individual and the practice of self-cultivation. The manner in which they evolved together philosophically during this period—their interdependence resulting from mutual exchanges and borrowings—requires broader attention that goes beyond the formal and official Confucian representation of that time, which was largely embodied in the anti-Buddhist discourse of the Neo-Confucian Cheng-Zhu school.

When it comes to Confucianism, from the thirteenth century onward, Zhu Xi's school triumphed as the new Confucian orthodoxy and political doctrine.

Following Han Yu's (768–824) and Zhu Xi's anti-Buddhist rhetoric, orthodox Neo-Confucians emphasized the ethico-political facets of Confucianism, regarding it mainly as the preeminent tool of governance, claiming the moral superiority of Confucianism, and officially identifying it as the ultimate symbol of Chinese culture. They considered Buddhism as a foreign doctrine that weakened Confucianism's rightful role in ordering and governing Chinese society (see chap. 1, sec. I).

When it comes to Buddhism, during the Song dynasty, Chan became Chinese Buddhism par excellence (Welter 2008, 7). Two of its five subschools prevailed: the Linji 臨濟 and the Caodong 曹洞. They promoted a version of Chan as a singular and independent tradition, outside the scriptures, distinct from the previous scholastic Buddhist tradition, and fostered new practices (see Foulk 1999, 188–219). As discussed in the introduction, section I, in the early Song, Qisong's Yunmen subschool was in competition with Linji for the status of the most influential Chan lineage. At a later stage, the Linji faction received support from official circles and assumed a dominant and "orthodox" role in Song Chan Buddhism (Welter 2011). The other three Chan subschools—the Yunmen 雲門, Guiyang 溈仰, and Fayan 法眼—all disappeared. Through his analysis of the tenth-century Chan master Yongming Yanshou's 永明延壽 (904–975) writings on the harmony between Chan and scholastic Buddhism, Albert Welter has contributed to our understanding of emerging Chan movements in the Five Dynasties and early Song period, before Qisong, and the ascendency of the Linji faction (Welter 2011). As explained by Tsai Chen-feng (2009, 177–213), in his criticism, Zhu Xi globally understood Buddhism rather as Linji Chan. Rightly, Welter, in his work on Yanshou's thought, emphasizes that not all Chan Buddhism in the Song period is reducible to Linji Chan, as Zhu Xi and his school suggested. This study argues that in the next century after Yanshou, Qisong of the Yunmen Chan defended and further developed the idea of the complementarity between Buddhist and Confucian traditions while also building a Confucianized presentation of Chan Buddhism.

II. WHY CREATE A SONG-DYNASTY DIALOGUE BETWEEN QISONG AND ZHU XI?

This chapter moves forward along this vein by presenting the viewpoint of the eleventh-century scholar-monk Qisong of the Yunmen school—one of the abovementioned three subschools assimilated by Linji—concerning issues directly related to Zhu Xi's twelfth-century commentary *On Buddhists* (*Shishi* 釋氏; Zhu Xi, *Zhuzi yulei* 朱子語類 126, *Zhuzi quan shu* [hereafter *ZZQS*],

18:3924–3966). In this context, chapter 6 examines Qisong's essay "Encomium of the Platform Sutra" ("Tanjing zan" 壇經贊; hereafter "TJZ"), the last and most complex essay of his collection *Fujiao bian*. It demonstrates that not only did Qisong advocate an all-inclusive Chan Buddhism as Yanshou had, but moreover, he promoted what may be called a Confucianized presentation of Chan: a "principled" nothingness. He wrote extensively on the complementarity of Buddhism and Confucianism within Chinese culture and how well they worked together to benefit a harmonious Chinese society. This feature of his other essays in the *Fujiao bian* has been widely explored in the previous chapters (1–5). Chapter 6 also introduces a new and complementary viewpoint: it argues that Qisong's interpretations provide pertinent answers avant la lettre to Zhu's criticism lodged one hundred years later.

In his article "Zhuzi dui fojiao de lijie ji qi xiangzhi" 朱子對佛教的理解及其限制 ("Zhu Xi's grasp of Buddhism, and its limitations"; Tsai 2012, 177–213), Tsai Chen-feng depicts Zhu Xi's understanding of the abovementioned notions—nothingness and principle—and his general disapproval of Chan Buddhism based on these concepts. He examines Zhu Xi's article *On Buddhists* (*Shishi* 釋氏), in which the Neo-Confucian scholar develops a philosophical critique of some major Buddhist concepts. On the Confucian side, his essay is important for our dialogue because prior Confucian anti-Buddhism criticism had been limited to socioeconomic, less elaborated arguments. The author intends here to render the Confucian anti-Buddhist discourse more effective through raising it to a doctrinal and philosophical level. Tsai notes that, in his judgment, the twelfth-century Confucian master understands Buddhism as primarily a foreign doctrine, harmful to the Chinese way (*dao* 道). As shown in chapters 1 to 5, Qisong depicts the harsh criticism directed against the Buddhist tradition by his eleventh-century contemporary Confucians in exactly the same way. It can be concluded that, in a sense, Zhu Xi's perspective reflects the pre-Song Confucian common view inherited from Han Yu (see chap. 1, sec. II). He does not recognize the emergence of an authentic and individualized Chinese Buddhism (as the eleventh-century collection *Fujiao bian* advocates in conceptual and argumentative terms), and he considers the Chinese scriptures as the result of "stealing" from Daoism ("The Buddhists first stole from Liezi 列子"; *Shishi*, ZZQS, 18:3925). Nor does he distinguish among the abovementioned different forms of Song Chan; instead, the Neo-Confucian scholar discusses Song Chan as the Linji Chan subschool.[1]

In connection with Zhu Xi's arguments advanced in his *Shishi*, the analysis of this chapter introduces Qisong's Confucianized Buddhist interpretation of the two notions and his ethico-moral approach to Chan Buddhism. As has been mentioned on numerous occasions throughout this book, his work was widely known during the Northern Song dynasty. His explanation of the Buddhist concepts not only provides a century-earlier meaningful response to Zhu Xi's recriminations but also highlights a genuinely Chinese, Confucianized dimension of his Chan, which belongs to one of the Song-dynasty subschools disregarded by Zhu Xi. As Linji did not emphasize ethico-moral training, the subject dear to Zhu's heart, yet was a predominant and powerful faction during Zhu Xi's time, we might also plausibly surmise that, for this reason, he purposely focused his criticism on it. His blanket condemnation of Buddhism, one century after the Northern Song scholar-monk wrote extensively about the complementarity between Confucianism and Buddhism, also suggests another thing: that, as a ruling class, the Neo-Confucians preferred to remain officially silent on Qisong's Confucianized vision of Chan or on a possible partnership with Buddhism and therefore were unwilling to see Buddhists as associates rather than competitors.

The piece investigated in this context is the "Tanjing zan" 壇經贊 ("Encomium of the Platform Sutra") included in the anthology *Fujiao bian*. Beyond addressing avant la lettre the issues raised a century later by Zhu Xi in *On Buddhists*, these essays, which offer a Confucian approach to Buddhism, bring light on a less understood and examined form of Chan that, to use the words of Welter, resisted interpreting Buddhism in terms dictated by Linji Chan (Welter 2011, 205)—what I call a cohesive and Confucianized Chan. Although Qisong's work was well known to the court and scholar-officials of Zhu's time, it is mentioned neither by him nor by the Northern Song Neo-Confucian masters that preceded him and had influenced him most—the Cheng brothers, who were still in their twenties when the Northern Song scholar-monk wrote his work. Yü Ying-shih affirms that the Cheng brothers strategically never mentioned Qisong in their works. However, he argues that they certainly knew his writings very well (see chap. 3, n. 30).

On the Chan Buddhist side, Qisong's view is significant for the following reasons: it was approved in 1062, by Emperor Renzong (r. 1022–1063) himself, to be included in the Song Buddhist canon, which implies that it was publicly widely known and respected (see Wang 2017, xxxiii, 108). Furthermore, as discussed in the introduction, section I, in the previously mentioned study, Tsai points out that the scholar-official Chen Shunyu 陳舜俞 (1026–1076), in his book *Duguanji* 都官集 (Collected works of a town official), recorded that Qisong's work had a positive impact on scholar-officials' perception of Buddhism as being compatible with Confucianism.

One might say that Zhu Xi's efforts to criticize Buddhism, and hence to stress the incompatibility between Confucianism and Buddhism, may be seen as some form of response to Qisong's efforts to demonstrate their complementarity in promoting the well-being of Chinese society. The short presentation of Zhu Xi's twelfth-century critique of Chan Buddhism before addressing the Northern Song scholar-monk's eleventh-century perspective is not anachronistic but aims to emphasize two key points. First, despite the development of five distinctive Chan subschools, the Confucian condemnatory discourse against Buddhism remained essentially unchanged from the Tang to the Northern and Southern Song dynasties. Second, despite some illustrious efforts to illustrate the common features of Buddhism and Confucianism, like that of the author of the *Fujiao bian*, the Neo-Confucians formally disregarded them while many of them privately appreciated and studied Chan. This clearly indicates the unwillingness on the part of Neo-Confucians to openly recognize either the existence of a full-fledged Chinese Chan Buddhism as an authentic feature of Chinese culture or the capacity of some charismatic Chan Buddhists—like those of the Yunmen school, or "lettered Chan" (see Gimello 1992, 381; introduction, sec. I)—to effectively contribute, alongside Neo-Confucians, to the moral education of Song-dynasty Chinese society. One might also justifiably assume that Zhu chose to remain silent on Qisong's moral, cohesive, and Confucianized Chan, as he did not wish to have this conversation about "officially" including Chan in the sphere of human relations and good governance, a domain that was traditionally reserved for the Confucian ruling class.

The next section presents the Northern Song scholar-monk's understanding of the Chan notions of nothing(ness) and principle in the form of an answer avant la lettre (one hundred years prior) to Zhu Xi's criticism. It provides a comparative analysis—Chan Buddhist and Neo-Confucian—of the notion of principle (*li* 理).

III. PRINCIPLE (*LI* 理): THE DIFFERENCE BETWEEN THE NONDUALIST (QISONG) AND DUALIST (ZHU XI) APPROACHES

The background of this examination is the inherent difference between the Northern Song scholar-monk's religious-nondualist and the Southern Song Neo-Confucian's rationalist-dualist views on these topics. It can be said that while Zhu "understands" by means of cognitive faculties, Qisong internally "realizes" the nothing(ness), principle, and authentic nature of things as religious experiences and as states of awareness, beyond the so-called ordinary separation of "internal" (self) and "external" (things) produced by consciousness (see chap. 5, sec. III.2). One may define the scholar-monk's "realization beyond separation" in Keiji Nishitani's terms, as both actualization and understanding of "the true reality of our self-together-with-all-things" (Nishitani 1960, 41). Unlike him, the Neo-Confucian master apprehends them "externally," through theoretical knowledge, within the field of consciousness, as external things— that is, originally outside one's self.[2]

The evaluation below concludes that while Qisong's point of view is all-inclusive and nondually encompasses both visions—religious and rationalist— that of Zhu has an external focus, and his center of attention remains from beginning to end the rationalist-metaphysical sphere. His understanding and criticism of Chan Buddhism are somehow weak and unidimensional because he discusses and criticizes Linji Chan as paradigmatic Chan. Nevertheless, for the reasons discussed earlier—the Yunmen was assimilated by the Linji subschool—it might be said that considering the latter as paradigmatic Chan was relevant during his time, almost a century after Qisong. Was this the result of the efforts of the subsequent Chan Buddhists to forge a pure identity for their Buddhist tradition and to clearly separate their practices from those of the Confucian tradition? Was the sectarian tendency triumphant over the Northern Song scholar-monk's inclusive and Confucianized vision?

Note also that in Zhu's view, the principle *li* 理 (discussed in the next section) has not only a theoretical, rationalist significance, but for him, principle is fundamentally ontological (metaphysical patterning of things) and ethical (good patterning of things). All principles of things and actions are present in potency in one's human nature, and therefore they become manifest in one's everyday relationships and good governance through the exemplary man's constant, outwardly oriented extension and knowledge and through the inner cultivation of reverence. In his view, the latter enables one to identify and understand one's egocentric feelings and interests and thus to separate from them. Julia Ching's explanation of this articulation in Zhu's thought is nuanced and insightful:

> Chu's [Zhu's] balanced method of both extension of knowledge and reverence would seem more "outer" oriented, since it takes the person out of himself, to the investigation of truth in the classical texts and in the natural universe. In fact, however, Chu's attention was focused on *xing* (nature), which he regarded as containing all principles (*li*) in potency, and which awaits the effort of being cleared from the obscuration cast upon by passions. It is a more passive principle, which must be acted upon, through the work of *xin*, the mind and heart, which controls both nature and emotions. For this

reason, Zhu placed much emphasis on quiet sitting, as a technique which consists in the restoration of man's pristine goodness. (Ching 1974, 174)

In a similar vein, Kirill Thompson also highlights the presence and importance of the cultivation of reverence in ancient Confucian thought as well as in Zhu Xi's Neo-Confucian perspective:

> It should come as no surprise that Confucius placed such a premium not just on the feelings, cultivations, and practices of filiality and fraternity but also on the reverential regard and deportment necessary in observances of ancestral sacrifices. He ascribed a special primacy to the feelings and expressions of reverential regard (*jing* 敬) operative in our sincere observances of ancestral rites and sacrifices, on the consideration that they purify our emotions and spirit and open our hearts so as to be resonant with ancestral spirits. I would argue that, for Confucius and Zhu Xi 朱熹 alike, it was this perceived catalyzing effect of reverential regard that made it crucial to their programs of cultivation, learning, and practice generally; for this opening resonance with the ancestral spirits would ground and vivify one's affections for and interactions with one's present relations against the living backdrop of a newly discerned fuller and richer tapestry of human connectedness.
> Noting how such reverential regard actuates one's resonance with ancestral spirits and vivifies one's interpersonal sensitivity and responsiveness, concentration, humility, alertness, and responsiveness—to be maintained in daily cultivation, learning, and practice.[3] (Thompson 2021, 16–17)

It is interesting to realize that Qisong's critique of this tendency in Confucianism (i.e., external focus) anticipated Lu Jiuyuan's 陸九淵 (1139–1192) disapproval of Zhu Xi's externalist and particularist orientation ("investigating things"), such as expressed in the latter's methodology of investigating things.[4] As discussed in chapter 1, section IV.2, in the *Great Learning*, the approach of "making one's natural knowledge complete" (*zhizhi* 至知) is defined as the "investigation of things" (*gewu* 格物), and Zhu Xi explains it in Neo-Confucian terms as "fully developing the understanding of all principles of coherence of things" (物格者, 物理之極處無不到也; Zhu, *Daxue zhangju, ZZQS*, 6:17).

In 1175, Lu Jiuyuan (Lu Xiangshan 陸象山) dramatically expressed his objections in a debate[5] with Zhu Xi at the Goose Lake Chan Buddhist Monastery, situated in the eastern part of today's Jiangxi province. Julia Ching (1934–2001) regarded this debate as "the conflict between learning and wisdom," as "an important event in the history of Chinese thought, chiefly because it marked the differences between two of the greatest representatives of the movement of thought known in the West as Neo-Confucianism. The differences which manifested themselves during this debate provoked repercussions during many centuries, particularly in Ming times, with the emergence of Wang Yang-ming 王陽明 (1472–1529) a self-proclaimed heir of Lu Chiu-yuan [Lu Xiangshan]. The impact of these differences would make itself felt even outside of China, particularly in Japan and Korea" (Ching 1974, 161). The main facets of Zhu's critical perception are outlined below.

III.1. Zhu Xi's Critical Perception of Chan Teaching in On Buddhists (Shishi 釋氏)

In his examination of Zhu Xi's *On Buddhists*, Tsai writes, "Master Zhu treats the concept of *kong* 空 (emptiness) as used in Buddhism as being equivalent to 'without principles' (*wuli* 無理). This is not only a criticism of original Buddhism, but a criticism of Chan scholarship (禪學)" (2012, 192).[6] Tsai also points out Zhu Xi's explanation of the Buddhist *kong* 空 (emptiness) as merely "nothing at all" (空無所有):

> Based on this understanding, Master Zhu also discusses Buddhism in terms of "*xu* 虛" [devoid of reality, void], and Confucianism in terms of "*shi* 實" [real, having real existence] [see *Shishi* 釋氏; *Zhuzi yulei* 126, ZZQS, 18: 3934]. His intent is that only Confucian teachings are "real and have principles" (*shi er youli* 實而有理), and Buddhist teachings are "devoid of reality and without principles" (*xu er wuli* 虛而無理). When he says that the Buddhists are "without principles (*wuli* 無理) and thus are *kong* 空 (empty)" [*Shishi*; ZZQS 18: 3934], the focus is on "*wuli* 無理 (without principles)," and it matters not whether the Buddhists use "*wu* 無 (nothing)," "*kong* 空 (empty)," or "*xu* 虛 (void)" to represent the meaning of "*wuli* 無理 (without principles)," the only difference is wording, and there is no theoretical significance. Therefore, in Zhu Xi's view, later Buddhist theories of *xing* 性 (natural tendencies) and *xin* 心 (the heart-mind) find no support for their arguments grounded on the notion of "*wuli* 無理 (without principles)." (Tsai 2012, 191)[7]

Indeed, Zhu Xi stresses, "'Without principles (*wuli* 無理),' this is 'empty (*kong* 空).' What they [Buddhists] call heart-mind (*xin* 心) and nature (*xing* 性)—these are just empty things, without principles (只是個空底物事, 無理)" (*Shishi*, ZZQS, 18:3934).

As mentioned earlier, Zhu Xi's criticism of the Buddhist perspective as lacking principle of coherence *wu li* (無理) is aimed at the Chan Buddhist tradition. It is worth remembering that in his view, Chan is principally embodied in the Linji tradition, which indeed is not concerned with investigating principle but rather with focusing on critical phrases (*huatou* 話頭; see Zhu, *Shishi*, ZZQS, 18:3958; Tsai 2012, 200).

Before proceeding further, let us briefly recall some major differences between the Confucian and Chan understandings of the term *principle* (*li* 理) (the Neo-Confucian theory of the principle of coherence is discussed in chap. 1, sec. IV.1; Qisong's theory of the universal principle, in chap. 2, sec. II.1, and chap. 3, sec. III.2). In what follows, this generic term *li*, which, roughly speaking, refers to the same multifaceted (metaphysical, ontological, spiritual, religious, etc.) aspect of reality in the scholar-monk's Chan work and Zhu's school of principle but is approached in different manners, is identified by the all-encompassing name *principle*: a real and subtle, significant level of reality, with metaphysico-ethical (Neo-Confucianism) and ethico-spiritual (Buddhism) implications. However, this denomination contextually entails two different meanings, which are the result of different approaches, and are translated as follows: the coherence principle in Zhu Xi's Neo-Confucian sphere[8] and the universal principle in Qisong's Chan Buddhist domain.[9] These different contextual translations highlight the existence of a fundamental difference between the two approaches to the same reality of *li* 理.

As is well known, the Buddhist perspective is the earlier one (see Chan 1964, 123–149). This section suggests that the Neo-Confucian viewpoint is inspired by the Buddhist one and represents an adaptation of this reality of principle to the specific Neo-Confucian ethico-moral and metaphysical focus and rationalist method.

As already mentioned, note that while Zhu's principle is metaphysical and ontological, in Qisong's understanding, it is religious (i.e., it entails nondual awareness of the universal principle and draws inspiration from Huayan Buddhist theory[10]). As he explains in the beginning of the essay "Guang yuanjiao" (0654b16-15), while developing his own ideas, he took inspiration from the manner of presentation of the *Huayan Sutra* and its central position: "By assimilating the branches, one returns to the root (攝末歸本門)." Zhu Xi's understanding belongs to the sphere of moral epistemology and of ethics as religion. The scholar-monk's universal principle of Chan is the root or common ground of everything, not a substantive reality (it is nondualist—that is, it lies beyond the duality of substantiality (*shi* 實)/insubstantiality (*xu* 虛)), which is the framework of Zhu Xi's analysis (see above), but a state of awareness of the intrinsic interdependence of all individual existences. Zhu's Neo-Confucian coherence principle belongs to the field of ethical dualism (the principle of moral coherence/perceptible appearance and behavior; see chap. 1, sec. IV). Julia Ching interprets his vision of the principle *li* (of heaven) and of its articulation with the nature *xing* and the heart-mind *xin* (of human and of the way):

> Zhu prefers to speak of *li* 理 (principle, being, goodness), which he also calls *xing* 性 (nature) in man. For him, *xin* 心 refers more to consciousness, to

the active side of man, which, on account of its very dynamism, is capable of evil, whereas *xing* 性, the more passive principle, is full of goodness. This interpretation of human nature and of the possibility of evil is consonant with his basic interpretation of reality itself, with its dualist tendencies expressed in the opposition of *li* 理 to *qi* 氣, the individuating, physical principle, which limits the potentiality for goodness. True, Zhu Xi also sees the spiritual legacy of the ancient sages as lying in "Mind"—the Mind of the Way (Daoxin 道心). He sees it in contrast to the "mind" of man (renxin 人心) which is full of qi 氣, and is subject to errors. To him, they represent two different realms, that of virtue, or Heavenly principle (tianli 天理) and that of human emotions or passions (renyu 人欲). (Ching 1974, 166)

To continue Ching's interpretation of Zhu's principle, I would add that the major difference between his vision and Qisong's view is the following: while the Neo-Confucian principle is integrated in a dual structure (*tianli* 天理/*qi* 氣), the author of the *Essays on Assisting the Teaching* highlights their nonduality—the universal principle and the social activities in the world are not two, also not one, but nondual.

From this specific conception of principle, Zhu derives his reasoning that Chan is unprincipled.[11] To better understand the root of his criticism as well as the Chan scholar-monk's different perspective, an interpretation of the Neo-Confucian scholar's conception is necessary and is provided below.

III.2. Zhu Xi's Dualist Moral View: Li 理 as Coherence Principle

I suggest that, within this Neo-Confucian moral structure, the translation principle of coherence or coherence principle for Zhu's term *li* 理 is justified not only philosophically but also etymologically. The Latin *cohaerentia*—organic order, structure—emphasizes the quality of constituting a unified whole. The Latin *principium*—source, foundations—has a moral resonance, exactly as does *li*. Translating *li* 理 as "coherence" disregards the strong moral connotation of this notion for Zhu Xi. First and foremost, he understands principle as principle of appropriate behavior: metaphysical potentiality included in the contingency of individuals. In his *Zhongyong zhangju* 1, the Neo-Confucian scholar writes, "Dao is the principle of coherence that all everyday things and affairs must follow. It is the moral quality of every nature. Every heart-mind is provided with this principle of coherence" (道者, 日用事物當行之理, 皆性之德而具於心; ZZQS, 6:32).

Translating it as merely the principle acknowledges this ethico-moral dimension but ignores the meaning of *li* as organic structure bestowed by heaven-earth. Heaven and earth are interlocked and indivisible, as are the two dimensions of their continuum, the coherence principle and functioning (*yong* 用; see next quotation), according to Zhu. He describes the structure of heaven-earth, as the principle of coherence (*li* 理) or *dao* 道, and its mode of functioning, vital breath (*qi* 氣)[12] or utensil (*qi* 器), and highlights their holistic unity and hierarchical dependency. But he does this within a dualist framework, with particular emphasis on their distinction:

> Within heaven-earth, there is the principle of coherence and the vital breath (天地之間, 有理有氣). The principle of coherence is the *dao* from beyond perceptible appearance (形而上之道也), that is, the root that gives birth to things. Vital breath is the utensil [things for use] within perceptible appearance (形而下之器也), that is, the utility (具) [use, utilization, way in which something can be used] that gives birth to things. Therefore, the birth of humans and things necessarily relies on the principle of coherence; and then, authentic nature occurs. The latter necessarily relies on vital breath; and then, perceptible appearance occurs. Even though the authentic nature and the perceptible appearance of a thing are not "outside" one another but form a single unity, the distinction between its *dao* and its utility quality is very clear. One cannot confuse them (雖不外乎一身, 然其道器之間分際甚明, 不可亂也。). (Zhu, ZZQS, 23:2755)

Consequently, when reflecting on his condemnation of Chan Buddhism as unprincipled, based on this organically/metaphysically moral and dualist (*li-qi* 理-氣) perspective, one observes that his analysis of the *li* 理 is founded on two premises: a dualist approach based on the relationships "nothing/something" (無/有), "*dao*/vital breath" (道/器), and "metaphysical potentiality/contingent utility" (本/具) and a metaphysical rationalist and moral interpretation of the knowledge.

It might be assumed that the main flaw in Zhu's criticism is his disregard for the different natures (dualist/nondualist) of the Confucian and Chan approaches to principle. The Neo-Confucian admits that he is primarily looking for (metaphysically) rational justification (有道理; see Zhu, Shishi, ZZQS, 18:3934) within the abovementioned dualist frame of reference. This is the position of the consciousness—namely, the dualist view defined earlier. He starts from a metaphysically rational and moral understanding of the (coherence) principle, as in his view the raison d'être of a thing (道理) has also a moral connotation. Based on this metaphysically rational premise, he sees the Buddhist state of nothingness (*wu* 無) or emptiness (*xu* 虛) as nonexistence—that is, the opposite of the state of material existence (somethingness (*you* 有)) and therefore separate from the apparent reality of everyday human existence and morality, which is the essence of the Neo-Confucian (coherence) principle. From these rational and moral premises flows for him the conclusion that Buddhists lack moral norms and moral restraint. In other words, their everyday reality is devoid of the (coherence) principle: "Every thing returns to nothing (一齊都歸於無)—they [the Buddhists] eat food all day, and yet they say they do not bite a single grain of rice. They wear clothes all day, and yet they say they do not put on a single string of silk" (Zhu, *Shishi*, ZZQS, 18:3930, cited in Tsai 2012, 190).[13]

From his two presuppositions (metaphysically rationalist and ethico-moral), Zhu infers the impossibility for Buddhists of gaining knowledge of real things, a rigorous rational process that he defines as "examining things" (格物) and "achieving the greatest possible knowledge" (致知; Zhu, *Daxue zhangju* 5, ZZQS, 6:20; *Shishi*, ZZQS, 18:3934). Obviously, the theoretical knowledge that he has in mind is the dualist kind: things and processes of everyday life are separate from and external to one's self, as objects of the knowing subject. This Confucian dualist separation between two states (existence, examining things of everyday life, and permanent connection with the real life versus nothingness, ascending to a higher level, and disconnection from real life) is convincingly illustrated in a quote by Cheng Hao 程顥 (1032–1085) in the Neo-Confucian anthology *Jinsilu* 近思錄 13.4, compiled by Zhu Xi and Lu Zuqian 呂祖謙 (1137–1181) (see also chap. 1). There, what the Neo-Confucians see as the disconnection of the Buddhists from real life is described as an endeavor to only "ascend to higher level" (上達; i.e., seek enlightenment, as this higher level is understood by Neo-Confucians to be metaphysical), instead of first "descending to the lower level of the groundwork" (下學; "lower level" is interpreted by them as pertaining to the material world, as concerning human affairs and the morality of everyday life) and then striving to move up. This distinction ascend/descend comes from the *Analects* 14.37, where Confucius highlights the necessary continuity between starting first with the groundwork until one is prepared to step up to a higher level: "They [Buddhists] [notes Cheng Hao 程顥] devote their efforts to ascending to a higher level (上達) without descending to the lower level of the groundwork (無下學). In this case, can their ascension to a higher level be correct? First, the two levels are thus disjoined (不相連屬). And all that is disconnected (有間斷), it is not the way (非道也)" (*Jinsilu* 近思錄, 13.4; ZZQS, 13:278).

Therefore, in the Neo-Confucian approach, coherence principles of things and affairs are to be understood starting from the external experience of concrete reality. The Confucian endeavor consists in first knowing principles—that is, probing coherence principles of things (i.e., of objects of knowledge, behaviors, and events) to the utmost (窮理)[14] in order, subsequently, to be able to follow principles (順理; that is, to practice ethico-moral behavior). Zhu Xi sees Chan Buddhist nothingness and Chan practice as separated from the social world and its everyday reality. Consequently, he concludes, the Chan practice of emptiness and nothingness is unprincipled (無理) and therefore unmoral.

III.3. Qisong's Nondualist and Moral View:
Li 理 as Universal Principle

Qisong's focus on *li* 理 and moral practice, a century before Zhu Xi, nullifies, so to speak, the Neo-Confucian's general view about the unprincipled and unmoral character of Buddhist training. The scholar-monk understands Chan practice as principled, and his conception is also based on a moral perspective, but a nondualist one that includes human ethics within the broader sphere of the religious. One could define it in Masao Abe's terms, as a "boundless solidarity of life between persons and other beings" (1986, 141). As explained below, far from denying it, Qisong also highlights the connection, mentioned above in the Neo-Confucian context, between the day-to-day level and the higher level, but from a nondualist position. That is, he starts not from the investigation of separate things (格物) that finally get united through one's knowledge (as in the Neo-Confucian perspective, where understanding principle is the result of one's complete rational, discursive, or intellectual knowledge (致知)) but from a Chan religious experience—namely, one's awareness of the fundamental unity of everything (unmediatedly experienced within one's self). One might clearly describe it using Nishitani's terms as "coming into contact with things as they really are" (1960, 29), not through representations but through the real manifestation of the universal principle, "which is actually concealed at the foundation of the self and everything in the world" (36).

Zhu laments what he sees as his contemporary Chan practitioners' lack of knowledge of the Buddhist scriptures and of moral purification through the practice of quiet sitting (不必看經不必靜坐; Zhu, *Shishi, ZZQS*, 18:3958). It is arguable that his criticism applies only to Linji Chan and not to the Northern Song scholar-monk's cohesive and Confucianized Chan. By contrast, in his collection of essays, far from neglecting the knowledge of scriptures, Qisong advocates for a holistic and inclusive Chan, in harmony with the scholastic Buddhist schools, including Huayan and Tiantai. He relates to the first (Huayan) through emphasizing the correlatives essence-function (*ti-yong* 體用) and root-shoots (*ben-mo* 本-末) and the universal principle of coherence (see chap. 2). As mentioned earlier, the monk also avows that he took the *Huayan Sutra* as a model. He includes the second (Tiantai) through emphasizing nature-appearance (*xing-xiang* 性-相). Furthermore, as seen throughout this book, his interpretation of Chan also emphasizes the complementarity of Confucianism and Buddhism.

In other words, the scholar-monk incorporates in his cohesive Chan view the scholastic Buddhist notion of universal principle and at the same time is inspired by the moral perspective of Confucianism. Consequently, he embraces "principle" as simultaneously and entirely existent in each individual phenomenon (thing, being, situation, etc.): as Chan nothingness, the common foundation that nourishes the interdependence of all living beings; but also as highest morality, which stems from this nothingness; and as the power source of the individual's moral practice of the observance of precepts (see below).

While the effects of the existence of principle in phenomena (things and affairs) are similar in both the Neo-Confucian's and the Chan scholar-monk's perspectives—perfection and spontaneous morality—their natures are different, as are the approaches used to achieve them: Confucian dualistic ethics and Buddhist nondualistic ethics. Note that the latter embraces the dualist view and goes beyond it. In his commentary *Zhongyong jie* (hereafter ZYJ), Qisong equates one's universal principle with one's authentic nature, which he considers as spiritual (*xing ling* 性靈). He proceeds thus to connect Buddhist notions with well-known Confucian ones, such as the *tianming*天命 ("what heaven endows with"):

> What heaven endows with (天命) is the dynamic ordering of the vital movements of heaven-earth (天地之數), and authentic nature is the spiritual authentic nature (性則性靈也). In other words, the human belongs to this dynamic ordering of the vital movements of heaven-earth, and fuses (生合) with the spiritual authentic nature. Authentic nature is therefore the universal principle, which is always with us (性乃素有之理也). The emotions originate from what one experiences and feels (情感而有之也). (Qisong, ZYJ 3, 666c18-1)

This quotation illustrates the abovementioned major difference between Qisong's understanding of the universal principle and Zhu's understanding of the coherence principle. Qisong considers it as spiritual/religious, as inherent in the human being, while the emotions (which are, for him, integral to the Confucian sphere) emerge and take shape at the moment of one's interaction with external things (see chap. 5). In Zhu Xi's Neo-Confucian view, it is this external interaction that generates the knowledge of the coherence principle. The paragraph above also illustrates Qisong's specific Chan perspective on the concrete moral reality of human affairs and relationships—the Confucian domain par excellence. He interprets this circumstantial moral reality (the domain of human interaction) as the sphere of emotions/feelings, which are externally generated. The scholar-monk's Chan Buddhist universal principle is beyond the sphere of emotions, requires a nondualist experience, and cannot be completely understood through emotions and intelligence, unlike Zhu's coherence principle, which is accessible through emotional (including intellectual) processing. Consequently, the Confucian dualist knowledge of the coherence principle, which pertains to the sphere of ethics and morality, is understood by Qisong as emanating from the emotions and how they are handled. He acknowledges this connection between the universal principle and emotions at the physiological level. To be able to grasp and experience the (universal) principle of their physiological lives, people, he remarks, need to manage and put their emotions in order. And this is possible, he notes, by using the Confucian tools—ritual behavior, music, laws, and political administration (*li* 禮, *yue* 樂, *xing* 刑, and *zheng* 政): "By promoting ritual behavior, music, laws and political administration, the emotions of humans are well placed. Thus, individuals do not do violence to their life, and they are able to grasp the universal principle of their life. The emotions do not trouble their authentic nature (性), and the universal principle of their authentic nature is rectified (禮樂刑政修。則人情得其所也。人不暴其生。人之生理得也。情不亂其性。人之性理正也。)" (Qisong, *ZYJ* 2, 0666b03-1).

Furthermore, it should be noted in passing that the last two paragraphs introduce another key notion for understanding this transhistorical conversation between Qisong and Zhu Xi—*xing* 性, which is closely linked to principle. It is translated here, in the context of the encounter between Qisong and Zhu Xi, as authentic nature (the Neo-Confucian perspective) and in chapter 5, section III (which focuses on the interdependence between emotions and nature in Qisong's thought), as nature-emptiness (the Chan view). In other words, in the scholar-monk's cohesive Chan vision, within everything there exists the same spiritual universal principle and authentic nature. It is clear from the arguments presented in this section that, contrary to what Zhu says about Chan Buddhists' lack of principle in general, Qisong not only admits the existence of principle but nondually equates it with authentic nature/nature-emptiness—a key component of his distinctive cohesive Chan thought. However, the author of the *Fujiao bian* views it differently because he relies on a broader approach. Note that the quote above points out a Confucian dimension incorporated in his thought: the integration of Confucian tools (ritual behavior, music, laws/punishments, and political administration) within the broader sphere of his cohesive Chan.

It is also important to stress another original interpretation of the universal principle the scholar-monk suggests. For him, as a fervent advocate not only of an inclusive Chan Buddhism but also of the compatibility between Confucianism and Buddhism, the spiritual/religious universal principle is the common source of all teachings—Buddhist, Confucian, and other. From it, all sages (Buddhist, Confucian, and other) draw inspiration when creating their different practices, and toward it all teachings converge. This is another facet of his nondualist vision. Due to their spiritual common root, for Qisong all learnings have a common goal—that is, "making people good (為善)": "The teachings provided by sages are different; however, they are identical in that they make people good" (聖人為教不同, 而同於為善也; "Yuanjiao" [hereafter "YJ"], 0649b28-10). In his view, the universal principle thus constitutes the source of the interdependence not only between different living beings but also between different teachings:

> Kindness and appropriate behavior (*ren yi* 仁義) [i.e., Confucian practice] are vestiges (footprints) of the method of good governance of society [for one lifetime] left by the first kings. If one discusses their practices starting from these footprints [concrete methods], their practices are different. If one discusses them starting from the universal principle, their practices are the same. The footprints stem from the universal principle, and the universal principle is the origin of the footprints. The footprints are the shoots, the universal principle is their root. The sage is searching for the root so he could set the shoots aside. (夫仁義者, 先王一世之治迹也。以迹議之, 而未始不異也. 以理推之, 而未始不同也。迹出於理, 而理祖乎迹。迹, 末也. 理, 本也. 君子求本而措末可也。) (Qisong, "YJ," 0649b13-16)[15]

In the scholar-monk's cohesive Chan vision, becoming conscious (*shi* 識), aware of the simultaneous presence of the universal principle within oneself and within others and all teachings, is the most valuable thing for the superior person (*junzi* 君子). Notice in the next quotation his Confucian *guwen* language. He justifies this claim by asserting that acquiring awareness of a shared universal principle is what leads one to become inclusive from within, to support inclusive communication with others, and to avoid excluding them and other teachings. Thus, becoming aware of the all-embracing presence of the universal principle constitutes for Qisong a means of describing the nondualist method and the nondualist experience of reality. According to him, the Chan practice is the everyday training that allows individuals to acquire awareness of the universal principle and to cultivate it:

> The exemplary person understands everything holistically (君子通而已矣). Why should he limit himself to one thing [i.e., a single teaching]?

The exemplary person should think about what connects [i.e., individuals and teachings]; why should he need to deny others [i.e., as Confucians deny the reliability of Buddhism]? Eating and drinking, and the married life—these are things the people consider precious and think they understand. But for the exemplary man these are not precious; what he considers as precious is being able to know the way and being aware of the principle. (君子通而已矣，何必苟專。君子當而已矣，何必苟非。飲食男女人皆能知貴。而君子不貴。君子之所貴。貴其能知道而識理也。) (Qisong, "YJ," 0650b14-10)

In the same context of his essay "Yuanjiao," the author describes the cohesive Chan practice—that is, the process of acquiring awareness of the universal principle—as the transformation (*hua* 化) people undergo when they are moved from the inside (感其內), from their heart-minds, and not from the outside (from contact with external things, as Qisong describes the Confucian approach to understanding the principle). In the first section of his article "Quanshu," the scholar-monk describes how individuals come to experience the universal principle with the same emphasis on the internal work that they do on themselves and that triggers their external transformation (i.e., worldview, moral behavior, and interaction with others). He explains the Confucian method as looking for the diverse coherence principles outside one's self, in one's outside relations with others and external reality, as fragments that would eventually come together as a unified whole—culminating in the understanding of the coherence principle of heaven (*tianli* 天理). Unlike the Neo-Confucian viewpoint, the Chan approach to the principle is an inward experience or realization of the common foundation of everything, which is all about the wholeness as nonduality, the complete or vast (*da* 大), the foundational (*zhu* 主), and the permanent (*chang* 常) (see next quotation: "The great principle is the foundation of the permanent way" (夫大理也者，固常道之主也)). In this cohesive Chan context, this is how he sees the Confucian practice and comprehension of the principle:

> Those who study nowadays (今學者) [i.e., Confucians] think that conformity with the model of appropriate behavior (適義) is the universal principle (*li* 理), and that following the model of appropriate behavior (行義) is the way (*dao* 道). But these are only the external dimensions (外事) of the way and the universal principle, that is, conduct within the specified limits on behavior (中節) [obviously, Qisong refers here to paragraph 1 of the classic *Zhongyong*, which he also interprets in his commentary; see *ZYJ* 3, 0666b21]. They do not grasp the great way and the great universal principle of the sages. The great principle (大理) [spiritual; see above] is primarily the foundation (主) of the permanent way (常道).[16] If all affairs are dealt with without taking into consideration their foundations, then are they dealt with how they really should be? (Qisong, "Quanshu" 1, 0652a16-2)

This investigation of the differences between the two perceptions of the principle (as Confucian coherence and as cohesive Chan spiritual omnipresence or profound environment) helps bring about a better understanding of Qisong's peculiar conception of the Chan nothingness—as principled (that is, as spiritually moral), to use Zhu Xi's term. Indeed, as discussed further below, he focuses on the ethical (moral) as a major dimension of his practice but not as its root. The latter is, for him, the Chan religious interdependence or nothingness—nothing means no independent thing (that is, interconnection, nonduality). This issue at the heart of his "Tanjing zan" 壇經贊 ("Encomium of the Platform Sutra") is addressed in the next section. It is arguable that his explanation of nothingness as the linchpin of the cohesive Chan practice, as well as his emphasis on ethico-moral practice highlighted below, make Zhu Xi's criticism (i.e., from the Confucian moral perspective, Chan is unprincipled and amoral) wholly unjustified in Qisong's case. It is obvious that Zhu Xi does not address his work, probably because he cannot consider it as representative of the Chan perspective of his Buddhist contemporaries.

IV. QISONG'S CHAN PRINCIPLED (*YOU LI* 有理) NOTHINGNESS (*WU* 無)

The notion of principle is one central issue surrounding this conversation between Qisong and Zhu Xi. As highlighted in section III.1, the overarching Chan notion of nothing(ness) (*wu* 無) is also part of this exchange. The following analysis examines what might be called Qisong's interpretation of principled (有理) nothingness. It could represent a clear response to Zhu Xi's criticism of Chan nothingness as without principle or unprincipled (*wu li* 無理; see *Shishi* 釋氏; *Zhuzi yulei* 126, ZZQS, 18:3934). As previously explained, in the Neo-Confucian scholar's vision, the term *principled* makes direct reference to morality and appropriate behavior (see sec. III.1).

This investigation, once again, brings to light Qisong's thought as a Confucianized vision of Chan or a principled form of Chan. It thus intends to demonstrate that, in his view, emptiness (*kong* 空) and its corollary, nothingness (*wu* 無; they are used interchangeably in this context), do not refer to an absolute emptiness (i.e., a nothing at all in a dualist sense of nothing/something, devoid of principle and out of touch with reality), as Zhu Xi depicts Buddhist nothingness/emptiness: "Without principles (*wuli* 無理), this is empty (*kong* 空). What they call heart-mind (*xin* 心) and nature (*xing* 性)—these are just empty things, without principles (只是個空底物事, 無理)" (Zhu, *Shishi*, ZZQS, 18:3934).

To the contrary, for Qisong, nothingness implies an experience that is totally embedded in the moral realm of everyday human affairs and human relationships. Therefore, the goal of this section is not only to look for already-existing responses to Zhu Xi's attacks in Qisong's thought but furthermore to describe the specific ethico-moral features of a less examined version of Song-dynasty Chan—the Northern Song scholar-monk's moral and principled Chan.

He clearly asserts, first, that the Chan Buddhists recognize and are aware of the existence of principle (as previously discussed) and, second, that nothingness (*wu* 無) is not at all separated from concrete reality—namely, from morality. This inquiry reveals Qisong's avant la lettre answer on this subject in his essay "Tanjing zan" 壇經贊 ("Encomium of the Platform Sutra"). He held in great esteem the *Platform Sutra of the Sixth Patriarch* (*Liuzu Tanjing* 六祖壇經), the major Chan text attributed to Huineng 惠能 (638–713). Actually, the scholar-monk identified his Chan school as the Platform Sutra school (Huang 1986, 11), and presumably, he prepared its mature Yuan-dynasty version, edited by Zongbao 宗寶 in 1291—*Platform Sutra of the Dharma Treasure of the Great Master, the Sixth Patriarch* (*Liuzu dashi fabao tan jing* 六祖大師法寶壇經; see Li and Ding 2010, 7–8). In what follows, reference is made to this version.

Let us start by pointing out Qisong's two main ideas concerning this issue—nondualist perspective and the *Platform Sutra*'s view. First, he interprets nothingness from a nondualist perspective. In this context, his approach translates into the idea that nothingness and existence are not different but the same thing. Existence here means for him everyday ethical interaction and ethical interpersonal relationships (this is also the Confucian ideal). Second, regarding this topic of nothingness, Qisong remains faithful to the *Platform Sutra*'s perspective. Thus, in this well-known "Encomium," he interprets the emergence of this nothingness as occurring within three significant contexts—namely, the three major elements of the Buddhist threefold way, which are addressed in the Chan context of the *Platform Sutra*: ethical discipline (*sīla, jie* 戒), concentration (*samādhi, ding* 定), and insight (*prajñā, zhihui* 智慧).

Ethical discipline involves precepts and morality and is the first dimension of the Buddhist habitual practice that Qisong addresses. In addition, he shows that nothingness is the pinnacle of ethical discipline. Nothingness and morality are therefore inseparable. To be more specific, in the sphere of ethical action, in his "Encomium" (0346c10-3), he refers to this moral nothingness in terms of (having) no form or (being) formless, without appearance (無相). "Form" in the framework nothingness-morality stands for finite, bounded, restricted, and therefore narrow—that is, following only separate, limited precepts and not being able to follow the totality of precepts. Concentration is the second dimension of practice to which the scholar-monk refers. In its context, he identifies nothingness as no-thought (無念). Within the articulation nothingness-concentration, "thought" stands for diverse, heterogenous, multifarious, and distracted. In the third context, that of nothingness and insight, he defines nothingness as not-dwelling (無住). In this frame of reference, dwelling means to be attached to self, to narrow thoughts, and to apparent reality, which is not the true reality. Each of his particular interpretations of nothingness—no-form, no-thought, and not-dwelling (no-self), as well as their strong connection with morality—is discussed in the ensuing sections.

IV.1. Nothingness and Precepts (Jie 戒): No-Form (Wu Xiang 無相)

The *Platform Sutra* explains the first abovementioned notion, no-form, as related to the moral precepts or ethical practice: "within the realm of form, remaining separate from form" (於相而離相; *Liuzu dashi fabao tan jing* 六祖大師法寶壇經, 0353a12-9). This phrase evokes the state of mind and focus of practice of one who is able in daily life to detach from arguing about the appearance of phenomena (*xiang* 相) and is not attached to them.[17] The difference between these appearances and forms emerges from likes and dislikes, from subjective and dual experiences, such as pleasure and displeasure, enjoyment and pain, and comfort and discomfort. The capacity to focus on no-form allows the individual to truly follow the precepts (obviously connected with the realm of form—that is, of distinctions). This is because within the (Chan) Buddhist context, the appearance or form of all things and affairs is primarily a mental product, which depends on the individual self's preconceptions, expectations, opinions, and so on. The well-known stance of Mahayana Buddhism is that form or appearance does not embody how things really are. The idea of no-form presented in the *Platform Sutra* suggests the identity at a subtle level, between reality (i.e., within the realm of form) and nothingness or relatedness (i.e., beyond the realm of form and embracing it).

Qisong further interprets this *Platform Sutra* concept of no-form and connects it even more clearly with the realm of everyday existence and with the Buddhist notion of great precepts. It can be said that, inspired by Song-dynasty Confucian culture, he considers the daily existence as rooted in the ethico-moral sphere of the major precepts that one honors—namely, the ethical discipline in everyday human interactions: "Considering the no-form [i.e., nothingness, detachment from phenomena] as essential, means to honor the

[Buddhist] great precepts (*dajie* 大戒) [i.e., karmic force or spiritual power to perform moral deeds, bestowed on laypersons and clergy during ordination ceremonies; see chap. 4]" (無相為體者, 尊大戒也。; Qisong, "TJZ," 0346c06-8). More importantly, he not only explains theoretically the meaning of the concept of no-form but also indicates the concrete practice one should follow so that one can experience the abovementioned connection between no-form and the precepts: "In order to be consistent with all the precepts, the best way is to focus on no-form" (資一切戒, 莫至乎無相; "TJZ," 0347a10-9). Note that in Qisong's view, the goal of practice is not the mere experience of nothingness, as Zhu Xi seems to assert about Buddhist practice in general, but the daily reality of being spontaneously consistent with all precepts in one's interactions with others. Nothingness as no-form is, in his perspective, a means to achieve this main goal, while focusing only on limited precepts is the source of the inability to completely follow all precepts.

Additionally, the highest stage of his practice is when one becomes able in daily life to fulfill what the *Platform Sutra* calls the "formless precepts" (無相戒). The *Platform Sutra* introduces the notion of "formless precepts" to describe the interiorization of morality.[18] Qisong provides a broader, unique interpretation of this perspective, deeply rooted not only in an abstract context but also in concrete everyday actions and interactions: he considers them as the "accomplished" precepts (無相戒, 戒之最也) and depicts them as consisting of performing good deeds free of attachments to personal interests, expectations, and opinions. No-form precepts means free of all forms of influences: "In order to cultivate good deeds and abandon evil ones, the best way is to focus on the no-form precepts" (生善滅惡, 莫至乎無相戒; Qisong, "TJZ," 0347a12-2). In his "Encomium" ("Tanjing zan"), the scholar-monk suggests this original interpretation of no-form, which, on one hand, strongly embeds the idea of formlessness in quotidian life and practice. Equally, on the other hand, his interpretation emphasizes the nonduality of perception: nothingness is daily reality (i.e., the world of dharmas (*fa* 法), physical and mental forms, affairs, and phenomena) and, conversely, daily reality is nothingness (i.e., one's inner, spiritual depth at which one is able to experience one's interrelatedness with all sentient beings). "The essential aspect of no-form," he emphasizes, "is what is called the embodiment of the [Buddhist] law" (無相之體, 法身之謂也。; "TJZ," 0347a19-1). That is to say, the experience of nothingness serves, in his view, precisely to accomplish the concrete Mahayana ideal of the bodhisattva practice within community (he focuses on its dimension of day-to-day ethical exchanges),[19] as well as the Confucian ideal of maintaining a stable and harmonious society. To reiterate, this is his particular understanding of nothingness: focusing on no-form precepts, which means cultivating good deeds and abandoning evil ones within the framework of no-form—namely, free of attachments to personal interests and expectations that arise from the concrete form (domain of interest) of particular precepts. The emphasis on ethics and morality is obvious.

IV.2. Nothingness and Concentration (Ding 定): No-Thought (Wu Nian 無念)

A second dimension of the nothingness that for Qisong is first of all embedded in everyday reality is the notion of no-thought (無念). He stresses its connection with the sphere of concentration (定). The *Platform Sutra* defines the concept of no-thought as follows: "When thinking, having no thoughts" (無念者, 於念而無念; *Platform Sutra*, 0353a12-14). This is not an unconscious state, a breaking off of one's contact with outer reality, but a state of focused awareness, among the highest forms of concentration, which no disturbing and parasitic thoughts can disrupt. A no-thought state implies that any mixed or erroneous thought that comes into one's mind will not be able to disturb one's state of concentration.[20] As in the case of the no-form, Qisong revisits this idea of no-thought and further interprets it: "Considering no-thought as [religious] teaching means to honor great concentration" (無念為宗者, 尊大定也。; Qisong, "TJZ," 0346c07-1). Again, he not only explains conceptually the idea of no-thought but also details the concrete practice one needs to follow in order to achieve what he calls great concentration (大定) or rectified complete concentration (正一切定; see below). He thus explains that successfully realizing the latter implies a practical exercise in nothingness, in the form of the method of no-thought: "In order to rectify all concentration, the best way is to focus on no-thought" (正一切定, 莫至乎無念; Qisong, "TJZ," 0347a11-1).

The *Platform Sutra* refers to concentration as the "one-practice samadhi" (*yixing sanmei* 一行三昧): all is one; the practice of one (i.e., one reality, one heart-mind, one form—see below). It illustrates concentration, as in the case of ethical discipline (precepts), in terms that also suggest its connection with daily existence. In the next quotation, this relation is implied by means of the formula "walking, stopping, sitting or lying down": "The one-practice samadhi is to always follow the one straight heart-mind, in any circumstance, when walking, stopping, sitting down or lying down" (一行三昧者, 於一切處行住坐臥, 常行一直心是也。; *Platform Sutra* 0361b01-7). Again, starting from this *Platform Sutra* view, the author of the "Encomium" proposes an original nondualist interpretation of the notion of one-practice samadhi, which further emphasizes that nothingness actually is precisely the realm of real phenomena (i.e., of human relations and affairs and of Confucian practice), and the phenomena (i.e., the phenomenal world) are nothingness[21]: "The one-practice samadhi—that is the one-form of the phenomenal world" (一行三昧者, 法界一相之謂也; Qisong, "TJZ," 0346c05-1). The use of the concepts of "one-form" (一相; the form that is the source of all different forms) and "phenomenal world" (法界) when discussing nothingness gives to the latter an anchoring point in the concrete ordinary reality of forms and phenomena (i.e., the reality of forms, patterns of daily existence and human relations). Again, as in the case of ethical discipline, the emphasis for Qisong is on tangible existence. One notes that this nuance doesn't exist in the *Platform Sutra*; it is his personal understanding. This shows the influence of the Song-dynasty Confucian culture on his Chan thought. He emphasizes that one-practice samadhi is not separated from the phenomenal world but actually is the phenomenal world. Furthermore, terms such as *one-practice, one heart-mind,* and *one-form* suggest achieving a state of nondual unity between an individual's heart-mind and body and between self and others. In his interpretation of the notions of the *Platform Sutra*, the scholar-monk further emphasizes this identity between nothingness (this time understood as one-practice samadhi, as no-thought and concentration) and human relations and ethics. Again, he accentuates the everyday dimension of the Chan practice of concentration and perceives the latter as the means for the individual to achieve personal moral development never separated from others but within community, as "a model of good deeds," as a moral leader: "In order to be a model of good deeds and become moral, the best way is to focus on the one-practice samadhi" (軌善成德, 莫至乎一行三昧; "TJZ," 0346c27). In addition, Qisong clearly stresses that "the one-practice samadhi is the beginning of morality" (一行三昧, 德之端也; "TJZ," 0347a09-15). This demonstrates that, in his view, the highest objective of the Chan practice of concentration, of no-thought, is developing ethico-moral behavior and contributing to the well-being of community.

*IV.3. Nothingness and Insight (*Hui 慧*):*
*Not-Dwelling (*Wu Zhu 無住*)*

The third dimension of nothingness that has, in Qisong's opinion, a strong connection with real existence is Chan wisdom or insight (*hui* 慧). The highest level of insight, called prajñā (般若), is insight into the nothingness of reality—that is, the interdependence of all sentient beings. On this point, Qisong explains that "the root of not-dwelling is what is called prajñā" (無住之本, 般若之謂也; "TJZ," 0347a18-9). Not-dwelling constitutes the Chan state of awareness. Following the *Platform Sutra*'s line of thought, he draws attention to the fact that Chan great insight (that is, complete, different from the ordinary, fragmentary insight into the true reality) belongs to the sphere of nothingness as not-dwelling (無住) and that not-dwelling is the foundation of the Chan way: "Considering the not-dwelling as the foundation [of one's ordinary life], means to honor great insight" (無住為本者，尊大慧也。; "TJZ," 0346c07-10).

The *Platform Sutra* explains the notion of not-dwelling through referring not only to nothingness but also to concrete reality:

> Not-dwelling is one's original nature [i.e., root, buddha-nature, which does not dwell either in the forms of external reality or in the thoughts of internal reality]. One's original nature is to consider all things of the world as empty (*kong* 空)—good and evil, attractive and ugly, and even one's enemies and friends, moments when one receives words that irritate and insult, times of dispute—and to not think to take revenge (無住者，人之本性。於世間善惡，好醜，乃至冤之與親，言語觸刺欺爭之時，並將為空，不思酬害). (*Platform Sutra*, 0353a13-6)

Nothingness is directly present in this image of not-dwelling: the individuals consider things as empty of permanence, and their thoughts are empty of revenge. Human relationships and quotidian ethics also have a strong presence in this image that vividly depicts, in detail, everyday interactions: enemies, friends, vexation, dispute, and revenge.

Yet, in this illustration, the *Platform Sutra* only suggests a connection between the practice of not-dwelling and mundane life, without special emphasis on the sphere of morality and ethical knowledge—the quintessential domain of Confucian interest. In his interpretation of the not-dwelling—that is, the experience of no-self—Qisong is not only inspired by the *Platform Sutra*'s ideas but also goes beyond them, precisely by focusing on the abovementioned ethico-moral perspective, which is also the foundation of Confucian training. It can be said that he thus asserts the strong connection of the Chan practice of not-dwelling with the daily human reality using language consistent with Confucian culture. According to his understanding, not-dwelling is neither a state detached from reality nor a passive one as the *Platform Sutra* might suggest (i.e., not thinking to take revenge; see above) but an active practice required, Qisong emphasizes, to obtain all knowledge (*tong yiqie zhi* 通一切智): "In order to obtain all knowledge, the best way is to focus on not-dwelling" (通一切智，莫至乎無住; "TJZ," 0347a11-10). In other words, as elements of reality, the various forms of knowledge are context bound and exist in relation with specific things and affairs: time, place, and human relations. The complete knowledge (一切智) can be achieved only when a person has attained the level of not-dwelling or no-self, does not dwell in their self as separate from other sentient beings, and therefore is aware of their interdependence with all. This active and focused awareness reflects the fact that one does not think to take revenge, for example. As mentioned earlier, in the Confucian view, acquiring "all knowledge" based on not-dwelling (that is, selfless knowledge) about the principles of everyday things and affairs is a major virtue whose development leads to understanding appropriate behavior and accomplished morality.

The Confucianized vision of Qisong's interpretation of Chan is also perceptible in the following idea: "In order to be able to probe the principles to the utmost and fully put into effect the authentic natures of everything in the world, the best way is to focus on the silent transmission" (天下之窮理盡性, 莫至乎默傳; "TJZ," 0347a15-13). He uses here an ancient Confucian term: fully putting into effect one's authentic nature (*jin xing* 盡性—see *Zhongyong* 22; *Mencius* 7A, 7B, *Jinxin shang, xia*). He also uses a term that, a generation after him, became a well-known Neo-Confucian term (probing the coherence principles to the utmost, 窮理—see, for example, Zhu Xi, *Daxue zhangju, jing* and *zhang* 5, *Lunyu jizhu* 7:20). About a century before the foundation of the Neo-Confucian school of principle by the Cheng brothers, Zhu Xi's most influential Northern Song masters, "fully understanding the coherence principles" and "entirely realizing the authentic natures" are terms present in the scholar-monk's work. They evoke the main goals of his moral Chan practice, substantially equivalent to those of the pre-Song Confucian practice and Song Neo-Confucian practice: knowledge, virtue, good governance, and harmonious human relations. On the one hand, their presence is tangible proof not only of the inclusive character of his interpretation of Chan Buddhism, which resembles the perspective of his predecessor, the tenth-century Chan monk Yongming Yanshou, but also of another characteristic, a specific feature of Qisong's approach—his Confucianized way of presenting the Buddhist practice and his effort to explain it to Confucian scholars in terms they recognize as their own. It might also be said that the abovementioned notions employed by him constitute the early embryos of a concrete Chan influence on Neo-Confucianism in the sphere of the practice of self-cultivation, a concrete training that did not exist before in Confucianism. Zhu Xi himself remarks that the scholars were only talking about this issue without concretely engaging in their own physical, mental, emotional training:

> In the beginning, the Buddhist school just talked about it, without developing the ability to preserve and nourish oneself (存養底工夫). Not until the Tang-dynasty did the Sixth Patriarch [*Platform Sutra*] start teaching

people how to develop the ability to preserve and nourish oneself (存養工夫). Initially, the [Confucian] scholars only talked about it, without personally engaging in the practice of this ability (physically, mentally, emotionally) (身上做工夫). Then Cheng Yi [程頤 (1033–1107)] began to teach them how to engage in this practice. This is why people say that Cheng Yi stole this training from the Buddhists and used it for his own [Confucian] purpose. (Zhu, *Shishi*, *Zhuzi yulei* 126, ZZQS, 18:3963–3964)

It is arguable that in this paragraph, Zhu Xi implicitly acknowledges that the Cheng-Zhu school integrated some Chan practice in its Confucian theoretical framework.

As shown above, a generation before Cheng Yi, the Northern Song scholar-monk already interpreted in Confucian terms the concrete elements of this Chan practice expounded in the *Platform Sutra*: no-form, no-thought, and not-dwelling. In the above quote, he also weaves together Confucian and Chan elements. The best way to achieve concrete goals like those of Confucians but based on a religious/spiritual practice, he writes, is by practicing Chan "silent transmission" (默傳). Yet he does not understand this method in a factionalist way, like the Linji Chan members, as a complete distrust in words, sutras, and theoretical knowledge, but again in an all-inclusive way. Inspired by Daoism (Zhuangzi, chap. "Waiwu" 外物: "Once one has got the meaning, one can forget the words" (得意而忘言)), he promotes a silent transmission understood as reliance on meaning, not on words (依義不依語; "TJZ," 0347b26-8).

And in agreement with Confucian tradition, he does not totally reject all texts but stresses the need to rely on those classics and scriptures (*jing* 經) best able to transmit meaning (依了義經) through words. Specifically, for him, these classics are those able to convey a complete understanding of the universal principle (以了義經盡理也; "TJZ," 0347b28-14). In accordance with his religious viewpoint, Qisong understands a perfect teaching like that of Huineng, the Sixth Patriarch, the presumed author of the *Platform Sutra*, who is for him an accomplished person (至人), as silent (默) or secret (密) teaching. Again, in his view, this notion does not mean something completely different from the previous Buddhist tradition, as it does for followers of the Linji faction. In complete agreement with the Chinese (Confucian and Daoist) culture in which he is rooted, the scholar-monk interprets Chan silent (i.e., complete, meaningful) teaching as a practice devoted to concrete training in no-form, no-thought, and not-dwelling, and he defines it as "a teaching that transforms individuals and that actively engages in all human activities, not a teaching indifferent and inactive" (至人密說變之、通之而不苟滯也; "TJZ," 0347c05-7). In this image, the ancient goals of Confucian tradition integrate perfectly into his Chan vision. Nevertheless, the concepts of meaning, principle, and the transmission of complete understanding have also a new Chan religious, nondualist connotation.

The foregoing analysis of Qisong's interpretation of the three dimensions of the Chan path leads to the conclusion that for each one he emphasizes its connection with the sphere of morality and ethics, ethical knowledge, and the everyday practice of human affairs.

V. CONCLUSION

This chapter develops an exchange between Qisong and Zhu Xi on two major notions: principle and nothingness. The first is equally important for Qisong's Chan as for Zhu's Neo-Confucianism, and the last one is the key component of Chan thought on which the Neo-Confucian master focuses his criticism. This dialogue includes two comparative perspectives. The first is Zhu's reproving perspective on Chan Buddhism, which he finds inferior to Confucianism. The second is the scholar-monk's integrative perspective built on the complementarity between Chan and Confucianism. Starting from different backgrounds, each of them tackles and explains the major features of the other.

This double comparison is relevant for the following reasons. On the one hand, it allows the examiner to capture the differences between the two thinkers regarding the contextual meanings they assigned to the terms *principle* (*li* 理) and *nothingness* (*wu* 無) in their comparisons of cohesive Chan (including general Buddhism) and (neo-)Confucian tradition. On the other hand, it reveals the borrowings and mutual influences between the two learnings during the Song-dynasty eleventh and twelfth centuries.

This chapter completes the series of steps of this multidimensional analysis (chaps. 1–6) of the scholar-monk's articles from the collection *Fujiao bian*. It focuses on two complex concepts of his cohesive Chan teaching—universal principle and nothingness—within the context of a transhistorical dialogue between Qisong and Zhu Xi. In this way, first, chapter 6 concludes an in-depth and progressive interpretation of the Northern Song monk's arguments advocating for the promotion of Buddhism as cohesive Chan, as complementary to Confucianism, and of his comparative explanation of major Song-culture concepts, common to both Confucian and Buddhist traditions or specific to his cohesive, nondual Chan teaching. Second, starting from this exchange between the two thinkers, this chapter suggests and demonstrates the important influence of Qisong's thought on a whole generation of Neo-Confucians who succeeded him and later established the Song-dynasty school of principle. It is arguable that this school integrates certain notions and ideas of the scholar-monk's argumentation into a Neo-Confucian form.

For instance, the Chan scholar-monk's interest in the chapter of the *Liji* entitled the *Zhongyong* and his examination of it in a commentary named *Zhongyong jie* 中庸解 (*Exegesis of the Mean*) certainly would contribute to Zhu Xi's deep interest in this section of the *Liji*, a century later, after Qisong. With his own commentary, the Neo-Confucian master gave this chapter a distinctive identity, independent of that of the *Liji*, and transformed it into one of the *Four Books*. The next and final chapter offers, in a comparative regard, a discussion of the *Zhongyong* and its major concepts of the emotions and proper behavior, through building another transcultural comparative dialogue, similar to the one assembled in this chapter. This time, the dialogue focuses on "interdependent ethico-spirituality," and it is between Qisong's eleventh-century and Zhu Xi's twelfth-century commentaries on the *Zhongyong*. The scholar-monk's commentary *Zhongyong jie* is not included in the *Fujiao bian*, but its structure and argumentative discourse are similar to those of the articles in the anthology *Fujiao bian* and, obviously, also focus on the articulations between the two traditions.

As regards Zhu Xi, even if he severely criticized Buddhism, as Julia Ching rightly mentions, it cannot be said that he was living in an intellectual vacuum, that he was unable to be open to the richness of other traditions. On the contrary, Zhu was a sympathizer of the Daoist tradition: "Lu Xiangshan, on his side, was to criticize Zhu Xi for showing Daoist influences, especially in maintaining that *Taiji*, the Great Ultimate, was at the same time *Wuji*, the Limitless. This was an example of the ideological aspect of the differences between the two thinkers. After all, neither of them lived in an intellectual vacuum, and their openness to insights coming from non-Confucian sources is witness to their greatness and a reason for the richness and depth which characterized the movement of thought known today as Neo-Confucianism" (Ching 1974, 171).

SEVEN

ETHICO-SPIRITUAL DISCIPLINE, EMOTIONS, AND BEHAVIOR DURING THE SONG DYNASTY

Zhu Xi's and Qisong's Commentaries on the *Zhongyong* in Comparative Perspective

I. INTRODUCTION

This last chapter, just like the other chapters of the book, provides an extensive discussion of a specific feature of Qisong's thought.[1] It discusses key issues that the Chan scholar-monk addresses in his eleventh-century commentary on the *Zhongyong*. By adopting, as in chapter 6, a comparative dialogical approach—in the form of a transhistorical conversation between Qisong and Zhu Xi on this chapter of the *Book of Rites* (*Liji* 禮記)—chapter 7 focuses on the issues of emotions and behavior in the context of interdependent spirituality (*zhongyong* 中庸). It proposes a new exploratory approach in the realm of philosophical ethics—namely, a comparative hermeneutics of two Song-dynasty commentaries on the Confucian classic the *Zhongyong*. This study also puts forward a fresh Song-dynasty perspective on this text, a point of view common to both the Neo-Confucian and Chan schools, as I will demonstrate, which focuses on emotions and what I call the "interdependent self." The development of this theme also offers new insight into Neo-Confucian and Chan views of ethics and spirituality.

Through a case study (namely, an examination of these interpretations of the *Zhongyong*), this chapter elaborates in some detail certain similarities between Song Neo-Confucian and Chan Buddhist traditions. It thus aims to make two complementary contributions: to illustrate the Confucian impact on the thinking of the Chan scholar-monk Qisong by examining the specific arguments that he uses to explain correspondences between Confucianism and Chan in his effort to promote the cooperation between them, and to provide evidence of Chan influence on the Cheng-Zhu school of principle (Cheng-Zhu Lixue 程朱理學).

Chapter 7 examines and interprets the nature and specific characteristics of Song-dynasty Neo-Confucian ethical spirituality starting from a parallel reading of two commentaries on the *Zhongyong* 中庸.[2] Initially a chapter of the *Liji* 禮記 (*Book of Rites*), the *Zhongyong* became during the Song one of the *Four Books* commented on by Zhu Xi 朱熹 (1130–1200), the leading figure of the Cheng-Zhu school. Kirill Thompson expounds Zhu Xi's major innovation:

> By recontextualizing *Zhongyong* in the *Sishu* [*Four Books*], Zhu Xi modified its range of significance from ritual conduct at court to the entire scope of personhood and life practice. He ramified the text by explicating its psychological and ontological roots for cultivated personhood and creative, transformative practice. He tapped these roots by prefacing and recasting the arguments of the text in light of the *renxin-daoxin* (human mind-dao mind) distinction (not dichotomy). He thus shifted the problematic of the text inward to the heart's core of ethical motivation and impulse with the theme of keeping vigilant without and cautious within on the belief that such introspective diligence would insure that one's responses to affairs would be balanced, on the mark, and harmony engendering. Apart from the human-mind-dao-mind distinction, these issues were already present in the original text, but Zhu put them on center stage, thus vitalizing the text and increasing its efficacy for moral personhood and practice. (Thompson 2010, 92)

The first commentary addressed in this chapter is the *Zhongyong jie* 中庸解 (*Exegesis of the Mean*; hereafter ZYJ),[3] written by the Chan Buddhist scholar-monk Qisong[4] in the time of the Northern Song dynasty. The second is the *Zhongyong zhangju* 中庸章句 (*Chapter and Verse of the Mean*; hereafter ZYZJ),[5] authored by Zhu Xi during the Southern Song. In light of the arguments put forward in the present chapter, I argue that during the Song the notion of *zhongyong* refers to an ethico-spiritual discipline, and I translate it as "taking action by constantly following the middle way." On the basis of the analysis of Qisong's and Zhu Xi's commentaries, I would suggest that this notion inseparably interweaves two correlative terms: *zhong* 中, which designates the ethico-spiritual capacity to conduct oneself according to the middle way (and equally designates the profundity of the human being where this capacity is to be found), and *yong* 庸, which designates the effort "to constantly make use of this ability in everyday life and actions."

This meaning of *zhongyong* illustrates the particular spirit of the Song dynasty (960–1279), an epoch marked by the renaissance of Confucianism and by multidimensional exchanges between members of the Cheng-Zhu school and Chan Buddhists.[6] Yü Ying-shih (2003, 1:116) describes this mutual dialogue in terms of the Confucianization of Northern Song Buddhism and the Buddhization of the Confucian literati. As Yü notes, Chan Buddhists promoted the reconstruction of the order of human relationships. With the emergence of the new school of Chan, Chinese Buddhism became socially involved, literally "entering the world" (*rushi* 入世). "Starting from the beginning of the Northern Song," Yü writes, "the social engagement of Buddhism becomes more profound, and the interest shown by prominent and virtuous monks in issues of daily life is often no less important than that of the Confucian literati and scholar-officials.... Also, because during the Song dynasty the sociopolitical status of the latter increases, the Buddhist monks need their support in promoting Chan doctrines" (2003, 1:116).[7] Morten Schlütter, in his study, also concludes that "Chan masters were active and willing participants in literati culture" (2008, 73). Qisong's interest in commenting on a Confucian text dealing with the Confucian middle way (i.e., the *Zhongyong*) is a perfect illustration of the participation of scholar-monks in literati culture.[8] As outlined below, this way is mainly concerned with human relations, particularly those involving political and civic leadership.

Through a parallel analysis of the two commentaries on the *Zhongyong*, I put forward that Qisong's marked interest in building philosophical bridges between Buddhism and Confucianism and his comparative developments led to the emergence of a new and ethico-spiritual feature in Cheng-Zhu Neo-Confucianism during the Song dynasty. I would offer that this profound dimension, which shares similarities with Chan Buddhist spirituality, was stimulated by the abovementioned exchanges between Confucian literati and Chan Buddhist monks, particularly by the scholar-monk's work. The parallel examination addresses first the ethico-spiritual nature of *zhongyong* practice and then the three specific dimensions of this practice, which entail overcoming the "independent self," cultivating an "interdependent" self, and developing interpersonal relationships.

II. THE NATURE OF THE SPIRITUALITY OF THE MIDDLE WAY (中庸之道)

II.1. *The Middle* (Zhong 中), *Emotions* (Qing 情), *and Constancy* (Yong 庸)

In what follows, I offer that a parallel reading of Zhu Xi's and Qisong's commentaries on the *Zhongyong* shows that the middle way means ethico-spiritual discipline. The latter allows one to become aware of one's own depth—that is, one's middle level (*zhong* 中) or authentic nature (*xing* 性)—and to become able to put it constantly into practice in everyday affairs (*yong* 庸). Both commentaries specify that this practice in everyday affairs requires managing one's own emotions and behavior. The inner practice of this spirituality concerns the emotions/feelings, while the outer relates to ordinary behavior. Their common source is the middle level, *zhong*. In his *Zhongyong zhangju* (*Zhuzi quanshu* [hereafter *ZZQS*], vol. 6), Zhu Xi describes these two dimensions of the middle way:

> Happiness, anger, grief, and enjoyment are emotions/feelings. The level at which they do not develop is authentic nature. Authentic nature does not pull to either side and does not take sides. For this reason, it is what is called the middle, *zhong*. When the emotions are developed in accordance with this rule of the middle, they are correct and without the slightest inappropriateness. Therefore, they are what is called harmonious. The authentic nature bestowed by heaven is the great root, [that is,] the source of all the individual principles of coherence of all the individual things in the world, and the intrinsic essence of the way. Pursuing the path means following authentic nature, which is the source of all things in the world, from antiquity to the present, and this is the practice of the way (喜、怒、哀、樂, 情也。其未發, 則性也, 無所偏倚, 故謂之中。發皆中節, 情之正也, 無所乖戾, 故謂之和。大本者, 天命之性, 天下之理皆由此出。道之體也。達道者, 循性之謂, 天下古今之所共由, 道之用也). (Zhu Xi, *Zhongyong zhangju* 1, *ZZQS*, 6:33)

I have opted for the translation of the central notion of *li* 理[9] as "principle of coherence"[10] (see also chap. 1, sec. IV, n. 37). I think this rendering is etymologically justified in this context. By comparison, the Latin *cohaerentia*, "organic order, structure," emphasizes the quality of constituting a unified whole. The Latin *principium*, "source, foundations," is morally and not ontologically significant—that is, it does not imply here a transcendent meaning but has a moral resonance (i.e., principle as natural rule governing human behavior, which originates in the natural order and not in the will), exactly as does *li* 理.

Qisong's view on this subject is consistent and complementary with Zhu Xi's. He warns, "When humans lose their *zhong* capacity, their authentic nature attaches to things; the feelings and emotions of happiness, anger, grief, fear, love and hate are born, and dependencies and desires develop (人失於中性接於物, 而喜怒哀懼愛惡生焉, 嗜欲發焉)" (Qisong, *ZYJ* 1, 0666a03-4). In other words, because of their emotional attachments and desires, human beings lose touch with their authentic nature—their profound, ethico-spiritual dimension—which is what makes them complete and gives them their full capacity to do good. The ethico-spiritual discipline needs constancy (*yong*) precisely in order to prevent this loss.

Thus, one's heart-mind comes to dwell in this depth, and this dwelling concretely enables one to deal with one's day-to-day affairs in a complete manner. It becomes obvious that in this context, dealing with one's day-to-day affairs in a complete manner means nothing other than achieving unity and accord between one's emotions/feelings and one's behavior. Both Qisong and Zhu Xi stress that the necessary preconditions for this harmonious life are both contact with one's own spiritual profundity or middle and also constancy; in other words, one "cannot abandon the practice of *zhongyong*" (中庸不可去), and one "does not want to give up mid-way" (不能半塗而廢; see Qisong, *ZYJ* 1; Zhu Xi, *ZYZJ* 11).

This ethico-spiritual (transmoral) source of Confucian moral practice is the first of several new features of Song-dynasty Neo-Confucianism that are uncovered and examined in the present chapter. In the context here, what is identified as transmoral is an effort to become complete, to acquire a sense of fullness[11]—in other words, to get and stay in touch with what might be called one's essential completeness (see Qisong's analysis of the completeness of the heart-mind in chap. 5, sec. II.2). Like Chan Buddhist practice, and unlike ancient Confucianism, the Song Neo-Confucian training promoted by the Cheng-Zhu school has an ethico-metaphysical nature, embodied in the idea of the principle of coherence (*li* 理),[12] or of authentic nature (*xing* 性), which shares essential similarities with the Chan Buddhist idea of buddha-nature (*foxing* 佛性). Zhu Xi's heart-mind-essence is the master of the body (*Jinsilu* 近思錄, 1:39), and the authentic nature present in human beings is the embodiment in humans of the coherence principle[13] bestowed (*fu* 賦) by heaven on all beings (*ZYZJ* 1, *ZZQS*, 6:32). The latter is the fundamental ordering principle present in everything, which is, the Neo-Confucian scholar explains in his *Daxue zhangju* 大學章句, *jing* 經, the source of the complete good: "The highest perfection, inherent in the coherence principles of all things" (事理當然之極; *ZZQS*, 6:16). The next section demonstrates that *zhongyong* discipline has a transmoral nature by showing that it possesses two specific features: it is characterized as a path of transformation through ethico-spiritual learning and as a practice of nonduality.

II.2. *Zhongyong* Spiritual Discipline as a Path of Transformation

The arguments introduced in this paragraph reflect the fact that the nature of this practice is beyond the philosophical or moral. Rather, it is spiritual as implied above in the sense that it enables one to accomplish oneself by acquiring one's fullness and completeness (*quan* 全), which might be described as one's transformative power and capacity to do good. In his eleventh-century commentary, Qisong clearly defines the *zhongyong* as "the way of establishing humans"[14] (夫中庸者立人之道也; *ZYJ* 1, 0666a17-7). He also states that the Confucian way of "the *zhongyong* is close to his own [cohesive Chan Buddhist] way" (中庸幾於吾道; *ZYJ* 5, 0667c14-12). Almost a century later, Zhu Xi, too, describes it as a path—as the successful completion of daily tasks and activities by individuals who are aware of their authentic nature or coherence principle, bestowed on them by heaven, and follow it (道, 猶路也. 人物各循其性之自然, 則其日用事物之間, 莫不各有當行之路, 是則所謂道也; Zhu Xi, *ZZQS*, 6:32). Only when a person is able to gain awareness of the coherence principle and follow it do they acquire and preserve a sense of fullness, of completeness—that is, an awareness of their authentic nature, in all moments of their daily life. In Qisong's words, this is "to become complete through following the *zhongyong*" (以中庸全; *ZYJ* 2, 0667c14-12). For Qisong, becoming complete means "one's commitment to do good, and the fact that one is able to do everything in this way" (全之者為善, 則無所不至也; *ZYJ* 2, 0666b11-11). Qisong stresses here the continuous and long-term character of this commitment, which for him implies constancy—that is, "to pay attention to one's fickleness" (慎其變; ibid.). Zhu Xi also stresses that practice is an effort to acquire completeness and perceives the latter in moral terms, as the recovery of a complete moral capacity (*quande* 全德) with which one has gradually lost contact (Zhu Xi, *Lunyu jizhu* 論語集注 12:1; *ZZQS*, 6:167).

From this, one can infer a second major dimension of the specific spirituality of the *zhongyong* path, also reflected in its second term—namely, one's ordinary behavior, *yong*: the requirement to carry out this completeness not in solitude but in everyday relationships with others. Also, Zhu Xi explains this concern for completeness in terms of developing unbiased—that is, complete (*zhou* 周)—relationships with others: "Complete, [that is,] concerns the whole. Partial, [that is,] biased, predisposed to favor. Both refer to the behavior of someone who is close to others, while 'being committed to the complete' means considering the relationship with others in a disinterested way, and 'being partial' means considering it from the bias perspective, in an interested way (周, 普遍也. 比, 偏黨也。皆與人親厚之意, 但周公而比私耳)" (*Lunyu jizhu*, 2:14, *ZZQS*, 6:78–79).

Thus, completeness denotes restoring contact with one's deep fullness or authentic nature, which profoundly unites one with others and impels one to answer to the needs of others. Getting in contact with this completeness and cultivating it therefore connotes having not an independent spirituality but an interdependent one. According to the thirteenth-century Zongbao 宗寶 version of the *Platform Sutra* prepared by Qisong (see Li and Ding 2010, 7, 8), in the Chan Buddhist tradition this type of ethical spirituality is expressed in the ultimate concern for the "constant practice of giving benefits to others" (常行饒益).[15] In the Neo-Confucian Cheng-Zhu school, Zhu Xi highlights it as the ultimate concern to "govern and provide service to the people" (經濟).[16]

In other words, it can be said that this transformative spirituality is a sense of fullness through which people carry out their usual daily affairs and tasks. This interpretation is fully consistent with the spiritual/material continuum present in both Neo-Confucianism and Chan Buddhism—namely, the unity of one's two interwoven dimensions: authentic nature (the principle of coherence), which is a gift from heaven, and individual natural capacities, which stem from the quality of an individual's life breath (qi 氣).[17] The latter designates the physical and psychological condition that one is born with. Both Neo-Confucians and Chan Buddhists see these dimensions as recoverable and restorable through practice. Zhu Xi stresses the organic fusion of these two human features in the following terms: "By using yin, yang, and the five elements, heaven gives life to the ten thousand things through a process of [natural] transformation; the life breath completes their physical appearance, and they also receive their coherence principle (天以陰陽五行化生萬物，氣以成形, 而理亦賦焉)" (ZYZJ 1, ZZQS, 6:32). He also acknowledges the major difference between the two dimensions: "Even if the authentic nature of individuals is entirely good, the life breath received by each of them is distinct; for this reason, some understand the way earlier, and others later; some follow it with difficulty, and others easily (蓋人性雖無不善, 而氣稟有不同者, 故聞道有蚤莫, 行道有難易)" (ZYZJ 20, ZZQS, 6:46). Through an emphasis on this difference, the Neo-Confucian scholar suggests the importance of restoring the completeness of the entity's authentic nature (coherence principle)/life breath and thus of embracing the fullness of life. However, despite initial differences, when completeness is acquired through practice, all individuals become the same, which Zhu Xi explains by quoting Mister Lü[18]: "Individuals step into the path in different ways, but they all reach the same level. This common orientation is *zhongyong* practice (所入之塗雖異, 而所至之域則同, 此所以為中庸)" (ZYZJ 20, ZZQS, 6:46). This transmoral transformation has, therefore, two intrinsically intertwined features. The first is hierarchical—like all living things, people are born with different abilities that require them to follow this process of change differently. The second is egalitarian—through this process of permanent learning and because the principle of coherence is potentially present in all, everyone can have access to one's deep level and maintain oneself at this level, which is the same for everyone.

It should also be noted that both Qisong and Zhu Xi perceive this deep transformation not as an esoteric process but as a dynamic and constant learning process (*xue* 學 or *jiao* 教).¹⁹ As already mentioned, this involves rules (*jie* 節) and therefore discipline, and it consists of learning how to follow them in order to change one's behavior (social relations), adapt oneself properly, and thus restore one's completeness. Qisong, the Chan monk, communicates rhetorically his confidence in this capacity to get in touch with the spiritual level:

> What is it that cannot be learned? *Zhongyong* is not obscure, nor useless. Therefore, by flawlessly following it one changes; by changing one fully understands. The rules are required in order to regulate the change; those who learn practice what they have already fully understood. Through changing and adapting to what is appropriate, one becomes a sage. When one fully understands the learning but does not follow it, one becomes a petty man. This is why it is said that *zhongyong* really lies in the practice of learning (孰不可學也? 夫中庸也, 非泯默而無用也. 故至順則變, 變則通矣. 節者所以制其變也, 學者所以行其通也. 變而適義, 所以為君子; 通而失教, 所以為小人. 故言中庸者, 正在乎學也). (Qisong, *ZYJ* 5, 0667b23-14)

Almost a century later, the Confucian Zhu Xi expresses a similar idea, quoting his predecessor Master Cheng, who also stressed the importance of practice and its constancy: "Not inclining to either side, this is what is called [capacity to conduct oneself according to the] middle, *zhong*; not being inconstant, this is what is called constancy in one's behavior, *yong*. The middle is the straight path of human beings; constancy in one's behavior is the precise rule of human beings (不偏之謂中, 不易之謂庸. 中者, 天下之正道, 庸者, 天下之定理)" (Zhu Xi, *ZYZJ* 1, *ZZQS*, 6:32). A major aspect of the nature of *zhongyong* spirituality that I have identified through the parallel analysis of the two commentaries is therefore the idea of constancy, a determined strength of will to pursue disciplined practice and transformation, also synonymous with permanent learning. Another central feature—that of nonduality and its practice—is addressed below.

II.3. *Zhongyong* Spiritual Discipline as the Practice of Nonduality

The abovementioned idea of a practice that is experienced in daily affairs and tasks reflects another feature of the particular nature of this ethical spirituality: it is embedded in everyday life, an aspect of the individual's life inseparable from everyday work, omnipresent and naturally experienced in every aspect of society—economic, social, and political—and in every moment of the everyday life of the individual. In Qisong's words, "One can stop drinking and eating; one can surrender one's power achieved through wealth and fame, but one cannot leave *zhongyong* (飲食可絕也, 富貴崇高之勢可讓也; 而中庸不

可去也)" (ZYJ 1, 0666a19-2). However, one should not forget that this practice of *zhongyong*—which concerns every aspect and every moment of one's daily life—also concerns a profound depth, or dual (Confucianism)/nondual (Buddhism) articulation transcendence/immanence present in everything, accessible to everyone, within daily affairs. Nonduality is therefore synonymous with completeness. In the following description, Qisong underlines the nondual nature of this discipline: "*Zhongyong* is not something made, not something one could describe as a concrete tool. It is as bright as the sun and the moon, though it cannot be seen; it is as obscure as the spirits, and therefore cannot be measured (夫中庸也者, 不為也, 不器也, 明於日月而不可睹也, 幽於鬼神而不可測也)" (ZYJ 2, 0666b08-11). A century later, Zhu Xi describes this spirituality interwoven with every single moment of human life using the central term associated with his school, the principle of coherence *li*, a term that, as I've shown elsewhere (see Arghirescu 2019), is imbued with moral and transmoral resonance:

> The pathway is the coherence principle that everyday things and affairs must follow; it is the moral quality of each authentic nature; each heart-mind is provided with this coherence principle; there is no thing without the way, and no moment; for this reason, one cannot separate oneself from it, not for the slightest moment; because what one can separate from, is something external, and not the pathway (道者, 日用事物當行之理, 皆性之德而具於心, 無物不有, 無時不然, 所以不可須臾離也。若其可離, 則為外物而非道矣). (ZYZJ 1, ZZQS, 6:31–32)

At first sight, one might suppose that this ethical spirituality as pathway, which is synonymous with awareness of the coherence principle, is something immanent, an inner reflection of a transcendent reality, as it is said that one cannot separate oneself from it. However, this interpretation is misleading because it is framed within dichotomies including immanent/transcendent and material/spiritual (i.e., life breath/authentic nature). Such dualism presupposes that the paired terms are separated and have a fixed or static substance—in other words, that there is a clear boundary between them.[20] And this is not how Zhu Xi describes their relation. He emphasizes the continuity between them, their inseparability and dual interdependency as principle of coherence or way (*dao* 道) and its mode of functioning, vital breath (*qi* 氣) or tools (*qi* 器), as the elements of the middle way, *zhongyong*:

> Within the heaven-earth, there is the principle of coherence and the vital breath. The principle of coherence is the *way* from beyond perceptible appearance, [that is,] the root that gives birth to things. Vital breath is the tool from within perceptible appearance, [that is,] the utility that gives birth to things. Therefore, the birth of humans and things necessarily relies

on the principle of coherence; and then authentic nature occurs. The latter necessarily relies on vital breath; and then perceptible appearance occurs. Even though the authentic nature and the perceptible appearance of a thing are not "outside" one another but form a single unity, the distinction between its *way* and its tool quality is very clear. One cannot confuse them (天地之間, 有理有氣。理也者, 形而上之道也, 生物本也;氣 也者, 形而下之器也, 生物之具也。是以人物之生, 必稟此理, 然後有性; 必稟此氣, 然後有形。其性其形, 雖不外乎一身, 然其道器之間分際甚明, 不可亂也). (Zhu Xi, ZZQS, 23:2755)[21]

Zhu Xi's perception of this ethico-spiritual pathway as a root that gives birth to everything implies that the middle way, *zhongyong*, or the practice to restore access to this single root, is the practice of dual interdependency. The latter refers to a specific level or depth in things, that is different from the level that corresponds to the two parts of a duality, between which there exists a relationship of opposition and contrast. Dual interdependency is ontologically different from the two extremes and encompasses them. The middle, *zhongyong*, or the way is a dimension of profundity, a "ground" and the root grounded in it, and therefore a complete unity of the immanent and the transcendent, which is a different reality from the two separated elements of the antinomy. Thus, this spirituality is neither transcendent nor immanent but dual interdependent. In Zhu Xi's words, "In the process of putting the way into effect the raison d'être of the ten thousand things is to be found; thus, one common root is characterized by ten thousand differences (道之用也, 一本之所以萬殊也)" (*Lunyu jizhu*, 4.15, ZZQS, 6:96). Moreover, this means that dual interdependent spirituality is simultaneously inside and outside, the thread that connects individuals at a trans-subjective—that is, nurturing rootlike (organic-like)—depth of reality. According to Zhu Xi's commentary on paragraph 4 of the *Zhongyong*, practicing the way is equivalent to becoming aware of and following the one and only principle of coherence of heaven (*tian li* 天理)—that is, the profound source of all principles of coherence of individuated beings and things: "The way is the obvious manifestation of the principle of coherence of heaven, namely the capacity to conduct oneself according to the middle; this is all (道者, 天理之當然, 中而已矣)" (Zhu Xi, ZYZJ 4, ZZQS, 6:34). The principle of coherence of heaven, which is ontologically different from the principles of things and, at the same time, contains all of them, gives us another image of the idea of organic, dual interdependency.

The interdependency Qisong refers to is nondual (see chap. 6, sec. IV). The idea of nonduality is not explicitly present in Qisong's *Zhongyong jie*; however, one clearly understands its implicit occurrence, as nonduality (emptiness/fullness) is a central notion of Chan Buddhism, and its practice is discussed at length (see, for example Hisamatsu 2002). In the Neo-Confucian context, the awareness of the dual interdependency between these different principles of human beings—which come together in the principle of coherence of heaven, their unique nurturing root—is synonymous with awareness of the interdependence of individuals at this level of depth, the so-called middle or authentic nature in Zhu Xi and Qisong's commentaries, their sameness pursuant to their connection at this deep level. Consequently, a notable difference between Qisong's interdependency and Zhu Xi's is that the first is nondual (rooted in one's inner level, beyond conceptual reasoning and embracing it), while the last is dual (rooted in conceptual reasoning and analysis of the external environment).

According to Zhu Xi, following the way means "not to be separate(d) [not to distance oneself] from the people" (*bu yuan ren* 不遠人), in the light of dual interdependency:

> When measuring the heart-minds of others against the same yardstick as one's own heart-mind, so that there is never a difference, it becomes evident that the way is not far away from humans. What you yourself dislike, do not impose on others; this is to not distance oneself from the people and to follow the way (以己之心度人之心, 未嘗不同, 則道之不遠於人者可見。故己之所不欲, 則勿以施之於人, 亦不遠人以為道之事). (Zhu Xi, ZZQS, 13:39)

What Zhu Xi clearly stresses here is the importance of gaining awareness of the existence of an effective attachment between individuals through the practice of the way. In other words, he points out that the highest level of practice of the *zhongyong* ethical spirituality can be reached only within everyday social life, the field of social relations, interpersonal connections, and the social environment. It may be deduced that, for Zhu Xi, this practice is precisely a training that starts externally with gaining awareness of the different principles of human beings, in order to finally get in touch with the deep level of their root, the one and only principle of heaven, and become internally aware of the profound connection between individuals on a deeper level of reality (for the reasons expressed above, I call this level ethico-spiritual—about the spiritual dimension of human beings, see also chap. 5, sec. II), and that this training must take place not within the isolated, inner world of oneself but within the outer world of everyday social activities and interactions with others.

A century earlier, Qisong also clearly noted these two dimensions—the principle of heaven (*tianli* 天理; about Qisong's Buddhist notion of principle, see chap. 6, sec. III) and social relations (*renlun* 人倫)—as the central issues around which the teaching provided in the *Zhongyong* text is structured, which for him is close to Chan teaching. Thus, from the very beginning of his commentary, Qisong synthetically mentions the concrete elements of *zhongyong* teaching and the precise function of each one. He notes that the teaching is intended to preserve and carry forward both dimensions (the principle of coherence of heaven and social relations):

> Some sages fearing that the principle of heaven may be destroyed, and that social relations may fall into confusion, created ritual behavior, music, laws and political administration, in order to regulate people's feelings and emotions of happiness, anger, grief, fear, love and hate, as well as [their] dependencies and desires; in order to guide people to behave according to humaneness, appropriate behavior, wisdom and fidelity to one's pledged word, the sages developed the content of their teaching (有聖人者, 懼其天理將滅而人倫不紀也, 故為之禮樂刑政, 以節其喜怒哀懼愛惡嗜欲也; 為之仁義智信, 以廣其教道也). (ZYJ 1, 0666a04-8)

This paragraph also amounts to an explicit illustration of Qisong's explanation of the dual interdependent character of Confucian everyday transmoral practice. The latter incorporates at a profound level the identity between inner and outer practice: the regulation of destabilizing, inner feelings, emotions, dependencies, and desires by means of external regulators and institutions (i.e., rituals, music, laws, and political administration) and gaining awareness of the inner dispositions (i.e., the spirit of humaneness, appropriateness of behavior, understanding, and fidelity to one's pledged word) by means of external teaching. As explained below, these inner dispositions are considered by both Zhu Xi and Qisong as already present from birth within one's heart-mind. Thus, this chiasmus that organizes the scholar-monk's description indicates not a paradoxical circumstance but precisely the interdependence between inner life and social life, as well as the interdependent character of everyday ethico-spiritual practice that, at an in-depth level, connects the inner and outer of the individual, the individual and others, into an essential completeness. Its specific dimensions (i.e., emotions and behavior) are analyzed in the following section.

III. THE SPECIFIC DIMENSIONS OF ZHONGYONG ETHICO-SPIRITUAL PRACTICE: THE REGULATION OF EMOTIONS AND BEHAVIOR

In their interpretation of the *Zhongyong* text, both Qisong and Zhu Xi make reference to the emotions/feelings as a major dimension of *zhongyong* practice—how we experience them and our awareness and regulation of them, as well as their influence on behavior—and both emphasize a social rather than a personal conception of the emotions, viewing them as concrete and particular social relationships between a given individual and others.[22] As discussed in this section, for both of them emotions should reside mainly within the interpersonal relationships and not within an inner closed self. Therefore, I suggest, the spiritual discipline has two interconnected goals. One is to focus on the transformation of the self (where emotions emerge and develop) from a limited self that is narrowly concerned with isolated personal sensibilities, passions, and urges to an endless self that is intimately interwoven with everyone. I show below that this first focus is determined by what is called the principle of overcoming the self, of surpassing oneself, and that Zhu Xi's commentary pays particular attention to it. The second goal is to focus on the renewal of human behavior, in particular where emotions forge social relationships. I show that this second focal point is determined by what is called the principle of service and that Qisong's commentary pays particular attention to it.

In what follows, first I argue that in Qisong's and Zhu Xi's view, *zhongyong* transmoral discipline focuses on the regulation of emotions/feelings as a way of opening the inner, closed self and that they refer to two distinct types of emotions/feelings: self-focused ones that are to be restrained and gradually eliminated, and other-focused ones that are to be cultivated and enhanced. Second, this analysis provides evidence advocating the idea that this discipline involves simultaneously developing these two different dimensions—that is, self- and other-focused. Both aspects are based on the premise that one's emotions determine one's behavior (social relations) and that regulating emotions is therefore vital for achieving and sustaining harmonious social relationships.

III.1. Self-Focused Emotions and the Principle of Overcoming the Self

As previously mentioned, the first paragraph of the *Zhongyong* introduces specific emotions/feelings: happiness, anger, grief, and enjoyment (喜, 怒, 哀, 樂). According to both Zhu Xi and Qisong, these emotions reflect primarily the unstable vital-breath side of the individual, which clouds one's awareness of the presence of the authentic nature within oneself. They are considered by Qisong as developed through the influence of one's "dependencies and desires" (*shiyu* 嗜欲) and by Zhu Xi as shaped by "personal desires" (*si yu* 私欲).

For both of them, these are personal or individual desires and tendencies. One can identify them as socially disengaging pleasant emotions (happiness and love) as well as socially disengaging unpleasant emotions (anger, grief, fear, and hate).[23] The emphasis on their personal or individual unidimensionality suggests that Qisong and Zhu Xi perceive them as self-focused—namely, oriented toward structuring an independent self, which considers inner feelings as primordial and relations with others only secondary. Indeed, happiness, anger, grief, fear, love, and hate are ego-focused and primarily express an individual's needs and desires. One can readily understand that when given priority and preference, when expressed overtly and explicitly in day-to-day behavior, not only are these emotions detrimental to interdependent and collaborative social interaction, but they also disconnect individuals from their spiritual depth (authentic nature), making it impossible for them to achieve completeness.

In his definition (cited at the beginning of this chapter) of *zhong* as an equanimous authentic nature that "does not pull to either side and does not take sides and, for this reason, it is what is called the middle," Zhu Xi refers to the self-focused emotions/feelings as present but not developed in *zhong*. He sees the regulation of the emotions as the effort to overcome, restrain, and eventually eliminate personal desires (i.e., make them present but not developed, or formless), which enables individuals to follow the principle of coherence of heaven, restore the completeness of the moral capacity (discussed above) of their original heart-mind, and make use of their humaneness:

> Those who conduct themselves according to humaneness are able to do so by means of the completeness of the moral quality of their heart-mind. The completeness of the moral quality of their heart-mind is nothing other than the coherence principle of heaven; however, this can be damaged by the human desires. Those who conduct themselves according to humaneness must work hard to overcome personal desires and thus return to ritual. In this way, their actions totally correspond to the coherence principle of heaven, and the completeness of the moral quality of their original heart-mind is completely restored (為仁者，所以全其心之德也。蓋 心之全德，莫非天理，而亦不能不壞於人欲。故為仁者必有以勝私欲而復於禮，則事皆天理，而本心之德復全於我矣). (Zhu Xi, *Lunyu jizhu*, 12:1, ZZQS, 6:167)

In his commentary *Lunyu jizhu*, Zhu Xi details the relationship between the heart-mind, spirit of humaneness, personal desires, and sense of fullness:

> The spirit of humaneness is the moral quality of one's heart-mind. When one's heart-mind doesn't go against the spirit of humaneness, one does not have personal inclinations anymore, and therefore the moral quality of one's heart-mind is complete. Master Cheng notes that ... when the slightest personal tendency arises, one's heart-mind loses contact with the spirit of humaneness (仁者，心之德。心不違仁者，無私欲而有其德也。程 子曰：「... 少有私欲，便是不仁」). (*Lunyu jizhu* 6.5, ZZQS, 6:111)

Therefore, Zhu Xi explains, in his *Zhongyong zhangju* 9, "The *zhongyong* discipline is impossible to develop without sufficiently practicing the spirit of appropriate behavior and the spirit of humaneness, and without being free of the slightest personal desires/tendencies (若中庸 ... 然非義精仁熟，而無一毫人欲

之私者, 不能及也)" (ZYZJ 9, ZZQS, 6:36). Also, in his commentary to the tenth paragraph of the *Zhongyong*, he states, "*Zhongyong* discipline is difficult to develop; as long as personal desires/tendencies are not overcome, it is impossible to acquire and preserve it (此則所謂中庸之不可能者, 非有以自勝其人欲之私, 不能擇而守也)" (ZYZJ 10, ZZQS, 6:37).

Constantly restraining self-focused emotions enables individuals to change their relationship with others (the social environment)—first, by opening an initially closed inner self, through the transfer of individual attention from the emotions residing in the self and from individual purposes to the emotions expressed through social relations and collective purposes; second, by regulating behavior in the same way, through the transfer of the source of action and behavior from personal choices and tendencies to mutual obligations aimed at preserving social harmony, interdependence, and connectedness. Through this practice, one is able to cultivate and focus on a sense of belonging, on feeling a real oneness with others, and thus gain access to a more profound level—that is, one's ethico-spiritual or ethico-metaphysical level. For this reason, it might be said that this work on self-focused emotions is subject to the principle of overcoming the closed self.

It becomes clear that Zhu Xi, in his clarifications referred to earlier, implies that the development of the self-focused emotions, essentially individual and private, undermines social relations and obscures one's access to one's authentic nature. At this depth are to be found what the Neo-Confucians call the "five natural dispositions (*wu xing* 五性)": the quality of being humane (*ren* 仁), appropriate behavior (*yi* 義,) ritual behavior (*li* 禮), (ethical) wisdom (*zhi* 智), and fidelity to one's pledged word (*xin* 信). As previously mentioned, it is important to note that, for Zhu Xi as for Qisong, these are not merely morally or emotionally acquired dispositions but transmoral/spiritual or metaphysical capacities, considered as naturally present at the profound level of the individual at birth, through which the self extends toward the other. Furthermore, to gain access to these profound dispositions, one needs to cultivate the so-called other-focused emotions/feelings. The latter are emotional actions and reactions that originate from the interaction between individuals and their social context. These are not the five natural dispositions but give access to them.

In *Lunyu jizhu* 6.2, quoting Master Cheng, Zhu Xi clearly draws attention to the metaphysico-spiritual nature of these capacities:

The accumulation of the vital essence of heaven-earth, the best of the five elements: this is the human being. His essential root is genuine and still. Even when this root is not yet manifest [expressed as a concrete form], the human being is already endowed with the five natural dispositions, [namely] quality of being humane, appropriate behavior, ritual behavior, wisdom, and fidelity to one's pledged word. After a human being's perceptible form comes to life, external things hit it, and agitate the depth of the human being (*zhong*). When the latter is agitated, the seven emotions arise, [namely] happiness, anger, grief, fear, love, hate, and desires. These emotions inflame, overflow, spill out, and make a hole in a person's authentic nature. For this reason, those who learn to restrain their emotions so that they suit their depth [will] correct their heart-mind, and nourish their human nature (天地儲精, 得五行之秀者為人。其本也真而靜。其未發也五性具焉, 曰仁, 義, 禮, 智, 信。形既生矣, 外物觸其形而動於中矣。其中動而七情出焉, 曰喜, 怒, 哀, 懼, 愛, 惡, 欲。 情既熾而益蕩, 其性鑿矣。故學者約其情使合於中, 正其心, 養其性而 已). (Zhu Xi, ZZQS, 6:109–110)

In a dialogue presented and further discussed below, Qisong provides a similar explanation concerning the source of the self-focused emotions and how they erode the profundity of human beings, or their authentic nature, thus disconnecting one from one's depth and from the abovementioned "five natural dispositions." He adds that this perspective of Song-dynasty scholars is essentially different from how these natural dispositions were viewed earlier by the Han scholars, who also interpreted the *Zhongyong* text and authentic nature using the five-elements approach. In Qisong's opinion, their "determinist," nonspiritual explanation is totally flawed, and to support this he offers a clear explanation of the ontological difference between emotions and authentic nature, which also contains a strong argument that a spiritual dimension and practice was absent in ancient and Han Confucianism and, one can say, was introduced in Neo-Confucianism during the Song dynasty. A student asks Qisong,

> Regarding Mister Zheng's[24] commentary on the phrase "what heaven endues with (*tianming* 天命) is what is called authentic nature."[25] He says that this is what heaven assigns to an individual at his birth; it is for this reason that it is called assigned authentic nature. The spirit of wood is the quality of being humane; the spirit of metal is appropriate behavior; the spirit of fire is ritual behavior; the spirit of water is wisdom; the spirit of earth is fidelity to one's pledged word. When examining Mister Zheng's doubtful explanation, it follows that if *tianming* gives birth to the individual, then his authentic nature comes from what one experiences [a response to an external stimulus, *gan* 感]. When the spirit of wood affects him, this produces the nature of humaneness; when the spirits of metal, water, fire and earth affect him, this produces the natures of appropriate behavior, ritual behavior, wisdom and fidelity to one's pledged word. In other words, one can acquire them without any practice. This is different from what Confucius says, that in order to acquire and perfect the natures of humaneness, appropriate behavior, ritual behavior, wisdom, and fidelity to one's pledged word, one needs the teaching.

I respectfully ask: What does this mean? (問曰, 鄭氏其解天命之謂性。云天命謂天所命生人者也, 是謂性命。木神則仁, 金 神則義。火神則禮, 水神則智, 土神則信。考夫鄭氏之義疑, 若天命生人, 其性則 從所感而有之也。感乎木神則仁性也, 感乎金水火土之神則義禮智信之性也。似 非習而得之也, 與子所謂仁義禮智信其於性也必教而成之不亦異乎。幸聞其所以 然). (Qisong, *ZYJ* 3, 0666c08-1)

Qisong's answer reflects a perspective similar to that of Zhu Xi, who makes a distinction between authentic nature or the principle of coherence and the emotions. According to Zhu Xi, the former is a person's ethico-spiritual depth, and this implies that in it are ontologically present the five natural dispositions, whereas the emotions are the transient result of external stimuli coming from external things as they continuously make contact with an individual's inner being. Like Zhu Xi a century later, Qisong clearly makes the same distinction. It could be argued that Zhu Xi was inspired by Qisong's commentary to the *Zhongyong*:

> What heaven endues with is the dynamic ordering of the vital movements of heaven-earth,[26] and authentic nature is the spiritual authentic nature (性靈). In other words, the human being belongs to this dynamic ordering of the vital movements of the heaven-earth, and fuses with the spiritual authentic nature. Authentic nature is therefore the [dynamic] coherence principle, which is always with us. The emotions originate from what one experiences and feels (天命則天地之數也. 性則性靈也. 蓋謂人以天地之數而生合之性靈者也. 性乃素有之理也. 情感而有之也). (Qisong, *ZYJ* 3, 0666c18-1)

Therefore, cleansing the self of all distracting self-focused thoughts and emotions—that is, emptying the self of ego-centered feelings—allows one to overcome one's closed self, to touch one's authentic nature. This empowers individuals to descend inwardly only to go beyond outward/inward, thus overcoming their separation from others and the external world. Starting from this Chan interpretation of the ancient *Zhongyong*'s concepts, Qisong develops its complement—the idea of cultivating specific other-focused emotions as a way to go beyond emotions and restore contact with the spiritual dispositions.

III.2. Other-Focused Emotions and the Principle of Service

Qisong further explains that the sage makes use, in his teaching, of the specific emotions/feelings that people experience in order to help them gain access to the deep level of their authentic nature and spiritual dispositions:

> The sage is aware that all human beings have an authentic nature, and in his teaching he uses the emotions/feelings of mutual affection, gratitude,

understanding of differences, assessing, and conforming, in order to bring to completion human beings' authentic natures. Thus, mutual affection can turn into the spirit of humaneness; gratitude can turn into the spirit of appropriate behavior; understanding of differences can turn into the spirit of ritual behavior; the capacity to assess can turn into wisdom; the capacity to conform can turn into fidelity to one's pledged word. How can one say that authentic nature comes from what one experiences as outside influences? When things don't yet have a concrete form, or an authentic nature, or life, how can they experience an outside influence? When one is born, why wait until one experiences the outside influence of things and of spirits, in order to have one's authentic nature? Metal, wood, water, fire and earth make things without having any knowledge about this process; why repeatedly talk about this? Mister Zheng's explanation is flawed, he didn't fully think it through. If what he said were true, why would the sage need to teach? (聖人以人之性皆有乎恩愛感激知別思慮徇從之情也, 故以其教因而充之. 恩愛可以成仁也. 感激可以成義也. 知別可以成禮也. 思慮可以成智也. 徇從可以成信也. 孰有因感而得其性耶? 夫物之未形也, 則性之與生俱無有也, 孰為能感乎? 人之既生也, 何待感神物而有其性乎? 彼金木水火土, 其為物也無知, 孰能諄諄而命其然乎? 怪哉鄭子之言也, 亦不思之甚矣. 如其說, 則聖人者何用教為). (Qisong, ZYJ 3, 0666c20-9)

As a matter of fact, Qisong describes the practice of getting in touch with the five natural dispositions present at the depth of the human being, which is achieved by cultivating in particular the interdependent, other-focused emotions such as mutual affection (*enai* 恩愛), gratitude (*ganji* 感激), understanding of differences (*zhibie* 知別), and the capacities to assess (*silü* 思慮) and to conform (*xuncong* 徇從). He stresses that the five dispositions are not these other-focused emotions, because they are spiritual; in other words, they originate in the depth of human beings and are not a result of the interaction between the individuals and their external world (as the Han Confucians affirm). However, Qisong notes, these emotions can "turn into" (*cheng* 成) the spiritual dispositions. In other words, the constant accumulation of practice at an ordinary level can bring one's awareness to a superior level, beyond the subjective limited awareness, to a limitless awareness. The result of cultivating these emotions is the gradual opening of one's self through connecting with others within society. When this opening is complete, one perceives one's self as endless, as intimately interconnected with everyone. The above passage suggests that this kind of practice is governed by a special principle, the Mahayana service principle. Cultivating these other-focused emotions can be associated with the genuine interest of bodhisattvas and of scholar-officials in serving others.

The constant practice of these specific emotions cultivates interdependence among individuals. It thus provides an efficient means of construing the self not as an individual or independent self but as an open and interdependent self, composed primarily of one's relationships with the other members of one's group, which focuses on the relation self-other. The interdependent self is not the inner self but the whole of one's relationships with others.[27] Additionally, this interdependent self mediates and regulates a specific type of behavior that involves serving others, one that cultivates this interdependence and maintains a cooperative social interaction. Therefore, it is important to note that the abovementioned spiritual dispositions all embody what may be referred to as the foundations of an "interdependent spirituality."

"Mutual affection" is interpersonal affinity and implies not only being constantly aware of others but also focusing on their needs and feelings, showing a sympathetic and hierarchical concern and kindness for others (which takes into account the differences between the individuals' social positions). Such behavior arises from the indissoluble connection between human beings as bearers of the same coherence principle (Neo-Confucianism) or universal principle (Qisong's cohesive Chan Buddhism). Due to this principle of coherence or universal principle, the character of this connection, which represents the unity of society, is ethico-spiritual or ethico-metaphysical (considered in their particular meanings in Chan Buddhism and Neo-Confucianism).[28] Mutual affection, in Qisong's view, is expressed concretely in the practice of generous and tolerant behavior: "In order to guide people to behave according to the quality of being humane, the sage teaches them generosity and tolerance (為之仁也, 教其寬厚而容物)" (Qisong, ZYJ 1, 0666a12-3).

There is therefore separateness between individuals, as people are distinct, each one having one's own social position and life; there is also social connection or intersubjectivity, which is a connection between different consciousnesses, created by the shared interest in common well-being, mutual friendships, or familial ties; and finally, there is also the spiritual (or metaphysical) connection between individuals, where at the deep level of the universal principle or the principle of coherence, they are nondually or dually interrelated (beyond the opposition subject-object and intersubjectivity and embracing it). The practice of mutual affection can assist one in getting in touch with one's essential root, where the spirit of humaneness (i.e., the quality of being humane) is present. Thus, the role of the quality of being humane within one's behavior becomes a role of immediate authority; in Zhu Xi's terms, one "follows" this quality/spirit of humaneness and lets oneself be guided by it. This implies that mutual affection, generosity, and tolerance become obligatory and necessary in one's behavior.

The emotion/feeling of gratitude is also a socially engaging emotion. It fosters interdependence in that the grateful individuals develop obligations and responsibilities, which, of course, influence their behavior. Gratitude, in

Qisong's view, is expressed directly in humans conduct when they fulfill their duties and honor their obligations. As Qisong notes, the practice of gratitude can assist one in getting in touch with the spirit of appropriate behavior: "In order to guide people to behave appropriately, the sage teaches them to carry on their occupations in a manner consistent with their duties (為之義也, 教其作事必適宜)" (Qisong, ZYJ 1, 0666a12-14). The role of the spirit of appropriate behavior becomes a role of immediate authority in relation with one's behavior; one "follows" this spirit of appropriate behavior.

Another emotion/feeling that Qisong endorses cultivating is the understanding of differences. The practice of the latter is context specific and can help one regulate (modify and adjust) one's behavior in accordance with particular interpersonal relationships. Equally, according to Qisong, this accumulation of knowledge arising from relations and interactions with others guides one to become aware of the presence of the spirit of ritual behavior in the depths of oneself and to concretely actualize it in one's everyday activities. Therefore, it is clear that, in Qisong's view, understanding differences is not cognitive or conceptual understanding but a social-relational understanding of the state of affairs, of social interactions and their conditions. It can be said that this emotion/feeling is a form of intuition, of instinctive feeling, through which one is able to effectively adjust oneself to various interpersonal circumstances and ethically fulfill one's role in the context of the hierarchical order. From an interdependent perspective, an understanding of differences means specific knowledge about others arising from interactions with them, such as differences in status or differences in age. The practice of this gives access to the spirit of ritual. Thus, the spirit of ritual assumes a role of immediate authority concerning one's behavior: as noted, one "follows" it. This implies that understanding differences and thus avoiding negligent behavior toward loved ones and enemies alike becomes obligatory and necessary in one's behavior: "In order to guide people to behave according to the spirit of ritual, a clear distinction between low and high, between inside and outside is established, to ensure that people do not behave negligently towards their loved ones, and towards their enemies (為之禮也, 有上下內外, 使喜者不得苟親, 怒者不得苟疎)" (Qisong, ZYJ 1, 0666a07-5).

The next emotion that Qisong advocates is a special capacity to assess, which, he says, allows access to the wisdom present in the very depths of one's being: "In order to guide people to behave according to wisdom, the sage teaches them how to connect things and understand change (為之智也, 教其疎通而知變)" (Qisong, ZYJ 1, 0666a13-8).

When individuals gain access to their source of wisdom, the role of the latter in relation to their behavior becomes a role of immediate authority. This implies that assessing, making connections, and understanding change become obligatory and necessary in one's comportment. Like all other emotions/feelings supported by Qisong, the capacity to (ethically) assess also contributes to forging an interdependent self, one focusing on cooperation and solidarity (that is, service). As suggested by the reference to a facility in grasping changing circumstances and connections, this ethical capacity refers not to a decontextualized knowledge but to a form of instinctive feeling, of vigilance and awareness, which pays particular attention to the changing nature of social relationships and focuses on the preservation of their harmony. This faculty to assess, which entails the ability to make connections and the vigilance to perceive change in situations, is relational and sociocentric because it helps individuals develop the quality of being observant of the context, of being watchful and careful, and thus fulfilling the role of voluntary control and regulation of feelings and behavior, and promoting one's primary task of adaptation, of interdependence. Because connecting things and understanding change refers to the social context, one can say that the practice of this ethical capacity to assess even the slightest movements within the social context is instrumental in forming the self as an open entity that is given shape not by inner thoughts and reflections, as in the case of a closed self, but by a constant evaluation of the exchanges within the social context. Through the practice of this quality, one gives primacy to one's flexibility and adaptability to social context and interpersonal communication; one's self dissociates from ego-focused emotions and focuses instead on other-focused emotions—that is, commitment to the service of others.

The capacity to conform is the last emotion/feeling in the same category and is closely linked with the previous one. It, too, helps one seek and restore contact with the very depths of one's being and, more precisely, with another potential present within these depths—that is, one's fidelity to one's pledged word, which could be interpreted as conformity between one's words and deeds. When one accesses within oneself the spirit of fidelity, the role of the latter in relation to one's behavior becomes a role of immediate authority. In other words, conforming and being free of any intention to deceive become attitudes obligatory and necessary in one's behavior: "In order to guide people to behave with fidelity to one's pledged word, the sage teaches them that when making a statement one has no intention to deceive (為之信也, 教其發言而不欺)" (Qisong, *ZYJ* 1, 0666a14-2). According to Qisong, connecting with all spiritual dispositions and putting them into practice is the aim of the teaching and the second side of the practice of *zhongyong*, which has the ultimate goal of restoring the deep unity of society.

Therefore, eliminating self-focused and socially disengaged emotions is one dimension of *zhongyong* ethico-spiritual practice, the one that focuses on limiting the sense of independent self generated by the ego. Zhu Xi's commentary centers on it. The second feature—namely, cultivating socially engaging emotions, which was discussed above—is central in Qisong's commentary. This parallel analysis illustrates that Qisong's and Zhi Xi's perspectives are intertwined.

IV. CONCLUSION

The present chapter is another piece of comparative scholarship on the philosophical exchanges between Song Buddhism and Song Confucianism. Like all other chapters, its main contribution is to elaborate in detail some of the similarities of Chan Buddhism and Confucianism, starting from the work of the Northern Song Chan scholar-monk. This chapter focuses on his commentary *Zhongyong jie* 中庸解 (*Exegesis of the Mean*) and explores the following topics: cultivating interdependent spirituality, interdependent self, and socially engaged emotions. The case study that serves as context for this investigation is a comparative analysis of Qisong's and Zhu Xi's commentaries on the *Zhongyong*.

This analysis has examined the interpretation of *zhongyong* practice during the Song dynasty, as reflected in these two complementary commentaries. It consists of two parts. The first presents arguments to prove that the nature of the *zhongyong* practice is ethico-spiritual. The second interprets and explains the practical content of this discipline: the particular role of emotions, the way in which different types of emotions are regulated in order to transform a self into an interdependent self, and the way in which emotions structure an interdependent type of behavior.

Furthermore, from this analysis of what I called an interdependent and ethical spirituality stems a supplementary finding: the evidence presented suggests a social orientation of the spirituality of the Cheng-Zhu Neo-Confucian school, which has deep connections with Chan's engaged practice. This specific feature of Neo-Confucian spirituality as interdependent and endowed with a sense of completeness in daily activities has not been explored previously.[29] The spirit of the Cheng-Zhu school is commonly presented in the scholarship as "turning inward" (Liu 1988, 19), as focusing on "the problems of human nature, personal cultivation, and man's place in the universe" (De Bary 1953, 105), and as having a tendency "to slide from questions concerning interaction with others to discussions of the inner state of the individual" (Nylan 1992, 72). This parallel interpretation of the two commentaries offers another picture of the Neo-Confucian school, quite different from this common image, by presenting new proof that supports the sociopolitically engaged character of its ethical spirituality and its connection with the spirituality of Qisong's cohesive Chan Buddhism.

CONCLUSION

FIRST, THE BOOK *BUILDING BRIDGES* aims to reveal and analyze the significance of Qisong's particular contribution to the Song Chan Buddhist tradition, which he made through his original and persuasive interpretation of the affinities and differences between Confucian and Chan practices and perspectives on social ethics and human interdependency. It argues that Qisong's Chan view is radically different from those of the previous Chan schools of the Tang dynasty, because it incorporates two specific characteristics whose investigation constitutes the core of this research: a Confucian feature and a cohesive facet. In addition, the study provides philosophical evidence that the encounter between Chan Buddhism and Confucianism embodied in his work written in *guwen* is decisively not a transcultural debate between an indigenous Confucian culture and an alien Buddhist culture destructive of the Chinese traditional values—as the unchanged Confucian rhetoric accuses even a century after Qisong—but rather a lively exchange between two Chinese traditions of equal salience in the landscape of Song-dynasty culture and society.

Moreover, Qisong's writings are important in the global cultural context of the Song dynasty because they prove that an effective process of reciprocal and mutual integration of the two traditions was already in place within Confucian as well as Buddhist spheres—but still encountering resistance on both sides—initiated at least since the Tang dynasty. Another task of this work is to provide a philosophical understanding of this process, in which Qisong is a leading participant, to illustrate the cohesive Chan-Confucian dynamic that contributes to the continuous recreation of the conceptual fabric of Song-dynasty culture and thought. As this analysis suggests, Qisong's project of combining both does not just spring out of nowhere but actually reflects the spirit of his time.

The investigation of his collection *Essays on Assisting the Teaching* unveils these objectives when expounding Chan Buddhism in an interdependent way. As constantly emphasized, this work is written in Confucian *guwen* style, in the context of the Song-dynasty Confucian culture, and uses arguments from Confucian classics such as the *Liji* 禮記, *Zhoushu* 周書 ("Hong Fan" 洪範), the *Analects* of Confucius, and *Mencius*.

The scholar-monk's emphasis on doing social good works, on communitarian practice and responsibility—his principal theme, already announced at the very outset of his collection, in his essay "Inquiry into the Teachings" ("Yuanjiao"; chap. 1), and further addressed in the "Extensive Inquiry into the Teachings" ("Guang yuanjiao"; chap. 2) and the following essays—reflects the major transformation that Chan Buddhism underwent starting from the Northern Song dynasty. Yü Ying-shih describes this transformation of Buddhist thought as its "entrance into the world (*ru shi* 入世)": "Buddhist thought enters into the world and becomes interested in this present world (life) (*ci shi* 此世). On the one hand, the Buddhists read the Confucian classics and interpret their connotations and values. On the other hand, they publicly acknowledge that the good governance of the country is the Confucians' responsibility, and that the survival of Buddhism as a social institution depends on the success of Confucian governance" (Yü 2003, 1:116). Qisong's view about a cohesive teaching indeed confirms Yü's perception.

It is especially noteworthy how the Chan scholar-monk introduces this idea of the interdependence of teachings not only in the context of the Buddhist schools but also to explain the connection between Confucianist and Buddhist teachings at a profound, nondual level, beyond the apparent difference between their footprints: "The people," observes Qisong, "are used to thinking that there is a competition between self and others (天下以彼我競), and therefore consider Confucianism and Buddhism in exclusive terms (儒佛之相是非). So, what people can understand is the fact that there exists a sphere of Confucian affairs, and a sphere of Buddhist affairs. How could they know that Confucianism and Buddhism interpenetrate just like the clay and the mould?" ("Guang yuanjiao," 0655a13-14).

Furthermore, it is arguable that, through his Confucianized and cohesive interpretation of Buddhist teaching, he makes clear that Confucianism is lacking in the specific practical aspect of training the heart-mind and in the spiritual dimension concerning issues of nonduality and ultimate transformation. The scholar-monk argues that through addressing what he sees as deficiencies of Confucianism, he assists (*fu* 輔) his own interpretation of cohesive Chan teaching (as the title of his writing indicates—*Fujiao bian* 輔教編, *Essays on Assisting the Teaching*). Thus, his endeavor to identify and explain insufficiencies of Confucianism brings the Northern Song monk back to a closer inspection of Chan Buddhism, which helps him discern clearly how the latter could work together with Confucianism on improving society. These authentically Chan dimensions of his thought are explored in his essays "On Filial Devotion" ("Xiaolun"), "Letter of Advice" ("Quanshu"), "Encomium of the Platform Sutra" ("Tanjing zan"), and *Exegesis of the Mean* (*Zhongyong jie*; chaps. 4 to 7). Qisong gradually introduces his Confucian readers to previously unknown Chan motives and perspectives, from simple features (chaps. 1 and 2) to increasingly complex ones (chaps. 3 through 6). It is arguable that, while the previous chapters focus on his first intention of demonstrating the reciprocal interrelationship between Confucianism and Buddhism, chapter 3 and the next ones concern mostly his second objective: teaching the meaning and practice of his cohesive (nondual) Chan Buddhism in the Song Confucian culture. Moreover, as argued in chapter 4, the Chan scholar-monk also infuses special meaning into the Buddhist practice of leaving the family and society: in his view, this is only temporary, in order to reenter them in a better state (morally and spiritually), and it is also a way to honor one's parents.

This book shows how the continuing contact between Buddhist and Confucian traditions stimulated the development of special perceptions of Chan, such as Qisong's Confucianized one, and the emergence of the Neo-Confucian philosophy of principle and of self-cultivation. It thus explores multiple features of this philosophical context of the Song dynasty: provides a philosophical understanding of this process of intellectual exchange in which Qisong was a leading participant; illustrates the originality of the cohesive Chan-Confucian dynamic that he unfolds in his writings, thus contributing to the continuous re-creation of the conceptual fabric of Song-dynasty culture and thought; and examines major dimensions of the scholar-monk's authentic, cohesive, and Confucianized Chan Buddhism, which would conceptually inspire a new generation of Song Neo-Confucians—that is, the founders of the Neo-Confucian school of principle.

In a sense, it can be concluded that his objective to create this partnership of cohesive Chan Buddhism and Confucianism did not succeed, given the disappearance of Qisong's Chan subschool in the next century as well as the future success of the Linji Chan school—a school with objectives completely different from those of the Confucian scholars and therefore not in competition with official Confucianism in the sphere of government.

In another sense, as his other purpose was to illustrate the efficiency of cohesive Chan Buddhist ideas when applied to governance, one might say that he indirectly did succeed in that, because a generation after Qisong, the founders of the Neo-Confucian school of principle did integrate Buddhist ideas such as universal principle, heart-mind, and spirituality into Song Neo-Confucianism (though, of course, without labeling them as being of Buddhist origin). However, it appears that this was not a partnership, as Qisong envisaged, but a certain assimilation of Buddhist ideas by Confucianism. Even if they did find inspiration in Buddhist views such as those of Qisong, the founders of the school of principle never recognized this source of stimulation. To the contrary, they affirmed that their new interpretation was in fact a legitimate new reading (Neo-Confucian) of ancient Confucianism—namely, of Mencius, for example. In other words, they absorbed the abovementioned Buddhist ideas while asserting that these were already latent in ancient Confucianism and that the Song-era Confucians had merely brought them to light.

One wonders what kind of impact on Buddhism this Confucian appropriation and reinterpretation of Buddhist ideas had, to which Qisong undoubtedly contributed. It is fair to say that it had a strategic importance for the safety of Buddhism's future, as after the foundation of the Neo-Confucian school and its assimilation of major Buddhist philosophical ideas, Buddhism no longer appeared to Confucian officials as a rival in possession of a more comprehensive philosophical doctrine. This was because, henceforth, one could find in Neo-Confucianism philosophical developments similar to some extent to those of Chan Buddhism advanced by Qisong in his collection *Fujiao bian*. The 955 suppression was the last anti-Buddhist repression in Chinese history. It might be said that this was an unexpected way in which Qisong beneficially assisted the Buddhist teaching, an unforeseen way in which his project succeeded.

This study also contributes to the analysis of the interaction that occurred in eleventh- and twelfth-century Song-dynasty China between Chan and Confucian approaches to the blossoming of the individual and the practice of self-cultivation. The manner in which they evolved together philosophically during this period—their interdependence resulting from mutual exchanges and exchanged views—requires broader attention that goes beyond the formal and official Confucian representation of that time, which was largely embodied in the anti-Buddhist discourse of the Neo-Confucian Cheng-Zhu school.

With regard to comparative textual research and conceptual archaeology, it might be argued that Song Buddhist scholarship and Song Confucian scholarship remain essentially separated at the present time. They do not yet pay close attention to their common cultural ground. However, the exchanges between the two traditions during the Song dynasty is a remarkable phenomenon with far-reaching consequences. The present study provides analysis and ideas to stimulate further dialogue between the two research areas.

NOTES

INTRODUCTION

1. Qisong was a scholar-monk—that is, first and foremost a Chan monk belonging to the Chan subschool Yunmen and a true scholar of the Confucian classics.
2. Approved in 1062, by Emperor Renzong (r. 1022–1063), to be included in the Song Buddhist Canon (Wang 2017, xxxiii, 108).
3. In their substantial studies of Qisong, both Huang Chi-chiang and Elizabeth Morrison provide in-depth presentations of his life (see sec. III below).
4. These articles are included in Qisong's anthology *Essays on Assisting the Teaching* (*Fujiao bian* 輔教編).
5. Translation slightly modified by Daniel Coyle (see Tsai 2018, 186–187; Tsai 2012, 177-178).
6. CBETA T08n0235_1. See Hsuan (2002) for an English translation.
7. CBETA T48n2008_1.
8. The Chinese graphs or morphemes, Christoph Harbsmeier explains, "offer glimpses of the range of imagery conjured up by the word in the writer's mind" (1998, 33)—as well as in the reader's mind, one might add. In other words, it can be said that, instead of functioning through precise categories (concepts), Chinese language and thought operate in a rather holistic or all-encompassing manner and are marked by an authentic fluidity, "functional flexibility," and "grammatical indeterminacy" (Harbsmeier 1993, 139, 142).
9. In the Chinese Electronic Tripitaka, Qisong's anthology *Fujiao bian* (*Essays on Assisting the Teaching*) is composed of three parts: Part 1—*Fujiao bian shang* includes the essays "Yuanjiao" ("Inquiry into the Teachings") and "Quanshu" ("Letter of Advice"); Part 2—*Fujiao bian zhong* is composed of the "Guang yuanjiao" ("Extensive Inquiry into the Teachings"); Part 3—*Fujiao bian xia* comprises the "Xiaolun" ("On Filial Devotion"), and the "Tanjiang zan" ("Encomium of the Platform Sutra") (see Bibliography).
10. About this concern of the Buddhist community during the tenth century, see Welter (1993, 68–69).
11. CBETA T52n2115_001, _002, and _003.

12. In section IV of this introduction, I explain in detail why I chose to translate the concept *xin* 心 as "heart-mind." This is the translation common in Confucian studies. Most Buddhological works simply use "mind" to translate it. However, this introduction often underlines in several contexts that Qisong's essays are written in *guwen*. His work has this special aim and therefore falls within a different context: he did not write a Buddhist text intended for a broad audience but wrote a study with wide Confucian resonances, proposed to Confucian readers.

13. I am grateful to a reviewer for suggesting this formula.

1. CHAN SCHOLAR-MONK QISONG ON THE AFFINITIES AND DIFFERENCES BETWEEN CHAN BUDDHISM AND CONFUCIANISM IN "INQUIRY INTO THE TEACHINGS" ("YUANJIAO" 原教)

1. Contemporary scholars consider Song Chan Buddhism as "an important and mature phase of Chan" during which its discourse, expression, and practical forms were completed. See Wang (2017, 21).

2. For a parallel between the thought of the Neo-Confucian Zhu Xi (1130–1200) and the Tang dynasty schools of Buddhism, see Makeham (2018).

3. This essay is in Qisong (2016a, 648c25). All translations from classical Chinese are the author's.

4. About this issue, see also Welter (1999, 21–61).

5. About Buddhism as an "illness" of Chinese society and the defeat of Buddhism with the help of developing the rites, see Liu (1967, 156–165).

6. See, for example, Bol (1992, 300–343).

7. For details about the cooperative nature of their project, see Tillman (1992, 118–131).

8. Zhou Dunyi 周敦頤 (1017–1073), Cheng Hao 程顥 (1032–1085), Cheng Yi 程頤 (1033–1107), and Zhang Zai 張載 (1020–1077).

9. Eric Zürcher refers to these eminent monks as a secondary elite, "the top layer of which was closely interwoven with the secular upper class" (1989, 27). Elizabeth Morrison also notes Qisong's emphasis on the ruler as dharma protector (2010, 155). And about the role of literati in sanctioning the interpretation of Chan, see Welter (2006, 18–19).

10. About Zhu Xi's attacks against the Chan teaching of sudden awakening as "completely neglecting the sociomoral importance of gradual cultivation," see Fu (1986, 394). See also *On Buddhists* (*Shishi* 釋氏; Zhu Xi, *Zhuzi yulei* 朱子語類 126, ZZQS, 18:3924–3966).

11. Yang Shi 楊時 (1053–1135), one of the Four Masters of the Cheng school, commented that the reason why Han Yu's and Ouyang Xiu's criticisms against Buddhism were ineffective was that "they didn't go beyond the level of human affairs." See Liu (1967, 171).

12. His *Fujiao bian* impressed the ministers and Emperor Renzong (Wang 2017, 195).

13. As Huang Chi-chiang observes, Qisong, a respected Chan literati-monk, "seems to have believed that the *Zhongyong* could help explain the compatibility between Buddhism and Confucianism and that it could be used to counter those Confucians who held Buddhism in contempt and attacked it" (2000, 316).

14. Qisong, *Tanjin wenji*, vol. 4, 鐔津文集卷第四.

15. This strategy also takes various forms in Chinese and other East Asian Buddhist apologists. Qisong interprets it as a common goal of teachings. Huang Chun-chieh, for

instance, identifies a similar idea as a method of putting to use the strategy of "assimilating Confucianism into Buddhism" (儒佛一致論) by equating the values inherent in Confucian and Buddhist doctrines (2020, 79). Charles Muller notes a similar approach in the work of the fourteenth-century Korean monk Kihwa: "Like Qisong, ... his aim is to point out the underlying unity of the three teachings and to reveal them as varying expressions of a mysterious unifying principle" (2015, 24). Timothy Brook (1993) also examines the "unity of the three teachings" in late-imperial China.

16. The discussion of the Five Precepts is a common topic in Buddhist apologetics. It is also highlighted in the specific context of Muller's study (see Muller 2015, 16). *Building Bridges* discusses the Five Precepts not in the broad historical context of East Asian Buddhism but in the limited sphere of the Song-dynasty texts and in the peculiar philosophical area of the interaction between Buddhism and Confucianism during this time—specifically, Qisong's eleventh-century Confucianized Chan Buddhist work and Zhu Xi's twelfth-century Neo-Confucian commentaries. This study suggests that Qisong made an original contribution to Song-dynasty philosophy by providing a new interpretation of these precepts in Confucian terms and by systematically demonstrating their complementarity with the Confucian Five Permanencies. What I call his Song intralinguistic translation or interpretation (see introduction, sec. VII) of the interdependence between the Five Precepts and the Five Permanencies is one of the leitmotivs of this book. The first five chapters build a five-layered, progressive philosophical hermeneutics of the Chan scholar-monk's new understanding. As John McRae mentions (1986, 206; see also n. 22 and the issues addressed in the following pages), this connection was previously suggested in Buddhist works, but without a substantial development. The present investigation provides textual, philosophical evidence that supports Huang Chi-chiang's opinion: "Qisong pushed a little further the parallel made between the Five Commandments and Five Constant virtues and maintained that Buddhism and Confucianism are identical in substance" (1986, 289).

17. About the role of the Chan monasteries in educating the laity, see Zürcher (1989, 39–49).

18. In his particular context, which focuses on a correlation between teachings and cosmogonic stages (see Gregory 1995, 24), the Tang-dynasty Buddhist scholar-monk Zongmi 宗密 (780–841) also mentions the five Buddhist vehicles in his *Inquiry into the Origin of Humanity* (*Yuanren lun* 原人論). He explains what he calls the first "teaching of heaven and man" (*tianren jiao* 天人教, "Teaching of Humans and Gods" in Peter N. Gregory's 1995 translation) in correlation with "experiencing the consequences" (*shou bao* 受報) and "generating karma" (*qi ye* 起業). One could compare and contrast Zongmi's first teaching with Qisong's two vehicles—the vehicle of heaven and the vehicle of man. For Zongmi's perception, see Gregory (1995, 110–127). Muller also notes that "the *Inquiry* is first and foremost a treatise on doctrinal taxonomy that takes up the critique of Confucianism only in its opening sections" (2015, 16).

19. In the context of Buddhist works, the translation "ten wholesome behaviors" for *shishan* 十善 is commonly used. I have chosen the generic term *Ten Goods* for the frequently mentioned reason that Qisong's text is written not in Buddhist style but in Confucian style. Of course, this is only an approximation of its original significance. Such approximations are an integral part of my effort to provide a two-sided (extralinguistic and intralinguistic) hermeneutical translation (see introduction, sec. VII). To uncover the multiple layers of meaning of this complex notion for his Confucian contemporaries who do not know

Buddhism, Qisong progressively interprets it further in each of his essays (see also chaps. 2–5). I wholeheartedly support Paul Ricoeur's vision on this matter:

> A good translation can aim only at a supposed *equivalence* that is not founded on a demonstrable *identity* of meaning. This equivalence can only be sought, worked at, supposed. And the only way of criticizing a translation—something we can always do—is to suggest another supposed, alleged, better or different one. And this, moreover, is what happens in the world of professional translators. As far as the great texts of our culture are concerned, [and of different cultures, I would say in an effort to extend the scope of Ricoeur's comment to my intercultural context] we essentially live on a few retranslations which are reworked over and over again. (2006, 22)

20. On this subject, see Zürcher (1989, 19–56).

21. The Ten Goods is a well-known Buddhist notion. Qisong's special achievement lies in his ability to present and explain these Buddhist notions in a comparative perspective, as supporting the Confucian vision and resonating with the Chinese classics.

22. McRae (1986, 206) also mentions the early Chan practice of correlating the five Buddhist precepts with the Confucian virtues.

23. About this movement, see also Skonicki (2014, 1–32).

24. On the role played by Buddhist monasteries in the secular elementary education of the laity, based on Confucian and secular texts, starting from the beginning of the Song, see Zürcher (1989, 39–87).

25. Chün-fang Yü also implies that "both Chan and Neo-Confucian masters regarded the classical tradition as their own heritage" (1989, 99); so does Zürcher (see n. 24). The present study provides philosophical and textual arguments on this issue through an investigation of what I call Qisong's *guwen* intralinguistic translation of Chan (Buddhist) values and practices. As mentioned in the introduction, Morrison also stresses "Qisong's commitment to Confucian classics," but from a perspective rooted in Qisong's writings on Chan lineage, *Chuanfa zhengzong lun* 傳法正宗論 (*Critical Essay on the True Lineage of the Dharma Transmission*; see Morrison 2010, 117).

26. About models of Chan leadership, see Yü (1989, 88–98).

27. For a study of the difference between Han-dynasty and Song-dynasty interpretations of this chapter, see Nylan (1992).

28. Usually, in texts written in the Buddhist style, *fo zhi jing* 佛之經 is translated as "Buddhist sutras." In keeping with Qisong's Confucian *guwen* intralinguistic translation of Chan ideas, I suggest here the broader formula "Buddhist classics." In Qisong's interpretation of Chan Buddhism written in Confucian *guwen* ancient style, the character *jing* 經 has an "inclusive" meaning and designates not only "sutras" but all types of classic texts: Confucian, Buddhist, Daoist, or any of the one hundred philosophical schools. Again, the term is introduced by the Chan scholar-monk in his first essay and gradually interpreted in the following essays. For him all the "classics" (writings) have a common feature: they are different "footprints" of the teachings, different perceptible footprints (approaches) of the same way, left by the sages. To preserve the inclusive context of his interpretation, I used the classical translation of this term and interpreted its several layers of meaning in this chapter and in chapter 2.

29. I am grateful to the anonymous reviewer who asked for more details about this translation. It is intended to reflect the Confucian resonances of Qisong's writings and to illustrate his intralinguistic translational effort. A difficult term to translate in the *guwen*

context of the whole paragraph is the character *tong* 通, which is a technical concept of the ancient Chinese (Confucian) texts. According to *Shuowen Jiezi*, the ancient Chinese dictionary from the Han dynasty—the first dictionary that gives the definition and graphic etymology of the characters—*tong* 通 means "enable communication" ("opening up lines of communication," in the *Shujing* 書經, *Classic of History*), relationships, exchanges (in the *Yijing* 易經, *Classic of Changes*), sharing or having in common with each other (in the classic *Liji* 禮記, *Book of Rites*), movement without obstruction, linking together, therefore harmony. It embodies the major characteristic of the ideal Confucian sage whose teachings aim to connect people, to build and preserve an all-inclusive, harmonious society. Qisong's term *xiao tong* 小通 (i.e., little inclusiveness, slightly inclusive, limited connectivity) is a direct allusion to the Confucian *da tong* 大通 (i.e., great, unlimited inclusiveness, connectivity, harmony)—a very familiar term to Confucians. *Xiao tong* 小通 (in the sentence mentioned: 如此豈小通哉?) is a rhetorical double negation, a common artifice in the Confucian *guwen* style, meant to strongly emphasize the opposite: "How could the Buddha's heart-mind be like this: only slightly inclusive?" The two elements of the double negation are, first, "How could?"—the question is interpreted as a negative assertion; and, second, "slightly." The double negative construction is not usual in English. This is why I translate the phrase not as "How could the Buddha's heart-mind be only slightly inclusive?" but as "The Buddha's heart is like this: it is very inclusive." In this paragraph, Qisong implicitly establishes a connection between the Confucian ideal of the sage and the goal of his teaching on the one hand, and the Buddhist ideal of the sage and the goal of the Buddhist teaching on the other: the teachings of all sages (Buddhist, Confucian, and other) adapt to all circumstances and therefore promote social harmony and inclusiveness. Moreover, Qisong sees all different sages who embody different teachings as sharing the same heart-mind (see chaps. 2 and 6). As discussed in the subsequent chapters and especially in chapter 6, the Buddha's heart-mind is an allusion to the Buddha's teachings. In Qisong's view, the latter embody the Buddha's heart-mind, exactly as the Confucian teachings embody the Confucian sage's heart-mind. According to the Chan scholar-monk, Buddhist teachings are also inclusive; all sages share the same heart-mind. The notion of *tong* 通 as inclusiveness is another central concept present in all of Qisong's essays, and I discuss at length its multiple layers of meaning in each of my chapters. Obviously, for him, unlike Confucian social and ethical inclusiveness, the (Chan) Buddhist nondual inclusiveness unfolds at a profound, spiritual level embodied in everyday life. This chapter (on the essay "Yuanjiao") is the introduction of this gradual philosophical development.

30. Here I draw inspiration from the theoretical structure proposed by Frederick J. Streng (1985, 82) for understanding religion as a means to ultimate transformation.

31. In his introductory note to the *Zhongyong zhangju*, Zhu Xi quotes the Cheng Masters: "This writing begins by evoking a unique natural principle of coherence (*li* 理). It dissipates itself in ten thousand things and events and they finally return to it. 'This principle dissipates itself and fills the world, wraps itself and pulls itself back so as to set itself aside in a remote place'" (其書始言一理, 中散 為萬事, 末復合為一理, 放之則彌六合, 卷之則退藏於密; Zhu 2002, 6.32). For an analysis of this note, see Arghiresco/u (2013, 39–44). For a presentation of the evolution of *li* as principle, see W. Chan (1964, 123–149). Chan emphasizes that, as a result of the Buddhists' challenge and for the first time in Chinese history, the Neo-Confucians built the entire Neo-Confucian system on this concept of principle as its "metaphysical foundation and rational basis." See the introduction in W. Chan (1967, xviii). For an exhaustive analysis of the meaning of *li* as "coherence" in pre-Song texts (Warring States and Han texts, Wang Bi, Guo Xiang, and Huayan 華嚴 and Tiantai 天台 Buddhism), see Ziporyn (2013).

32. The novel dimension of the Neo-Confucians' method—that is, cultivating "reverence" (*jing* 敬), which is directly inspired by Chan—is not examined in the present essay.

33. As earlier explained, in the context of this book, what makes the particularity of Qisong's project is his effort to translate intralinguistically and therefore "critically" (Chan) Buddhist thought into the *guwen* matrix of the Confucian tradition. Moreover, his effort to make this Confucian tradition sensitive to the (Chan) Buddhist reality has a simultaneous and complementary result: it enriches (Chan) Buddhist thought in its whole. To shed light on the particularity of this philosophic project, I am developing chapter by chapter an archaeology of the Confucian foundations of Qisong's concepts—that is, a philosophical hermeneutics of his "inclusive" Chan Buddhist philosophy in Confucian terms. This archaeology includes a close philosophical interpretation of Qisong's text and of how it fits in Song-dynasty Confucian culture. The context in which the particularity of Qisong's view is illustrated is not the Buddhist apologetic tradition (Chinese, Korean, or Japanese) but the very Chinese Confucian context (Chinese classics), the Chinese culture from which Qisong's thought emerged. Also, my focus is not to investigate the way in which his ideas have influenced or interacted with other Buddhist thinkers but to explore the Song-dynasty intracultural ties between Qisong's ideas and Zhu's Neo-Confucian thought.

34. Also see Zhu Xi's commentary to the sixteenth paragraph of the *Zhongyong* (Zhu 2002, 6:41).

35. Translation by Wing-tsit Chan, slightly modified.

36. I translate *qi* 氣 as "vital breath" because this term emphasizes the dynamism of natural life, the holistic character of the substrate of the world, neither matter nor spirit but both, and suggests the interconnectedness of things, which in Zhu Xi's thought is effectively realized through sharing a common coherence principle of heaven.

37. I thank an anonymous reviewer for bringing this issue to my attention.

2. AN ELEVENTH-CENTURY CONFUCIANIZED AND COHESIVE FORM OF CHAN

1. See T52n2115-2, 0654b23-2.

2. This quotation is from Qisong's "Tanjing zan" ("Encomium of the Platform Sutra"). Note that this essay, included in the *Fujiao bian* (*Essays on Assisting the Teaching*), is very famous and appears twice in the Tripitaka Collection: as an article of Qisong's anthology *Fujiao bian*, and also at the beginning of the mature version of the *Platform Sutra*, known as the *Platform Sutra of the Dharma Treasure of the Great Master, the Sixth Patriarch* (*Liuzu dashi fabao tanjing* 六祖大師法寶壇經), presumably edited by Qisong himself (see the introduction, sec. III). To highlight the importance of this essay and its double presence, for this quotation I give its *Platform Sutra* reference.

3. Welter also notes, in passing, that Qisong had close affinities with Yanshou's interpretation of Chan (Welter 1993, 104, 175; 2011, 12, 26).

4. Aside from Confucianism, Qisong mentions, in passing, that Nagarjuna's thought was also a source of inspiration for him (see "GYJ," 0654b07).

5. For a detailed presentation of its twelfth-century Neo-Confucian meaning, see Arghiresco/u (2013).

6. For a philosophical analysis of these chapters (ancient and twelfth-century Neo-Confucian meaning), see Arghiresco/u (2013, 97–121, 165–187, 199–206).

7. The same idea can be found in Mencius 4.A.12 (*Li Lou shang* 離婁上).

8. For other discussions of *quan* 權 in Early China, see *quan* as "weighing in the context of the human action" (Vankeerberghen 2005, 47–89), as "weighing the way" in *Analects* 9:30 (Berthrong 2005, 3–18), and as "externally varying from standard ethical action while internally holding to correct principles" (Ing 2017, 38).

9. Qisong, "Tanjing zan" 壇經贊, ("Encomium of the Platform Sutra"), CBETA T48n2008-1, 0346a13.

10. On this particular topic, see Bol (1992, 176–211).

11. About the nonduality of Chan Buddhism, see Arghirescu (2020b, 7–11).

12. About Zhou Dunyi's thought, see J. Adler (2014, 37–76).

13. About Zhang Zai's thought, see Kasoff (1984, 125–147).

3. QISONG'S "LETTER OF ADVICE" ("QUANSHU" 勸書)

1. I want to express my deep appreciation to an anonymous reviewer who provided me with insightful comments on this topic.

2. Yü Ying-shih notes the existence of this mutual dialogue during the Song dynasty. He describes it as a process of Confucianization of Northern Song Buddhism and Buddhization of the Confucian literati. With the emergence of the new school of Chan, Chinese Buddhism became socially involved, literally "entering the world" (*rushi* 入世). "Starting from the beginning of the Northern Song," Yü points out, "the social engagement of Buddhism becomes more profound, and the interest shown by prominent and virtuous monks in issues of daily life is often no less important than that of the Confucian literati and scholar-officials.... Also, because during the Song dynasty the sociopolitical status of the latter increases, the Buddhist monks need their support in promoting Chan doctrines" (2003, 1:116).

3. About this issue, see Li and Ding (2010, 7–8). For a different perspective, see Schlütter (2007).

4. Welter notes that the new early Song Chan "did not challenge conservative Confucians to accept Buddhism as part of China's *wen* tradition" and "did not suggest that Buddhism be admitted alongside Confucianism as a legitimate expression of China's cultural values" (2006, 172). To a certain extent, Welter's characterization is as true for Qisong as it is for Zanning. However, Qisong explicitly and philosophically advocated for his cohesive Chan Buddhism as complementary to Confucianism and a legitimate expression of the Song-dynasty cultural landscape.

5. Morrison (2010, 155) notes Qisong's emphasis on the ruler as dharma protector.

6. About Zhu Xi's twelfth-century criticism of the Buddhist specific meaning of the moral goodness (*shan* 善), see Tiwald (2018, 137).

7. To simplify and standardize references, all the quotations from ancient Confucian classics come from one standard source: the ZZQS. All the *Four Books* (*Daxue, Lunyu, Mencius* and *Zhongyong*) are included in the vol. 6 of Zhu Xi's collected works *Zhuzi quan shu* 朱子全書 (here abbreviated as ZZQS, 6), together with Zhu Xi's commentaries to these *Four Books*.

8. In the context of Qisong's thought, I follow Frederick Streng's definition of *religion*—"a means to ultimate transformation, of change from disharmonious, evil, state of existence to harmony, enlightenment" (Streng 1985, 16).

9. For a study of the difference between Han-dynasty and Song-dynasty interpretations of this chapter, see Nylan (1992). In the context of her study, Nylan translates "Hong Fan" 洪範 as "Great Plan."

10. Liu quotes Ouyang Xiu, who, in the introduction to his "Treatise on Rites and Music," acknowledges that "the rites and music failed to meet the needs of the people and became 'expressions without reality': empty, lifeless, and mere formalities" (Liu 1967, 163).

11. About the development of the concept of heart-mind within the Neo-Confucian context after the Song dynasty, and about the Buddhist influence on this process, see Qian (1980), De Bary (1986), and Ng (1999, 89–120).

12. For an analysis of the main themes of his commentary, see Arghirescu (2020b).

13. For a translation and philosophical interpretation of the *Zhongyong*, see Ames and Hall (2001). For a philosophical translation of the *Zhongyong zhangju*, Zhu Xi's commentary to the *Zhongyong*, and a comparative, intercultural hermeneutics (Chinese/Western) of the main moral themes of Zhu Xi's twelfth-century interpretation of the *Zhongyong*, see Arghiresco/u (2013).

14. See, for instance, Han Yu's 韓愈 (768–824) part 5 of his essay "Yuandao" 原道 ("Inquiry into the Dao"), in Han (1986, 17).

15. For an analysis of Qisong's understanding of the connection between Confucian human relationships and the Buddhist Five Precepts and Ten Goods, see Arghirescu 2020b.

16. I thank an anonymous reviewer who provided the following insight: This notion of "not dwelling" seems inspired by the book of Zhuangzi, especially chapters 2 and 17. The anonymous reviewer notes that in chapter 1, Zhuangzi shows how everything and everyone has a different perspective. This is dwelling on a limited and specific perspective. The enlightened person can grasp all of the perspectives and can respond to things on the hinge or axis of the way. I totally agree that this seems to be a transcendent view that anticipates the Chinese Buddhist perspective.

17. For an exhaustive analysis of the meaning of *li* as "coherence" in pre-Song texts (Warring States and Han texts, Wang Bi, Guo Xiang, and Huayan 華嚴 and Tiantai 天台 Buddhism), see Ziporyn (2013).

18. In this context, I would like to draw attention to the complex meaning of the term *shu* 數. The translation I suggest here ("the dynamic ordering of the vital movements") is still reductive.

19. Welter distinguishes a "principled" Buddhism as one type of Buddhist practice during the early Song dynasty. He proposes the addition of a Buddhist school of principle that focuses on a moral and principled approach, and he repositions the monk Yanshou 延壽 (904–975) as an advocate of this school. See Welter (2011, 203–220). Qisong's thought could also be described as a form of "principled Buddhism," as he also holds the principle in high esteem. However, this is only an aspect of his multifaceted, cohesive Chan. Welter considers Qisong as a Confucian monk (*ruseng* 儒僧) and Yanshou as a doctrinal Buddhist (*jiaoli seng* 教理僧).

20. Willard Peterson (1986, 13–31) explores the *li* as coherence in the teachings of Neo-Confucians Cheng Yi 程頤 (1033–1107) and Zhu Xi 朱熹 (1130–1200).

21. It should be emphasized that "seeing one's nature" (*jian xing* 見性) is in fact *xian xing* 見性 and means to realize, manifest, or express one's nature (*xing* 性). The latter cannot be seen or perceived by sensory perception. I am grateful to the anonymous reviewer who stressed the importance of emphasizing here this special Chan meaning of *jian* 見.

22. Zheng Xuan 鄭玄 (127–200) was an Eastern Han Confucian scholar who annotated the Confucian texts, including the three classics on the rites *Sanli* 三禮.

23. The opening phrase of the classic *Zhongyong*.

24. For a translation of the Guodian version of "The Five Aspects of Conduct" with an emphasis on Guodian religion and on the religious function of major concepts of the *Wuxingpian*, see Holloway (2009).

25. About the Guodian concept of *wuxing* "as a challenge to contemporary concepts of *wuxing*, in which the author consciously attempts to redefine *xing* in terms of moral attributes, and not amoral natural processes," see Brindley (2019, 187–196).

26. In this regard, see also Zhu Xi and Lü Zuqian, *Jinsilu* 近思錄 13.3. The Neo-Confucians use the term *mie* 滅 to translate *nirvana*.

27. Obviously, Qisong refers here to paragraph 1 of the classic *Zhongyong*, which he also interprets in his commentary; see *Zhongyong jie* 3, 0666b21.

28. The great principle is spiritual (see sec. III.2).

29. For an in-depth explanation of this Huayan Buddhist notion, see Fazang 法藏 (643–712), *Huayan fa putixin zhang* 華嚴發菩提心章, CBETA T45n1878-1, 0652c29.

30. Yü Ying-shih affirms that the Cheng brothers strategically never mentioned Qisong in their works. However, he argues that they certainly knew Qisong's work very well, as it was officially recognized by Emperor Renzong. Yü Ying-shih's point is that, during the 1070s, the "discussions on Chan" (*tanchan* 談禪), Qisong included, were a common topic of debate among members of the Luoyang school (the political adversaries of Wang Anshi) and that the young Cheng brothers attended these meetings organized by Han Wei 韓維 (1017–1098) and elder Confucian scholars. Yü Ying-shih quotes a comment by Cheng Yi from the book *Surviving Works of the Two Cheng Brothers* (*Er Cheng yishu* 二程遺書) about a meeting he attended in 1080 (see introduction, sec. VI).

31. Posthumous name Yang Wengong 楊文公, a scholar-official in the Imperial Academy, influenced by the Linji Chan school, who edited the *Jingde chuandeng lu*.

32. I am grateful to an anonymous reader for raising this point.

4. QISONG ON BUDDHIST FILIAL DEVOTION (XIAO 孝)

1. CBETA T52n2115_003.

2. I am grateful for the comment of an anonymous reviewer who suggests that a parallel examination of this essay of Qisong and of Zhu Xi's edition of the *Xiaoxue* 小學 (Elementary learning), published in 1187, might also be interesting. Childhood education was a major interest for Song scholars. It expressed the fundamentals of the Neo-Confucian educational philosophy, starting with prenatal influences in the womb (see De Bary 2008, 401–404). Theresa Kelleher argues that what Zhu chose to include in the *Elementary Learning* reflects his attempt to reform people's values and behavior through education and ritual. In his preface to the *Elementary Learning*, Kelleher stresses, Zhu states that his purpose was to reestablish the learning that the "ancients" had developed for young people. This consisted in specific, concrete modes of behavior that were both practical and ritualistic, such as sweeping and sprinkling, learning how to converse with elders, and relating affectively to the human beings around oned—loving parents, respecting elders, and esteeming teachers. Mastery of these then prepared a person to advance to the next level—pursuit of the goals of the *Great Learning*: cultivating the self, regulating the family, ruling the country, and establishing peace in the world (Kelleher 1989, 220). Another connected Neo-Confucian study that focuses on shaping ritual behavior is Zhu Xi's *Family Rituals*. According to Patricia Buckley Ebrey, this book deserves careful reading because of the importance of the ritual described in

it. These rituals expressed and reproduced the key principles underlying the family system: the relationships between ancestors and descendants, men and women, parents and children, and families linked through marriage (Buckley Ebrey 1991, xiv).

3. Except where the translator is indicated, all translations from the classical Chinese are my own.

4. Zhou Dunyi 周敦頤 (1017–1073), Cheng Hao 程顥 (1032–1085), Cheng Yi 程頤 (1033–1107), and Zhang Zai 張載 (1020–1077).

5. About the inclusion of Buddhist monks as "an essential party in the cycle of exchange linking ancestors and descendants," see Teiser (1988, 197).

6. In *Hongming ji* 弘明集, juan 1, CBETA T52n2102_001, 0002b17, 0002c16, 0003a07. For an English translation, see Keenan (1994).

7. For a theoretical explanation of this type of religious life, see Streng (1985, 64).

8. For a philosophical interpretation of this ancient paragraph and of its Song-dynasty Neo-Confucian commentary by Zhu Xi, see Arghiresco/u (2013, 253–260).

9. For a philosophical translation of this ancient paragraph and of its Neo-Confucian commentary by Zhu Xi, see Arghiresco/u (2013, 365–366).

10. For a philosophical translation and interpretation of this classic, see Rosemont and Ames (2009, 22–63).

11. For a philosophical interpretation of this paragraph and of its commentary by Zhu Xi, see Arghiresco/u (2013, 275–301).

12. About a theoretical development of the concept of "spiritual ideal" as a basis for the reconstruction of society, see F. Adler (1929, 27).

13. For a theoretical development on the notion of spiritual discipline, see Streng (1985, 88–101).

14. CBETA T24n1484_001 and _002. For the English translation, see Muller and Tanaka (2017). About the origins of the sutra, see "Origins of the Sutra: Its Structure and Content," in Muller and Tanaka (2017, xvii–xxi).

15. I adopt here Keith N. Knapp's translation of the term *yang* 養 ("nurturing with food or physical care"), which preserves the polysemy of this concept. See Knapp (2004, 44).

16. The six destinies include three good destinies, i.e., heavenly destiny (*tian dao* 天道), human destiny (*ren dao* 人道), and asura destiny (*Axiuluo dao* 阿修羅道), and three evil destinies, i.e., animal destiny (*chusheng dao* 畜生道), hungry ghost destiny (*egui dao* 餓鬼道), and hell destiny (*diyu dao* 地獄道).

17. CBETA T24n1484_002, 1006b09; *The Brahma's Net Sutra*, translation in Muller and Tanaka (2017, 55).

18. In the English translation, the paragraph referred to is paragraph 21 (Muller and Tanaka 2017, 56).

19. CBETA T17n0784_001. For an English translation and a discussion concerning the dating and significance of this sutra, see Sharf (1996, 360–371).

20. For a discussion of the place of the Mulian myth in Chinese Buddhist mythology, see Teiser (1988, 113–167).

21. CBETA T16n0685_001. For an English translation, see Bando (2005, 17–23).

22. For a philosophical translation and interpretation of this chapter, including its commentary by Zhu Xi, see Arghiresco/u (2013, 345–352).

23. Brook Ziporyn (2013, 185–259) explores the meaning of the principle (*li* 理) in Tiantai and Huayan Buddhism.

24. For a theoretical analysis of the concept of "action" in the context of Indian Buddhism, see "Karma and Avijnapti-rupa" in Hirakawa (1990, 185–196).
25. For an interpretation of this term, see Knapp (2004, 44–72).
26. Knapp (2004, 44–72) explains how this Confucian notion of "reverent caring" is reflected in early medieval tales.
27. CBETA T03n0174_001 菩薩睒子經, 0438a20.
28. In the *Analects* 8.1, Confucius considers Wu Taibo as an example of perfect moral quality (*zhi de* 至德).
29. Historical figures without direct descendants praised by Confucius in the *Analects* (5.22, 7.14, 16.12, 18.8) and by Mencius (5.B.1) because they chose to hold on to the moral quality of humaneness (*ren* 仁) and starved themselves to death on a mountain.
30. Translation by Rosemont and Ames (2009, 116).
31. Mencius, *Gongsun chou, shang* 公孫丑上, 2.A.6, *ZZQS*, 6:289.
32. Translation from the Chinese by Bando (2005, 21).
33. See also Teiser's explanation of this episode as "showing the failure of ancestral food offerings" and as a way in which "Buddhism was domesticated in China . . . through the inclusion of monks as an essential party in the cycle of exchange linking ancestors and descendants" (1988, 196–197).
34. Translation by Muller and Tanaka (2007, 42). Translation slightly modified.

5. HEART-MIND (*XIN* 心), EMOTIONS (*QING* 情), AND NATURE-EMPTINESS (*XING* 性) IN QISONG'S THOUGHT

1. About Li Ao and the *Fuxing shu*, see Barrett (1992).
2. The Song-dynasty Buddhist collection *Song gaoseng zhuan* 宋高僧傳 (Biographies of eminent monks of the Song) compiled by Zanning 贊寧 (919–1001) mentions their student-master relationship. See *Song gaoseng zhuan, juan* 17, *Tang Langzhou Yaoshan Weiyuan zhuan* 唐朗州藥山惟儼傳, CBETA T50n2061_017, 0816a19.
3. For a contemporary commentary on the *Heart Sutra* and on the five skandhas, see Sheng-Yen (2001, 45–51).
4. Qisong uses here the notion *jingshen* 精神, which is an ancient Chinese term that occurs frequently in the *Huainanzi*. In its ancient understanding, it means "a form of *qi*, one even more rarefied, potent, and dynamic than essence itself," the vital force associated in the *Huainanzi* "with properties of consciousness and having the ability to oversee or coordinate the various mental activities of perception and cognition" (Major 2010, 878, 233–260). Note that the meaning of the ancient notion is essentially different from Qisong's interpretation.
5. For a philosophical interpretation of the ancient Confucian meaning of this paragraph and of its Song-dynasty Neo-Confucian explanation, including Zhu Xi's commentary to it, see Arghiresco/u (2013, 45–62).
6. A philosophical commentary on this phrase, including its Neo-Confucian interpretation, can be found in Arghiresco/u (2013, 62–74).
7. See the *Heart Sutra* 般若波羅蜜多心經 and Sheng-Yen's commentary (2001, 36–39).
8. For a study of the difference between Han-dynasty and Song-dynasty interpretations of this chapter, see Nylan (1992).

9. It should be reemphasized that "seeing one's nature," *jian xing* 見性, is in fact *xian xing* 見性 and means to realize, manifest, or express one's nature, *xing* 性 (see chap. 3, sec. III.2 and n. 23).

6. QISONG ON UNIVERSAL PRINCIPLE (*LI* 理), NOTHINGNESS (*WU* 無), AND THE "ENCOMIUM OF THE PLATFORM SUTRA" ("TANJING ZAN" 壇經贊)

1. Welter (2011, 219) also notes that Zhu Xi's school of principle reduces all of Buddhism to the Linji Chan.

2. Nishitani develops this difference as the contrast between "[seeing] things merely as objects, that is, as 'external' things outside of the 'internal' self" and "the real manifestation of that is actually concealed at the foundation of the self and everything in the world" (1960, 29 and 36).

3. About how one's resonance with ancestral spirits vivifies one's everyday interpersonal sensitivity in Zhu's thought, see also his commentary to paragraph 16 of the ancient *Zhongyong* (Arghiresco/u 2013, 249–251).

4. I would like to express here my sincere gratitude to an anonymous reviewer for this captivating comment and the suggested reading: Julia Ching's 1974 article "The Goose Lake Monastery Debate (1175)," *Journal of Chinese Philosophy* 1:161–178.

5. At the beginning of this article, Ching also highlights the approximate nature of the translation in English, "its equivalence without identity," to paraphrase Paul Ricoeur (what this book calls its extralinguistic side, which includes consistent interpretations before and after the de facto translation of the paragraphs):

> I wish to mention how the English word "debate" can only be used in a modified sense to suit the Chinese context. This word usually connotes formal and public presentations, in an organized and systematic fashion, of certain arguments for and against a given proposition. In this Chinese context, however, the event represented rather scholarly discussions highlighting certain differences between two men on the subject of the Confucian quest for sagehood. If I use the word, it is for lack of a better one in English and because the semi-formal and semi-public occasion, and the arguments which were expressed, gives the event certain characteristics which resemble those of a debate. (1974, 161)

6. This paragraph from Tsai 2012 is translated from the original Chinese by Daniel Coyle and Yahui Anita Huang (unpublished translation of Tsai 2012). Tsai 2018 translated by Daniel Coyle is an abbreviated version of Tsai 2012.

7. Translation from the original Chinese by Daniel Coyle and Yahui Anita Huang (unpublished translation of Tsai 2012) slightly modified. Tsai 2018 translated by Daniel Coyle is an abbreviated version of Tsai 2012.

8. Willard Peterson (1986, 13–31) explores *li* as coherence in the teachings of Neo-Confucians Cheng Yi 程頤 (1033–1107) and Zhu Xi 朱熹 (1130–1200).

9. Brook Ziporyn (2013, 185–259) examines *li* in Tiantai and Huayan Buddhism.

10. See, for example, Fazang 法藏 (643–712), *Huayan fa putixin zhang* 華嚴發菩提心章, CBETA T45n1878.

11. On Zhu Xi's understanding of principle, see also Arghirescu (2019, 52–70).

12. I translate *qi* as "vital breath" because this term emphasizes the dynamism of natural life and the holistic character of the substrate of the world, neither matter nor spirit but both, and suggests the interconnectedness of things, which in Zhu's thought is effectively realized through sharing a common coherence principle of heaven.

13. Translation by Daniel Coyle and Yahui Anita Huang (unpublished translation of Tsai 2012) slightly modified.

14. See Zhu Xi, *Daxue zhangju* 5, ZZQS, 6:20: "The wonderful power of the heart-mind has the capacity to understand, and each of the myriad things of reality has a coherence principle. It is only when these coherence principles are not probed to the utmost that understanding remains incomplete (蓋人心之靈莫不有知, 而天下之物莫不有理, 惟於理有未窮, 故其知有不盡也)."

15. For an in-depth interpretation of this paragraph in the context of the complementarity between Confucianism and Buddhism advocated by Qisong, see chapter 3, section III.2.

16. One notes again the term *changdao* 常道 as a powerful Daoist allusion (Laozi, par. 1).

17. About no-form in this context, see also the interpretation of Guo (1983, 33).

18. On this subject, see also Faure (1991, 237).

19. Welter (2011, 34) presents the Chan monk Yangshou (904–975) as an "advocate of Bodhisattva practice" who, like Qisong a century later, was a Buddhist practitioner free of sectarian bias.

20. See also Guo Peng's interpretation (1983, 33).

21. Nishitani explains that "a realization of nothingness is not simply a conscious, 'subjective' phenomenon; it is rather the real manifestation of that is actually concealed at the foundation of the self and everything in the world. On the field of consciousness, it is hidden and cannot really emerge" (1960, 36).

7. ETHICO-SPIRITUAL DISCIPLINE, EMOTIONS, AND BEHAVIOR DURING THE SONG DYNASTY

1. This chapter is a revised version of an article originally published in *Philosophy East and West* (Arghirescu 2020b, doi:10.1353/pew.2020.0016).

2. For a translation and philosophical interpretation of the *Zhongyong*, see Ames and Hall (2001). For a complete philosophical translation of the *Zhongyong zhangju*—Zhu Xi's commentary to the *Zhongyong*—and a comparative, intercultural hermeneutics (Chinese/Western) of the main moral themes of his twelfth-century interpretation of the *Zhongyong*, see Arghiresco/u (2013).

3. Qisong, *Tanjin wenji*, vol. 4, 鐔津文集卷第四 (*Collected Works of Qisong*) in CBETA T.52, no. 2115-4. For a general examination of Qisong's interpretation of the *Zhongyong* and his goal to synthesize Buddhism and Confucianism, see Huang (2000, 315–331). In her study on Qisong's writings on Chan lineage, Elizabeth Morrison mentions Qisong's commentary on the *Zhongyong* as proof that "he does not dismiss Confucian teachings as 'merely' provisional." And she highlights Qisong's involvement in Confucian studies as an indication that he defines himself as "the inheritor of the wisdom of many sages" (Morrison 2010, 116, 129).

4. About the Confucian elite patronage of Qisong and his reputation as a brilliant *guwen* 古文 writer, see Huang (1999, 315–316). Morrison interprets Qisong's use of plain *guwen* as

his own distinctive way of defending the Buddhist faith and as an expression of "his sincere admiration for and engagement with the Confucian tradition" (Morrison 2010, 114).

5. Zhu Xi, *Zhuzi quan shu* 朱子全書, ZZQS, 6:29–60. Except where the translator is indicated, all translations from classical Chinese are the author's.

6. About the government patronage of Buddhism, especially of the Chan school, and the harmonious cooperation among bureaucrats (prefects), local elites, and Buddhist institutions for the welfare and the prosperity of a given region, see Schlütter (1999, 135) and Huang (1999, 297–316).

7. "*Daoxue jia 'pifo' yu songdaifojiao de xindongxiang* (道學家「闢佛」與宋代佛教的新動向)."

8. The Tiantai Buddhist monk Zhiyuan 智圓 (976–1022) also discussed the complementarity between Buddhism and Confucianism and commented on the classic *Zhongyong*. See Shinohara (1994, 38).

9. For a presentation of the evolution of *li* as principle, see Chan (1964, 123–149). However, Wing-tsit Chan emphasizes a single dimension of Cheng Yi's method of understanding principle: its "strictly rationalistic basis which is a far cry from neo-Taoism or Buddhism" (140). The view I'm advocating here is different from the traditionally accepted perspective he embraced. Also, for a discussion of five meanings of *li*, see Cheng (1986, 169–174).

10. For an exhaustive analysis of the meaning of *li* as "coherence" in pre-Song texts (Warring States and Han texts, Wang Bi, Guo Xiang, and Huayan 華嚴 and Tiantai 天台 Buddhism), see Ziporyn (2013).

11. In the Western context, Charles Taylor (2007, 5) also defines the condition or activity that embodies the spiritual as a sense of fullness.

12. In fact, at the beginning of the Northern Song, it was the Huayan Buddhist thinkers that rediscovered the term *principle* (*li*) and "maintained that the unitary and pure principle was the basis of reality." See Gregory (1999, 9).

13. About the idea of *li* as principle, see Chan (1964, 123–149).

14. I am indebted to an anonymous reviewer for improving the translation of this quotation.

15. *Platform Sutra*, CBETA T.48, no. 2008, 352b25.

16. Zhu Xi, *Zhuwengong wenji, juan* 4, ZZQS, 20:358–359. Also quoted in Yü (2003, 2:57).

17. I translate *qi* as "vital breath" because this term emphasizes the dynamism of the natural life and the holistic character of the substrate of the world, neither matter nor spirit but both, and suggests the interconnectedness of the things, which in Zhu Xi's thought is effectively realized through sharing a common coherence principle of heaven.

18. Lü Zuqian 呂祖謙 (1137–1181).

19. One should not forget that the term *jiao* 教 traditionally connotes "religious/spiritual learning and teaching," with direct reference to the three Chinese spiritualities (i.e. Daoist, Confucian, and Buddhist).

20. See Milton Scarborough's study on the difference between duality and nonduality (Scarborough 2009, 6).

21. Zhu Xi, *Zhuwengong wenji* 58, *Da Huang Daofu* 答黃道夫.

22. For a theoretical analysis of emotions as social relationships, see De Rivera and Grinkis (1986, 351–368).

23. For a cultural presentation of these emotions, see Parkinson, Fischer, and Manstead (2005, 72–86).

24. Zheng Xuan 鄭玄 (127–200), Eastern Han Confucian scholar who annotated the Confucian texts, including the three classics on the rites *Sanli* 三禮. I am grateful to Kirill Thompson for the following ideas. Probably, in the former Han when Zheng Xuan was commenting on the *Zhongyong*, some of the cultural/intellectual information surrounding the *Zhongyong* had been lost. Apparently, Zheng had heard of a correlation between the *wuxing* theory and the *Zhongyong* through Zisi's school. But, as Qisong notices, the materialistic *wuxing* theory is inconsistent with the *Zhongyong* system of thought. Now we have the *Wuxingpian* in hand from the Mawangdui and Guodian excavations. In the *Wuxingpian*, the *wuxing* are practice of the five virtues of Confucius. They are not the materialistic *wuxing*. Indications are, the reviewer notes, that the *Wuxingpian* was produced and used by the Zizi school; also, Zhu Xi ascribed the authorship of the *Zhongyong* to Zisi. Maybe the text indeed is a product of Zisi's thought (school). It is clear that Zheng Xuan did not have knowledge of the *Wuxingpian* and made the strange interpretation of *tianming zhi wei xing* 天命之謂性 in light of the *wuxing* (earth, wood, fire, water, and metal) simply because he had heard that *wuxing* was also related to Zisi's thought. About the *Wuxingpian*, see also chap. 3, sec. III.2.

25. The opening phrase of the classic *Zhongyong*.

26. I am grateful to an anonymous reader for drawing my attention to the complex meaning of the term *shu* 數. The translation I suggest here ("the dynamic ordering of the vital movements") is still reductive.

27. For a cultural analysis of the different construals of the self in different cultures (Western and non-Western) and an examination of the interdependent construal, see Markus and Kitayama (1991, 224–253).

28. About the idea of the spiritual character of the unity of society and the principle of service in the Christian context, see Frank (1987, 43).

29. For an extensive collective study on Confucian spirituality, see Tu and Tucker (2003). See also Bloom and Fogel (1997), a collection of essays that explores the religious dimensions of Confucian and Neo-Confucian thought and practice.

BIBLIOGRAPHY

PRIMARY SOURCES

Chen Shunyu 陳舜俞. 1972. *Duguan ji*: "Mingjiao dashi hangye ji" 都官集. 明教大師行業記. In *Siku quanshu zhenben sanji*, ed. Wang Yunwu, 8:16. Taipei: Shangwu yinshuguan.

Fanwang jing 梵網經 (*Brahma's Net Sutra*). 2016. CBETA T24n1484_001 and _002. Chinese Electronic Tripitaka Collection. tripitaka.cbeta.org.

Fazang 法藏. 2016. *Huayan fa putixin zhang* 華嚴發菩提心章. CBETA T45n1878. Chinese Electronic Tripitaka Collection. tripitaka.cbeta.org.

Gu Hongyi 顧宏義, trans. with notes. 2009. *Xin yi Jingde chuandeng lu (shang)* 新譯景德傳燈錄(上). Taipei: Sanmin.

Han Yu 韓愈. 1986. *Han Changli wenji jiaozhu* 韓昌黎文集校注. Shanghai: Shanghai guji chubanshe.

Heart Sutra 般若波羅蜜多心經. 2016. CBETA T08n0251. Chinese Electronic Tripitaka Collection. tripitaka.cbeta.org.

Hongming ji 弘明集. 2016. *juan* 1. CBETA T52n2102_001. Chinese Electronic Tripitaka Collection. tripitaka.cbeta.org.

Ouyang Xiu 歐陽脩. 2001. "Ben lun" 本論 (On the root). In *Ouyang Xiu quanji* 歐陽修全集 (Complete works of Ouyang Xiu), vol. 17. Beijing: Zhonghua shuju.

Platform Sutra of the Dharma Treasure of the Great Master, the Sixth Patriarch (*Liuzu dashi fabao tanjing* 六祖大師法寶壇經). 2016. CBETA T48n2008. Chinese Electronic Tripitaka Collection. tripitaka.cbeta.org.

Pusa shanzi jing 菩薩睒子經 (*Bodhisattva Syama Sutra*). 2016. CBETA T03n0174_001. Chinese Electronic Tripitaka Collection. tripitaka.cbeta.org.

Qisong 契嵩. 2016a. *Fujiao bian shang*: "Yuanjiao," "Quanshu" 輔教編上 (原教, 勸書) (*Essays on Assisting the Teaching*, part one: "Inquiry into the Teachings," "Letter of Advice"). In Qisong 契嵩, *Tanjin wenji juan di yi* 鐔津文集卷第一 (Collected works of Qisong, juan 1). CBETA T52n2115_001. Chinese Electronic Tripitaka Collection. tripitaka.cbeta.org.

———. 2016b. *Fujiao bian xia*: "Xiaolun," "Tanjing zan" 輔教篇下 (孝論, 壇經贊) (*Essays on Assisting the Teaching*, part three: "On Filial Devotion," "Encomium of the Platform Sutra"). In Qisong 契嵩, *Tanjin wenji juan di san* 鐔津文集卷第三 (Collected works of Qisong, juan 3). CBETA T52n2115_003. Chinese Electronic Tripitaka Collection. tripitaka.cbeta.org.

———. 2016c. *Fujiao bian zhong*: "Guang yuanjiao" 輔教編中 (廣原教) (*Essays on Assisting the Teaching*, part two: "Extensive Inquiry into the Teachings"). In Qisong 契嵩, *Tanjin wenji juan di er* 鐔津文集卷第二 (Collected works of Qisong, juan 2). CBETA T52n2115_002. Chinese Electronic Tripitaka Collection. tripitaka.cbeta.org.

———. 2016d. *Zhongyong jie* 中庸解 (*Exegesis of the Mean*). In Qisong 契嵩, *Tanjin wenji juan di si* 鐔津文集卷第四 (Collected works of Qisong, juan 4). CBETA T52n2115_004. Chinese Electronic Tripitaka Collection. tripitaka.cbeta.org.

Si shi er zhang jing 四十二章經 (*Sutra in Forty-Two Sections*). 2016. CBETA T17n0784_001. Chinese Electronic Tripitaka Collection. tripitaka.cbeta.org.

Wang, Meng'ou 王夢鷗. 1970. *Liji jin zhu jin yi* 禮記今注今譯 (Interpretation with commentary in modern language of the Liji). Edited by Wang Yunwu 王雲五. Taipei: Taiwan Commercial Press.

Yulanpen jing 盂蘭盆經 (*Ullambana Sutra*). 2016. CBETA T16n0685_001. Chinese Electronic Tripitaka Collection. tripitaka.cbeta.org.

Zanning 贊寧. 2016. *Song gaoseng zhuan* 宋高僧傳 (Biographies of eminent monks of the Song). CBETA T50n2061_017. Chinese Electronic Tripitaka Collection. tripitaka.cbeta.org.

Zhu Xi 朱熹. 2002. *Zhuzi quan shu* 朱子全書 (*The Collected Works of Master Zhu*). 27 vols. Shanghai: Shanghai gu ji chubanshe; Hefei: Anhui jiaoyu chubanshe.

SECONDARY SOURCES

Abe, Masao. 1986. "The Problem of Evil in Christianity and Buddhism." In *Buddhist-Christian Dialogue, Mutual Renewal and Transformation*, edited by Paul O. Ingram and Frederick J. Streng, 139–154. Honolulu: University of Hawaii Press.

———. 1992. *A Study of Dogen: His Philosophy and Religion*. Edited by Steven Heine. Albany: State University of New York Press.

Adler, Felix. 1929. *An Ethical Philosophy of Life: Presented in Its Main Outlines*. New York: D. Appleton.

Adler, Joseph Alan. 2014. *Reconstructing the Confucian Dao: Zhu Xi's Appropriation of Zhou Dunyi*. Albany: State University of New York Press.

Ames, Roger T., and David L. Hall. 2001. *Focusing the Familiar: A Translation and Philosophical Interpretation of the Zhongyong*. Honolulu: University of Hawaii Press.

Arghiresco/u, Diana. 2013. *De la continuité dynamique dans l'univers confucéen (Lecture néo-confucéenne du Zhongyong 中庸, nouvelle traduction du chinois classique et commentaire herméneutique)*. Paris : Éditions du Cerf.

Arghirescu, Diana. 2012. "Zhu Xi's Spirituality: A New Interpretation of the Great Learning." *Journal of Chinese Philosophy* 39 (2): 272–289.

———. 2019. "The Neo-Confucian Transmoral Dimension in Zhu Xi's Moral Thought." *Philosophy East and West* 69 (1): 52–69.

———. 2020a. "Song Neo-Confucian Conceptions of Morality and Moral Sources (Zhu Xi): Connections with Chan Buddhism." *Journal of Chinese Philosophy* 47 (3–4): 193–212.

———. 2020b. "Spiritual Discipline, Emotions and Behavior during the Song-Dynasty: Chan Monk Qisong's and Zhu Xi's Commentaries on the *Zhongyong* in Comparative Perspective." *Philosophy East and West* 70 (1): 1–26.

———. 2021. "New Insights into the Mutual Exchange between Confucianism and Buddhism in East Asia." *Comparative and Continental Philosophy* 13 (1): 220–234.

Bando, Shojun, trans. 2005. *The Ullambana Sutra*. In *Apocryphal Scriptures*, 19–23. Berkeley, CA: Numata Center for Buddhist Translation and Research.

Barrett, T. H. 1992. *Li Ao: Buddhist, Taoist or Neo-Confucian?* Oxford: Oxford University Press.

Berthrong, John H. 2005. "Weighing the Way: Metaphoric Balances in Analects 9:30." In *Interpretation and Intellectual Change: Chinese Hermeneutics in Historical Perspective*, edited by Ching-I Tu. New Brunswick, NJ: Transaction.

Bloom, Irene, and Joshua A. Fogel. 1997. *Meeting of Minds: Intellectual and Religious Interaction in East Asian Traditions of Thought*. New York: Columbia University Press.

Bol, Peter. 1992. *"This Culture of Ours": Intellectual Transitions in T'ang and Sung China*. Stanford, CA: Stanford University Press.

Brindley, Erica. 2019. "'Sagacity' and the Heaven-Human Relationship in the *Wuxing* 五行." In *Dao Companion to the Excavated Guodian Bamboo Manuscripts*, edited by Shirley Chan, 187–196. Cham: Springer.

Brook, Timothy. 1993. "Rethinking Syncretism: The Unity of the Three Teachings and Their Joint Worship in Late-Imperial China." *Journal of Chinese Religions* 21 (1): 13–44.

Buckley Ebrey, Patricia, trans. 1991. *Chu Hsi's Family Rituals: A Twelfth-Century Chinese Manual for the Performance of Cappings, Weddings, Funerals, and Ancestral Rites*. Princeton, NJ: Princeton University Press.

Chan, Alan K. L., and Sor-hoon Tan, eds. 2004. *Filial Piety in Chinese Thought and History*. New York: Routledge.

Chan, Wing-tsit. 1964. "The Evolution of the Neo-Confucian Concept Li 理 as Principle." *Tsing Hua Journal of Chinese Studies* 4 (2): 123–149.

———, trans. 1967. *Reflections on Things at Hand*. New York: Columbia University Press.

Ch'en, Kenneth K. S. 1973. *The Chinese Transformation of Buddhism*. Princeton, NJ: Princeton University Press.

Cheng, Chung-Ying. 1986. "Chu Hsi's Methodology and Theory of Understanding." In *Chu Hsi and Neo-Confucianism*, edited by Wing-tsit Chan, 169–196. Honolulu: University of Hawaii Press.

Ching, Julia. 1974. "The Goose Lake Monastery Debate (1175)." *Journal of Chinese Philosophy* 1:161–178.

De Bary, W. Theodore. 1953. "A Reappraisal of Neo-Confucianism." In *Studies in Chinese Thought*, edited by Arthur F. Wright, 81–111. Chicago: University of Chicago Press.

———. 1986. *Neo-Confucian Orthodoxy and the Learning of the Mind-and-Heart*. New York: Columbia University Press.

———. 2008. "Neo-Confucian Education." In *Sources of East Asian Tradition: Premodern Asia, Volume 1*, edited by W. Theodore de Bary, 1:402–408. New York: Columbia University Press.

De Bary, W. Theodore, and Irene Bloom. 1999. *Sources of Chinese Tradition: From Earliest Times to 1600*. 2nd ed. New York: Columbia University Press.

De Bary, W. Theodore, and John W. Chaffee, eds. 1989. *Neo-Confucian Education: The Formative Stage*. Berkeley: University of California Press.

De Rivera, Joseph, and Carmen Grinkis. 1986. "Emotions as Social Relationships." *Motivation and Emotion* 10 (4): 351–369.

Faure, Bernard. 1991. *The Rhetoric of Immediacy: A Cultural Critique of Chan/Zen Buddhism*. Princeton, NJ: Princeton University Press.

Foulk, Griffith T. 1999. "Sung Controversies Concerning the 'Separate Transmission' of Ch'an." In *Buddhism in the Sung*, edited by Peter N. Gregory and Daniel A. Getz, 220–294. Honolulu: University of Hawaii Press.

Frank, S. L. 1987. *The Spiritual Foundations of Society: An Introduction to Social Philosophy*. Translated by Boris Jakim. Athens: Ohio University Press.

Fu, Charles Wei-hsun. 1986. "Chu Hsi on Buddhism." In *Chu Hsi and Neo-Confucianism*, edited by Wing-tsit Chan. Honolulu: University of Hawaii Press.

Gadamer, Hans-Georg. 2013. *Truth and Method*. Translation revised by Joel Weinsheimer and Donald G. Marshall. London: Bloomsbury.

Gimello, Robert M. 1992. "Marga and Culture: Learning, Letters, and Liberation in Northern Sung Ch'an." In *Paths to Liberation: The Marga and Its Transformations in Buddhist Thought*, edited by Robert E. Buswell Jr. and Robert M. Gimello, 371–437. Honolulu: Kuroda Institute.

Gregory, Peter N. 1995. *Inquiry into the Origin of Humanity: An Annotated Translation of Tsung-mi's* Yüan jen lun *with a Modern Commentary*. Honolulu: Kuroda Institute.

———. 1999. "The Vitality of Buddhism in the Sung." In *Buddhism in the Sung*, edited by Peter N. Gregory and Daniel A. Getz, 1–20. Honolulu: University of Hawaii Press.

Groner, Paul. 1990. "The Fan-wang ching and Monastic Discipline in Japanese Tendai." In *Chinese Buddhist Apocrypha*, edited by Robert E. Bushell Jr., 251–290. Honolulu: University of Hawaii Press.

Guang, Xing. 2010. "A Buddhist-Confucian Controversy on Filial Piety." *Journal of Chinese Philosophy* 37 (2): 248–260.

Guo Peng 郭朋. 1983. *Tanjing jiaoshi* 壇經校釋 (The *Platform Sutra* redacted and annotated). Beijing: Zhonghua Book Company.

Halperin, Mark. 2006. *Out of the Cloister: Literati Perspectives on Buddhism in Sung China, 960–1279*. Cambridge, MA: Harvard University Press.

Harbsmeier, Christoph. 1998. *Science and Civilisation in China*. Vol.7, pt. 1, *Language and Logic*. Cambridge: Cambridge University Press.

Heidegger, Martin. 1971. *On the Way to Language*. New York: Harper & Row.

Hirakawa, Akira. 1990. *A History of Indian Buddhism: From Sakyamuni to Early Mahayana*. Translated by Paul Groner. Honolulu: University of Hawaii Press.

Hisamatsu, Shin'ichi. 2002. *Critical Sermons of the Zen Tradition: Hisamatsu's Talks on Linji*. Translated by Ives Christopher and Tokiwa Gishin. Basingstoke: Palgrave Macmillan.

Holloway, Kenneth W. 2009. *Guodian: The Newly Discovered Seeds of Chinese Religious and Political Philosophy*. New York: Oxford University Press.

Hsuan Hua 宣化. 2002. *The Vajra Prajna Paramita Sutra: A General Explanation*. Burlingame, CA: Buddhist Text Translation Society.

Huang, Chi-chiang 黃啓江. 1986. "Experiment in Syncretism: Ch'i-sung (1007–1072) and Eleventh-Century Chinese Buddhism." PhD diss., University of Arizona.

———. 1997. *Beisong fojiaoshi lungao* 北宋佛教史論稿. Taipei: Shangwu yinshu guan.

———. 1999. "Elite and Clergy in Northern Sung Hang-chou: A Convergence of Interest." In *Buddhism in the Sung*, edited by Peter N. Gregory and Daniel A. Gets, 295–339. Honolulu: University of Hawaii Press.

———. 2000. "Chung-yung in Northern Sung Intellectual Discourse: The Buddhist Components." In *Classics and Interpretations: The Hermeneutic Traditions in Chinese Culture*, edited by Ching-I Tu, 315–337. New Brunswick, NJ: Transaction.

Huang, Chun-chieh 黃俊傑. 2017. *Dongya rujia renxue shilun* 東亞儒家仁學史論 (Discussing humanity in East Asian Confucianisms: A history). Taipei: National Taiwan University Press.

———. 2020. *The Debate and Confluence between Confucianism and Buddhism in East Asia*. Translated by Jan Vrhovski. Göttingen: V&R Unipress.

Hucker, Charles O. 1985. *A Dictionary of Official Titles in Imperial China*. Stanford, CA: Stanford University Press.

Ing, Michael D. K. 2017. *The Vulnerability of Integrity in Early Confucian Thought*. New York: Oxford University Press.

Jan, Yün-hua. 1991. "The Role of Filial Piety in Chinese Buddhism: A Reassessment." In *Buddhist Ethics and Modern Society: An International Symposium*, edited by Charles Wei-hsun Fu and Sandra A. Wawrytko, 27–39. New York: Greenwood.

Kaplan, Uri. 2019. *Buddhist Apologetics in East Asia, Countering the Neo-Confucian Critiques in the* Hufa lun *and the* Yusok chirui non. Leiden: Brill.

Kasoff, Ira E. 1984. *The Thought of Chang Tsai (1020–1077)*. Cambridge: Cambridge University Press.

Keenan, John P. 1994. *How Master Mou Removes Our Doubts: A Reader-Response Study and Translation of the Mou-tzu Li-huo lun*. Albany: State University of New York.

Kelleher, Theresa M. 1989. "Back to Basics: Chu Hsi's Elementary Learning (Hsiao-hsüeh)." In *Neo-Confucian Education: The Formative Stage*, edited by W. Theodore de Bary and John W. Chaffee, 219–251. Berkeley: University of California Press.

Knapp, Keith N. 2004. "Reverent Caring: The Parent-Son Relationship in Early Medieval Tales of Filial Offspring." In *Filial Piety in Chinese Thought and History*, edited by Alan K. L. Chan and Sor-hoon Tan, 44–72. New York: Routledge.

Liu, James T. C. 1967. *Ou-Yang Hsiu, an Eleventh-Century Neo-Confucianist*. Stanford, CA: Stanford University Press.

———. 1988. *China Turning Inward: Intellectual-Political Changes in the Early Twelfth Century*. Cambridge, MA: Harvard University Press.

Li Zhong Hua 李中華 and Ding Min 丁敏. 2010. *Xin Yi Liuzu Tanjing* 新譯六祖壇經. Taipei: Sanmin shuju.

Major, John S., ed. 2010. *The Huainanzi: A Guide to the Theory and Practice of Government in Early Han China*. New York: Columbia University Press.

Makeham, John, ed. 2018. *The Buddhist Roots of Zhu Xi's Philosophical Thought*. New York: Oxford University Press.

Markus, Hazel Rose, and Shinobu Kitayama. 1991. "Culture and the Self: Implications for Cognition, Emotion, and Motivation." *Psychological Review* 98 (2): 224–253.

McRae, John. 1986. *The Northern School and the Formation of Early Ch'an Buddhism*. Honolulu: University of Hawaii Press.

Morrison, Elizabeth. 2010. *The Power of Patriarchs: Qisong and Lineage in Chinese Buddhism*. Leiden: Brill.

Mugitani, Kunio. 2004. "Filial Piety and 'Authentic Parents' in Religious Daoism." In *Filial Piety in Chinese Thought and History*, edited by Alan K. L. Chan and Sor-hoon Tan, 110–121. New York: Routledge.

Muller, Charles. 2000. "*Tiyong* and Interpenetration in the *Analects* of Confucius: The Sacred as Secular." *Bulletin of Toyo Gakuen University* 8:15–29.

———. 2015. *Korea's Great Buddhist-Confucian Debate: The Treatises of Chong Tojon (Sambong) and Hamho Tuktong (Kihwa)*. Honolulu: University of Hawaii Press.

———. 2016. "The Emergence of Essence-Function (*Ti-yong*) 體用 Hermeneutics in the Sinification of Indic Buddhism: An Overview." *Critical Review for Buddhist Studies* 19:111–152.

Muller, Charles, and Kenneth K. Tanaka, trans. 2017. *The Brahama's Net Sutra*. Moraga: BDK America.

Ng, On-Cho. 1999. "An Early Critique of the Philosophy of Mind-Heart: The Confucian Quest for Doctrinal Purity and the Doxic Role of Chan Buddhism." *Journal of Chinese Philosophy* 26 (1): 89–120.

Nhat Hanh, Thich. 1987. *Being Peace*. Edited by A. Kotler. Berkeley, CA: Parallax.

Nishitani, Keiji. 1960. "What Is Religion?" In *Philosophical Studies of Japan*, 2: 21–64. Tokyo: Japan Society for the Promotion of Science.

———. 1982. *Religion and Nothingness*. Berkley: University of California Press.

Nylan, Michael. 1992. *The Shifting Center: The Original "Great Plan" and Later Readings*. Nettetal: Steyler Verl.

Parkinson, Brian, Agneta H. Fischer, and Antony S. R. Manstead. 2005. *Emotion in Social Relations: Cultural, Group and Interpersonal Processes*. New York: Psychology Press.

Peterson, Willard. 1986. "Another Look at Li 理." *Bulletin of Sung and Yüan Studies* 18:13–31.

Qian Mu 錢穆. 1980. "*Zhuzi xinxuelun* 朱子新學論." In *Zhongguo xueshu sixiang shi luncong* 中國學術思想 史論叢. Taipei: Dongda.

———. 2006. *On Translation*. Translated by Eileen Brennan. London: Routledge.

Rosemont, Henry. 2008. "Family Reverence (Xiao 孝) as the Source of Consummatory Conduct (Ren 仁)." *Dao: A Journal of Comparative Philosophy* 7:9–19.

Rosemont, Henry, and Roger Ames. 2009. *The Chinese Classic of Family Reverence, a Philosophical Translation of the* Xiaojing. Honolulu: University of Hawaii Press.

Scarborough, Milton. 2009. *Comparative Theories of Nonduality: The Search for a Middle Way*. New York: Continuum.

Schlütter, Morten. 1999. "Silent Illumination, Kung-an Introspection, and the Competition for Lay Patronage in Sung Dynasty Ch'an." In *Buddhism in the Sung*, edited by Peter N. Gregory and Daniel A. Getz, 109–147. Honolulu: University of Hawaii Press.

———. 2007. "Transmission and Enlightenment in Chan Buddhism Seen through the *Platform Sutra*." *Chung-Hwa Buddhist Journal*, no. 20, 379–410.

———. 2008. *How Zen Became Zen: The Dispute over Enlightenment and the Formation of Chan Buddhism in Song-Dynasty China*. Honolulu: University of Hawaii Press.

Sharf, Robert H. 1996. "The Scripture in Forty-Two Sections." In *Religions of China in Practice*, edited by Donald D. Lopez, 360–371. Princeton, NJ: Princeton University Press.

Sheng-Yen. 2001. *There Is No Suffering: A Commentary on the Heart Sutra*. New York: Dharma Drum.

Shih, Heng-ching. 1992. *The Syncretism of Ch'an and Pure Land Buddhism*. New York: Peter Lang.

Shinohara, Koichi. 1994. "Zhiyuan's Autobiographical Essay, 'The Master of the Mean.'" In *Other Selves: Autobiography and Biography in Cross-Cultural Perspective*, edited by Phyllis Granoff and Koichi Shinohara, 35–72. Oakville: Mosaic.

Skonicki, Douglas. 2011. "A Buddhist Response to Ancient-Style Learning: Qisong's Conception of Political Order." *T'oung Pao* 97:1–36.

———. 2014. "'Guwen' Lineage Discourse in the Northern Song." *Journal of Song-Yuan Studies* 44:1–32.

Streng, Frederick J. 1967. *Emptiness: A Study in Religious Meaning*. Nashville: Abingdon.

———. 1985. *Understanding Religious Life*. 3rd ed. Belmont: Wadsworth.

Taylor, Charles. 2007. *A Secular Age*. Cambridge, MA: Belknap Press of Harvard University Press.

Teiser, Stephen F. 1988. *The Ghost Festival in Medieval China*. Princeton, NJ: Princeton University Press.

Thompson, Kirill Ole. 1991. "How to Rejuvenate Ethics: Suggestions from Chu Hsi." *Philosophy East and West* 41 (4): 493–513.

———. 2002. "Ethical Insights from Chu Hsi." In *Varieties of Ethical Reflection: New Directions for Ethics in a Global Context*, edited by Michael Barnhart, 49–65. Lanham, MD: Lexington Books.

———. 2007. "The Archery of 'Wisdom' in the Stream of Life: 'Wisdom' in the *Four Books* with Zhu Xi's Reflections." *Philosophy East and West* 57 (3): 330–344.

———. 2010. "Zhu Xi's Transformation of the *Zhongyong*." In *East Asian Confucianisms: Interactions and Innovations, Dong ya ru xue: Hu dong yu chuang xin: Proceedings of the Conference of 1–2 May 2009*, 87–105. New Brunswick, NJ: Confucius Institute at Rutgers University.

———. 2012. "Guodian: The Newly Discovered Seeds of Chinese Religious and Political Philosophy. By Kenneth W. Holloway. Oxford: Oxford University Press, 2009." *Philosophy East and West* 62 (2): 311–316.

———. 2021. "Mining the Emotions, Deepening *Ars Contextualis*: A Personal Reflection on the Power of Sensitive Reading." In *One Corner of the Square:*

Essays on the Philosophy of Roger T. Ames, edited by Ian M. Sullivan and Joshua Mason, 15–26. Honolulu: University of Hawaii Press.

Tillich, Paul. 1990. *The Encounter of Religions and Quasi-Religions*. Edited by Terence Thomas. Lewinston, NY: Edwin Mellen.

Tillman, Hoyt Cleveland. 1992. *Confucian Discourse and Chu Hsi's Ascendency*. Honolulu: University of Hawaii Press.

Tiwald, Justin. 2018. "Zhu Xi's Critique of Buddhism: Selfishness, Salvation, and Self-Cultivation." In *The Buddhist Roots of Zhu Xi's Philosophical Thought*, edited by John Makeham, 122–155. New York: Oxford University Press.

Tsai Chen-feng 蔡振豐. 2012. "Zhuzi dui fojiao de lijie ji qi xiangzhi" 朱子對佛教的理解及其限制 (Zhu Xi's grasp of Buddhism, and its limitations). In *Dongya Zhuzixue de quanshi yu fazhan* 東亞朱子學的詮釋與發展 (East Asian Zhu Xi studies: interpretations and developments), edited by Tsai Chen-feng, 177–213. Taipei: Taiwan daxue chuban zhongxin.

———. 2018. "Zhu Xi's Grasp of Buddhism and Its Limitations." Translated by Daniel Coyle. *Contemporary Chinese Thought* 49 (3–4):186–206.

Tu, Weiming, and Mary Evelyn Tucker, eds. 2003. *Confucian Spirituality*. Vols. 1 and 2. New York: Crossroad.

Vankeerberghen, Griet. 2005. "Choosing Balance: Weighing (Quan 權) as a Metaphor for Action in Early Chinese Texts." *Early China* 30:47–89.

Wang, Youru. 2017. *Historical Dictionary of Chan Buddhism*. London: Rowman and Littlefield.

Welter, Albert. 1993. *The Meaning of Myriad Good Deeds: A Study of Yung-ming Yen-shou and the Wan-shan t'ung-kuei chi*. New York: Peter Lang.

———. 1999. "A Buddhist Response to the Confucian Revival: Tsan-ning and the Debate over *Wen* in the Early Sung." In *Buddhism in the Sung*, edited by Peter N Gregory and Daniel A. Getz. Honolulu: University of Hawaii Press.

———. 2006. *Monks, Rulers and Literati: The Political Ascendency of Chan Buddhism*. Oxford: Oxford University Press.

———. 2008. *The Linji lu and the Creation of Chan Orthodoxy*. Oxford: Oxford University Press.

———. 2011. *Yongming Yanshou's Conception of Chan in the Zongjing lu: A Special Transmission within the Scriptures*. Oxford: Oxford University Press.

———. 2016. "Confucian Monks and Buddhist Junzi: Zanning's Topical Compendium of the Buddhist Clergy (Da Song seng shi lüe) and the Politics of Buddhist Accommodation at the Song Court." In *The Middle Kingdom and the Dharma Wheel: Aspects of the Relationship between the Buddhist Samgha and the State in Chinese History*, edited by Thomas Jülch, 222–277. Leiden: Brill.

Yü, Chün-fang. 1989. "Ch'an Education in the Sung: Ideals and Procedures." In *Neo-Confucian Education: The Formative Stage*, edited by W. Theodore de Bary and John W. Chaffee, 57–104. Berkeley: University of California Press.

Yü, Ying-shih 余英時. 2003. *The Historical World of Zhu Xi: A Study of the Political Culture of Song Intellectuals* 朱熹的歷史世界 宋代士大夫政治文化的研究. Vols. 1 and 2. Taipei: Yunchen wenhua.

Zhang Hongsheng 張宏生, trans. 1996. *Fujiao bian (Essays on Assisting the Teaching)* 輔教編. Kaohsiung: Foguang wenhua shiye.

Ziporyn, Brook. 2013. *Beyond Oneness and Difference*. Albany: State University of New York Press.

Zürcher, Eric. 1989. "Buddhism and Education in T'ang Times." In *Neo-Confucian Education: The Formative Stage*, edited by W. Theodore de Bary and John W. Chaffee, 19–56. Berkeley: University of California Press.

INDEX

Abe, Masao, 8, 24, 98, 221
affairs (*shi* 事), 53, 101, 109, 118, 120, 218, 225, 228, 232–233; everyday, 30, 38, 50, 55, 57, 64, 72, 184, 227, 240; human, 36, 53, 65, 87, 144, 171, 179, 219, 222; ordinary affairs, 67–69; sociopolitical, 76, 91, 122, 192, 206. See also phenomena
affection, 38, 70, 102, 187–188, 189; mutual, 253–255
Analects of Confucius, 12, 44, 47, 65, 115, 127, 129, 154, 220; classic, 94; Confucian devotion, 142; Confucius' 97, 260. See also *Lunyu*
ancestors, 127, 132, 140, 142, 158, 272, 273; Ancestors' temple, 132; Ancestors' ritual, parents-, 141; ancestor worship, 128; ancestral spirits, 133; ancestral worship, 132, 134
assisting (*fu* 輔), 169, 260
authentic nature (*xing* 性), 5, 31, 49, 55, 68–69, 80, 100, 104–108, 111, 115; aware of, 87; buddha-nature, 42, 117; Chan Buddhist, 70, 102, 123–124; cultivating, 204; of humans, 52, 109–110; nature-emptiness, 184; original nature, 42, 72; spiritual, 118
awakening/awakened (*jue* 覺), 46, 62, 74; complete, 207; of the heart-mind, 182; individual, 38; religion of, 8; state of, 206–207. See also enlightened

behavior: appropriate, 30–31, 39, 91, 104, 115–118, 163, 218; bad, 100; ego-centered, 101; external, 52, 112, 134; filial, 148; good, 16, 44, 54, 83, 113, 154, 175; human, 103, 181, 192; kingly, 45, 99; monk's, 78; moral, 64, 221, 225; ritual, 110–111, 223, 251–252; rules of, 182; unethical, 145
benefits (*yi* 益), 107, 204, 243
bian 變 : change, 51, 67, 180, 244, 256; transformation, 78, 80, 135, 140, 182–183
Bodhidharma, 10
Bodhisattva Syama Sutra (*Pusa shanzi jing* 菩薩睒子經), 31, 151
Book of Changes (易經 *Yijing*), 50, 129, 180, 189, 267
Book of Documents (*Shangshu* 尚書), 65
Book of Rites (*Liji* 禮記), 65, 100, 119, 127, 201, 237, 260, 267
Boyi and *Shuqi* 伯夷叔齊, 155
Brahma's Net Sutra (*Fanwang jing* 梵網經), 138
branches, 29–30, 58, 84, 207, 217. See also root
Buddha, 3, 47, 60, 63, 73, 74, 77, 78, 87, 124, 151–152; action of, 76; becoming a, 149, 199; children, 126; disciple, 158; heart-mind, 46, 67, 69, 267; origin, 48; teachings, 5; the way of, 201
buddha-nature (*foxing* 佛性), 41–42, 88, 117, 150, 232, 241

289

cause, 31, 51, 174, 180–181; accessory cause, 201–202; fundamental cause, 201–202; good and evil, 199; karmic cause, 56, 106, 139–140, 146, 161, 168, 195–196, 198, 203–204; way of, 199–200

Chan: Chan "houses," 9; Confucianized Chan, 89, 94, 102, 117–119, 212; cohesive Chan, 23, 27, 31, 63, 68, 86, 165, 197; engaged, 28; inclusive Chan, 23, 107, 211; lineage, 10–11, 22, 62; moral Chan, 60, 233; nondual Chan, 84, 89; principled, 226–227; socially engaged Chan, 7, 19, 28, 58, 89, 258; sub-schools, 2, 9, 38, 85, 114, 210; unprincipled Chan, 218–219, 221, 226

change, 50–51, 54, 67, 256–257; positive change, 100; process of, 80, 243; vital, 70

charity, 18, 147–148, 150

cheng 誠, 40, 50, 65–66, 70–71, 73, 135, 148–149. *See also* sincerity

Cheng brothers (Cheng Yi, Cheng Hao), 13–14, 20, 35, 48, 127, 212, 233

Chen Shunyu 陳舜俞 (1026–1076), 2–3, 27, 212

Classic of Poetry (*Shijing* 詩經), 133

cohesive, 2, 5, 21–23, 27, 61; Chan practice, 31, 119, 121, 197; instruction, 81–82; teaching, 31, 76, 81, 86–88, 235

community, 25, 76–77, 95, 98, 142, 229; harmony of, 97; life, 128, 137; well-being of, 76, 96, 231. *See also* individual

comparative hermeneutics, 28, 74, 79, 237; comparative interpretation, 62, 91

compassion(ate), 51, 141, 154, 157

complete(ness), 29, 31, 37, 139, 148, 182, 186, 199–200; filial devotion, 132; good, 194; man, 60, 64; moral quality, 139, 155, 242; (perfect) sincerity (*zhicheng* 至誠), 50, 71, 73, 135, 194; (true) reality (*zhishi* 至實), 193; understanding/knowledge (*zhizhi* 知至), 53, 80, 194–197; way (*zhidao* 至道), 67, 69, 137–138, 143, 153–154, 156. *See also* highest state

concentration (*ding* 定), 39, 73, 94, 228, 230–231. *See also* no-thought

condition, 89, 146; accessory, 202. *See also* cause

Confucianization, 20, 34, 239

"Confucianized" dimension, 2, 6, 22, 31, 61–62, 74, 79, 123; Buddhism, 13, 41, 90–91; Chan, 5, 12, 77, 89, 94, 96, 211–212

Confucian monks (*ruseng* 儒僧), 22, 270

conscience, 159–160

consciousness (*shi* 識), 16, 80, 82, 198, 217, 219, 255; causal, 200, 205; field of, 179, 181–182, 188, 214; non-consciousness, 193; self-consciousness, 167, 172–174, 187, 192–193, 206; spiritual consciousness (神明, 神識), 17, 108, 170; state of, 183

constancy (*chang* 常), 70, 84, 118, 124, 197, 225, 243; constancy (*yong* 庸), 45, 239–242, 244

cultivation (*xiu* 修), 51, 93, 197–198, 215; Buddhist, 24; Confucian, 38, 118; individual, 48, 80, 96–97, 205; inner, 214; of one's nature, 200; of the people, 115; self-cultivation, 6, 67, 105, 123, 127, 137, 209, 233; of spirit, 83

dao 道, 35–36, 67, 81, 85, 89, 178, 188; complete, 139; functioning of, 50; great, 64, 87; of heaven, 49, 66, 128; kingly, 45, 99; natural, 38; permanent, 124; of the spirit, 52. *See also* way

Daoism, 4, 211, 234

Daoji 道紀 (550–577), 152

Daopi 道丕 (889–955), 153

Daxue (*Great Learning*), 37, 43, 72, 80, 95; *Daxue zhangju*, 49, 53, 55, 215, 220, 241

de 德: complete moral quality, 139, 144, 194, 242; great moral quality, 50, 130; luminous moral power (*mingde* 明德), 96; moral ideal, 137, 159–160; moral nature, 50, 71; moral order, 128–131; moral power, 46, 96; moral quality, 88, 129, 131, 145, 153; ordinary morality, 87, 176

death-birth (life), 51–52, 56, 67, 70; cycle of, 139, 152, 165, 168

INDEX

deeds, 52, 56, 67, 173–174; bad, 77, 90, 104, 171–172, 175, 187–189, 190; good, 44, 63, 65–66, 86–88, 134, 161; universal good, 151–152
desires, 39, 55, 97, 107–110, 186–187, 252; attachment to, 189; personal/individual, 48, 121, 167, 251; self-centered, 130, 249–250
Diamond Sutra, 5
difference/differentiation (*yi* 異), 41, 88, 119, 183; differentiation, 73, 78, 102, 194; different practices, 224; different ways, 243. *See also* sameness
discipline, 54; ethical, 94, 227–228, 230–231; School of, 157; self-, 101; spiritual, 2, 24, 30, 138–139, 144, 146, 238; transmoral, 249
dualism, 217, 245

emotions/feelings/sentiments (*qing* 情), 39, 51, 73, 101, 108, 110, 168; beyond, 73, 106, 121, 223; dependence on, 180; filial sentiments, 151, 157; negative, 73, 154, 190, 199; other-focused, 249, 251, 253–254; positive, 154, 188, 196; rectify, 151; self-focused, 249–252
Emperor Renzong, 10, 35, 59, 95, 212
emptiness (*kong* 空), 173–174, 178, 182; concept of, 216; field of, 24, 140, 148, 172, 176, 203; level of, 188, 193; nature-, 30, 54, 166–167, 185–186, 200; state of, 184. *See also* nothingness
enlightened (*ming* 明), 16, 73–74, 78; constantly, 207; individuals, 200–201; unenlightened, 116; way, 149. *See also* awakening/awakened
enlightenment, 38, 137, 150–151, 205, 220; achieving, 153, 155, 161; sudden and gradual, 85
essence (*ti* 體), 16–17, 240; essence-function paradigm, 16, 221
ethico-metaphysical, 241, 251, 255
ethico-spiritual, 217, 238–241, 246, 248, 251
ethics/ethical, 6, 88, 118; Buddhist ethics, 211, 222; Confucian ethics, 105, 131–132, 210; Ethical Culture movement, 159; ethical discipline (*jie* 戒), 227, 231, 238; ethical interrelationships, 24, 95; ethical knowledge, 53, 232; ethical standard, 160; ethical values and practice, 4, 89, 99, 106, 113, 163, 197, 228; ethical wisdom, 110–111; ethics as religion, 128, 217; family ethics, 17, 19
exemplary individual (*junzi* 君子), 37, 47, 99, 103, 105, 119, 149, 201, 224–225; ancient, 44, 116, 154–155; sovereign as, 45
expedient (*quan* 權), 69, 119, 124; great, 87; level, 121–122; means, 68, 85–86, 116; practice, 162. *See also* real
extinction (*mie* 滅), 113–114, 179–180

family, 43, 96, 113, 126, 131, 136, 145; broad, 150; ethics, 17; leaving the, 152–155, 261; primacy of, 151; relationships, 127, 159, 202
Fayan 法眼 Chan subschool, 2, 210
filial devotion (*xiao* 孝), 5, 17, 24, 70–71, 125; accomplished, 149, 155; Buddhist, 29, 107, 136–141, 155–156; Buddhist practice of, 126–127, 142, 144–147, 148–150; complete, 142, 145, 161; Confucian, 128–129, 131–132, 133–135, 153; great, 162, 164; model of, 143, 136; moral duty of, 151, 202; partial, 165
Five Blessings (*wu fu* 五福), 54–55, 192
Five Elements (Five aspects of conduct) (*wu xing* 五行), 110–111, 243, 251–252
Five natural dispositions, 42, 251–254
Five Permanencies, 30, 39–40, 42, 57, 60, 71, 89. *See also wuchang* 五常
footprints (*ji* 迹): interdependent, 88; of the methods, 79, 81, 87, 119, 176–177, 224; of teachings, 12, 64, 67–68, 260, 266; of the way, 72, 76–77
form: beyond (*xing er shang* 形而上), 49, 51; concrete, 111, 196–197, 251; corporeal, 17, 108, 120, 170; formless, 42; no-form, 228–230, 234; one-form, 231
Four Books, 6, 35, 103, 236, 238
Four Masters, 35, 127, 264
Four Noble Truths (*si di* 四諦), 89
function/functioning, 177, 180, 219, 221; practice, 146, 152; of the way, 50, 240, 246

good (*shan* 善): actions, 39, 53, 56–57; behavior, 54, 83, 175; common, 122, 130; complete, 80, 194, 241; deeds, 52, 63, 66, 70, 88, 90, 151–152; goodness, 215, 217–218; governance, 34, 37–38, 41, 43, 45, 99; individuals, 38, 43, 48, 95; making people good, 30, 37, 42–43, 98, 224

governance: exercise of, 95; good, 34, 37–38, 45, 99–100, 119, 213; perfect, 195

gratitude, 253–254; acts of, 139; debt of, 162; emotion/feeling of, 255; practice of, 256

Guiyang 潙仰 Chan subschool, 2, 210

guwen style, 2–4, 12–13, 19, 24–25, 27–28, 39–40, 62–64, 259, 260

Han Yu 韓愈 (768–824), 3, 18, 27, 33, 210–211; Ancient Style movement, 40, 62; criticism, 35–36, 38, 47, 57, 120

harmony; between teachings, 14, 18, 210, 221; ethico-moral, 130; familial, 159; harmonious continuity of life, 66, 129–130; of human relationships, 187–188, 251, 257; organic, 66, 130, 195; social, 42–43, 46, 51, 63–64, 97–98, 100, 102, 137, 145, 160

heart-mind (*xin* 心), 12–13, 29, 30–31, 70, 80, 87; Buddha's, 69; cultivating, 89–90; (heart-)mind of human 人心, 72, 117, 218; (heart-)mind of the way 道心, 217–218; marvelous, 60, 67; original, 100; rectifying, 53, 55, 65, 72, 73, 91, 117; see the, 82; sincere, 45–46, 148; touching the, 45, 51–52, 54, 112–113

heaven-earth, 50, 53, 102, 130–131; movements of, 108, 222, 253; natural order of, 70–71; unity, 67. See also nature

Heidegger, Martin, 26–27

hermeneutical/interpretive translation, 22–26, 28–29; extralayer of, 23–24; intralayer of, 23–25, 33, 62

heterodox Buddhism, 33, 35

hierarchy, 90, 115–118; hierarchical distinctions, 102–103; relationships, 95, 219, 243; of schools, 89; social order, 148, 255–256

highest state, 80, 87, 194, 231

holism/holistic, 47, 224; Chan, 221; unity, 219; way, 46

Hong Fan 洪範, 44–45, 54–55, 65, 99, 191–192

Huayan school, 22, 66–67, 84, 86–87, 94, 107–108, 119, 221

Huayan Sutra, 29, 58, 67, 84, 217, 221

Huineng 惠能 (638–713), 60, 64, 94, 105, 152, 156, 227, 234

impartiality, 66, 68, 70

individual, 36, 41–42, 55, 63, 67; enlightened, 73–74, 200; good, 38, 43–44, 48, 97; heart-mind, 71, 77, 192, 231; interdependent, 131; self, 109, 140, 184; suffering, 89; transformation of, 30, 34, 49–50, 98, 105, 146; well-being of, 5. See also community

insight (*zhihui* 智慧), 73, 94, 227–228, 231–232

interculturality, 11, 25, 101, 128

interdependence, 40, 43, 148, 209, 231; between emotions and nature, 183–184, 188–189, 223–224; Buddhist, 32, 56, 71, 107, 109, 119, 167–168, 217; mutual, 126; nondual, 90, 192, 206–207; principle of, 198; of teachings, 260–262. See also relatedness of beings

interrelatedness, 31, 88, 95, 102, 138–139, 154–155, 173

"investigation of things," (*gewu* 格物), 53, 101, 215, 221

Jingde Era Record of the Transmission of the Lamp (*Jingde chuandeng lu* 景德傳燈錄), 10, 156, 271

Jinsilu 近思錄 (*Reflections on Things at Hand*), 35, 38, 53, 55, 220, 241

karma, 17, 29, 31, 180; essence of, 147; good karma, 147, 149; karmic causes, 56, 106, 139, 146, 167, 171, 203; karmic effect, 193, 196; karmic law, 168, 189, 196; karmic potency, 162; karmic result, 158, 161; karmic retribution, 82, 190–192

kindness, 39–40, 43, 88, 119, 224; complete, 68; feeling of, 104; great, 162; quality, 122, 163; virtue, 70–71. See *ren* 仁

knowledge (*zhi* 知), 69, 108; complete knowledge 至知, 53, 80, 194–197; ethical, 232, 235; extension of, 214–215; natural knowledge, 52, 55. *See also* "investigation of things"

law: Buddhist, 78, 155, 229; cosmic law, 131–132; ethico-moral law of life, 129; karmic, 168, 180, 189, 196; law of heaven, 129–131; law of life, 131–132, 134, 145; moral, 128, 132, 134, 136; natural, 70–71, 131, 138
lettered Chan, 2, 213
li 理 (principle), 109, 119–121, 124, 209, 213–214; of coherence, 49, 51, 53, 218–219, 246; of heaven, 247–248, 250; inner essence of, 146–147; school of, 6; universal, 31, 66–69, 84, 94, 100, 106–107, 221; without, 216, 226. *See* principle
life: continuity of, 71, 129, 132, 135, 145, 171; inner, 103, 136, 159; natural universal order of, 24, 49, 129–130; organic, 50–51, 145–147, 159, 185, 199; organism-focused, 145; root of, 146; social, 48, 50, 130, 179, 199, 247; spiritual, 145–146
Linji Chan subschool, 2, 19, 38, 84–85, 210–212
lixue 理學, 6, 237. *See also* school of principle
loyalty (*zhong* 忠), 43, 70–71, 159, 202
Lu Jiuyuan 陸九淵 (1139–1192), 215
Lunyu, 6; complete knowledge, 194; Confucian classics, 28, 65, 109, 116, 160; cultivation, 205; filial devotion, 127, 129, 242, 246, 250–225; *Lunyu juzhu*, 42, 55, 105, 115. *See also Analects of Confucius*

Mahayana, 5, 38, 84, 170, 228–229, 254
marvelous(ness) (*miao* 妙), 66–69, 80, 85–86, 139, 179; great (*damiao* 大妙), 183; heart-mind, 60, 73, 87; ordinary, 67–69; way, 113, 146, 180
mean (middle) (*zhong* 中), 23–24, 31–32, 65; middle of ordinary affairs (事中), 68; middle of the universal principle (理中), 69; middle way, 45–46, 94, 99, 238–240, 245–246; potency of the middle, 66–67
means, 48; expedient, 69, 85, 116, 124; real, 86; temporary, 117–118; of transformation, 49, 52–53, 55–56
merits: hidden merits, 170–172; transfer of, 96, 141, 147
ming 命, 114, 116; *tianming* 天命 ("what heaven endows with"), 110, 222, 240, 252–253
moral quality/power (see *de* 德), 46, 49, 96, 129, 139; complete (至德), 144, 194; great (大德), 50, 130–131; moral nature, 71; small (小德), 130
mourning, 156–157
Mouzi lihuo lun 牟子理惑論 (*How Master Mou Removes Our Doubts*), 127, 151
movement (*dong* 動), 50, 135; of the heart-mind, 180, 182–184, 186, 188–189; signs of, 80, 182–183; of the world, 71, 73, 108, 184, 186
Mulian, 142, 158

name/reputation/status (*ming* 名), 91, 115–117, 201; rectification of names, 123
nature, 50, 53, 66–67, 71, 128–131. *See also* heaven-earth
Neo-Confucianism, 13–14, 19, 216–217; Cheng-Zhu, 98, 123, 127; Korean, 13–14
no-ego, 24, 148; experience of, 232–233; field of, 187; no-self, 138–139, 148, 155, 167, 204
no-form (*wu xiang* 無相), 227–230, 234
nonduality, 58, 73: nondual awareness, 73, 148, 217; nondual correlation, 67, 82, 174, 184, 188; nondual interdependence, 90, 184, 188, 192, 206–207; nondual unity, 36, 231; practice of, 244–246; of the teachings, 4, 19, 81, 85, 123
not-dwelling (*wu zhu* 無住), 108, 228, 231–234
nothingness (*wu* 無), 220–222, 226–228, 231–232; "principled" nothingness, 211, 221, 226–227
no-thought (*wu nian* 無念), 228, 230–231, 234

order: cosmic, 132; higher, 117, 179; of life, 24, 49, 129–130, 145; moral, 128–129, 131; natural, 66, 70–71, social, 102, 148

organic, 49–50; growth, 50, 52, 195, 199; life, 51–52, 145–147, 159, 185; nature, 131; order, 218, 240

Ouyang Xiu 歐陽修 (1007–1072), 18, 75–76, 97, 159

parents: death, 158; filial devotion for, 43, 70, 135, 138, 141, 161; honor the, 154–155, 164, 261; illustrious, 155, 163; mourning, 157; nurture, 139, 153; service to, 147–148, 153, 162, 202

peace, 41, 100, 113, 157, 165; live peacefully, 37, 43, 45, 95, 97, 99, 154;

phenomena (*shi* 事), 73, 87, 119, 173, 196; appearance of, 228; correlation of, 67; manifest, 147; natural, 191–192; phenomenal reality, 183–184, 189, 194. *See also* affairs

philosophical hermeneutics, 6, 8, 11, 21, 25–26; Qisong's, 19

Platform Sutra, 7, 42, 60, 64, 81, 83, 87, 149, 229; school, 94, 227

position/situation (*wei* 位), 96, 102, 116, 130, 132

practice, 160, 244; Chan, 96, 122, 138, 167, 232; Confucian, 98, 113, 119; ethical, 4, 89, 163, 197, 228; principled, 221; of self-cultivation, 6, 105, 123, 127, 209, 233, 262; spiritual, 106, 132, 146–147, 179, 234; *zhongyong*, 247, 258

prajñā, 227, 231

precepts, 38, 58, 73, 158, 161–163; accomplished, 229; Five Precepts, 17, 30, 39–41, 57, 60, 107; formless, 42, 229–230; great, 160, 164, 229; practice of, 73, 107, 158, 162–163

principle, 6, 58, 119–121, 123, 146: of coherence, 49, 51, 53; follow 順理, 221; probing to the utmost 窮理, 233; universal, 66–69, 73, 84, 107–108; without principles (unprincipled) *wuli* 無理, 216, 226. *See also li* 理

purification, 54, 113–114, 221

qi 氣, 17, 51, 218–219, 243, 245–246. *See also* vital breath

real (*shi* 實), 186, 216–217: means, 85–86; method, 87. *See also* expedient

reality: external reality, 173, 179, 225, 232; higher level of, 36, 49, 51, 247; nondual, 87, 178; phenomenal, 184, 189; true reality, 73, 80, 86, 194, 214; ultimate reality, 80, 182–183

reason, 8, 173, 179, 182, 205–206

rectification (*zheng* 正), 40, 45, 70, 99, 103; of feelings/emotions, 31, 151, 165; of the heart-mind, 53, 55, 65, 72, 123–124, 201; of names (*zhengming* 正名), 31, 115, 117, 123; of nature, 73, 100, 195–196, 240; of the spirit, 55

Rectifier of Buddhists, 73–74, 77–79

relatedness of beings, 51, 150, 165, 228–229. *See also* interdependence

relations: causal, 107, 181, 198; ethical, 24, 89, 95, 160, 227; family, 127, 132, 134, 142, 151, 153; five permanent, 102, 106, 116; hierarchical, 89, 95, 102–103, 115, 202, 256; interdependent, 97, 131, 250, 255; interpersonal, 53, 55, 89, 170, 186, 227, 239, 255–256; nondual, 149, 193–194; norms of, 57, 71, 202; organic, 130–132, 159; social, 30, 34, 38–39, 46, 130, 244, 247–249

religion/religious, 8, 24, 71, 77, 66, 68, 134; ethico-, 98, 121–122, 131–132, 135–138, 142–143; ethics as religion, 128, 131–132, 217; philosophico-, 19, 54, 79, 128; religious authority, 11; religious experience, 10–11; as ultimate concern, 24, 71, 243; as ultimate transformation, 24, 80, 130

ren 仁: 仁政, governance based on, 95; humaneness, 42, 110–112, 250–255; kindness, 39–40, 43, 70, 104, 119, 122, 163; 仁學, learning to be human, 16

resonance (*ying* 應), 55, 159, 189–190

response (*ying* 應), 110, 189–192, 198–199, 252

retribution (*baoying* 報應), 29, 51–52, 82, 174, 190–193; heavy, light, 190. *See also* Five Blessings and Six Perils

reverence/reverential regard, 132–135, 214–215; Confucian, 134–135, 142, 214; cultivation of, 215, 268; feeling of, 133

Ricoeur, Paul, 23–24, 26, 266
righteousness (*yi* 義), 66, 75, 101, 111; concrete, 95; great, 154
ritual (*li* 禮), 31, 72–73, 97, 100, 114, 116–117, 127; Confucian, 100–104, 223; ritual behavior, 110–111, 163, 238, 251–252; spirit of, 39, 42, 256
root, 29–30, 58, 80, 84, 116, 119, 156, 219; common root, 23, 61, 64, 79, 88, 175–176; correcting the, 207; great root (*da ben* 大本), 57, 60, 177, 185, 240; of the marvelous, 182; three, 146. See also branches

sadness, 41, 156, 191
sage (*sheng ren* 聖人), 36, 68, 72; Buddha/Buddhist, 3, 41, 56–57, 60, 63–64, 78; capacity of, 44, 47, 74, 85; Confucius/Confucian, 51, 66, 71, 104, 112, 143; great, 89–90; heart-mind of, 12, 76–77, 88; undertaking of, 82; way of, 69–70, 184–185
samadhi, 230–231
sameness (*tong* 同), 41, 82, 85, 97. See also difference
Sandai (Three Dynasties), 43–44
scholar-official, 2, 79, 95, 118, 122, 163, 212
school of principle, 5–6, 91, 109, 127, 203, 217, 233, 237, 261–262. See also *lixue* 理學
self, 58, 86; authentic, 204; field of, 138, 172–174; independent, 173, 239, 249, 255, 258; individual self, 8, 104, 108–109, 140, 184; interdependent, 97, 237, 239, 255, 257–258; no-self, 24, 138, 148, 155, 160, 185, 187; self-centeredness, 53, 97, 122, 139, 167, 179, 200; self-cultivation, 6, 67, 97, 105, 123, 137; self-transcendence, 49, 51
Sengyou 僧祐 (445–518), 17
sentient beings, 74, 81–84, 138–141, 148, 162, 170
sincerity, 50, 66, 70; Chan, 71, 145, 147–150; complete, 50, 71, 73, 135, 194; Confucian, 133–135. See also *cheng* 誠
Six Paramitas/perfections (*liu du* 六度), 89
Six Perils (*liu ji* 六極), 54–55
solidarity, 24, 51, 97–98

Song dynasty, 1, 164, 209–210, 262; Chan, 2, 6–7, 21, 34, 85; Confucian culture, 11, 19, 56, 58, 76, 126, 169, 231; Northern, 79, 91, 168, 212, 227; school of principle, 235; society, 207, 259; thought, 29, 208, 237, 261
Song gaoseng zhuan 宋高僧傳 (Biographies of eminent monks of the Song), 2, 151–153
sovereign, 43, 45, 63, 102, 190, 191; first, 101; good, 99; position of, 115–116
spirit/spiritual (*shen* 神), 17, 49, 51–52, 54–55; quintessential spirit (*jingshen* 精神), 49, 54, 66, 83, 113, 140–141, 175; spirit *lingshen* 靈神, 66, 83; spirits and ghosts (*guishen* 鬼神), 67, 70, 83, 112, 132–133, 147, 175; spiritual brightness, 177; spiritual discipline, 238–239, 241, 249; way of spirit, 49, 52, 57, 112, 115, 174, 176
stimulus/stimuli: external (外感); inner (感內); mutual stimuli. See response
Sutra in Forty-Two Sections (*Si shi er zhang jing* 四十二章經), 141
syncretism, 8, 10, 22, 61, 85–86

Ten Good Deeds, 17, 89, 171
ten thousand practices (*wan xing* 萬行), 89
ten thousand things (*wanwu* 萬物), 36, 41, 45, 66, 72–73, 182–183
testimony, 4, 193: auspicious, 190–191; Buddhist testimony (*zheng* 證), 197–198, 205; Confucian testimony (*zheng* 徵), 192
three lives (*san shi* 三世), 51–52, 54–57, 71, 79, 106, 109
transcendence (*xing er shang* 形而上), 49–51; self-transcendence, 49, 51
transformation, 48–52; emotional, 106; of the heaven-earth, 50, 108, 130, 131, 195; organic, 52; real, 121; soteriological, 79–80; spiritual, 136, 140; transformation-growth, 195; ultimate, 24, 79–80. See also transformative
transformative, 45, 154, 242–243; practice, 79–80, 82, 238
translation, 2, 4, 13, 17; hermeneutical translation, 22–29; transcultural translation, 26–27

transmigration, 97
transmoral: capacity, 251; nature, 117, 241; practice, 248–249; transformation, 243
Twelve Links of Conditioned Arising (*shier yuan* 十二緣), 89

Ullambana Sutra, 142, 158
ultimate concern, 24, 59, 71, 243
universal principle, 31, 66–69, 73, 84, 87, 94
utensil, 219

vehicle, 39, 85, 140; of heaven, 58, 84; of man, 49
vital breath, 17, 51, 219, 245–246, 249. See also utensil and *qi* 氣
vow, 42, 161, 221

way: of causes, 199–200; complete, 139, 194; Confucian, 3, 38–39, 66, 84, 176, 181; forgotten, 81, 177–178; of fruits, 199–200; of heaven, 49, 128, 181; of humans, 87, 112, 134, 162, 174–176, 181, 202; kingly, 45, 99; marvelous, 113, 179–180; middle, 24, 45–46, 94, 99, 238–239, 245–246; permanent, 118, 124, 225; of spirit, 52, 87, 112, 115, 174–175, 181. See also *dao* 道
wisdom/insight, 39, 70, 73, 94, 110–111, 227, 231–232, 251–252

wuchang 五常, 30, 39–40, 42, 57, 60, 71, 89. See also Five Permanencies
Wu Taibo 吳泰伯, 154, 273

Xiaojing 孝經 (Classic of filial devotion), 127, 129, 131, 153, 156–159

Yao and Shun, 75, 104
yin, yang, 51, 243
Yongming Yanshou 永明延壽 (904–975), 61, 210, 233
Yunmen 雲門 Chan subschool, 2, 62, 209–210, 213–214

Zanning 贊寧 (919–1001), ix, 2, 77–78, 151–152
Zhang Zai 張載 (1020–1077), 91, 264, 269, 272
Zheng Xuan 鄭玄 (127–200), 111, 270, 277
Zhiyuan 智圓 (976–1022), 21, 65, 94
Zhizang 智藏 (458–522), 153
Zhongyong 中庸 (classic), 6, 31, 36, 44, 49–50, 53, 65–66, 71, 103, 129–131, 177–178, 194–195; *Zhongyong jie*, 23, 41, 45, 99–100, 110
zhongyong (middle way), 24, 238–239: practice of, 241–246, 257–258; spirituality, 244, 247–250
Zhou Dunyi 周敦頤 (1017–1073), 91, 264, 269, 272
Zongmi 宗密 (780–841), 15, 265

DIANA ARGHIRESCU is Research Director of the Observatoire de l'Asie de l'Est and Lecturer in the Department of Philosophy at the Université du Québec à Montréal, Canada. She teaches Chinese philosophy and comparative philosophy. She is author of *De la continuité dynamique dans l'univers confucéen: Lecture néoconfucéenne du Zhongyong*, a philosophical translation and interpretation of Zhu Xi's commentaries, and translator of *Xu Fuguan in the Context of East Asian Confucianisms*, by Chun-chieh Huang. Arghirescu has contributed to the collaborative project *Dao Companion to Zhu Xi's Philosophy* and has also published in *Philosophy East and West*, the *Journal of Chinese Philosophy*, *Comparative and Continental Philosophy*, and *Taiwan Journal of East Asian Studies*.

www.ingramcontent.com/pod-product-compliance
Lightning Source LLC
Chambersburg PA
CBHW021347300426
44114CB00012B/1109